# From Voting to Violence

# From Voting to Violence

*Democratization and Nationalist Conflict*

Jack Snyder

*W. W. Norton & Company* · *New York* · *London*

The text of this book is composed in Adobe Garamond
with the display set in Torino.
Composition by Tom Ernst.
Manufacturing by The Courier Companies, Inc.
Book design by Chris Welch.
Maps by John McAusland.


Library of Congress Cataloging-in-Publication Data


Snyder, Jack L.
    From voting to violence : democratization and nationalist conflict / Jack Snyder.
        p.    cm.
    Includes bibliographical references and index.
    **ISBN 0-393-04881-0**
        1. Democratization.  2. Nationalism  I. Title.

JC421 .S557  2000

320.54'09'049—dc21                                         99-049208


W. W. Norton & Company, Inc., 500 Fifth Avenue, New York, NY 10110
www.wwnorton.com


W. W. Norton & Company Ltd., 10 Coptic Street, London WC1A 1PU


1 2 3 4 5 6 7 8 9 0

# Contents

6 Nationalism and Democracy in the Developing World 265

7 Averting Nationalist Conflict in an Age of
Democratization 313

# Maps

# Acknowledgments

Many of the people I thank below have characterized my views on democratization and nationalism as "provocative." I suspect that means they want to keep a safe distance from any allegation that implies they have made a significant impact on this book. But I will thank them anyway.

My arguments about nationalism were developing while I was working on a parallel research project on the connection between democratization and the increased risk of international war. Edward Mansfield, my co-author in a series of articles on that theme, made the research a pleasure and a learning experience. Mansfield's carefully designed statistical tests also helped me to see that the assertive behavior of Europe's democratizing great powers was part of a more general pattern with broad implications for the study of nationalism.

Karen Ballentine was my co-author on another article, "Nationalism and the Marketplace of Ideas," *International Security* (Fall 1996), which presented many of the basic arguments that I have adapted for this book. Those arguments, developed by both of us through numerous give-and-take conversations and revisions, have left their mark on almost every chapter of this book. Ballentine was also an exacting critic who deserves as much credit for her skepticism about this book's weaknesses as for her contribution to whatever strengths it may have. I also profited a great deal from her entirely separate work on ethnic federalism.

Chaim Kaufmann, after plowing through two early draft chapters, made a huge impact on the overall shape of this study with his terse comment: "I'm not having fun yet." Because Kaufmann read those chapters, you don't have to. The fun now starts sooner, I hope.

Among those who offered extremely useful comments on chapters at various stages of development were Michael Brown, Rogers Brubaker, Valerie Bunce, James Fearon, Sumit Ganguly, John Hall, Stuart Kaufman, Jan Kubik, Karen Peabody O'Brien, Barry Posen, Stephen Saideman, Sherrill Stroschein, Ashutosh Varshney, and three anonymous Norton reviewers. Fiona Adamson, Robert Jervis, Ronald Rogowski, and Leslie Vinjamuri made especially productive suggestions for improving the "Marketplace of Ideas" article. Robin Bhatty, Chip Gagnon, and Anne Nelson were extraordinarily generous in sharing information, references, files, and ideas, and allowing me to plunder shamelessly their extensive expertise. Chaim Kaufmann, Roy Licklider, Barbara Walter, and Anne Pitsch of Ted Gurr's Minorities at Risk project helped me devise a list of ethnic conflicts. Ian Bremmer generously allowed me to refer to his unpublished work that categorizes the nationalisms of post-Communist states.

I profited tremendously from conversations with Columbia University's creative and varied faculty working on nationalism and related topics. In particular, I learned a great deal from participating in a series of workshops in Eastern Europe on nationalism curriculum with colleagues Karen Barkey and Alexander Motyl, and from co-teaching a course on war and race with Anthony Marx. A similar source of stimulating ideas that shaped these pages has been my annual debates with Stephen Van Evera at the MIT-sponsored Seminar XXI.

Teresa Lawson, as she always does, devised a seamlessly logical way to reorganize some egregiously misshapen chapters and saved me from countless logical lapses. Claire Ehlers reminded me of all the historical facts and jargon that second-year undergraduates have not learned yet, while also maintaining an acute running commentary on the substance of my argument. At Norton Books, Sarah Caldwell displayed an astonishing array of skills, performing at Lawson-like levels in the developmental editing stage, and showing tenacity and good taste in the final selections of art, maps, and tables. Kathy Talalay, the copy editor, was alert not only to stylistic errors but also to opportunities to update the text in light of late-breaking Balkan developments. Norton's Roby Harrington bears the responsibility for convincing me to undertake this impossibly ambitious book. I've never met a more recklessly persuasive guy.

While I was writing this book, I received research grants for several closely related projects: from the Harry Frank Guggenheim Foundation and from the United States Institute of Peace for research on democratization and war, from the Pew Foundation for workshops on nationalism curriculum, from the Ford Foundation for a book on civil wars, and from the Carnegie Corporation for a project evaluating the strategies of nongovernmental organizations for promoting democracy and preventing ethnic conflict.

One of the more entertaining aspects of working on this project was soliciting suggestions for potential titles from my creative friends. Catherine Romano came up with "Adolescent Democracies: Gotta Love 'em, Wars and All." Randall Schweller's was the most concise: "Run! It's a Democracy!" But my wife Nina wins the prize for suggesting the title that we actually used. This book is dedicated to her.

Jack Snyder
New York City
June 1999

# From Voting to Violence

# 1

## Transitions to Democracy and

## the Rise of Nationalist Conflict

The centerpiece of American foreign policy in the 1990s was the claim that promoting the spread of democracy would also promote peace. Noting that no two democracies have ever fought a war against each other, President Bill Clinton argued that support for democratization would be an antidote to international war and civil strife.[1] Yet paradoxically, the 1990s turned out to be a decade of both democratization and chronic nationalist conflict.

While the world would undoubtedly be more peaceful if all states became mature democracies, Clinton's conventional wisdom failed to anticipate the dangers of getting from here to there. Rocky transitions to democracy often give rise to warlike nationalism and violent ethnic con-

---

[1] See his 1994 State of the Union address, "Transcript of Clinton's Address," *New York Times*, January 26, 1994, A17. On the absence of war between democracies, see Michael Doyle, "Liberalism and World Politics," *American Political Science Review* 80:4 (December 1986), 1151–1169.

flicts. Since the French Revolution, the earliest phases of democratization have triggered some of the world's bloodiest nationalist struggles.

Spreading the benefits of democracy worldwide is a worthy long-run goal. However, strategies for accomplishing this must be guided by a realistic understanding of the politics of the transition. Naively pressuring ethnically divided authoritarian states to hold instant elections can lead to disastrous results. For example, international financial donors forced free and fair elections on the leaders of the small central African country of Burundi in 1993, and within a year some 50,000 Hutu and Tutsi were killed in ethnic strife there. And yet many other democratic transitions succeed without triggering nationalist violence. Understanding the conditions that permit such successful transitions should be the first step toward designing policies to pave the way toward democracy. To that end, this book explains why democratization often causes nationalist conflict, and why it sometimes does not. Drawing on that analysis, I prescribe ways to make democratic transitions less dangerous.

## Liberal Optimism Confronts the Nationalist Revival of the 1990s

When the Berlin Wall came down in 1989, a euphoric vision briefly captured the American imagination. Liberalism had triumphed over its two ideological competitors in the twentieth century, communism and fascist nationalism, and no new challengers were in sight. Empires and dictatorships were collapsing. Democratization was sweeping formerly authoritarian countries in Latin America, southern Europe, and Eastern Europe, and even making inroads in East Asia. Virtually everywhere states were adopting market economies. Global economic interdependence was continuing to deepen. Liberal, American-based mass news media and popular culture were achieving global reach. This victory of liberalism, it was claimed, would usher in "the end of history."[2]

Believing that all good things go together, liberal commentators argued that war was becoming obsolete, at least among the liberalizing countries

[2] Francis Fukuyama, "The End of History," *The National Interest* 16 (Summer 1989), 3–18.

that were establishing the dominant global trend.[3] A learned tome published in 1990 concluded that nationalism, commonly defined as the doctrine that each cultural group should have its own state, was rapidly heading into the dustbin of history because states organized around single nations could no longer cope with an increasingly interdependent, globalizing world.[4] Residual stumbling blocks in the path of triumphant liberalism could be overcome with the help of an energetic set of international institutions—United Nations troops to keep the peace, and International Monetary Fund experts to lure countries into the liberal fold and to enforce the rules of fiscal prudence. In keeping with this vision, President Clinton explained that promoting democratization would be a watchword of U.S. foreign policy—because democracies never fight wars against each other, they trade freely with each other, and they respect the human rights of their citizens.[5]

This vision tarnished quickly. War has been endemic since the collapse of the Berlin Wall. Nor have these been trivial wars at the periphery of the international order: the world's oil supply was at risk in the 1991 Gulf War; in June 1991 the Yugoslav army battled Slovenian separatists scarcely a hundred miles from Vienna, and NATO's air forces mounted a sustained bombing campaign throughout Serbia during the 1999 Kosovo conflict. Nationalist rhetoric, far from being discredited, came back into vogue. A quarter of the electorate in Russia's fledgling democracy voted in 1993 for the party of a neofascist anti-Semite, Vladimir Zhirinovsky (only a third voted for Hitler in 1932). In civil wars from Somalia to Bosnia, the armed forces of the liberal international community were bedeviled, attacked, and held hostage by local thugs. Ethnic mayhem in 1994 caused over half a million deaths in Rwanda, after Belgian peacekeepers were killed on the first day of the genocide campaign against the Tutsi minority.

As a result, the conventional wisdom was soon turned on its head: *The Atlantic Monthly* relabeled the post-Communist world as "the coming anar-

[3] John Mueller, *Retreat from Doomsday: The Obsolescence of Major War* (New York: Basic Books, 1989).

[4] E. J. Hobsbawm, *Nations and Nationalism since 1780* (Cambridge: Cambridge University Press, 1990), Chapter 6.

[5] In addition to the 1994 State of the Union address, see also the article by Clinton's national security adviser, Anthony Lake, "The Reach of Democracy," *New York Times*, September 23, 1994, A35.

chy," and the eminent Harvard political scientist Samuel Huntington announced that the future would hold in store a "clash of civilizations."[6] In the view of such pundits, cultural conflicts, whether along the fault lines of whole civilizations or simply among intermingled ethnic groups, would become the defining cleavages of international relations in the coming era. News media and political leaders commonly attributed these grim developments to "ancient hatreds" between inimical cultures, simmering for centuries and boiling over as soon as the lid of the cold war was lifted off the pot. This account was simple, intuitive, and reinforced daily by the justifications offered by perpetrators of ethnic slaughter. For Western politicians looking for an easy excuse to limit their involvement in unseemly struggles, the story of ancient hatreds also had the advantage of portraying these disputes as hopelessly intractable. But even those who retained the vision of spreading liberal democracy to unaccustomed corners of the globe considered age-old ethnic prejudices to be liberalism's major foe. President Clinton, in his 1993 presidential inauguration speech, remarked that "a generation raised in the shadows of the cold war assumes new responsibilities in a world warmed by the sunshine of freedom but threatened still by ancient hatreds."[7]

The good news is that this view is largely incorrect. Most of the globe's recent strife is not due to ancient cultural hatreds. In some cases, the warring groups had experienced no armed conflict until relatively recently. Serbs and Croats, for example, never fought each other until the twentieth century, and then largely because the Nazis installed an unrepresentative regime of murderers in Zagreb.[8] In other cases, occasional conflicts between cultural or ethnic groups have been interspersed with long interludes of

---

[6] Robert D. Kaplan, "The Coming Anarchy," *The Atlantic Monthly* 273:2 (February 1994), 44–76; Samuel Huntington, "The Clash of Civilizations," *Foreign Affairs* 72:3 (Summer 1993), 22–49.

[7] Quoted in Susanne Hoeber Rudolph and Lloyd I. Rudolph, "Modern Hate," *The New Republic* 208:12 (March 22, 1993), 24. Clinton later acknowledged that his "ancient hatreds" remarks were erroneous. See Katharine Seelye, "Clinton Blames Milosevic, Not Fate, for Bloodshed," *New York Times*, May 14, 1999, A12.

[8] The first armed conflict pitting Serbs against Croats was World War I, when half of the Austro-Hungarian forces invading Serbia were Croats. However, a quarter of this invasion force were Serbs from the border districts of Croatia, a group whose traditional occupation had been frontier guards against the Ottomans. Since Serbs fought on both sides, World War I can hardly be classified as an example of an ancient ethnic conflict. Dimitrije Djordjevic, "The Yugoslav Phenomenon," in

amicable relations, therefore cultural differences cannot in themselves be a sufficient explanation for the recent fighting. Few serious scholars attribute nationalism and ethnic conflict primarily to ancient cultural hatreds.[9]

The bad news, however, harbors a deep irony: the very trends that liberals saw as bringing the end of history have in many instances fueled the revival of nationalism. The end of the authoritarian Soviet empire spurred the aspiring leaders of many of its intermingled nations to establish their own national states, whose conflicting claims to sovereignty and territory often gave rise to disputes.[10] Elections often sharpened these ethnic and national differences. Nationalist demagogues exploited the increased freedom of the press in some newly democratizing states to hijack public debate for illiberal ends.[11] Painful adjustments to a market economy and to international interdependence provided further opportunities for nationalist politicians who promised protection in a strong state, or who distributed a shrinking economic pie along ethnic lines. At the same time, the globalization of media and culture often repelled rather than attracted those who failed to prosper in a Westernized world.[12] Moreover, as some critics argue, international organizations sometimes caused more conflict than they averted with their inept strategies of peacekeeping and their strict philosophies of economic reform.[13]

Though surprising to liberal optimists, these developments of the

---

Joseph Held, *The Columbia History of Eastern Europe in the Twentieth Century* (New York: Columbia University Press, 1992), 310.

[9] Although ethnic conflicts are a prevalent feature of the post–cold war landscape, they do not necessarily represent an increasing proportion of all conflicts. Myron Weiner, "Bad Neighbors, Bad Neighborhoods: An Inquiry into the Causes of Refugee Flows," *International Security* 21:1 (Summer 1996), 21–22, points out that between 1969 and 1992 the proportion of nonethnic refugee-causing conflicts increased.

[10] Placing the Soviet collapse in comparative perspective is Karen Barkey and Mark Von Hagen, eds., *After Empire: Multiethnic Societies and Nation-Building* (Boulder, CO: Westview, 1997).

[11] Jack Snyder and Karen Ballentine, "Nationalism and the Marketplace of Ideas," *International Security* 21:2 (Fall 1996), 5–40.

[12] Huntington, "The Clash of Civilizations," 25–62; Mark Juergensmeyer, *The New Cold War? Religious Nationalism Confronts the Secular State* (Berkeley: University of California Press, 1993).

[13] Richard K. Betts, "The Delusion of Impartial Intervention," *Foreign Affairs* 73:6 (November/December 1994), 20–33; Susan Woodward, *Balkan Tragedy* (Washington, DC: Brookings, 1995), Chapter 3.

1990s actually echoed long-standing patterns in the history of national-ism, which I explore in subsequent chapters. Far from being an outmoded throwback, nationalism is largely a reaction to the social changes of the modern era. Western Europe went through these changes between the French Revolution and the Second World War, an age that saw the rise of modern nationalism and of popular warfare. During that period, democ-ratization, economic development, and a revolution in the means of com-munication fueled nationalism, which often took a militant form. States being dragged by social change into a transition to democracy have been more likely to participate in wars and more likely to start them than have states whose regimes did not change.[14] The end of the cold war increased the prevalence of nationalism by unleashing this dangerous transition toward democratic, market societies in the post-Communist states.

Though democratization heightens a state's risk of war, historical evi-dence shows that three out of four democratizing states nonetheless avoided war in the decade after their democratization. Moreover, once liberal democracy became entrenched, no mature democracies have ever fought wars against each other. In those countries where transitions to democracy were fully consolidated during the 1990s, the rights of ethnic minorities tended to improve, and ethnic conflicts were rare.[15]

The central message of this book, consequently, constitutes a paradox. On the one hand, the successful unfolding of a global, liberal-democratic revolution might eventually undergird a more peaceful era in world poli-tics. On the other hand, the transition to democratic politics is meanwhile creating fertile conditions for nationalism and ethnic conflict, which not only raises the costs of the transition but may also redirect popular politi-cal participation into a lengthy antidemocratic detour. The three most nearly successful attempts to overturn the global balance of power through aggression—those of Napoleonic France in 1803–15, Kaiser Wilhelm's Germany in 1914–18, and Adolf Hitler's Germany in 1939–45—all came

[14] Edward D. Mansfield and Jack Snyder, "Democratization and the Danger of War," *International Security* 20:1 (Summer 1995), 5–38; Mansfield and Snyder, "Democratization and War," *Foreign Affairs* 74:3 (May/June 1995), 79–97.

[15] Ted Robert Gurr, *Peoples versus States: Ethnopolitical Conflict and Accommodation at the End of the 20th Century* (Washington, DC: US Institute of Peace, forthcoming); see also Ted Robert Gurr and Will H. Moore, "Ethnopolitical Rebellion: A Cross-Sectional Analysis of the 1980s with Risk Assessments for the 1990s," *American Journal of Political Science* 41:4 (October 1997), 1079–1103.

on the heels of failed attempts to democratize. Popular nationalistic energies, unleashed and perverted by the miscarriage of democratic reforms, created the conditions that made possible these bids for global hegemony. Thus, the process of democratization can be one of its own worst enemies, and its promise of peace is clouded with the danger of war.

To promote democratization without heeding these risks would be self-indulgent idealism. Yet to try to hold back the global social processes that may stimulate nationalism—including demands for increased mass participation in politics, the collapse of outworn empires, and the globalization of the economy and communications—would be equally unrealistic. Instead, one of the key tasks for the international community will be to distinguish the circumstances that make for a safe transition to liberal democracy from those that lead to backlash, nationalism, and war. Insofar as astute policy choices can help to create the more favorable conditions, understanding the pitfalls of democratization is the first step toward avoiding them. This is an analytical task for everyone who is engaged with the seminal issues of our day: political leaders in the advanced democratic states and in transitional states, journalists, human rights activists, scholars, citizens, and even nationalists themselves, insofar as they want to avoid costly missteps in the pursuit of their nations' goals.

In this introductory chapter, I will first define what I mean by the terms nationalism and democratization; second, summarize the evidence that nationalist conflict correlates with the early phases of democratization; third, challenge the view that ancient popular rivalries explain this correlation; fourth, briefly sketch my own alternative explanation, which highlights the role of persuasion by nationalist elites; fifth, discuss the practical implications of this theory for policy choices; and finally, provide a road map to the historical and contemporary case studies that constitute the bulk of the book.

## What Are Nationalism and Democratization?

### Nationalism

In everyday usage, a variety of very different phenomena may all be labeled as manifestations of nationalism, including ethnic riots, aggressive foreign policies of fascist states, patriotism in democracies, and the peaceful seeking of special rights for cultural groups. To avoid confusion, social scientists typically like to define terms more narrowly and precisely than is common in everyday discourse.

The most widely used scholarly definition of nationalism is by Ernest Gellner, who defines nationalism as the doctrine that the political unit (the state) and the cultural unit (the nation) should be congruent.[16] According to this view, nationalism holds that the state, which is the organization that exercises sovereign authority over a given territory, should rule on behalf of a particular nation, defined as a group of people who feel they share a common culture. This formulation is theoretically clear and historically plausible. Many self-proclaimed nationalist movements have had as their central aim the acquisition of a state by a culturally distinct people (like Croatian nationalists did in 1991), the inclusion of cultural brethren in an existing state (Hungarian nationalists in the 1930s), or the domination of an existing state by a single cultural group (Estonian nationalists in the 1990s). Indeed, in an age when conflicts rooted in ethnic nationalism are such a dominant concern, it is tempting to highlight cultural distinctions in the very definition of nationalism.

Yet this definition would seem to leave out phenomena that common usage, including usage by self-described nationalists, normally calls nationalism. For example, defining nationalism strictly in terms of shared culture would seem to exclude militant loyalty to a state's political institutions or other principles not based on culture, such as the universalistic principles embodied in the U.S. Constitution. Similarly, defining the aim of nationalism as achieving a sovereign state would seem to exclude the seeking of political rights short of sovereign statehood by cultural groups, such as those Québecois nationalists who seek a form of autonomy within the Canadian federal state. Moreover, nationalists often do not stop at getting their own state. They frequently attempt to enshrine distinct cultural values in that state, discriminate in favor of coethnics living within its borders, try to incorporate ethnic brethren and historic national territories into the state, and militantly guard against encroachments by historic enemies of the nation.[17] In some cases, the nation-state adopts a "nationalistic"

---

[16] Ernest Gellner, *Nations and Nationalism* (Ithaca: Cornell University Press, 1983), 1–7.

[17] Rogers Brubaker, *Nationalism Reframed* (Cambridge: Cambridge University Press, 1996), Chapters 3 and 4.

view of neighboring nation-states as inferior, hostile, and deserving of domination.[18] Everyday usage assumes that these broader meanings are an integral part of the thing people call nationalism. I will try to show that common parlance links these phenomena not out of confusion but because they have related causes, dynamics, and consequences, which a theory of nationalism and nationalist conflict ought to try to capture. To accommodate this, Gellner's definition, though a useful starting place, needs to be broadened.

I define nationalism, therefore, as the doctrine that a people who see themselves as distinct in their culture, history, institutions, or principles should rule themselves in a political system that expresses and protects those distinctive characteristics.[19] A nation is, therefore, a group of people who see themselves as distinct in these terms and who aspire to self-rule. Nationalist conflict is defined as organized, large-scale violence motivated or justified by a nationalist doctrine.

By this definition, not all ethnic groups are nations; nor are all nations ethnic groups. There are many peoples who consider themselves to be culturally or historically distinct, for example the Cajuns of Louisiana, but who lack a doctrine that claims a right to self-rule for the group. Based on wide-ranging historical research, Anthony Smith distinguishes between an ethnic group, or *ethnie* (which has a distinctive consciousness based on a common language or culture, myths of common ancestry, or a common historical experience), and a nation (which seeks self-rule for such a group).[20] Ethnic conflict involves nationalism only when a goal of the conflict is to establish or protect self-rule by the ethnic group.[21]

---

[18] John Mearsheimer, "Back to the Future," *International Security* 15:1 (Summer 1990), 5–56, calls this "hypernationalism."

[19] Snyder and Ballentine, "Nationalism and the Marketplace of Ideas," 9–10.

[20] Anthony D. Smith, *The Ethnic Origins of Nations* (Oxford: Blackwell, 1986), Chapters 1 and 2.

[21] The most ambitious expression of the demand for self-rule is the achievement of sovereign statehood, whereby the nation establishes a bureaucratic apparatus that monopolizes the legitimate use of force within the territory it governs (Gellner, *Nations*, 3–5). Some nationalist movements, however, seek more limited forms of self-rule, involving autonomous authority for the nation over a narrower range of issues such as educational and language policy, a separate legal code, taxation, or control over local police forces. The Québecois political movement, for example, would remain nationalist by my definition if it sought to expand or protect the scope of self-

Although nationalist doctrine derives political authority from the right of a distinct people to rule themselves, nationalists do not necessarily hold that legitimate political processes require democratic voting. Rather, the right to self-rule means that the national group should not be ruled by an alien people or alien institutions. It also means that the nation's rulers, no matter how they are chosen, must justify their policies in terms of the welfare, security, and fulfillment of the national aims of the sovereign people. This ambiguity between rule by the people and rule in the name of a people constitutes one of the main attractions of nationalist doctrine to elites who seek to rule undemocratically in an era of rising demands for a mass role in politics.

Nations may distinguish themselves from each other not only on the basis of distinctive cultural traditions, but also on the basis of distinctive political traditions, political institutions, and political principles.[22] Thus, scholars commonly divide nationalisms into two types, ethnic and civic, based on the nature of their appeals to the collective good and on their criteria for including members in the group.[23] Ethnic nationalisms, like those of the Germans and the Serbs, base their legitimacy on common culture, language, religion, shared historical experience, and/or the myth of shared kinship, and they use these criteria to include or exclude members from the national group.[24] For example, German law offered citizenship to people of German ancestry who reside in Russia, while it denied it to many Turks who have lived in Germany all their lives. Civic nationalisms, like those of the British, the United States, and for the most part the French, base their appeals on loyalty to a set of political ideas and institutions that are perceived as just and effective. Inclusion in the group depends primarily on birth or long-term residence within the nation's territory, though sufficient knowledge of the nation's language and institutions to participate in the nation's civic life may be a criterion for the naturalization of resident aliens.

---

rule of the distinct Québecois nation, even while remaining within the sovereign state of Canada.

[22] Indeed, given Gellner's extremely broad definition of culture as "a system of ideas and signs and associations and ways of behaving and communicating," a nation's political ideas and habits would count for him as culture. Gellner, *Nations*, 7.

[23] Liah Greenfeld, *Nationalism: Five Roads to Modernity* (Cambridge: Harvard University Press, 1992); Rogers Brubaker, *Citizenship and Nationhood in France and Germany* (Cambridge: Harvard University Press, 1992).

[24] Smith, *Ethnic Origins*, 22–31.

This distinction between civic and ethnic nationalism is especially crucial in countries like contemporary Ukraine, where ethnic Russians and Ukrainians live intermingled. In those conditions, basing political loyalties on cultural or linguistic differences would be intensely divisive. Consequently, Ukraine's leaders have for the most part prudently promoted a civic-territorial form of national loyalty.

These categories are ideal types: no actual nation is purely civic or purely ethnic. Ethnic groups that seek political goals normally set up administrative institutions that function at least partly according to legal criteria, not just cultural norms. Conversely, civic states are often built on some discernible ethnic core, and over time, civic nations generate their own civic culture and shared historical myths.[25] Nonetheless, nations can be placed on a continuum between the civic and ethnic ideal types depending on whether loyalty to and inclusion in them is based primarily on institutions or on culture. A definition of nationalism that is broad, yet distinguishes between ethnic and civic variants, permits the investigation of the causes and consequences of both types.[26]

In short, this definition of nationalism highlights popular self-rule as a universal goal of nationalists but avoids smuggling democracy into the very definition of nationalism. It also allows the exploration of the cultural basis of political loyalty but avoids the mistake of equating nationalism with ethnicity. Thus, it features some of the elements of nationalism that are central to understanding the causes of nationalism and its consequences for violent conflict.

### Democratization

The term democratization distinguishes between mature democracies and democratizing states. In mature democracies, government policy, includ-

---

[25] Ibid., 153–54.

[26] Although this definition of nationalism is broad, it does not subsume all types of political loyalty. There are many doctrines of supreme political loyalty that are based on alternative criteria for alignment and enmity, other than nations—e.g., social classes; smaller-scale kinship groups such as clans; local communities of individuals with face-to-face relationships; transnational religions; status groups such as the aristocracy; professional organizations such as guilds and knightly orders; family dynasties, empires, networks of patronage and personal reciprocity; or organizations that stand for universalistic moral principles.

ing foreign and military policy, is made by officials chosen through free, fair, and periodic elections in which a substantial proportion of the adult population can vote; the actions of officials are constrained by constitutional provisions and commitments to civil liberties; and government candidates sometimes lose elections and leave office when they do. Freedom of speech, freedom to organize groups to contest elections, and reasonably equitable representation of varied viewpoints in the media are presumed to be preconditions for a free and fair election. I define states as democratizing if they have recently adopted one or more of these democratic characteristics, even if they retain important nondemocratic features.[27]

The category of democratizing states is a very broad one. It includes states like the Czech Republic in the early 1990s, which made a transition from complete autocracy to virtually complete democracy. However, it also includes the former Yugoslavia just before its breakup in 1991, when elections were contested for the first time in circumstances of somewhat freer speech, yet electoral fairness and the rule of law were hardly well established.[28]

[27] Snyder and Ballentine, "Nationalism and the Marketplace of Ideas," 6 (fn. 5). For the purpose of a quantitative study of the relationship between democratization and war, the findings of which I occasionally invoke in this book, Edward Mansfield and I identified specific thresholds for several types of institutional change from an autocracy to a mixed regime and from a mixed regime to a democracy. We labeled states crossing any one of these thresholds as democratizing. See Edward D. Mansfield and Jack Snyder, "Democratization and the Danger of War," 8–10. We relied on the categories and case codings of Ted Gurr's Polity II and III databases. However, in narrative discussions of cases in this book, I do not rely solely on these particular quantitative thresholds. Rather, I describe qualitatively the specific changes in institutions or civil liberties that warrant the designation of democratization.

[28] Though democratization is a broad term, scholars sometimes employ a still broader term—that is, increased political participation. Political participation may take democratic forms, such as voting or joining a political party, but it may also take nondemocratic forms, such as rioting, striking to express political demands, or forming mass-based paramilitary movements. See Samuel Huntington, *Political Order in Changing Societies* (New Haven: Yale University Press, 1968). Where these latter forms of political participation are prevalent, democratic elections are not "the only game in town," and perhaps not even the main game. Historically, one important form of increased mass political participation was the formation of nationalist societies and pressure groups, whose repertoire often featured rallies, lobbying, intimidation, and other nonelectoral methods. These operated in democracies, such as the

At what moment does a successfully democratizing state become a mature democracy? When can its democracy be termed consolidated? Some scholars use the "two turnover rule" to define democratic consolidation: that is, a democracy is considered consolidated when power has changed hands twice as a result of free and fair elections. Others say that democracy is consolidated when it is "the only game in town": that is, when no significant political party or group seeks to come to power by means other than winning a free and fair election.[29] Finally, others measure the degree to which the country has achieved the institutional and legal characteristics of a mature democracy, using indicators such as competitive politics, regular elections, broad participation, constraints on arbitrary use of executive power, free speech, and respect for civil liberties, including minority rights. When a country achieves a high enough score on almost all of these dimensions, it is said to have consolidated its democracy.[30] States that have crossed this line by any of the above criteria are mature democracies, no longer democratizing states.[31]

## The Link between Democratization and Nationalist Conflict: Some Evidence

Diverse evidence points to a connection between democratization and conflicts fueled by nationalism. As more people begin to play a larger role in politics, ethnic conflict within a country becomes more likely, as does international aggression justified by nationalist ideas.

---

Nazis in the Weimar Republic; in democratizing states, such as the German Navy League before World War I; and in states untouched by significant democratization, such as the nationalist Chinese Kuomintang movement of Chiang Kai-shek.

[29] See Juan Linz and Alfred Stepan, *Problems of Democratic Transition and Consolidation* (Baltimore: Johns Hopkins University Press, 1996), Chapter 1.

[30] Both Gurr and Freedom House aggregate scores across multiple dimensions in this way. See Mansfield and Snyder, "Democratization and the Danger of War" and "Democratic Transitions, Institutional Strength, and War" (manuscript, 1999), for a discussion of the precise cutoff points used to distinguish mixed regimes from mature democracies.

[31] Thus, to predict the international behavior of consolidated democracies, one should look to the theory of the democratic peace among mature democracies, not to the hypotheses about the war-proneness of democratizing states contained in this book.

Most of the states undergoing bloody ethnic conflicts that dominated the news of the 1990s experienced a partial improvement in their political or civil liberties in the year or so before the strife broke out. Most of these conflicts occurred in states that were taking initial steps toward a democratic transition, such as holding contested elections and allowing a variety of political groups to criticize the government and each other. Freedom House, an independent research and advocacy organization, makes widely used annual rankings of every state's degree of democracy and civil liberties, including press freedoms. By these measures, partial democratization and partial increases in press freedom occurred before the outbreak of ethnic conflict in the former Yugoslavia, before the escalation in the fighting between Armenians and the former Soviet republic of Azerbaijan, and in Russia, the perpetrator of the war against the ethnic separatist Chechens. In Burundi, the ethnic minority Tutsi military government agreed to accept elections in 1993 and to share governmental offices with the long-oppressed Hutu majority. When, inevitably, the elections installed a Hutu President who tried to insert some of his coethnics in the military establishment, a conflict spiral touched off by mutual fears and retaliation left some 50,000 dead. Though neighboring Rwanda held no election, its Hutu-dominated government allowed an increase in press freedom on the eve of the 1994 genocide against the Tutsi minority.[32]

A systematic study of every ethnic conflict during the period from 1990 to 1998 noted that ethnic political assertiveness peaked during the wave of transitions toward democracy that followed the collapse of the Soviet empire from 1989 to 1991.[33] By mid-decade, this tide of democratization had slackened or in some cases reversed itself, and correspondingly the number of ethnic conflicts also diminished.[34] Where democracy was successfully consolidated, as in much of South America and the northern part of Eastern Europe, minority rights were increasingly being guaranteed through peaceful means. Meanwhile, fewer countries were entering the dangerous category of semidemocratic regimes, where

---

[32] Freedom House, *Freedom in the World* (New York: Greenwood Press, annual yearbooks for 1989–94).

[33] Gurr, *Peoples versus States* (forthcoming).

[34] Larry Diamond, "Is the Third Wave Over?" *Journal of Democracy* 7:3 (July 1996), 96.

minority rights were more likely to suffer than to improve. Thus, democratic consolidation reduced ethnic conflict, but the initial steps in the rocky transition to democracy increased it, especially in new states.[35]

Democratic transitions have also tended to coincide with involvement in international wars over the past two centuries. The chance of war in any given decade for the average state has been about one in six, whereas for democratizing states it has been about one in four during the decade following democratization. The democratizing states were more likely to be the attackers than the target of aggression in these wars. The most war-prone states are those at the beginning stages of democratization, rather than those that have nearly completed the consolidation of democracy. Especially at risk for war are newly democratizing countries that lack a strong centralized state to lay down firm rules for regulating popular participation in politics and for enforcing state authority.[36] Similarly, domestic political opposition to free trade rises significantly at the beginning of democratization, whereas successful consolidation of democracy tends to make states free-trading. Thus, the rise in nationalistic and uncooperative thinking affects economic relations as well as military matters.[37]

This pattern of war-proneness during the early stages of democratization echoes the history of virtually every great power. France, Britain, Germany, and Japan all fought aggressive wars, fueled in part by popular nationalism, on the heels of their initial phase of democratization.

[35] Gurr, *Peoples versus States* (forthcoming).

[36] See three studies by Mansfield and Snyder, "Democratization and the Danger of War," "Democratization and War," and "Democratic Transitions, Institutional Strength, and War." Although the databases used for these studies did not measure nationalism directly, we presented logical arguments and narrative historical evidence suggesting that nationalism was at least one of the factors causing this link. On the failure to consolidate and the heightened incidence of war, see Alexander Kozhemiakin, *Expanding the Zone of Peace? Democratization and International Security* (New York: St. Martin's, 1998), Chapter 5. For studies showing variations in the strength of the link between democratization and war, see William Thompson and Richard Tucker, "A Tale of Two Democratic Peace Critiques," *Journal of Conflict Resolution* 41:3 (June 1997), 428–54, and other articles in that issue; John Oneal and Bruce Russett, "Exploring the Liberal Peace," paper presented at the International Studies Association meetings, April 1996, revised and shortened as "The Classical Liberals Were Right," *International Studies Quarterly* 41 (1997), 267–94.

[37] Edward D. Mansfield, "Democratization and Commercial Liberalization," paper presented at the 1996 annual meeting of the American Political Science Association.

By today's standards, France was not a full-fledged democracy in the years immediately following the French Revolution of 1789: it had no stable rule of law, elections were irregular, and only some Frenchmen could vote. Nonetheless, the elected assembly was the focal point of the nation's politics, and the press was, at least for a time, free and lively. Under these free-wheeling conditions, one of the revolutionary factions, led by the newspaperman Jacques-Pierre Brissot, discovered that the best way to win popularity and power was to hype the foreign threat. Brissot was swept into power through his allegations of a conspiracy linking the Austrian monarchy to the French king and aristocracy. Soon the assembly and the Paris political clubs (which nowadays we would call "civil society") were demanding war. The troops of revolutionary France marched to the frontier in the name of liberty, equality, and fraternity, as well as national defense.[38]

In comparison, British politics during the decades of partial democratization following the First Reform Bill of 1832 were far less volatile. Nonetheless, even here, public opinion among the newly enfranchised middle classes, inflamed by the nationalistic press, pushed the reluctant British cabinet into the Crimean War against Russia in 1853.[39]

World Wars I and II can similarly be attributed in part to the imperfect beginning stages of German and Japanese democratization. Before 1914, Germany had universal suffrage, an elected legislature that controlled the national budget, and habitual voter turnouts above 90 percent. However, it was not a full democracy, since the hereditary monarch, rather than the voters, picked the ministers who ran the executive branch of government. Over a million German voters were members of nationalist organizations like the Navy League, which demanded an aggressive policy of imperial expansion that led Germany into confrontation with Europe's great powers. Despite Germany's defeat in World War I, middle-class voters once again helped install a belligerent nationalist government in the waning days of the unstable Weimar Republic, voting heavily for the Nazis in 1932. Japan, too, experimented with electoral democracy in the 1920s. Japanese public opinion, encouraged by a relatively free press,

[38] T. C. W. Blanning, *The Origins of the French Revolutionary Wars* (London: Longman, 1986).

[39] Norman Rich, *Why the Crimean War?* (Hanover, NH: University Press of New England, 1985).

turned sharply in favor of forceful imperial expansion on the heels of the 1929 economic depression and the Japanese military invasion of Manchuria in 1931.[40] Thus, the turbulent early stages of democratization in Germany and Japan were closely tied to the origins of both world wars.

Although these episodes may seem like ancient history, Argentina's ill-fated 1982 invasion of the Falkland Islands, owned by Great Britain, was spurred by a similar dynamic. The Argentine military regime, its popularity waning, had recently allowed more freedom of the press, which was in turn effectively exploited by nationalist voices clamoring for a seizure of the islands. Hoping that a successful military gambit would enhance its popularity and position it well for democratic elections that increasingly seemed inevitable, the Argentine military dictatorship gambled on attacking the sovereign territory of a nuclear-armed great power and NATO member.[41]

Thus, there are strong indications that nascent democratization and its close cousin, press liberalization, heighten the risk of nationalist and ethnic conflict in our own time, just as they have historically. What accounts for this correlation?

## Why Democratization Increases the Risk of Nationalist Conflict

Two contending views, which I label the "popular-rivalries" and the "elite-persuasion" arguments, offer opposite explanations for the correlation between democratization and nationalist conflict. The former contends that long-standing popular nationalist rivalries precede democratization. In this view, democratization gives expression to the long-held, popular aspirations of an already-formed nation, which are incompatible with the aspirations of other nations. The "ancient hatreds" argument is one form of this popular-rivalries explanation.

[40] Jack Snyder, *Myths of Empire* (Ithaca: Cornell University Press, 1991), Chapters 3–4; Louise Young, "War Fever: Imperial Jingoism and the Mass Media," in *Japan's Total Empire: Manchuria and the Culture of Wartime Imperialism* (Berkeley: University of California, 1998).

[41] Richard Ned Lebow, "Miscalculation in the South Atlantic," in Robert Jervis, et al., *Psychology and Deterrence* (Baltimore: Johns Hopkins University Press, 1985), 98–99; Jack Levy and Lily Vakili, "Diversionary Action by Authoritarian Regimes," in Manus Midlarsky, ed., *The Internationalization of Communal Strife* (London: Routledge, 1992), 118–46.

I argue the opposite. Before democratization begins, nationalism is usually weak or absent among the broad masses of the population. Popular nationalism typically arises during the earliest stages of democratization, when elites use nationalist appeals to compete for popular support.[42] Democratization produces nationalism when powerful groups within the nation not only need to harness popular energies to the tasks of war and economic development, but they also want to avoid surrendering real political authority to the average citizen. For those elites, nationalism is a convenient doctrine that justifies a partial form of democracy, in which an elite rules in the name of the nation yet may not be fully accountable to its people. Under conditions of partial democratization, elites can often use their control over the levers of government, the economy, and the mass media to promote nationalist ideas, and thus set the agenda for debate. Nationalist conflicts arise as a by-product of elites' efforts to persuade the people to accept divisive nationalist ideas.

It matters which of these two views is correct, because each points toward different prescriptions for averting nationalist conflict. If the popular-rivalries view is right, the preferred solution should often be to partition democratizing ethnic groups into separate states, even if it means moving populations.[43] Much of Eastern Europe has already undergone a vast "unmixing of peoples" in the twentieth century, most of it as a result of extermination and forced emigration during and immediately after the two world wars.[44] Why not, in this view, move people before the fighting rather than afterward? Where partition of a multiethnic state is impractical, the closest substitute would have to be adopted: powersharing between largely self-governing nationalities. Under this scheme, sometimes called "consociational democracy," people would have rights not only as individuals but also as members of a national or ethnic group,

---

[42] For related arguments, see V. P. Gagnon, "Ethnic Nationalism and International Conflict: The Case of Serbia," *International Security* 19:3 (Winter 1994/95), 130–66; V. P. Gagnon, "Ethnic Conflict as Demobilizer: The Case of Serbia" (Cornell University, Institute for European Studies Working Paper no. 96.1, May 1996); Paul Brass, *Language, Religion and Politics in North India* (Cambridge: Cambridge University Press, 1974).

[43] For a discussion of the conditions in which partition is necessary, see Chaim Kaufmann, "Possible and Impossible Solutions to Ethnic Civil Wars," *International Security* 20:4 (Spring 1996), 136–75.

[44] Rogers Brubaker, *Nationalism Reframed*, Chapter 6.

which would govern its own internal affairs and have group rights to pro-portional representation in the bureaucracy and the legislature.[45] However, if the elite-persuasion view is correct, such separation measures might serve to lock in divisive national identities, unnecessarily heightening distrust between groups. When this is the case, a better solution would be to take advantage of the fluidity of national identity during the formative stages of democratization to promote more inclusive, civic identities and cross-ethnic political alignments.

I will first summarize and assess the popular-rivalries view, in part because it seems so plausible, indeed commonsensical, to most American readers. Then I will briefly summarize my own elite-persuasion argument, which will be presented more fully in Chapter 2.

### Predemocratic popular rivalries: A simple but usually erroneous explanation

A very simple explanation for the link between democratization and nationalist conflict sees nationalism as deeply rooted in popular attitudes that long precede democratization. If people of different cultures natu-rally want their own state, and if they inhabit the same territory, giving them the vote will unavoidably put them at loggerheads. In principle, these conflicting aims might cause conflict even if the contending groups had no predemocratic history of violence toward each other. However, if people of different cultures had learned through long-term rivalries to hate or distrust each other, that would make the rivalry even worse: the democratic process would express those entrenched popular animosities.[46]

In the popular-rivalries view, national strivings can be suppressed by empires and authoritarian regimes, whereas democratization gives voice to the true nationalist preferences of the average voter. Elections become a census rather than a deliberative process. Democratization will tend to

[45] Arend Lijphart, *Democracy in Plural Societies* (New Haven: Yale University Press, 1977).

[46] Hurst Hannum, *Autonomy, Sovereignty, and Self-Determination* (Philadelphia: University of Pennsylvania, 1996), discusses problems arising out of demands for eth-nic self-determination; Daniel Byman and Stephen Van Evera, "Hypotheses on the Causes of Contemporary Deadly Conflict," *Security Studies* 7:3 (Spring 1998), esp. 33–35, discuss the conflictual consequences of the "tyranny of the majority" and of historic grievances of "hardened groups" in democratizing multiethnic societies.

produce either the tyranny of the majority or a pitched battle between the competing state-building goals of rival nations. Democratization, in this view, may also give rise to international conflicts, if a newly democratic nationalizing state seeks to capture foreign territory where its ethnic brethren reside.

Many Americans, steeped in Woodrow Wilson's doctrine of national self-determination, take for granted that humanity is divided into distinct peoples, each of whom has the natural desire to rule itself in its own way.[47] When the Soviet Union collapsed, for example, many Americans with Wilsonian instincts saw it as quite natural that each of the fifteen ethnically titled constituent republics of the USSR should exercise its democratic right to self-determination. This seemed all the more just because of the long history of Soviet repression of what U.S. cold warriors called the "captive nations": mass deportations of some non-Russian ethnic groups to Siberia and Central Asia, systematic campaigns of terror or starvation against others, and dictatorial rule from Moscow over all the subject nations at the periphery of the empire. Emerging from this history, the formerly captive nations had ample reason to desire self-rule rather than rule by Moscow.

But where ethnic groups live side by side in the same towns and regions, one group's aim to establish self-rule in its own state is sure to be incompatible with that of others.[48] Every successor state to the Soviet Union except Armenia houses a substantial minority, including the Russians who populated many of the cities and industrial enterprises of the non-Russian Soviet republics.[49] Under these circumstances, democratic self-determination by ethnic groups becomes a recipe for conflict if each group tries to establish a state in which it monopolizes citizenship rights and in which policies on linguistic or economic issues serve the interests of the dominant ethnic group. Because so few states in the former Soviet empire or in the developing world are ethnically homoge-

---

[47] For a critique of this view, see David Laitin, *Identity in Formation* (Ithaca: Cornell University Press, 1998), 12.

[48] Hurst Hannum, "Rethinking Self-Determination," *Virginia Journal of International Law* 43:1 (Fall 1993), 1–69, points out the elusiveness of self-determination doctrine on the question of the boundaries of the self-determining unit.

[49] Robert Kaiser, *The Geography of Nationalism in Russia and the USSR* (Princeton: Princeton University Press, 1994). Armenia, which had the smallest minority population even in Soviet times, expelled most of its Azerbaijani minority before independence.

neous, Wilsonians should not be surprised if many new democracies are conflict-prone.[50]

Despite the clear logic behind this popular-rivalries view, I argue that in most cases it gets the facts exactly backward. Mass nationalism is rarely well developed before democratization. More commonly, it rises during the earliest phase of democratic change. In the era before the majority of the population takes an active part in political life, their sense of belonging to a nation is usually weak. Typically, they are aware of cultural, linguistic, religious, and regional differences across groups, but they attach political significance to these differences only intermittently, if at all. At that stage of social development, politics is a matter for elites. It is true that cultural legacies or administrative arrangements based on nationality in the authoritarian regime may load the dice in favor of the *later* development of a particular form of nationalism, once the broader population becomes politically active. Even so, in most cases, this consciousness does not crystallize until people start to speak out in public and form mass political organizations along national lines.

For example, it would be wrong to view Serbia's war for autonomy from the Ottoman Empire in the early nineteenth century as an outpouring of ancient popular nationalist sentiment. As I show in Chapter 4, this struggle was more a commercial enterprise by a multiethnic cabal of pig-traders than a war of national liberation. Serbian national consciousness took shape only gradually from the 1860s to 1914, when Serbia had a surprisingly democratic though disorderly political system with nearly universal suffrage, competing parties, and a free press. The wars and hatreds of that period made a lasting impact on the national consciousness, in part because the public was already playing a role in political life. As in most of the European states, according to historian Miroslav Hroch, "the process of nation-forming acquired an irreversible character only once the national movement had won mass support."[51]

---

[50] Clifford Geertz, "Primordial Sentiments and Civil Politics in the New States," in Geertz, ed., *Old Societies and New States* (New York: Free Press of Glencoe, 1963), 123. According to one survey, fewer than 10 percent of states are populated almost entirely by members of a single national group. Walker Connor, *Ethnonationalism* (Princeton: Princeton University Press, 1994), 96.

[51] Miroslav Hroch, "Real and Constructed: The Nature of the Nation," in John Hall, ed., *The State of the Nation: Ernest Gellner and the Theory of Nationalism* (Cambridge: Cambridge University Press, 1998).

In short, nations are not simply freed or awakened by democratization; they are formed by the experiences they undergo during that process. The type of political experiences, institutions, and leadership that prevails during the initial phases of democratization can be decisive for the formation of national identity. How people are included in the political life of their state determines the kind of national consciousness that they develop, as well as the degree of nationalist conflict that democratization brings. Consequently, it is of immense practical importance, as well as academic interest, to explore in detail what forces shape the kind of nationalism that emerges from the crucible of democratization. Purported solutions to ethnic conflict that take predemocratic identities as fixed, such as partition, ethnofederalism, ethnic powersharing, and the granting of group rights, may needlessly lock in mutually exclusive, inimical national identities. In contrast, creating an institutional setting for democratization that de-emphasizes ethnicity might turn these identities toward more inclusive, civic self-conceptions.

### Elite persuasion: Selling nationalism in democratizing states

Democratization gives rise to nationalism because it serves the interests of powerful groups within the nation who seek to harness popular energies to the tasks of war and economic development without surrendering real political authority to the average citizen. In predemocratic societies, military, economic, and cultural elites preferred to rule without taking the risk of arousing popular nationalist sentiments. However, with the rise of mass armies, commercial capitalism, and inexpensive printing in the eighteenth and nineteenth centuries, rulers who could attract the active support of their people gained a valuable advantage in competition against other states and against rival elites at home. In a growing number of countries, old elites either granted some democratic reforms, or else rising new elites forced such changes. Despite the pressures for democratization, both the old and new elites were typically reluctant to allow full democratic rights, since this could have endangered their parochial economic interests as well as their positions of power in society. Nationalism, a doctrine of rule in the name of the people but not necessarily by the people, provided a way for elites to be popular without being fully democratic.

A very effective tool for containing popular pressure for democratization is the use of nationalist doctrine to exclude so-called enemies of the nation from enjoying democratic rights. Nationalist elites commonly argue that ethnic minorities, the working classes, rival elites, or other political opponents should be excluded from political participation, often alleging that these groups lack the proper national credentials and are in league with foreign powers. This tactic not only justifies curtailing the democratic rights of these purported "enemies within," but just as important, it has a chilling effect on freedom of expression among all citizens.[52]

The prospects for elite attempts at nationalist persuasion depend in part on the timing of democratization relative to the development of the country's economy and political institutions. Exclusionary nationalism is most likely to prevail when the democratizing country is poor, when its citizens lack the skills needed for successful democratic political participation, and when its representative institutions, political parties, and journalistic professionalism are weakly established during the early phase of the democratic transition. In these conditions, nationalist elites are more able to hijack political discourse. Moreover, in such a barren and unpromising political landscape, threatened elites are likely to have little confidence that a fully democratic regime could reliably guarantee to protect their interests after they surrender power. Under these conditions, gambling on staying in power at the crest of a nationalist tide will seem an attractive alternative. Conversely, exclusionary nationalism is less likely to thrive in countries like nineteenth-century Britain or contemporary South Africa that democratize after the necessary economic resources, citizenship skills, or political institutions are already in place.

These outcomes depend on both the motivation and the opportunity of elites to promote nationalist doctrines. The strength of an elite's *motivation* depends on the adaptability of its interests to a more democratic setting. The more the elite feels threatened by the arrival of full democracy, the stronger is its incentive to use nationalist persuasion to forestall that outcome. The elite's *opportunity* to sell exclusionary nationalism depends to a large extent on the character of the political institutions of the democratizing state. For example, where the state's bureaucracy is strong, yet its institutions for democratic participation and public debate are weak, state elites will be able to use their administrative leverage to promote national-

---

[52] Gagnon, "Ethnic Conflict as Demobilizer"; on the role of racial exclusion, see Anthony Marx, *Making Race and Nation* (Cambridge: Cambridge University Press, 1998).

ism during the early phase of democratization. Conversely, when representative and journalistic institutions are already well developed during early democratization, nationalist arguments can be checked through more effective scrutiny in open public debate.

Together these two factors, the adaptability of elite interests and the strength of the country's political institutions during early democratization, determine the intensity of the democratizing country's nationalism and the form that nationalist exclusions are likely to take. Representing the resulting possibilities as a schematic simplification, this yields four types of nationalism: counterrevolutionary, revolutionary, ethnic, and civic (see Table 1.1). Three of these four entail severe exclusions of different kinds and are likely to lead to intense nationalist conflicts.

*Counterrevolutionary* nationalism is likely to emerge when elite interests are not adaptable, and when administrative institutions are strong, but representative institutions are weak. In that situation, my theory predicts that attempts at nationalist persuasion will be intense and effective. Threatened ruling elites will justify excluding political opponents from power by portraying them as revolutionary enemies of the nation. As in Germany before World War I, nationalism will take a counterrevolutionary form.

Conversely, *revolutionary* nationalism will emerge when state institutions have already collapsed, and opportunistically adaptable elites seek to establish a popular basis for restoring power to the state. Under those conditions, I predict that nationalist persuasion will be used effectively to rally support against foes at home and abroad. As in the French Revolution, nationalism will take an intensely exclusionary revolutionary form.

*Ethnic* nationalism is likely when democratization begins in a setting where the basic building blocks of political or administrative institutions have never been laid down. In this institutional desert, elites will by default be constrained to base appeals to loyalty on the only available alternative, traditional popular culture. As in nineteenth-century Serbia, an intensely exclusionary nationalism will take an *ethnic* form.

These three types of exclusionary nationalism—counterrevolutionary, revolutionary, and ethnic—are likely to produce violent nationalist conflicts with the excluded groups inside the country and with any of these groups' purported foreign allies. The fourth variant of nationalism, the civic type, is more moderate and inclusive.

Nationalism will take an inclusive *civic* form when elites are not partic-

ularly threatened by democratization, and when representative and journalistic institutions are already well established before the mass of the
population gains political power. Under those conditions, as in Britain in
the eighteenth and nineteenth centuries, nationalists lack both the motive
and the opportunity to purvey divisive doctrines. While civic nationalisms are not predicted to be pacifistic, they have far less reason to fall
prey to the kind of reckless, ideologically driven conflicts characteristic of
the other three types.

**Table 1.1 Relationship of Political Institutions and Elites' Interests to the
Type of Nationalism during the Early Phase of Democratization.**

| *Nationalist Elites' Interests* | *Strength of the Nation's Political Institutions* | |
|---|---|---|
| | *Strong* | *Weak* |
| *Adaptable* | Civic: strong representative institutions (Britain) | Revolutionary (revolutionary France) |
| *Unadaptable* | Counterrevolutionary: strong administrative institutions (pre–World War I Germany) | Ethnic (pre–World War I Serbia) |

## Making Choices in Today's World

These explanations for the connection between democratization and
nationalism have significant implications for designing strategies to manage contemporary nationalism. The ethnic conflicts of the 1990s spurred
a number of sharp policy debates among politicians, journalists, and
scholars. Understanding how democratization causes nationalist conflict
sheds new light on each of those debates.

The most general debate revolves around the nature of the coming
epoch, whether it will be wracked with ethnic conflict, or whether it is
heading toward an inclusive democratic peace. The analysis advanced in
this book suggests that both perspectives are likely to be right. The democratic peace will prevail within and between states wherever democracy is
quickly and successfully consolidated. Meanwhile, nationalism will be on

the rise in the many states that find themselves newly embarking on democratization, stuck in between autocracy and democracy, suffering from the consequences of failed democratization, or simply anticipating its unsettling effects. Insofar as great powers like China and Russia may face these dangers, dealing with democratization as a cause of nationalist conflict should remain high on the agenda of the international community.

More concretely, the management of these transitions provokes sharp differences of opinion. Some argue that international organizations, nongovernmental human rights groups, and powerful democratic states ought to press all dictators to democratize immediately. *New York Times* editorials routinely insist that the authoritarian leaders of such countries as Congo and Malaysia should immediately announce multiparty elections. My theory suggests skepticism about that advice. Given the postcolonial pattern of patronage and political alignment in such countries, factionalism in politics during their democratization often follows ethnic lines.[53] And given that starting point, effective institutions for channeling social cleavages in other directions need to be well developed before democratization can be part of the solution rather than part of the problem.

Some argue that the international community should press for powersharing between groups in multiethnic societies, with ethnic groups, not just individuals, enjoying rights.[54] My theory suggests that this is a last resort because it runs the risk of unnecessarily politicizing and locking in inimical cultural distinctions. Wherever possible, democratizing states should try to promote civic identities and guarantee rights at the individual level. For the same reasons, ethnically based federalism and regional autonomy should be avoided, since they create political organizations and media markets that are centered on ethnic differences.

Some argue that multiethnic states with a history of intercommunal conflict ought to be partitioned before the conflict recurs, even if this means moving people to new homes.[55] My theory suggests that partitions might be necessary where ethnic conflicts during formative periods of

---

[53] Mahmoud Mamdani, *Citizen and Subject: Contemporary Africa and the Legacy of Late Colonialism* (Princeton: Princeton University Press, 1996), 300.

[54] Arend Lijphart, "The Power-Sharing Approach," in Joseph V. Montville, ed., *Conflict and Peacemaking in Multiethnic Societies* (New York: Lexington, 1991), 491–510.

[55] Chaim Kaufmann, "Possible and Impossible Solutions to Ethnic Civil Wars," *International Security* 20:4 (Spring 1996), 136–75.

democratic development have already created entrenched institutions, ideas, and interests based on invidious ethnic distinctions. But for states that have not undergone significant levels of democratization, such partitions should be unnecessary if leaders are willing to adopt a strategy of civic institution-building *before* embarking on democratization. The gradual development of the rule of law, an impartial bureaucracy, civil rights, and a professional media, *followed* by the holding of free elections, should be able to create a civic national identity that trumps "ancient hatreds."

Many human rights organizations argue that individuals responsible for human rights abuses in waning authoritarian systems, especially their leaders, ought to be punished for their crimes against humanity. My theory, however, highlights the incentive that this creates for still-powerful elites to play the ethnic card in a last-gasp effort to forestall this fate. Indeed, democratization has proceeded most smoothly where authoritarian elites were given a "golden parachute" into a safe retirement, as in South America and northeast Europe. Where elites have felt most threatened, notably in Rwanda, human rights disasters have only intensified. Punishment is a prudent strategy only when the human rights abusers are too weak to wreak such havoc.

Finally, advocacy groups like Human Rights Watch propose greater freedom of speech and a more active "civil society" as antidotes to manipulative governments that foment ethnic conflict.[56] Yet in many infant democracies, the newly freed press becomes a vehicle for nationalist appeals. Weak democratic institutions often make society uncivil.[57] Unfettered speech and a vibrant civil society are forces for peace only when conditions are favorable, that is, when media audiences are sophisticated and journalists are professionalized. Projects to foster those preconditions need to precede proposals to unleash vigorous debate in a free press.

These are controversial prescriptions that run counter to the current conventional wisdoms of the international human rights community as

[56] Human Rights Watch, *Slaughter among Neighbors* (New Haven: Yale University Press, 1995).

[57] Sheri Berman, "Civil Society and the Collapse of the Weimar Republic," *World Politics* 49:3 (April 1997), 401–29; Margaret Levi, "Social and Unsocial Capital," *Politics and Society* 24 (March 1996), 45–56; Sidney Tarrow, "Making Social Science Work across Time and Space," *American Political Science Review*, 90:2 (June 1996), 389–98.

well as many of the natural instincts of the American public. Nonetheless, I believe that the theoretical logic and case-study evidence presented in the coming chapters should make even the most avid proponent of spreading democracy and human rights think more carefully about devising prudent ways and means of pursuing those ends.

## The Plan of the Book

The next chapter fleshes out my elite-persuasion explanation for the correlation between democratization and nationalist conflict. It also discusses some possible alternative explanations. To probe the plausibility of these arguments, I examine historical as well as contemporary cases of democratization. I rely on a combination of two strategies: tracing causal processes within cases and comparing across cases.

Chapters 3 and 4 present historical case studies of the four types of nationalism: counterrevolutionary Germany before the two world wars, civic Britain in the eighteenth and nineteenth centuries, revolutionary France, and ethnic Serbia in the century before 1914. These four cases have been focal points for much of the theoretical and historical literature on nationalism, and for good reason. Britain and France, the two earliest cases of nationalism, created a form of political loyalty that other states felt compelled to emulate. France and Germany carried out nationalist aggression on a continental scale. Serbia spans two centuries as the quintessential example of divisive ethnic loyalty. Any theory of nationalism must come to grips with these seminal instances. I devote all of Chapter 3 to the German case, which provides an exceptionally rich laboratory illuminating many of the mechanisms through which democratization causes nationalism and nationalist conflict. Chapter 4 sketches the other three cases and concludes by comparing all four types of nationalism. These paradigmatic cases illustrate patterns that help in assessing the contemporary case studies presented in subsequent chapters.

Chapter 5 examines the impact of democratization on nationalism and ethnic conflict in the post-Communist states. It is important to analyze these cases both because of their intrinsic contemporary significance and because they constitute a hard test for my theory. Many of the post-Communist states democratized, yet not all of them experienced intense nationalist conflicts. Thus, this set of cases presents a challenge to see how well each state's distinctive pattern of democratization can explain the degree of its nationalism.

Chapter 6 discusses the relationship between democratization and nationalism in the contemporary developing world. It begins with a broad overview of the conditions that have led to intense nationalist and ethnic conflicts in some democratizating states, and contrasts them with the conditions that have led to peaceful transitions in others. Then I look in more detail at a few cases that illuminate key issues for my theory. A comparison of the closely parallel cases of Sri Lanka and Malaysia shows how unfettered democratization triggered ethnic strife in the former case, whereas in similar circumstances, a scheme imposed by an authoritarian leader averted ethnic conflict in the latter one. Sketches of Rwanda and Burundi show the dangers of liberalization in states lacking an adequate institutional foundation, while the case of India illustrates the consequences that ensue when those foundations begin to atrophy.

Chapter 7 draws out the practical implications of the analysis, assessing various prescriptions for averting nationalist conflict. Overall, I argue that the international community should pursue a patient and sometimes indirect strategy for promoting the spread of well-institutionalized civic democracies. Shortcuts on the road to the "democratic peace" could wind up as detours to a counterrevolutionary nationalist backlash or to rivalrous ethnic pseudodemocracies.[58]

---

[58] For a related argument, see Fareed Zakaria, "The Rise of Illiberal Democracy," *Foreign Affairs* 76:6 (November/December 1997), 22–43.

# 2

## Nationalist Elite Persuasion in

## Democratizing States

Democratization produces nationalism when powerful elites within a nation need to harness popular energies to the tasks of war and economic development, but they also want to avoid surrendering real political authority to the average citizen. For those elites, nationalism is a convenient doctrine that justifies a partial form of democracy: the elites rule in the name of the nation but are not fully accountable to its people. The form of nationalism that emerges during democratization, and the intensity of the conflicts that it unleashes, depends in large part on the interests of that nationalist elite, the strength or weakness of the institutions through which it rules, and its power over the media.

After presenting my argument, I discuss how I test my theory against other explanations of the link between democratization and nationalist conflict, including the popular-rivalries account.

### Elite Persuasion: Promoting Popular Loyalty to the Nation

Not all successful modern states are democracies, but with very few exceptions, all have had to find some way to attract the active loyalty of the majority of their people. Before the latter part of the eighteenth century, dynasties and empires could successfully rule over politically passive populations, extracting enough economic surplus from them to maintain mercenary forces or an armed aristocracy. Rulers rarely claimed to govern in the interests of their populations. It hardly mattered that monarchs and subjects often spoke different languages and lacked a common national identity.[1]

This changed with the advent of commercial capitalism, mass armies, and inexpensive printing.[2] As wealth from trade, and later from industry, spread more widely throughout society, the most successful states were those that convinced their mercantile populations to submit to taxation or to lend their wealth voluntarily to the state. This gave the state the wherewithal to fight wars on a grand scale and to further promote commerce. States that could win the enthusiastic support of their people gained a significant advantage in the raising of large armies and the financing of navies. For the first time, nationalism, the doctrine that the interests of the state and the people were one, was a valuable commodity in the marketplace of ideas. The concurrent development of cheap commercial publications provided the perfect medium for selling this message.

States that enjoyed the active loyalty of their people, like Britain by the mid-eighteenth century and France after the Revolution of 1789, were powerhouses that threatened to overwhelm those that lagged behind in attracting a nationalist following. Both then and now, countries that are

---

[1] Ernest Gellner, *Nations and Nationalism* (Ithaca: Cornell University Press, 1983), Chapter 2.

[2] Charles Tilly, ed., *The Formation of National States in Western Europe* (Princeton: Princeton University Press, 1975); Tilly, *Coercion, Capital, and European States, AD 990–1990* (Cambridge: Basil Blackwell, 1990); Barry Posen, "Nationalism, the Mass Army and Military Power," *International Security* 18:2 (Fall 1993), 80–124; Benedict Anderson, *Imagined Communities: Reflections on the Origins and Spread of Nationalism* (London: Verso, 1983); Michael Mann, "The Emergence of Modern European Nationalism," in John A. Hall and Ian Jarvie, eds., *Transition to Modernity* (Cambridge: Cambridge University Press, 1992), 137–66.

more democratic tend to win their wars, even taking into account differences in size and wealth.[3] Thus, rulers either harnessed national sentiment or else risked being replaced by rival elites who insisted on forging a popular state that could tap national enthusiasm. Through emulation of this magic formula invented by the Western powers, nationalist ideas and movements emerged even in those central and east European lands where commercial capitalism, industry, and literacy lagged behind. Nationalism spread to countries like Germany and Serbia as the ideology that would justify a strong, modernizing state and would protect the interests of its people from foreign domination, providing government ostensibly for the people, but not necessarily by the people.[4]

The need for popular support of the state presented a pair of opposite challenges to leaders and would-be leaders: how to promote popular loyalty while still containing popular demands. The problem of getting a large group of people to contribute to a common end—the so-called collective action problem—has been a major preoccupation of contemporary social science. In small, face-to-face groups, people cooperate on collective tasks relatively easily because they know that whatever help they give will be reciprocated on another occasion. People learn that they sink or swim together, and that shirking is self-defeating. However, in larger groups like a nation, collective action faces serious barriers. People don't necessarily understand that they share a common fate. Indeed, they may feel that some members of the group are more threatening than outsiders, or that these members are not likely to pull their weight for the collective good. People will be wary about cooperating, prudently choosing to husband their own resources and to avoid pooling resources with those who may exploit them. Even in times of foreign threat, keeping a son at home to work the fields and to protect the local village may seem more prudent than sending him off to protect the nation.

Overcoming the disincentives for national collective action may be dif-

[3] David Lake, "Powerful Pacifists: Democratic States and War," *American Political Science Review* 86:1 (Spring 1992), 24–37.

[4] Hans Kohn, *Prelude to Nation-States: The French and German Experience, 1789–1815* (Princeton: D. Van Nostrand, 1967); Liah Greenfeld, *Nationalism: Five Roads to Modernity* (Cambridge: Harvard University Press, 1992); Alexander Gerschenkron, *Economic Backwardness in Historical Perspective* (Cambridge: Belknap, 1962).

ficult, even in parts of today's world. For example, Kurdish clans in northern Iraq who share a common ethnic nationality have recently found it impossible to cooperate with one another, even in the face of a military threat from their arch foe, Iraqi dictator Saddam Hussein. With the balance of power among the clans shifting, each clan concluded that the greatest threat came from other clans rather than from Saddam. Consequently, none was willing to risk pooling resources, coordinating strategies, or allowing another clan to gain disproportionately from joint action to safeguard national autonomy.[5]

To overcome the barriers to collective action in a large group like a nation, elites need two kinds of tools: effective institutions (which embody the habit of working together toward collective ends), and unifying ideas (which convince people that they share common goals and a common fate).

### Building national institutions

Institutions are repeated patterns of behavior around which expectations converge.[6] When behavior is institutionalized, people can predict how others will behave based on past patterns of regularized activity. These predictable regularities shape the environment in which people calculate the costs and benefits of their own behavior. In large complex groups like nations, specialized, formal institutions are needed to carry out the various tasks that enable collective action: legislatures establish group norms, chief executives propose policies around which collective efforts can converge, immigration services verify group membership, bureaucracies monitor contributions to group tasks and provide information and standards, courts act as third-party guarantors of contracts for group members, and police enforce compliance with group norms. The Kurds have been unable to rally around their nation largely because they lack strong institutions of this type.

---

[5] For background on Kurdish factionalism, see Michael Gunter, *The Kurds of Iraq* (New York: St. Martin's, 1992), Chapter 3.

[6] Walter Powell and Paul DiMaggio, eds., *The New Institutionalism in Organizational Analysis* (Chicago: University of Chicago Press, 1991); Andrew Schotter, *The Economic Theory of Social Institutions* (Cambridge: Cambridge University Press, 1981), 9.

In simpler or less organized groups, the same tasks may be carried out with varying effectiveness by less specialized, informal institutions, such as decentralized cultural habits and practices. For example, when police and courts are weak, popular cultures often develop informal rules governing retaliation by clan members against outsiders who harm a member of their group. Although such feuding may seem lawless, in fact it is overseen and regulated by clan elders in ways that can some-times provide an effective informal substitute for formal institutions.[7] Because shared cultural practices of this type may serve as catalysts in the crystallization of national institutions, ethnic bonds may facilitate the formation of a nation. However, as the Kurds have learned, a shared culture offers no guarantee that effective national institutions will emerge.

### Promoting nationalist ideas

Ideas also play a central role in promoting collective action by shaping the kind of groups that people can imagine joining, their assessments of the costs and benefits of collective action, and their feelings of moral obliga-tion. Who is part of our group? Which outsiders pose the greatest threat? How did a certain group behave in the past? What is their character now, and what do they plan for the future? Who will be an effective, reliable ally against them? Answers to these questions hinge in part on facts, but in the social realm, facts almost never speak for themselves. Facts require interpretation and the application of moral judgments. The ideas set forth by nationalist politicians give people a simple guide from which to make interpretations and judgments.

All nationalist elites have some incentive to propound ideas that exag-gerate the threat emanating from rival nations and also the benefits that will flow from rallying the nation to contain that threat. Such ideas, if they can be made persuasively, facilitate collective action by members of

---

[7] Christopher Bloehm, *Blood Revenge: The Anthropology of Feuding in Montenegro and Other Tribal Societies* (Lawrence: University Press of Kansas, 1984); on intra-group self-policing as a key factor explaining why ethnic conflict is not more com-mon, see James Fearon and David Laitin, "Explaining Interethnic Cooperation," *American Political Science Review* 90:4 (December 1996), 715–35.

the community. Inherently, these exaggerations heighten the risk of conflict between nations. If both sides are laboring under these biased perceptions, then each side will see the other as more threatening than it
really is yet more easily defeated by united opposition than the true prob-
abilities may warrant. Thus, aggression looks more necessary and more
likely to succeed than it really is. The extent of these conflict-causing
biases varies tremendously, depending in part on the kind of social groups
that nationalist elites must rely upon for support.

### Self-interested elite groups as the kernel for national institutions and ideas

Effective institutions and unifying ideas are indispensable for collective
action in a large group like a nation, but they are difficult and costly to
provide. To overcome these difficulties, nationalists need an institutional
base from which to build a constituency. These nationalists need to start
from some smaller group that already has the habit of mutually beneficial
cooperation, which can serve as the kernel for wider collective action.
People studying collective action in settings of high risk and cost (e.g.,
revolutions, rebellions, and resistance movements) have found that the
inclination to shirk is most often overcome by mobilization through
small-scale social networks of people who trust each other. Their trust is
based on a history of repeated interactions in other activities.[8] History
shows that the small-group kernel for nationalist collective action may
come from almost any group: the ruling dynasty of the prenational
regime, the dominant faction of a region, a cohesive and privileged economic group, a religious or cultural elite, a part of the military officer
corps, intellectuals sharing a common education or outlook, prominent
figures in an ethnic group, or the leaders of a powerful clan.

[8] Sidney Tarrow, *Power in Movement: Social Movements, Collective Action and
Politics* (Cambridge: Cambridge University Press, 1994), 22; Pierre Birnbaum, *States
and Collective Action* (Cambridge: Cambridge University Press, 1988), 58, citing
Charles Tilly, *La Vendée* (Paris: Fayard, 1970); Samuel Popkin, "Political Entrepreneurs
and Peasant Movements in Vietnam," in Michael Taylor, *Rationality and Revolution*
(Cambridge: Cambridge University Press, 1988), 9–62; Ian Lustick, "Writing the
Intifada," *World Politics* 45:4 (July 1993), 560–94; Roger Petersen, *Resistance and
Rebellion: Lessons from Eastern Europe* (Cambridge: Cambridge University Press,
forthcoming).

Those who incur costs to promote collective action normally do so because they anticipate a private benefit.[9] Even if some nationalists may be motivated entirely by the force of their own ideals, motivating the small groups that provide the resources and cadres for national institution-building and campaigns of persuasion means promising them selective incentives: disproportionate power, privileges, subsidies or protectionism for their economic activities, and preservation of their groups' accustomed ways. Privileged groups who take the lead in forming the nation's ideas and institutions try to lock in their advantages by defining the national identity in ways that reflect their own parochial interests and habitual practices. Competing visions of a country's national identity normally reflect differences in the interests or outlooks of groups that are vying to mobilize national sentiment—for example, the antithetical American nationalisms of the slave-holding agrarian Confederacy versus the wage-labor industrializing North. Similarly, in pre-1914 Germany, Prussian landowning aristocrats and army officers appealed to rural Germans by offering a vision of German nationalism centered on pre-industrial traditions, high tariffs against agricultural imports, and the conquest of land in central Europe, whereas heavy industrialists and the German navy appealed to the urban middle classes by offering a vision of commercial, high-technology, overseas expansionist nationalism.[10]

In short, the first problem faced by nationalist elites is to create the possibility of effective collective action on a national scale. The solution is to build institutions and disseminate ideas from a small group that already has the habit of working together and can derive parochial benefits from promoting collective action on a national scale. As I will explain below, the likelihood that nationalist mobilization will produce conflict with other nations is determined in part by the nature of these founding interests. Once popular nationalist energies have been mobilized, a second problem arises: how to contain popular demands to participate in politics.

[9] Michael Hechter, "The Emergence of Cooperative Social Institutions," in Michael Hechter, Dieter Opp, and Reinhard Wippler, eds., *Social Institutions: Their Emergence, Maintenance, and Effects* (New York: Aldine de Gruyter, 1990), 20; Russell Hardin, *Collective Action* (Baltimore: Johns Hopkins University Press, 1982), 31; Jack Knight, *Institutions and Social Conflict* (Cambridge: Cambridge University Press, 1992), 5–9.

[10] Woodruff Smith, *The Ideological Origins of Nazi Imperialism* (New York: Oxford University Press, 1986).

### The dangers of successful persuasion:
### Containing popular demands through exclusions

Sometimes nationalist elites are all too successful in unleashing popular enthusiasm for mass participation in the nation's political life. Once the majority of the nation has been convinced that legitimate authority stems from national self-rule, it is a short step to the conclusion that the average voter ought to determine the policy of the state. Yet this is likely to conflict with the interest of the nation-forming group, which wants to continue gaining private benefits from its investment in national collective action. The ideology of national self-rule serves the privileged group's interest in promoting loyalty to the state it controls, but the actuality of democratic government may not. Consequently, the nationalists have an incentive to establish institutions that block full democratic accountability and promote ideas that justify infringements on civic freedom.

The typical strategy for accomplishing this is to contend that opponents who demand greater democratic freedoms are playing into the hands of the nation's enemies by weakening its common front. Serbian president Slobodan Milosevic is just the latest in a long line of nationalist demagogues who tried to discredit his liberal opponents by branding them as tools of a foreign enemy. In this way, self-interested nationalists can open up a distinction between the populist goal of national self-rule and the democratic goal of individual civic rights.[11] Branded as traitors, the ethnic groups or social classes that support rival elites can be excluded from the rights of citizenship. Indeed, even members of the faction in power who choose to speak out for the rights of excluded groups can find their own rights in jeopardy. In cases where the truth is hard to prove, the most effective defense against charges of treason is often to become more nationalist than one's demagogic critics. As a result, democratizing states, from the French Revolution down to present day Serbia, often fall victim to a nationalist bidding war in which even the liberals must prove themselves the most militant defenders of the nation.

In short, promoters of nationalism face the two-sided problem of drumming up enthusiasm for the nationalist project yet damping down

[11] V. P. Gagnon, "Ethnic Conflict as Demobilizer: The Case of Serbia" (Ithaca: Cornell University, Institute for European Studies Working Paper No. 96.1, May 1996).

expectations that ruling *in the name of* the people will mean ruling *by* the people. How successful the nationalist elites are in this two-sided project depends largely on the tools of persuasion that they command.

## When and Why Nationalist Elites Are Persuasive

Nationalism is an attractive doctrine for elites in democratizing countries, but it would seem to be a hard program to sell to the public. In most instances, the broad mass of the population is not already strongly inclined toward militantly nationalist attitudes at the outset of the democratization process. As I mentioned above, nationalist appeals are often based on untruths or exaggerations, propounded by self-interested groups that aim to derive private benefits from the fruits of public coop-eration. Nationalist programs are often overtly hostile to the full granting of civic rights. In addition, it is hardly a secret that adopting a program of militant nationalism carries with it the likelihood of costly conflicts with neighboring nations. In many nationalist conflicts, all sides wind up worse off as a result of the struggle. Even the instigators suffer huge death tolls, severe economic disruptions, and derailments of their political goals. Hutu killers in Rwanda wound up in squalid refugee camps in Zaire. In the former Yugoslavia, the Serbian nation has been paid back in kind for campaigns of "ethnic cleansing" implemented in its name; its economy has been ruined by war and sanctions, and Serb leaders are indicted war criminals. Likewise, the brand-name aggressive nationalists of history—in Napoleonic France, Nazi Germany, and Imperial Japan—provoked over-whelming international opposition, which drove them out of business and incurred heavy costs for the popular masses who had rallied to their appeals of national glory or racial superiority.

Why is militant nationalism still attractive, despite its dubious track record in the twentieth century? How can people be convinced to run grave risks and suffer heavy costs to contribute to the purported welfare of their national group, especially when the truthfulness of nationalist claims and the benefits to the group of belligerent nationalism are highly problematic? Why don't publics in democratizing states throw their sup-port more often to liberal democrats, social welfare movements, or more moderate civic nationalists, whose programs would presumably carry greater benefits to the average citizen?

The answer is, of course, that sometimes such moderate forces do prevail in democratizing countries. On balance, however, the early phase of democratization creates especially favorable conditions for the success of nationalist persuasion campaigns. This is because elites who benefit from nationalism often retain partial control over powerful governmental, economic, and media resources, despite the rise in mass politics. In this setting, democratic institutions, including the institutions that govern public debate, are often too weak to check the influence of nationalist mythmakers. Democratization typically creates both the motive and the opportunity for elites to sell nationalist ideas to the public.

The breakup of an authoritarian regime threatens powerful groups, often including military bureaucracies and economic interests that derive a parochial benefit from war and empire. To salvage their position, these threatened interests try to recruit mass support, commonly resorting to nationalist appeals that allow them to seem popular without being truly democratic. Exploiting what remains of their levers of influence, they may succeed in establishing terms of inclusion in politics that force opposition groups to accept nationalism as the common currency of public discourse. Ambitious opponents of the old regime, including ethnic minorities as well as rising classes from the majority cultural group, may also find a nationalist platform attractive. If they head a successful nationalist movement, they will wind up as leaders of a national state.

This competition to rally popular support around elite interests takes place in a setting where democratic institutions are highly imperfect. In a perfect democracy, the average voter who would suffer from reckless nationalist policies should be able to get accurate information about those risks and should have the power to punish reckless politicians through the ballot box. That helps explain why no mature democracies have ever fought a war against each other.[12] In well-functioning democracies, moreover, people develop norms of bargaining and conflict-resolution. They can make use of legal channels and other institutions to increase the likelihood that people will stick to their agreements. These habits and institutions can be used to avert conflict within the state and to mitigate conflicts of interest with other democratic states. Mature democracies also enjoy a well-regulated marketplace of ideas, in which dangerous ideas are

[12] Dan Reiter and Allan C. Stam III, "Democracy, War Initiation, and Victory," *American Political Science Review* 92:2 (June 1998), 377–90.

routinely held up to public scrutiny by critics and by experts who have professional incentives to evaluate proposals objectively.[13]

However, these happy solutions typically emerge only in the long run. Effective democratic institutions take time to establish themselves. When powerful groups feel threatened by democracy, they seek to keep their states' institutions weak and manipulatable. Thus, the practices of many newly democratizing states are only loose approximations of mature democracy. Limited suffrage, unfair constraints on electoral competition, disorganized political parties, corrupt bureaucracies, or partial media monopolies may skew political outcomes in newly democratizing states away from the patterns that full democracy should produce. Though elites in newly democratizing states need to reach out for mass support, the weakness of democratic institutions allows them to avoid full accountability to the public. Nationalist ideas, which help to perpetuate this semidemocratic state of affairs, are harder to refute in public debate because partial media monopolies prevent a full airing of evidence and argument. Likewise, nationalist forces are harder to oppose through the democratic process, since privileged elites often rig the game to their advantage. Thus, none of the mechanisms that produce the democratic peace among mature democracies operate in the same fashion in newly democratizing states. Indeed, most of them work in reverse.

Although the weakness of various kinds of democratic institutions contributes to this outcome, flaws in the media of mass communications are especially important in creating opportunities for successful nationalist persuasion in many democratizing states. Nationalism is an idea, and it wins the day only if it prevails in the arena of public discourse. The following sections show how the structure of that arena affects the success of nationalist myths.[14]

[13] Bruce Russett, *Grasping the Democratic Peace* (Princeton: Princeton University Press, 1993); Anne-Marie Burley, "Law among Liberal States: The Act of State Doctrine," *Columbia Law Review* 92:8 (1992), 1907–96; Jack Snyder, "Democratization, War, and Nationalism in the Post-Communist States," in Celeste Wallander, ed., *The Sources of Russian Conduct after the Cold War* (Boulder, CO: Westview, 1996), 24–28.

[14] I define myths as assertions that would lose credibility if their claim to a basis in fact or logic were exposed to rigorous, disinterested public evaluation. The assertion that the Holocaust never happened is an example of a myth, in this sense. Nationalist myth-making, then, is the attempt to use dubious arguments to mobilize support for nation-

## *Nationalist mythmaking in the marketplace of ideas*

Elites in democratizing states have strong incentives to define politics in nationalist terms, but to succeed in this, they must first create a market for nationalist ideas. At the outset of the process of democratization, the public in most cases is not already mobilized around nationalist themes. What conditions allow elites to persuade the public to accept these ideas?

Just as elites can exploit the weakness of democratic institutions in the early phases of the transition to democracy, so too can they take advantage of the immaturity of forums for public debate in order to promote nationalist ideas. In new democracies, elites can often hijack the mass media, just as they can manipulate elections, rig the courts, and corrupt the state bureaucracy. However, their ability to do this depends on three factors: their ability to control sources of information, the ease of dividing the public into segments that can be targeted with nationalist messages, and the level of journalists' independence and professionalism.

The early phase of democratization normally coincides with increases in press freedom. Conventional wisdom holds that such increases in the freedom of speech should reduce the ability of ruling elites to promote nationalist thinking, since critics are better able to scrutinize and refute incorrect, dangerous ideas.[15] Based on an analogy to a competitive economic marketplace, this classical liberal view has its roots in John Stuart Mill's argument that truth is most likely to emerge from no-holds-barred debate.[16] In fact, this conventional wisdom is often *not* true of newly

---

alist doctrines or to discredit opponents. Similarly, John Zaller, *The Nature and Origins of Mass Opinion* (Cambridge: Cambridge University Press, 1992), 313, defines "elite domination" of opinion as "a situation in which elites induce citizens to hold opinions that they would not hold if aware of the best available information and analysis."

[15] Human Rights Watch, *Slaughter among Neighbors* (New Haven: Yale University Press, 1995).

[16] On the benefits of a free market of ideas, see John Stuart Mill, *On Liberty* (Cambridge: Cambridge University Press, 1989), part 2. Mill himself argued only that unconstrained debate was a guarantee that superior ideas would not be permanently suppressed; even he did not contend that the invisible hand of competition would automatically lead to the victory of the best idea, let alone of truth. For a critique, see Robert Weissberg, "The Real Marketplace of Ideas," *Critical Review* 10:1 (Winter 1996), 107–21. More generally on politics as a market competition, see Gary Becker, "A Theory of Competition among Pressure Groups for Political

democratizing states. Increases in press freedom often lead to outbursts of nationalist mythmaking because democratizing states are likely to have highly imperfect political marketplaces where nationalist myths are fueled rather than refuted.[17]

Whether nationalist myths can be successfully sold depends in large measure on the structure of the marketplace of ideas in which they are advanced. As in standard economic analysis, the structure of the market comprises the degree of concentration of supply, the degree of segmentation of demand, and the strength of institutions regulating market interactions, including those that provide information or regulate advertising. In a situation of "perfect competition" in the marketplace of ideas, there would be no monopolies of information or media access. All citizens would be exposed to the full range of ideas through direct debates between those who promote competing ideas. Factual claims would be subject to public scrutiny and comment by knowledgeable experts. Under those conditions, it may indeed be true that, on balance, unfettered debate tends to discredit ill-founded myths by revealing their factual inaccuracies, their logical contradictions, or the hidden costs of policies.[18] However, when waning authoritarian power is newly challenged by the forces of mass politics, then competition in the political marketplace is likely to be highly imperfect, and opportunities for nationalist mythmaking abound.

Continuing with the analogy to economic markets, imperfect competition occurs when there are few sellers, when potential sellers face high barriers to enter the market, and when products are differentiated for sale

---

Influence," *Quarterly Journal of Economics* 98:3 (August 1983), 371–400. On the sphere of public debate, see Jürgen Habermas, *The Structural Transformation of the Public Sphere* (Cambridge: MIT Press, 1989).

[17] The following analysis is adapted from Jack Snyder and Karen Ballentine, "Nationalism and the Marketplace of Ideas," *International Security* 21:2 (Fall 1996), 5–40, which has a fuller discussion of the market analogy. In this analogy, ideas are advertisements for political leaders and their policies. In most contexts, it is more helpful to view politicians, rather than ideas per se, as the commodities offered in the marketplace.

[18] On the role of free debate in the democratic peace, see Stephen Van Evera, "Primed for Peace: Europe after the Cold War," *International Security* 15:3 (Winter 1990/91), 27; Dan Reiter and Allan C. Stam III, "Democracy, War Initiation, and Victory," *American Political Science Review* 92:2 (June 1998), 377–90.

to segmented markets. Market segmentation may occur because consumers have long-established distinctive tastes, because targeted advertising artificially creates differentiated preferences, or because political
barriers limit exchange between market segments. When sellers are few
and markets are segmented, there may be the appearance of competition
in the market, but in fact some sellers may be able to establish near
monopolies in particular market segments. Under these conditions, sellers
may engage in either competitive advertising, collusion to divide up market share, or a combination of the two.[19] Rivalry is more likely when barriers to entry are falling, or in a "young industry," where "sellers may not
have learned what to expect of rivals" and "may be scrambling to secure
an established place in the industry, in the process inadvertently starting a
price war."[20] To achieve socially beneficial outcomes under imperfect
competition, regulation is needed to break up partial monopolies, pro-
hibit collusion, and insure truth in advertising.

The political marketplace in newly democratizing states often mirrors
that of a young, poorly regulated industry where barriers to entry are
falling. Elites often retain partial monopoly control over the media, and
the market is divided into segments by national identity. This kind of
imperfectly competitive market may yield the worst of both worlds. On
the one hand, elites have no alternative but to compete intensely for the
mobilization of mass support. On the other hand, by targeting captive
ethnic or national market segments, they can avoid debating in a common forum where ideas are publicly and rigorously scrutinized by competitors and expert evaluators. Thus, market conditions in newly
democratizing states often create both the incentive for nationalist advertising and the conditions for its success.

[19] Paul Samuelson, *Economics*, 15th ed. (New York: McGraw-Hill, 1995), Chapters
9 and 10, esp. 152; Edwin Mansfield, *Microeconomics*, 4th ed., (New York: W. W.
Norton, 1982), Chapters 11–12, esp. 323, 344–46, 353–55; James W. Friedman,
*Oligopoly Theory* (Cambridge: Cambridge University Press, 1983), 138–45; Robert
Kuenne, *The Economics of Oligopolistic Competition* (Oxford: Blackwell, 1992), 469–76.

[20] Richard Leftwich and Ross Eckert, *The Price System and Resource Allocation*, 9th
ed. (Chicago: Dryden, 1985), 407. The same uncertainty that fuels rivalrous behavior in a "young industry" typically characterizes periods of democratization and, in
the absence of shared norms or effective enforcement mechanisms, often produces
the same results. See Adam Przeworski, *Democracy and the Market* (Cambridge:
Cambridge University Press, 1991).

## Partial Monopolies of Supply

What conventional wisdom fears most is a complete governmental monopoly over the press. In this situation, the government can propagate any nationalist myth without having to face countervailing arguments. While perfect monopoly is hardly desirable, it is not the only—and perhaps not the most—dangerous condition for nationalist mythmaking. In conditions of perfect monopoly, the audience is often skeptical. In Communist and other authoritarian states, for example, people tend to discount propaganda precisely because they know that it comes from a monopolistic source, and they typically turn to informal networks and stratagems for reading between the lines of official discourse.[21] Moreover, perfect monopolists often lack a motive to mobilize their population's nationalism. Facing no active opposition and ruling without popular consent, they have little need to compete for the mantle of popular legitimacy by whipping up mass enthusiasms. Indeed, unleashing mass nationalism would only hinder their goal of depoliticizing domestic politics and would introduce needless complications into their management of foreign relations.[22] For this reason, dictatorships are likely to play the nationalist card only when their power is already slipping, and they are compelled to gamble on a popular appeal.

More dangerous than pure monopolies, and especially prone to nationalist mythmaking, are situations of partial media monopoly, which often occur during the earliest stages of democratization. In these conditions, governments and other elites often enjoy residual market power as a legacy of authoritarian monopoly control: the state or economic elites of the threatened ruling circles may still control key components of the mass media or have the resources to shape its content. Nationalist militaries may invoke their monopoly of specialized expertise to exaggerate foreign threats; the government may tendentiously regulate broadcast media in what it calls "the public interest"; private economic lobbies may buy jour-

[21] Ellen Mickiewicz, *Split Signals: Television and Politics in the Soviet Union* (New York: Oxford University Press, 1988); Bruce Allyn and Steven Wilkinson, *Guidelines for Journalists Covering Ethnic Conflict* (Cambridge: Conflict Management Working Paper, January 1994), 17–18; Ithiel de Sola Pool, "Communication in Totalitarian Societies," in Pool, Wilbur Schramm, et al., *Handbook of Communication* (Chicago: Rand McNally, 1973), 462–511.

[22] Stanislav Andreski, "On the Peaceful Disposition of Military Dictatorships," *Journal of Strategic Studies* 3:3 (December 1980), 3–10.

nalists, ostensibly neutral experts, and media access. In such conditions, the arena of public debate may seem open and competitive, but in fact information may be heavily controlled and slanted. This often creates the worst of both worlds, in which elites have a strong motive to engage in competitive public persuasion, and they control the means to distort the content of public debate.

A German example is instructive. During the Weimar Republic that was established following Germany's defeat in the First World War, powerful industrial interests deployed their resources to feed a steady diet of nationalist news to readers in Germany's towns and small cities in an effort to foster a mass middle-class constituency that would defend the capitalist order against the working classes. For example, Alfred Hugenberg, the chairman of the board of directors of Krupp Steel during World War I and the chairman of the German National People's Party during the Weimar Republic, established the Telegraph Union wire service, which gave him control over half of Germany's press.[23] By providing loans, reduced-rate newsprint, and accounting services to inflation-ridden papers, Hugenberg achieved substantial control over many papers while maintaining their facades of independence. Though even small cities often had multiple newspapers, Hugenberg's service fed them all the same nationalist-slanted copy.

The impact of this kind of partial monopoly over the supply of information is multiplied when the political market is divided into captive segments.

### Segmentation of Demand

A well-constituted marketplace of ideas depends not only on the expression of diverse views by different groups in society, but also on individuals being exposed to diverse ideas. A highly segmented marketplace has the former, but not the latter. In a segmented marketplace of ideas, individuals in one market segment lack exposure to ideas expressed in other segments, or exposure is filtered through sources that distort those ideas.

Demand in the marketplace of ideas is especially likely to be segmented in newly democratizing states. Sometimes this segmentation reflects the cultural divisions of traditional society or the legacy of authoritarian policies of divide-and-rule. Politicians in transitional states often use their con-

---

[23] Modris Eksteins, *The Limits of Reason: The German Democratic Press and the Collapse of Weimar Democracy* (London: Oxford University Press, 1975).

trol over the levers of persuasion to exploit latent divisions of this kind in a strategy of nationalist exclusion. These divisive efforts are often successful in new democratizers, which typically lack well-established integrative media institutions that link segments of society in a common public discourse.

Without a unifying nonpartisan media, narrow market segments are susceptible to domination by a single, myth-purveying supplier. For example, nationalist groups in the newly democratic Weimar Republic, including those backed by heavy industrial cartels, competed for mass electoral support against labor parties and liberals not so much by preaching to the constituencies of their opponents but by exploiting partial propaganda monopolies to mobilize their own. Hugenberg had only 50 percent of the overall Weimar media market, but he enjoyed a virtual monopoly over the flow of news to papers in Germany's small cities and towns, the locations that later voted most heavily for Hitler.[24] Exploiting Hugenberg's priming of middle-class opinion, Hitler succeeded not by winning over liberal, socialist, or undecided opinion in open debate, but by cornering the nationalist market segment through skillful penetration of grassroots voluntary organizations, such as veterans groups and beer-drinking societies.[25] Hitler attained a dominant position in the Reichstag with only one-third of the vote, and he used this as a platform for an unconstitutional seizure of the media and other state powers: monopolizing one segment of the market had been enough for a decisive outcome in a splintered polity.[26]

Scholars who tout the rationality of public opinion attach two crucial qualifications, one on the supply side and the other on the demand side: the public responds rationally to events within the limits of the informa-

[24] Ibid., 80–81; Thomas Childers, *The Nazi Voter* (Chapel Hill: University of North Carolina Press, 1983), 157–59.

[25] Richard Bessel, "The Formation and Dissolution of a German National Electorate," in Larry Eugene Jones and James Retallack, eds., *Elections, Mass Politics, and Social Change in Modern Germany* (Cambridge: Cambridge University Press, 1992), 404, 412–13; Peter Fritzsche, "Weimar Populism and National Socialism in Local Perspective," in Jones and Retallack, *Elections*, 301–4; Wolfgang Mommsen, "Government without Parties," in Jones and Retallack, eds., *Between Reform, Reaction, and Resistance: Studies in the History of German Conservatism from 1789 to 1945* (Providence: Berg, 1993), 359, 372.

[26] E. J. Feuchtwanger, *From Weimar to Hitler* (London: Macmillan, 1993), 298, 313–14.

tion and analysis that it receives, and given its predispositions.[27] John Zaller, for example, shows that American voters rely for their opinions on perceived experts whom they believe share their own values. [28] In this view, experts do not tell people what to care about, but they do shape people's estimates of the costs and feasibility of various means for pursuing the ends that they themselves value. Consequently, demand reflects not only the preferences of consumers but also the extent to which consumers with similar predispositions are isolated in separate market segments, each dominated by a single supplier.

Often the ethnic segmentation of the market is not a spontaneous reflection of language or traditional social organization, but rather the modern artifact of elite strategies of divide-and-rule. For example, colonial rulers, such as Joseph Stalin in Central Asia or the Belgians in Rwanda, frequently highlighted or even created ethnic cleavages in order to split local populations and insure the dependence of native functionaries. [29] Likewise, German chancellor Otto von Bismarck and his successors in the late nineteenth century segmented Germany's political marketplace of ideas through their nationalistic electoral propaganda, which divided the Protestant middle classes from socialist workers and Catholics, whom Bismarck labeled "enemies of the Reich." The belligerent tone of the bourgeois press, middle-class pressure groups and associations like the Navy League, and the National Liberal political party were all shaped by the nationalist themes around which elections were fought. Militarist ideas—including the notions of a need for territorial conquests, Germany's victimization by the encircling great powers, the superiority of German Protestant culture, and the spiritual benefits of war—thus became standard fare in right-wing, middle-class, Protestant thinking. In this way, electoral tactics erected high walls between segments of German society and continued to shape political discourse and electoral strategies down through the Weimar period of the 1920s. [30]

[27] Benjamin Page and Robert Shapiro, *The Rational Public* (Chicago: University of Chicago Press, 1992). Consumers' level of education, which presumably affects their sophistication about propaganda, seems to have mixed effects. Page and Shapiro, 178, 203–5, 313–30.

[28] Zaller, *The Nature and Origins of Mass Opinion.*

[29] Gérard Prunier, *The Rwanda Crisis: History of a Genocide* (New York: Columbia University Press, 1995), Chapter 1; Rogers Brubaker, *Nationalism Reframed* (Cambridge: Cambridge University Press, 1996), Chapters 3 and 4.

[30] Dirk Stegmann, "Between Economic Interests and Radical Nationalism," in

Sometimes elites segment the marketplace in a way that inadvertently loads the dice in favor of nationalist ideas. Tito's decentralizing reforms of the 1960s put Yugoslavia's media in the hands of regional leaderships, which in the 1980s fell into the hands of nationalists like Milosevic. As a result, Prime Minister Ante Markovic, who strove to hold Yugoslavia together under a program of liberal reform, had virtually no access to the Serb and Croat television markets, which were locally controlled.

Segmentation of demand, in short, may be shaped by a number of factors: the pre-existing preferences or experiences of groups sharing a common outlook; differentiated preferences induced by targeted advertising; division of media markets by language or region; or divisions imposed by political boundaries, as in federal systems. Such factors may be overridden if political discourse is channeled into a wider framework by broad-based parties or nonpartisan media institutions. However, such unifying institutions take time to develop and are often lacking in new democracies.

### Media Institutions and Norms

Where markets are imperfect, increased freedom of speech will tend to exacerbate nationalist mythmaking unless institutions and norms correct the flaws in the market. A well-institutionalized marketplace of ideas requires antimonopoly regulations guaranteeing media access, the training of journalists in the verification of sources as well as in the separation of fact from opinion, and the development of expert evaluative institutions whose prestige depends on maintaining a reputation for objectivity. Without such regulatory institutions, free speech by itself will not guarantee that a range of voices is effectively heard, that competing arguments are forced to confront each other on the merits, that participants in debate are held accountable for the accuracy of their statements, that factual claims are scrutinized, that experts' credentials are verified, that hidden sources of bias are exposed, and that violators of the norms of fair debate are held up to public censure.[31]

Regulation entails some risk of abuse, the severity of which depends in part on how it is carried out. In centralized forms of regulation, a state

---

Jones and Retallack, *Between Reform*, 170; Brett Fairbairn, "Interpreting Wilhelmine Elections: National Issues, Fairness Issues, and Electoral Mobilization," in Jones and Retallack, *Elections*, 22–23.

[31] For various approaches to regulating speech and media, see Judith Lichtenberg, ed., *Democracy and the Mass Media* (Cambridge: Cambridge University Press, 1990), esp. 52, 127–28, 144–45, 186–201.

official or governmental body decides who has access to the media and
what are the ground rules for its use. In contrast, decentralized regulation
is achieved through routines of professional behavior in institutions such
as the professional media, universities, think tanks, and legislative oversight bodies. Both forms of regulation may be useful antidotes to market
imperfections, and both may be used in combination. Decentralized regulation is generally preferable, since centralized regulation creates the risk
that the state will exploit its regulatory power to establish its own media
monopoly. However, where decentralized institutions are weak or lack the
required professional norms, centralized regulation, especially if it is subject to democratic control or held accountable to international standards,
may be less dangerous than an imperfect, unregulated marketplace.

Similarly, the regulation of the content of speech, such as the banning
of hate speech, is more subject to abuse than the establishment of norms
of debate, which set standards for how people are expected to argue their
case. The latter would include the professional journalist's norm of distin-
guishing facts from opinion, the scholar's norm of citing sources of
alleged facts, and the League of Women Voters' norm of expecting candidates to debate issues in a common forum in front of a panel of disinterested expert questioners. Establishing strong norms of debate is generally
better than regulating the content of speech, which can easily become an
excuse for self-serving government censorship.

Regulation is not a panacea. Indeed, skeptics dispute how well media
institutions structure public debate even in the most mature democracies.
Nevertheless, there is substantial evidence that effective evaluative institutions do have an impact on public views. Studies show that, apart from
the influence of a popular president, American public opinion is swayed
most strongly by the media testimony of experts who are perceived as
credible and unbiased.[32]

If the marketplace of ideas is imperfect even in mature democracies, its
flaws are even more grave in new democracies. An integrated public sphere,
in which one idea confronts another on its merits, does not get created
overnight. Without the functional equivalents of institutions like the *New
York Times*, the public television *News Hour*, the Brookings Institution, and
the Congressional Budget Office, discussion may be open, but an

---

[32] Page and Shapiro, *The Rational Public*, 339–54; for a skeptical view, see Robert
Entman, *Democracy without Citizens* (New York: Oxford University Press, 1989).

exchange and evaluation of contending views before a common audience may not occur. In many newly democratizing societies, press laws are biased and capriciously enforced.[33] The middlemen of the marketplace—journalists, public intellectuals, and public-interest watchdogs—tend to perform poorly in the initial stages of the expansion of press freedom. Instead of digging out the truth and blowing the whistle on fallacious arguments, journalists in emerging markets are often beholden to a particular party or interest group, make little attempt to distinguish between fact and opinion, and lack training in the standards of journalistic professionalism.[34] Thomas Jefferson said that if forced to choose, he would rather have a free press than a democratic government; yet assessing the actual state of the press in young America, he also remarked that "a suppression of the press could not more completely deprive the nation of its benefits, than is done by its abandoned prostitution to falsehood. Nothing can now be believed which is seen in a newspaper. Truth itself becomes suspicious by being put into that polluted vehicle."[35]

Even if a new democracy has a responsible elite press, its ability to impose a coherent structure on discourse may not penetrate to the grass-roots level, where markets are segmented. Weimar's liberal, Jewish-owned, mass circulation newspapers were objective and even erudite, but their ideas failed to penetrate beyond Berlin or Hamburg. Even in those urban centers, workers read the liberal press only for the sports, feature stories, and entertainment listings, ignoring the political views of the "class enemy."

**Market Forces That Promote Nationalist Mythmaking**
In summary, under conditions of incipient democratization, the increased openness of public debate often fosters nationalist mythmaking and ethnic conflict because opportunistic governmental and nongovernmental elites exploit partial monopolies of supply, segmented demand, and the weakness of regulatory institutions in the marketplace of ideas. The

[33] See the periodic country studies by Article 19 and Freedom House.

[34] Phillip Knightly, *The First Casualty* (New York: Harcourt, Brace, Jovanovich, 1975), 21–25; Michael Schudson, *Discovering the News: A Social History* (New York: Basic, 1978); Laura Belin, "Russia: Wrestling Political and Financial Repression," *Transition* 1:18 (October 6, 1995), 59–63; John A. Lent, ed., *Newspapers in Asia* (Hong Kong: Heineman Asia, 1982), 176, 211.

[35] Letter to John Norvell, June 14, 1807, in Merrill D. Peterson, ed., *The Portable Thomas Jefferson* (New York: Viking, 1975), 505.

greater these market imperfections (that is, the stronger the media market position of rivalrous partial monopolists, the greater the consumer segmentation, and the more dependent and partisan the media institutions), then the greater the likelihood for nationalist mythmaking to dominate public discourse, and the greater the likelihood for mythmaking to promote conflict. Conversely, the more perfect the marketplace and the more integrated the public sphere, the less effective is nationalist mythmaking.

## How Nationalist Persuasion Causes Violent Conflict

Successful campaigns of nationalist persuasion tend to provoke violent conflict both at home and abroad because they provoke enemies and hinder the development of coherent strategic policies. Not surprisingly, exclusionary forms of nationalism often make enemies of the excluded groups and their allies abroad. At the same time, nationalist myths confuse the strategic thinking of the nation in ways that make it more belligerent. Even when the costs and risks of militant nationalist policies become apparent, the weakening of central authority in newly democratizing states typically hinders leaders' ability to pull back from reckless commitments. Political coalitions in newly democratizing states are often held captive by the policy preferences of nationalist veto groups, including military and protectionist economic interests that have a stake in assertive policies. Competing elites' nationalist rhetoric may also trap these coalitions in nationalist bidding wars for popular backing. Coalition leaders may lack the power to enforce discipline on these political forces. While the strength and mix of these factors may vary, as a whole they explain why nationalist persuasion in democratizing states promotes violent conflict. The following sections briefly outline each of these causal mechanisms.[36]

### *Exclusions that provoke enmity*

Nationalist persuasion campaigns often identify a neighboring nation, an ethnic minority, or some other social group as an "enemy of the nation,"

---

[36] For an overview of a broader range of factors that affect the likelihood that nationalism will give rise to violent conflict, see Stephen Van Evera, "Hypotheses on Nationalism and War," *International Security* 18:4 (Spring 1994), 5–39. In particular, he includes a number of important strategic factors that I omit here.

to be excluded from full rights of citizenship, disarmed, dominated, or expelled from the nation's midst. If the excluded group has the ability to resist, this inevitably heightens the likelihood of violent conflict. Moreover, excluded groups, whether ethnic minorities or other factions that are branded as enemies of the nation, naturally seek alliances with like-minded foreign states that may also bridle at the nationalist policies of the democratizing state. Insofar as the civic form of nationalism is less exclusionary than other types, it is less likely to provoke such conflicts.

### Inaccurate and biased strategic assumptions

To mobilize support, nationalists often portray other nations as more threatening, more implacable, more culpable for historic wrongs, yet also more easily countered by resolute opposition than they really are.[37] Once this skewed picture of the national foe has succeeded in generating mass enthusiasm for national collective action, it tends to live on as a distorted assumption, guiding strategic discourse and calculations. Insofar as this imagery heightens the nation's feeling of insecurity yet also increases its optimism about militant solutions to security problems, violent conflict becomes more likely.

### Logrolling nationalist veto groups

Typically, the power of central authorities begins to weaken in newly democratizing states. The old authoritarian state is breaking up, leaving behind the fragments of its ruling class as still powerful interest groups. Some of these groups, including the military bureaucracy and dominant economic interests, may have self-serving reasons to lobby for policies of military expansion or for the exclusion of foreign economic competition, which could cause tensions with other states. These elite groups may become even further committed to nationalism, foreign expansion, or economic protectionism as a result of their rhetorical appeals for popular support. Consequently, political coalitions in newly democratizing states are especially likely to be conglomerations of veto groups, at least some of which have a stake in assertive foreign policies and nationalist political rhetoric.

When this occurs, the ruling coalition of the partially democratizing

---

[37] Jack Snyder, *Myths of Empire: Domestic Politics and International Ambition* (Ithaca: Cornell University Press, 1991), 5–6.

state tends to make decisions by "logrolling," to use the term from American politics that denotes a mutual back-scratching alliance among narrowly self-serving interests. In logrolling, each group in the coalition agrees to support the others on the issue that each cares about most. For example, the ruling coalition in Germany before World War I was the nationalist "marriage of iron and rye," in which aristocratic landowners supported a fleet-building program that industrialists desired in exchange for big-business support of high agricultural tariffs.

In a logroll, the coalition partners focus on the concentrated benefits that each of them expects to gain on their issue of most intense concern. None of them is primarily concerned with the more diffuse costs of these policies, which are dispersed among the various coalition partners and among groups outside the coalition.[38] Since logrolling works by giving each group what it wants most, policies leading to war and expansion are likely even if only one coalition partner favors them. In the German elite coalition before World War I, several groups insisted on policies that embroiled Germany with powerful neighbors. The navy and heavy industry demanded a fleet that alienated Britain, the landowners obtained agricultural tariffs that sowed discord with grain-exporting Russia, and the army got its preferred offensive war plan, which threatened all of Germany's neighbors.

Logrolling is to some degree a feature of all political systems, but it is especially likely in partially democratized states such as pre-1914 Germany. Since mature democracies have strong mechanisms of accountability to the average voter, logrolls that impose huge costs and risks on the citizenry are likely to provoke strong and effective opposition. Democracy, when it works correctly, confers power on the taxpayers, consumers, and military conscripts, all of whom would have to pay the diffuse costs that are side effects of the logroll. In newly democratizing states, however, the power of elite groups is likely to be strengthened vis-à-vis the weakened autocratic center, yet the power of mass groups is not yet institutionalized in the manner of a mature democracy. Thus, democratizing states are especially at risk for unchecked logrolling among elite interest groups, which can fuel violent nationalist conflicts.

### *Popular nationalist bidding wars*

To survive in an era of democratization, privileged elites must attract a degree of popular support, often through the use of nationalist rhetoric.

[38] Ibid., 44–46.

However, rising alternative elites may seize upon this rhetoric and try to turn it against the old elites, triggering a nationalist bidding war. For example, in Germany before World War I, mass middle-class nationalist groups such as the Navy League argued that if Germany were really encircled by national enemies, as the ruling elites claimed, then the government's ineffectual policies were endangering the nation. The old elite should step aside, they argued, and let the more vigorous middle classes reform Germany's army, toughen its foreign policy, and use coercion to break up the encircling alliance of France, Russia, and England. The "iron-and-rye" government felt compelled to outbid these middle-class critics, so in an attempt to gain nationalist prestige in the eyes of the domestic audience, the German government trumped up a series of international crises, such as the showdowns with France over control of Morocco in 1905 and 1911. This reckless and counterproductive strategy served only to tighten the noose around the neck of the German elites and pushed them toward a decision to launch a preventive war in 1914.[39]

In short, campaigns of nationalist persuasion in newly democratizing states tend to promote violent nationalist conflicts through several mechanisms. These mechanisms work more strongly in some democratizing countries than in others, and consequently their intensity of nationalist conflict varies. The next section explores some different types of nationalism that arise in newly democratizing states, as well as their causes and their varying consequences for conflict.

### Four Types of Nationalism: Their Causes and Consequences

Nations follow different routes toward democratization, and consequently their nationalisms differ radically, depending on which groups in society take the lead in mobilizing support for nationalism and what tools are available for that task. I classify nationalisms into four different types—ethnic, civic, revolutionary, and counterrevolutionary—based on the nature of their appeals to the collective good and their criteria for including members in the group.

---

[39] Geoff Eley, *Reshaping the German Right* (New Haven: Yale University Press, 1980), Chapter 10; James Retallack, "The Road to Philippi: The Conservative Party and Bethmann Hollweg's 'Politics of the Diagonal,' 1909–1914," in Jones and Retallack, *Between Reform*, 286–87.

Ethnic nationalisms, like those of the Serbs and the Estonians, base their collective appeals on common culture, language, religion, shared historical experience, and/or the myth of shared kinship, and they use these criteria to include or exclude members from the national group. Civic nationalisms, like those of the British and the United States, base their appeals on loyalty to a set of political ideas and institutions that are perceived as just and effective. Inclusion in the group depends primarily on birth or long-term residence within the nation's territory. Revolutionary nationalisms, like that of France in the 1790s, base their appeals on the defense of a political revolution that brings to power a regime that governs in the name of the nation, and exclude those who are seen as trying to undo that change. Counterrevolutionary nationalisms, like that of Germany before 1914, base their appeals on resistance to internal factions that seek to undermine the nation's traditional institutions. They exclude any social classes, religions, cultural groups, or adherents to political ideologies that are by this criterion "enemies of the nation."

These categories are ideal types. Many real cases fall in the gray areas between the pure types. In these more complex cases, the collective appeals and patterns of exclusion may be mixtures of those found in the ideal types. For example, several post-Communist transitions combine aspects of the ethnic and the counterrevolutionary patterns: in these cases, former Communist officials have tried to use appeals to exclusionary ethnic nationalism in order to forestall a shift to full mass democracy. Even in such hybrid cases, understanding the forces shaping the ideal types helps to reveal the strands of causality affecting these outcomes.

The four types have different causes and produce different consequences for the intensity and objectives of nationalist conflict. Civic nationalism, because it is the most inclusive, produces the least violent conflict within societies. Each of the other three forms of nationalism is likely to provoke violent conflict with the groups that it excludes and with their foreign allies. The following sections outline these different causes and consequences.

### *Causes of the four types of nationalism*

Because some of the states that are now on the cusp of democratization are potential great powers, which type of nationalism they develop could decide their future patterns of conflict and cooperation in much of the globe. What factors will determine whether Russia and Ukraine adopt culturally inclusive civic nationalisms, as opposed to ethnically divisive nationalisms? Should we heed predictions of a "Weimar Russia," which might recapitulate the conditions that fostered Hitler's rise to power in Germany in the 1920s?[40] Or, as the title of one recent study of China's growing nationalism put it, "will China become another Germany?"[41] Might the trade, human rights, and military policies of the established democracies influence the development of Chinese democracy and nationalism, and if so, what policies should they be?

Answering such practical questions requires a great deal of knowledge about these contemporary states, but it also requires knowledge of the historical paths that commonly lead to the development of different types of nationalism, both benign and militant. To know whether contemporary Russia and China are likely to relive any of the tribulations of German- or Serbian-style nationalism means developing a theory about the causes of these different types of nationalism. It is obvious that today's Russia and China are not exactly the same as Germany and Serbia; they will not relive identically those archetypal experiences with nationalism. Therefore, to gain insights from the past that might illuminate the future, we must extract historical lessons not in the journalistic form of one-to-one analogies, such as "Weimar Russia," but as broader generalizations about types of cases that capture underlying similarities, despite particular differences of historical setting and details.

The type of nationalism that is forged during the process of democratization is shaped to a significant degree by the level and timing of the country's social and economic development. A country's level of wealth and the skills of its population have a direct impact on the kind of nationalism that it develops. A country's pattern of development also affects the shape of its nationalism indirectly, through development's effect on two other factors that mold the country's nationalism during the democratic transition: (1) the adaptability of the skills and assets of powerful governmental or economic elites to a situation of increasing democracy, and

[40] Stephen E. Hanson and Jeffrey S. Kopstein, "The Weimar/Russia Comparison," *Post-Soviet Affairs* 13:3 (1997), 252–83.

[41] John Garver, *Will China Be Another Germany?* (Carlisle Barracks, PA: U.S. Army War College National Strategy Institute, 1996).

(2) the strength of democratic institutions at the moment when political participation begins to expand.

### Level and Timing of Social and Economic Development

The most general influence on the development of a country's nationalism during democratization is its level and timing of socioeconomic development. Transitions to democracy are almost always successfully consolidated when they occur in states that have high levels of per capita income, roughly $6,000 in the purchasing-power equivalent of 1985 dollars. At these levels of income, almost all states other than oil sheikdoms have large middle classes and highly literate populations with the skills needed to participate effectively in democratic deliberations.[42] The more advanced the state in these terms, the more likely it is to develop a civic form of nationalism, or temper its nationalism with civic features, such as effective guarantees of civil rights to ethnic minorities. The large size of the highly literate, reasonably prosperous, urban middle class helps to explain the relative peacefulness of the post-Communist democratic transitions in the Czech Republic, Poland, Hungary, and Estonia, despite widespread predictions of ethnic conflict in the latter two cases.[43]

Transitions to democracy are rarely consolidated in countries where per capita income is below $1,000, the middle class is tiny, and civic skills are lacking. Traditional patronage networks often dominate the politics of such states. If democratic elections are held under those conditions, a likely outcome is mobilization along ethnic lines in a form of patronage politics based on cultural cleavages. For example, elections in Burundi and Kenya in the 1990s followed this pattern. Indeed, at very low levels of socioeconomic development, the mobilization of even ethnic nationalism is hard to sustain. The capacity of these societies for mass-scale collective action is so low that patronage networks tend to focus on smaller-scale ties among personal cronies, strongmen, clans within the broader ethnic group, or other localized networks. For these reasons,

[42] Adam Przeworski and Fernando Limongi, "Modernization: Theories and Facts," *World Politics* 49:2 (January 1997), 155–83.

[43] For supporting social and income measures, see World Bank, *Social Indicators of Development* (Baltimore: Johns Hopkins University Press, 1995). On the politics of civic inclusion in Estonia, see David Laitin, *Identity in Formation* (Ithaca: Cornell University Press, 1998).

post–Soviet Central Asia remains at the prenationalist stage of social development, just as Western Europe was prenational before the French Revolution.

Intermediate levels of socioeconomic development are the zone in which revolutionary or counterrevolutionary nationalisms are more likely. In these states, a successful democratic opposition movement may sweep the old elite from power but then find that it lacks a sufficient base of middle-class or working-class support to sustain a civic outcome without resorting to revolutionary nationalist appeals. Alternatively, the rising democratic opposition may be too weak to force the old elites from power, but just strong enough to compel them to reach out for mass support by playing the nationalism card as a counterrevolutionary tactic. In the post-Soviet world, for example, counterrevolutionary nationalist appeals by former Communist leaders met with some success in Serbia, Slovakia, and Romania, whose populations were more rural and less politically sophisticated than the more advanced Czechs and Hungarians.

A high level of development may serve as a substitute for other favorable conditions, such as supportive elites and a tradition of civic institutions, that normally facilitate democratic consolidation and civic nationalism. For example, in Poland and Hungary, political reforms in the late Communist period had created some institutions to facilitate civic dialogue; in contrast, the unreformed Communist regime in Czechoslovakia left no such legacy. When the latter regime abruptly collapsed, Czech civil society groups and democratic institutions had to be formed from scratch. In a less educated society with a weaker white-collar class, a democratic transition in such an institutional void would be a recipe for revolutionary nationalism, but the sophisticated Czechs were able to invent a working civil society almost overnight.[44]

As a rule, states like Britain and the United States that got an earlier start in economic development have been more likely to form civic nationalisms. Later developers like Germany have been more likely to go through revolutionary or counterrevolutionary nationalist phases, whereas very late developers like Serbia and the other Balkan states have been more likely to form ethnic nationalisms. In part, this is because of development's direct effects on wealth and the political skills of the middle class. However, the

[44] John Glenn, *Framing Democracy in Eastern Europe* (Stanford: Stanford University Press, forthcoming).

timing of development also works as an underlying factor that shapes the nature of elite interests and the strength of the country's political institutions. These interests and institutions in turn affect the kind of nationalism that develops along with democratization.

Early developers like Britain have been somewhat more likely to have elites with adaptable interests and strong political institutions that can regulate mass political participation in the initial phase of their democratic transitions. This has been conducive to civic outcomes. Later developers have typically had weaker political institutions or less flexible elites during the initial phase of the democratic transition. These circumstances fostered more exclusionary forms of nationalism. In some cases, these historic trajectories of political and economic development remain relevant to the contemporary wave of democratizations. For example, a good predictor of the prevalence of militant, exclusionary nationalism in the post-1989 politics of the various East European states is the percentage of that country's workforce engaged in agriculture in the 1920s, a good indicator of late development.[45] Nonetheless, the timing of development is only one background factor that influences elite interests and institutional strength. It fosters tendencies, not inescapable outcomes. The next section explains how different patterns of elite interests and institutional strength, whatever their sources, produce different forms of nationalism.

### Adaptability of Elite Interests and Strength of Political Institutions

The type of nationalism that emerges in a democratizing state is shaped by the adaptability of its elite interests to democracy and by the strength of its political and administrative institutions. Inclusionary civic nationalism arises where elite interests are adaptable to democracy and where representative political institutions are already strong when political participation starts to expand. In contrast, the exclusionary forms of nationalism—ethnic, revolutionary, and counterrevolutionary—arise where the threat posed by democratization to elite interests is high, or where democratic political institutions are weak, or both.

[45] Herbert Kitschelt, "Formation of Party Cleavages in Post-Communist Democracies," *Party Politics* 1:4 (1995), 456. For a demonstration of the contemporary relevance of the concept of early and late development in the area of international political economy, see Peter Katzenstein, *Between Power and Plenty* (Madison: University of Wisconsin Press, 1978).

These interests and institutions affect both the motivation and the opportunity of elites to promote different kinds of nationalist doctrines during the initial phase of democratization. Elites are highly motivated to promote exclusionary nationalist myths under two circumstances. First, the more the elite feels threatened by the arrival of full democracy, the stronger is its incentive to use exclusionary nationalist persuasion to forestall that outcome. Second, the weaker the democratic institutions that the elite commands as tools for governing, the more the elite must rely on exclusionary nationalist ideas as a basis for mobilizing national collective action.

An elite's opportunity to sell exclusionary nationalism depends to a large extent on the character of the political institutions of the democratizing state. Where the state's bureaucracy is strong, yet its institutions for democratic participation and public debate are weak, state elites will be able to use their administrative leverage to promote exclusionary nationalism during the early phase of democratization. Conversely, when representative and journalistic institutions are already well developed during early democratization, exclusionary nationalist arguments can be checked through more effective scrutiny in open public debate. Where both representative and administrative institutions are weak, the easiest route for elites to gain popular support for building national institutions is often through the propagation of exclusionary cultural or revolutionary themes. Under these conditions, institutional checks on nationalist mythmaking are likely to be extremely weak.[46]

***Civic nationalism: Adaptable elite interests, strong political institutions.*** The development of civic nationalism is likely when elites are not particularly threatened by the emergence of a democratic system, and when the representative and journalistic institutions needed to make democracy

---

[46] Which social cleavages are most opportune for exploitation as criteria for exclusion depends in part on the cultural legacies of the predemocratic society and on social divisions during the democratic transition. Where the population can be differentiated by language or culture, exclusion by ethnicity is feasible. Where political factions are based on status groups or classes, nationalist doctrine may emphasize exclusion based on support for or opposition to revolutionary change. Nationalist elites activate or heighten such cleavages; they rarely create them out of nothing. Nonetheless, some cleavage that creates a useful basis for exclusion is bound to be present in any newly democratizing society where elites' motivation and opportunity for nationalist mythmaking is high.

work are already fairly well developed during the initial phase of the democratic transition. These favorable conditions might arise in a number of ways. They could be a legacy of an elite representative regime, which is subsequently broadened to include the mass of the population. For example, in nineteenth-century Britain and in South Africa during the era of apartheid (1950s–1980s), privileged elites enjoyed a system of elite electoral politics, elite political parties, rule of law, and relatively free public debate before this system was opened to participation by the majority of the population. Such favorable conditions might also be imposed through conquest, as in Germany after World War II or to some extent in India by the British colonial regime. In relatively wealthy countries with a large and highly skilled middle class, these conditions might be quickly created during the transition itself, as in the Czech Republic. Or they could emerge through intermittent accretions, as in much of South America. In Argentina, Brazil, and Chile, for example, liberal institutions began to develop in periods of democratization, were stripped of power by military dictatorships, and then re-emerged in a stronger form during later periods of democratization. Thus, the preconditions of civic nationalism are not forged in any single mold.

Nonetheless, one particular pattern—the historical pattern of early development—has been especially conducive to civic nationalism. States that developed their economy and their political system relatively early, as Great Britain did, enjoyed two advantages that eased their transition to democracy and made more likely the development of civic nationalism. First, their elites were relatively unthreatened by the process of democratization because they shared many commercial interests with the rising middle class. In Britain's case, this was because the landed aristocracy had been the main source of investment capital for the boom in the textile industry in the early nineteenth century.[47] Second, in the British pattern of early development, this economically dynamic coalition of commercial and landowning elites had a stake in strengthening representative institutions and free speech, which protected them from arbitrary actions by the monarch. Thus, liberal institutions became entrenched among the elite before the mass of the population began to play a major role in politics. In sum, when elite interests are adaptable, and liberal institutions precede

---

[47] Alexander Gerschenkron, *Economic Backwardness in Historical Perspective* (Cambridge: Belknap, 1962).

mass politics, nationalism is likely to be inclusive and will probably take a civic form. Though other civic nationalisms may not exactly replicate the British pattern, it is generally the case that the earlier the nation's start on economic and political development, the more likely it is to have a consolidated democracy and a civic form of nationalism.

In contrast, late developing countries normally lack these advantages. In the typical patterns of late development, economic change and pressures for democratization arise abruptly. Demands for democratic participation arise before the creation of institutions that can accommodate them. This rapid change commonly poses threats to elites. The weakness of representative institutions in the suddenly democratizing state means that these elites are neither able to move with confidence toward democratic consolidation, nor are they firmly constrained by democratic accountability. Militant exclusionary nationalism, in one form or another, is an ideological solution to problems that elites face in this setting. Thus, counterrevolutionary nationalism arises where threats to inflexible elite interests are high, and where elites can deploy strong administrative institutions on behalf of a campaign of nationalist persuasion. Revolutionary nationalism arises where elites are adaptable but an institutional void compels them to use nationalist ideology to establish a popular basis for their rule. Finally, ethnic nationalism arises where state institutions are so weak that elites must base their rule on popular cultural identities, which state elites then lock in place. The pattern of late development may not be the only factor shaping these outcomes, but it is an important one that helps show the underlying causes at work.

***Counterrevolutionary nationalism: Unadaptable elite interests, strong administrative institutions.*** Elites who are threatened by democratization and who control administrative levers of powers are often tempted to use exclusionary nationalism to limit democratic accountability while cloaking themselves in the popular mantel of national self-rule. In this situation, the nationalist doctrine may simultaneously seek the exclusion of putative class, factional, and cultural enemies of the nation, and also promote a confrontation with the nation's foes abroad. Thus, in the 1870s, German chancellor Otto von Bismarck simultaneously labeled the working class, the socialists, the Catholics, and the Poles as enemies of the true German nation. Likewise, on the eve of the 1994 Rwanda genocide, militants in the Rwandan Hutu regime directed nationalist doctrinal attacks toward Rwanda's Tutsi minority, Hutu moderates, and their foreign allies in Uganda and the great powers. Similarly, former Communist leaders seeking to hold onto positions of power in democratizing post-Communist Romania, Slovakia, and Serbia tried with varying degrees of success to combine cultural and class appeals in their strategies of exclusionary nationalism. Thus, counterrevolutionary nationalism is opportunistic in its exclusions, resorting to any and every available ploy to divide potential popular opposition.

It would be an oversimplification to reduce the causes of counterrevolutionary nationalism to any single pattern of late development. Nonetheless, it is worth emphasizing the particular pattern of late industrialization that shaped the nationalisms of Germany, Japan, and Italy, the aggressor powers in World War II. For example, German industrialization, instead of developing gradually in the textile sector, took off abruptly in the iron and steel sectors in the 1860s. Capital investments were amassed by large banks or by the state, not by the more decentralized efforts of the old landed elite, which remained on the sidelines of the commercial revolution. The resulting rapid economic change produced a large, politically demanding working class before the middle class had won its battle with the old elite for liberal political rights. In these conditions, inflexible elite interests were doubly threatened by democratization. The old elite feared the rising political power of both the middle-class commercial revolution and also the working-class revolution. Meanwhile, the new and relatively weak commercial class feared the rapid growth of a politically conscious working class and sought the power of the old regime to defend against this threat.[48] Nationalism served as an ideology to bind the old elite to the rising commercial elite and to discredit the working class as unpatriotic. The state administrative institutions commanded by these elites were strong, but democratic institutions, whose development these elites hindered, were too weak to contain the exclusionary nationalist persuasion campaigns mounted by the threatened elites.[49]

***Revolutionary nationalism: Adaptable elite interests, weak institutions.*** In another pattern of late development, institutions for democratic participation may lag behind the demands of a population that is already highly mobilized to play a role in politics. Under these conditions, such as those

---

[48] Barrington Moore, *Social Origins of Dictatorship and Democracy* (Boston: Beacon, 1996).

[49] Gerschenkron, *Economic Backwardness*; Snyder, *Myths of Empire*, Chapter 3.

of the French Revolution, opportunistically adaptable elites may find that appeals to nationalism rooted in alleged foreign conspiracies may be the quickest route to the re-establishment of state authority in the wake of institutional collapse. Since authority rests so heavily on nationalist ideology, the incentives for a nationalist bidding war can be very powerful, and nationalist conflicts correspondingly extreme.

*Ethnic nationalism: Unadaptable elite interests, weak institutions.* In the most extreme form of belated development, where state institutions are still in their infancy when pressure for mass political participation arises, ethnic nationalism is especially likely. Lacking effective democratic or administrative institutions to attach the citizenry to the state, political entrepreneurs will by default attempt to create loyalty through cultural attachments. Granting equal civic rights to ethnic minorities would thus threaten the nationalist ideology of the state elite, which becomes locked into a rigid definition of state interest centering on the special position of the dominant ethnic group. Once political alignments become attached to particular cultural loyalties, this creates a situation of unadaptable interests and weak institutions—that is, the opposite of the situation that gives rise to civic nationalism. Nineteenth-century Serbia is the classic example.

In short, the conjuncture of two determining factors—the adaptability of interests and the strength of political institutions—yields four patterns for the development of nationalism in democratizing states: civic, ethnic, revolutionary, and counterrevolutionary.

### International Influences

My theory mainly focuses on the internal characteristics that shape the development of a country's nationalism. However, for practical reasons, it is also important to know whether international influences can affect the trajectory of nationalism in newly democratizing states. Consistent with the logic of the theory just presented, I argue that international actors can indeed influence the development of a people's nationalism by affecting the incentives that elites face and by shaping the institutions that channel mass politics during a democratic transition.

There is strong evidence that the international setting does affect the outcome of democratic transitions. Statistical research suggests that democratic transitions are more likely to become consolidated and less likely to provoke international wars when they take place in international regions

that are already composed mainly of mature democratic states.[50] Many of
the democratizations that occurred in the wave following World War I
failed to consolidate civic nationalism and instead degenerated into counterrevolutionary, ethnic, or revolutionary forms. In part, this was due to
the ineffective economic and military alliance policies of leading liberal
democracies, such as Britain and the United States; in part, it was also due
to the influence of illiberal great powers like Germany and Russia on the
political developments in smaller powers nearby. In contrast, the latest
wave of democratization since 1989 has seen a higher success rate for civic
nationalisms in northeastern Europe and in South America because of the
greater dominance of the liberal great powers and the better institutionalization of their forms of economic and military cooperation.

In the concluding chapter, I will discuss at greater length how international trade, foreign military competition and cooperation, and the international flow of ideas can affect the development of a state's nationalism.

### *The effect of the four types of nationalism on violent conflict*

The four types of nationalism give rise to different degrees and types of
violent conflict. Civic nationalism normally leads to less internal conflict
within the state and to more prudent policies abroad. The three exclusionary forms of nationalism entail a greater likelihood of violence,
though the patterns of their violence differ. The ethnic pattern may produce intense conflict, but this is likely to be limited to the establishment
of domination in the ethnic homeland. Revolutionary and counterrevolutionary nationalism are likely to produce higher levels of open-ended conflict with rival states (see Table 2.1).

Because civic nationalism is inclusive within the territory of the state,
it is less likely to yield violent domestic conflicts. At least as an ideal type,
civic nationalism seeks to accommodate all citizens within a nondiscrimi-
natory legal and institutional framework. Admittedly, actual states that
approximate the civic model may discriminate against some racial or ethnic groups, such as the Irish in the British union and the African
Americans and Native Americans in the United States, and sometimes

[50] John R. Oneal and Bruce Russett, "Exploring the Liberal Peace: Interdependence,
Democracy, and Conflict, 1950–85," originally presented at the April 1996 meeting of
the International Studies Association.

**Table 2.1 Relationship of Political Institutions and Social Interests to the Type of Nationalism, and Their Consequences for Violent Conflict**

| *Nationalist Elites' Interests* | *Strength of the Nation's Political Institutions* | |
|---|---|---|
| | *Strong* | *Weak* |
| *Adaptable to Democracy* | Civic: strong representative institutions (Britain) → low internal conflict; cost-conscious foreign policy | Revolutionary (revolutionary France) → open-ended external conflict |
| *Not adaptable* | Counterrevolutionary: strong administrative institutions (pre–World War I Germany) → open-ended external conflict | Ethnic (pre–World War I Serbia) → high conflict until domination of ethnic homeland is achieved |

these exclusions may lead to violent conflict. If so, these deviations prove my point rather than undermine it. However, sometimes civic states may find themselves in conflict with ethnic minorities not as a consequence of deviations from civic ideal, but precisely *because* they are civic. This is most likely to occur in relatively weakly institutionalized civic states when mass groups are first gaining admission to the democratic process. If ethnic minorities within the civic state clamor for group rights or political autonomy, this may be seen as a dangerous challenge to the new democracy's insecure civic principles. For example, such sensitivities have been a factor in the violent conflict between the secular Indian state and the Muslim majority in Kashmir.[51] However, civic nationalism should reduce violent conflict once democracy is consolidated, insofar as ethnic demands can be effectively accommodated as normal interest-group lobbying in the peaceful democratic process.[52] In short, inclusive civic nationalism dampens internal violence, except when civic principles are

[51] Sumit Ganguly, *The Crisis in Kashmir* (Cambridge: Cambridge University Press, 1997).

[52] Ted Robert Gurr, *Peoples versus States: Ethnopolitical Conflict and Accommodation at the End of the 20th Century* (Washington, DC: US Institute of Peace, forthcoming).

unevenly applied or when weak civic states fear that the legitimacy of their civic principles is coming under a severe challenge.

As a rule, states embodying civic nationalisms are also the most prudent in their foreign relations. Most mature democracies either have civic nationalisms—like Britain, France, and the United States—or else their historic nationalisms have been tempered by civic features, like that of today's Germany.[53] The peace among mature democracies underscores the mutual compatibility of these civic nationalisms. To be sure, the example of the British empire shows that civic nationalism may underpin a policy of military expansion. Yet Britain's imperial policy was regulated by prudent calculation and democratic self-criticism. Compared with its German, Japanese, and Russian competitors, civic Britain more astutely extricated itself from self-defeating imperial ventures when their costs rose.[54] Civic nationalisms are not pacifist, but they are cost-conscious compared to the other types.

Ethnic nationalism is of course likely to provoke violent conflict within a culturally diverse society. Such conflicts should be greatest when the nation is fighting to achieve statehood or to bring foreign territories inhabited by ethnic brethren under the control of the homeland state. Conflict may also be intense after the achievement of statehood, when the nation is attempting to assimilate, expel, or impose its domination on ethnic minorities in the territory it controls.[55] However, once that process has culminated in a homogenized state or a sustainable pattern of domination, ethnic expansionism has reached its natural limits, and the nation should no longer be prone to violent conflict.

In contrast, the military expansionism of revolutionary and counter-revolutionary nationalisms has no such natural limits. All three of the unlimited, reckless attempts to overturn the European balance of power, twice by Germany in the first half of the twentieth century and once by revolutionary France, were energized by these types of nationalism.

Revolutionary nationalism combines defensive vigilance against enemies of the revolution with the possibility of spreading the benefits of political transformation to potential revolutionists abroad. In the short

---

[53] On the recent moderation of German ethnic nationalism, see Rogers Brubaker, *Citizenship and Nationhood in France and Germany* (Cambridge: Harvard University Press, 1992), Chapters 8 and 9.

[54] Snyder, *Myths of Empire*, 9, 153–55, 209–10, 311.

[55] Brubaker, *Nationalism Reframed*, Chapters 3 and 4.

term, the revolutionary state is weakened by internal turmoil, but the popular energy that it unleashes creates a long-term threat for neighbor states. In this situation of intense mutual fear, neighboring states often think in terms of preventive aggression to kill the revolution in its infancy, so that their own populations won't be inspired to revolt. In turn, revolutionary nationalists often conclude that spreading the revolution abroad is the best way to secure the revolution at home.[56] In this situation, the revolutionary state's goals for conquest are not necessarily limited to a finite set of historic or cultural objectives but are spurred by a more open-ended competition for security.

Counterrevolutionary nationalism arises when threatened elites attempt to fend off internal political change by unifying the nation against its external foes. This form of nationalism should therefore present its peak danger when elites are most threatened by social change, and in particular, when they begin to lose control of the self-contradictory process of nondemocratic mass mobilization. Insofar as counterrevolutionary nationalism perpetually needs external enemies to serve as internal unifiers, it too, like revolutionary nationalism, lacks any clear limits on the rivalries that it provokes with other nations.

## Alternative Explanations for the Link between Democratization and Nationalist Conflict

Scholars have identified many factors that plausibly contribute to nationalism or nationalist conflict: the rise of the modern state, economic change, the development of cheap printing methods, political repression of minorities, socioeconomic inequality, security threats, and more.[57] My focus on democratization and the selling of nationalist doctrines to the mass public is not intended to compete with most of these arguments but to complement them. Insofar as such factors affect the level and timing of

[56] Stephen Walt, *Revolution and War* (Ithaca: Cornell University Press, 1996).

[57] E. J. Hobsbawm, *Nations and Nationalism since 1780* (Cambridge: Cambridge University Press, 1990); Ernest Gellner, *Nations and Nationalism*; Anderson, *Imagined Communities*; Ted Robert Gurr, *Minorities at Risk* (Washington, DC: US Institute of Peace, 1993); Anthony D. Smith, *The Ethnic Origins of Nations* (Oxford: Blackwell, 1986); Barry Posen, "The Security Dilemma and Ethnic Conflict," *Survival* 35:1 (Spring 1993), 27–47.

development, threaten elite interests, or affect the weakness or strength of democratic institutions, they can be seen as part of a broader context shaping the type of national identity that emerges during the democratization process. I argue that these factors affect nationalism through persuasion and mythmaking in the initial stages of democratization. Whatever background factors may contribute to nationalism, nationalist agitation and propaganda are always a necessary condition for the development of a mass nationalist movement.[58]

Similarly, I do not claim that nationalism and nationalist myths are the only cause of conflict between nations. The rational pursuit of conquest, as well as security fears, imbalances of power, reckless leaders, misperceptions, and a whole host of other factors may cause conflict between social groups, including nations. These factors can create conflict independent of nationalism, or they may interact with nationalism to increase or dilute its effects. If a conflict can be easily explained in terms of such factors, then nationalism may be superfluous to understanding the outcome. However, while I do not claim that my theory explains every case of nationalist conflict, I do claim that it identifies a central feature in many cases of nationalist conflict that have concerned scholars and spurred contemporary public debates.

Some theories do compete directly with my elite-persuasion theory. These are theories that, like mine, try to explain why democratization and nationalist conflict tend to coincide, but these competing explanations posit a different causal sequence or mechanism connecting democratization and nationalism. Insofar as some of these competing theories may have opposite policy implications from my own, it is important to demonstrate that my account is the correct one. The main competing theory that I examine in the case studies is the popular-rivalries theory. Less systematically, I also take into account economic and strategic explanations of the link between democratization and nationalist conflict.

### Popular rivalries and other cultural explanations

The argument that most directly contradicts my own is that the character of a country's nationalism and the intensity of nationalist conflict is deter-

---

[58] Miroslav Hroch, *Social Preconditions of National Revival in Europe* (Cambridge: Cambridge University Press, 1985), 11–13; Elie Kedourie, *Nationalism* (London: Hutchinson, 1960).

mined mainly by popular rivalries between cultural groups that precede the democratization process (such as "ancient hatreds"). In this view, democracy causes violent conflict between nations because these peoples express their long-standing, conflicting aspirations for statehood or their engrained fears and hatreds through the ballot box.[59] This popular-rivalries theory holds that the best predictors of the intensity of nationalist conflict during democratization are a history of violence between the national groups and an ethnically intermingled demographic pattern. In contrast, my elite-persuasion theory would expect national identity to become salient in politics only after the onset of the early phase of democratization. Thus, a predemocratic history of ethnic violence should not be an insurmountable barrier to civic coexistence if elite interests and institutional factors are otherwise favorable. I predict that long-standing cultural identities will become rallying points for nationalist rivalries in newly democratizing states only if political institutions are weak. In the case studies in the following chapters, I show that, for the most part, popular nationalism developed during the process of democratization, not before; that demography and a history of predemocratic group conflict are inaccurate predictors of conflict during democratization; and that traditional culture becomes the basis for politics only under the conditions that my theory would expect.

It matters which of these two theories is correct because at least some of the policy prescriptions that follow from them are opposite. For example, the popular-rivalries theory prescribes powersharing schemes or ethnic partitions as means of disentangling rival ethnic groups, whereas my theory warns that such putative remedies might needlessly lock in inimical ethnic identities. However, these two approaches do agree on one prescription: it is dangerous to unleash democratization before effective antidotes to nationalist conflict are in place.[60]

The popular-rivalries theory rests on a view of culture as traditional and relatively unchanging. Many contemporary scholars take a different

---

[59] For commentaries on this kind of approach, see Daniel Byman and Stephen Van Evera, "Hypotheses on the Causes of Contemporary Deadly Conflict," *Security Studies* 7:3 (Spring 1998), esp. 33–35, and Susanne Hoeber Rudolph and Lloyd I. Rudolph, "Modern Hate," *The New Republic* 208:12 (March 22, 1993), 24–29.

[60] Byman and Van Evera, "Hypotheses on the Causes of Contemporary Deadly Conflict," 49.

view of culture, portraying it as an ever-changing arena in which people invoke or invent symbols in order to create meanings that shape patterns of social relations.[61] These symbols may draw on cultural traditions, cultural borrowings, new ideas, or a synthesis of these elements. This view of culture as an arena of active discourse and changing practices shares with my own approach an emphasis on the role of persuasion in shaping attitudes about the nation at crucial junctures of historical change. However, the elite-persuasion theory that I present in this book places greater stress on persuasive arguments about rationalistic calculations of costs and benefits than do most culturalist accounts.[62] In that sense, my argument might be seen as competing with such accounts. However, it might also be viewed as complementary to such cultural approaches insofar as all of these are part of a broader orientation emphasizing diverse kinds of ideas, persuasion, and mythmaking.

### Industrialization and commercial capitalism

Another direct challenge to my theory is the view that democratization is simply a side effect of economic changes that are the actual causes of nationalism and nationalist conflict. For example, in one of the most influential theories of nationalism, Ernest Gellner argues that industrialization causes nationalism because the industrial economy can work only if there is a common language and culture to facilitate its complex interactions.[63] Whereas a patchwork of local dialects and cultures did not hinder agricultural economies, whose operation depended little on symbolic communications, Gellner contends that the arrival of industrialism set off a Darwinian struggle to determine whose culture would survive as the lingua franca of the emerging national market. Industrialization is also a cause of democratization because it increases per capita income and fosters the growth of the middle class. Thus, if Gellner's theory is right,

---

[61] Brubaker, *Nationalism Reframed*, Chapter 1; Eric Hobsbawm and Terence Ranger, eds., *The Invention of Tradition* (Cambridge: Cambridge University Press, 1983).

[62] For some arguments about ethnic conflict that combine culture, mass persuasion, and rational calculation, see James Fearon and David Laitin, "Violence and the Social Construction of Ethnic Identities," manuscript, January 1999.

[63] Gellner, *Nations and Nationalism*, Chapter 3.

industrialization tends to cause both nationalism and democratization. If so, then democratization might coincide with the rise of nationalism, not because democratization causes nationalism, but because they are both caused by industrialization.

Gellner's argument is easy to refute. The rise of nationalism preceded the arrival of industrialism in its earliest instances, eighteenth-century Britain and France, and also in many industrial latecomers during the nineteenth century. However, a variation on Gellner's theory proposed by Michael Mann comes closer to my own argument and fits the facts better than Gellner's original formulation. Instead of refuting Mann's argument, I incorporate it into my own theory. Mann argues that nationalism first arose not with nineteenth-century industrialization but with the intensification in the eighteenth century of pre-industrial commerce.[64] Social and economic changes associated with early capitalism put more resources and skills in the hands of a larger proportion of the population. This made the people more politically aware and demanding, and consequently forced rulers to bargain with their populations.[65] Thus, commercial development led to broader participation in politics, which in turn created the possibility of nationalism, the doctrine of national self-rule. Unlike Gellner's argument, Mann's variation on it is entirely consistent with my own approach. It helps to explain why elites in commercial, democratizing societies have such a strong incentive to co-opt mass support and thus to adopt strategies of nationalist persuasion.

### Strategic theories of democratization as a cause of preventive war

Strategic theories imply that democratization coincides with nationalist conflicts because it destabilizes power relationships between nations. In this view, democratization may create incentives for preventive aggression. The early phase of a democratic transition may disrupt and weaken the state in the short run but strengthen it by mobilizing popular energies in the long run. This gives neighbors an incentive to attack while they still have a chance of winning. Strategic approaches contend that the rise

---

[64] Michael Mann, "The Emergence of Modern European Nationalism," 137–66.

[65] On commerce and democratization, see Dietrich Rueschemeyer, Evelyne Stephens, and John Stephens, *Capitalist Development and Democracy* (Chicago: University of Chicago Press, 1992).

of nationalist feeling is mainly a side effect of heightened security fears in such circumstances.[66] However, statistical findings show that democratizing states are somewhat more likely to be the initiators of international wars than to be the targets of aggressions.[67] This is the reverse of what the preventive war argument predicts, so this argument fails as a general theory of the link between democratization and nationalist conflict. Nonetheless, since strategic factors may play a role in particular cases, I assess their impact when they are relevant in the case studies.

### Tracing Causal Relationships and Selecting Cases

In the introductory chapter, I summarized statistical evidence suggesting that democratization is a cause of nationalist and ethnic conflict, especially in the early stages of the transition in states with weak political institutions. In the following chapters, I present case studies to demonstrate that democratization gives rise to nationalism and nationalist conflict in the manner predicted by my theory of elite persuasion. By tracing causal processes within cases and comparing across cases, I show that the following main predictions generally hold true:

- Popular nationalism generally arises (or at least greatly intensifies) during the earliest phase of the process of democratization, or in direct anticipation of democratization, and rarely before it.[68]

---

[66] This line of argument is not fully laid out in any single source, but the logic of it follows from arguments found in Posen, "The Security Dilemma and Ethnic Conflict"; Posen, "Nationalism, the Mass Army and Military Power"; Walt, *Revolution and War*; Byman and Van Evera, "Hypotheses on the Causes of Contemporary Deadly Conflict"; and Van Evera, "Hypotheses on Nationalism and War."

[67] Edward D. Mansfield and Jack Snyder, "Democratic Transitions, Institutional Strength, and War," manuscript, 1999.

[68] Nationalism or ethnic conflict that arises in anticipation of potential democratization supports my theory, even if no democratic institutional changes have yet been adopted. For example, in 1991, international donors and human rights groups pressed the authoritarian ethnic minority government of Kenya's president Daniel Arap Moi to institute multiparty democracy. In response, government-backed minorities instigated ethnic violence in order to demonstrate that democratization would destabilize the country (Gurr, *Peoples versus States*). The mere prospect of

- Elite persuasion is the central mechanism promoting popular nationalism in most of these cases.
- The success or failure of such attempts at persuasion is strongly influenced by the structure of the marketplace of ideas, defined in terms of partial monopolies of supply of political information, the segmentation of demand, and the strength of institutions that scrutinize and integrate public debate.
- The type of nationalism that emerges during democratization (and the intensity and nature of nationalist conflict) depends primarily on the level and timing of economic development, the adaptability of elite interests, and the strength of the country's political and administrative institutions.
- These correlations are not simply side effects of economic or strategic factors.

To test these hypotheses, I examine cases studies in three domains. First, I look at the four cases from European history that have played the central role in the development of existing theories of nationalism: Germany, Britain, France, and Serbia. The first test of a good theory is whether it can explain what other theories have tried to explain.[69] These cases include the two earliest instances of nationalism, the cases that triggered the three major hegemonic wars of modern history, as well as exemplars of the main paradigmatic types of nationalism. By tracing causes within each case and by comparing across them, I show in Chapters 3 and 4 that my theory can explain the type of nationalism that emerged in each case and the pattern of violent conflict that resulted from it.

Second, in Chapter 5, I look at the relationship between democratization and nationalism in all the post-Communist countries. This is an especially good test of my arguments for several reasons. The class of cases was chosen because of a change in the causal variable (the early phase of

---

increased political participation led the threatened elite to adopt the kind of polarizing tactics that my theory would predict. See also Colin Kahl, "Population Growth, Environmental Degradation, and State-Sponsored Violence: The Case of Kenya, 1991–1993," *International Security* 23:2 (Fall 1998), 80–119, esp. 111.

[69] Imre Lakatos, "Falsification and the Methodology of Scientific Research Programs," in Imre Lakatos and Alan Musgrave, eds., *Criticism and the Growth of Knowledge* (New York: Cambridge University Press, 1970).

democratization), which simultaneously affected the majority of the cases in the class, almost in the manner of a laboratory experiment. Thus, I followed the methodologists' rule of choosing cases "on the independent (or causal) variable."[70] Moreover, since this class includes cases with democratization and without democratization as well as cases with violent conflict and without any violent conflict, it is well suited for comparing across cases to show covariation between cause and effect. I study almost all cases within this class, and thus avoid the temptation of picking only cases that fit my theory. Furthermore, several of these cases seem on first inspection to be anomalous for my theory—that is, democratization did not lead to nationalist conflict despite the existence of weak institutions and ethnic divisions in society. Thus, this is a particularly challenging set of cases against which to test my arguments. I show that the factors highlighted by my theory go a long way toward explaining the nature and intensity of the nationalism that emerged in each of these countries, and why nationalist violence emerged in some countries but not in others. I trace the emergence of violent nationalist conflicts in three cases (Yugoslavia, the Caucasus, and Russia) in some detail, and then compare these with shorter accounts of the cases without nationalist violence.

Third, I examine in Chapter 6 the effects of democratization on nationalist conflict in the developing world in recent decades. These cases taken as a whole do not constitute a tidy lab experiment in the same way that the post-Communist cases do. Nonetheless, they permit me to set up some illuminating tests. I conduct some broad comparisons to explain why the recent wave of democratization in the 1980s and 1990s has led to nationalist conflict in some developing countries, but not in others. Then I look in somewhat more detail at a few cases that permit more rigorously structured comparisons across cases or within a case. Thus, I contrast two countries with many similar features, showing how democratic politics spurred ethnic conflict in Sri Lanka, whereas the squelching of democratization averted ethnic conflict in Malaysia. Next, a short case study of India allows me to trace the effects of declining civic institutions on ethnic violence. Finally, the ethnic violence between Hutu and Tutsi in Rwanda and Burundi illustrates the unintended consequences of international efforts to promote democracy, free speech, and powersharing.

[70] Gary King, Robert Keohane, and Sidney Verba, *Designing Social Inquiry* (Princeton: Princeton University Press, 1994), 129.

In presenting the longer cases, I begin with the outcomes: namely, the type of nationalism that the case exemplifies and the degree of nationalist violence that it caused. After discussing whether long-standing popular rivalries or other competing explanations can account for this outcome, I proceed to discuss the main causal variables of my own theory: the level and timing of development, the adaptability of elite interests, and the institutional context of the democratic transition, including the strength of democratic, administrative, and media institutions. Then I trace the impact of these factors on elites' political strategies, the pattern of persuasion in public debate, and its impact on nationalism and violence. In presenting the shorter cases, however, I sometimes vary this sequence in order to focus on the elements that are most distinctive to the case or most relevant to a comparison with other cases.

The final chapter applies the lessons of these historical and contemporary case studies to the problem of devising strategies for dampening nationalist violence during democratic transitions. While the diverse tests presented in this book can hardly be called definitive, they provide more than enough evidence to warrant a critical interrogation of many of the conventional wisdoms underpinning contemporary thinking about foreign affairs.

# 3

## How Democratization Sparked

## Counterrevolutionary German Nationalism

German nationalism was the driving force behind both World Wars and the racist Nazi attitudes that led to the extermination of millions of Europe's Jews. This calamitous form of nationalism was a by-product of the flaws in the semidemocratic political system of Imperial Germany (1870–1914) and the failure of democracy in the Weimar Republic (1918–1933). These two historical episodes not only shed light on the mechanisms by which democratization can lead to nationalist conflict, but also exemplify the particular dynamics of the counterrevolutionary form of nationalism.

Germany's aristocratic and economic ruling elites promoted aggressive German nationalism as a strategy for maintaining their dominant position in an era of rapid industrialization and social change. Beginning in the 1860s, German steel and railroad production boomed, creating a large working class strongly influenced by socialist ideas. In part to forestall the potential revolutionary threat from these workers, German chancellor Otto von Bismarck and his successors cultivated a base of mass political support among the Protestant middle classes, especially in small towns and rural areas. Grounding this appeal in an exclusionary form of German nationalism, Bismarck and the ruling elites of the German Empire portrayed workers, socialists, Catholics, and Poles as enemies of the true German people. Using nationalism to divide the population, the dominant elites tried to prevent both a working-class revolution and an alliance between industrial workers and other mass groups that might have demanded a fully democratic political system.[1]

Although the Parliament (or Reichstag) was elected by universal male suffrage, the chancellor and his ministers were chosen by the hereditary emperor (or kaiser) and allied with aristocratic and industrial elites. These elites used their control over foreign policy, their ability to shape domestic policy, the prestige of the army, the financial resources of business groups, and their influence over the media to establish a nationalist political agenda. Ruling in the name of the people rather than by the people, these elites were able to use nationalism as the central element in their strategy for fending off the emergence of liberal democratic accountability. As my theory would expect, the pattern of late economic development created both the motive and the opportunity to promote counterrevolutionary nationalism: elites were threatened by demands for mass political partici-pation, democratic institutions were only partially developed, and elites could exploit their influence over administrative and media institutions to lead mass politics in a pseudodemocratic direction.

In the long run, however, the ruling elites lost control of the mass nationalism that they had unleashed. Fed a steady diet of nationalist pro-paganda from the government and from media controlled by business interests, middle-class nationalists increasingly outbid elite nationalists by issuing demands for ever more militant foreign and domestic policies. These grassroots nationalist groups swept Hitler into power when the Great Depression discredited the business and governmental elites at the end of the Weimar Republic.

In presenting this argument, I first trace the development of German nationalism and its role in provoking a series of foreign wars; second, assess some competing explanations for these developments; third, explain the role of elite persuasion in fostering militant nationalism dur-

[1] For related arguments, see Hans Ulrich Wehler, *The German Empire, 1871–1918* (Leamington Spa/Dover, NH: Berg, 1985).

ing the eras of Chancellor Otto von Bismarck (1862–90) and of Kaiser Wilhelm (1888–1918); and finally, analyze the impact of nationalist mythmaking in public debates and mass media in the Weimar Republic from 1918 to 1933.

## War and Nationalism in Germany, 1864–1945

Germany was often at war in the century before World War II and, in every instance, was the principal instigator of the fighting. Although popular with the German people, the wars of national unification from 1864 to 1871 were not fueled by mass nationalist movements, which developed only in the late 1890s. These insatiable nationalist movements did, however, help drive Germany toward war in 1914 and played a central role in Hitler's rise to power in 1933.

Germany's predecessor, Prussia, instigated three wars in the middle of the nineteenth century—first seizing the province of Schleswig-Holstein from Denmark in 1864, then defeating the Austro-Hungarian Empire to gain influence in South Germany in 1866, and finally provoking an ill fated attack by France in 1870. With these three short, victorious wars, Chancellor Otto von Bismarck incorporated several South and West German principalities into a new German nation-state, ruled by the Prussian monarch under a constitution that established a Germany-wide legislature, the Reichstag, elected by universal male suffrage (see map).

These wars were not caused by a spontaneous upsurge of grassroots German nationalism, but rather were part of a strategy of the traditional elite to shape a national consciousness. The precursors of German nationalism are found in the early nineteenth century when Romantic intellectuals, notably Johann Herder, began stressing the role of a common language in defining the political community. This emerging nationalist idea also had an economic dimension. In 1841, the German economist Friedrich List published his book on the *National System of Political Economy*, which argued in favor of railroad building and protective tariffs to promote the development of what he considered the natural economic unit: the unified, culturally defined nation.[2] During urban political tur-

---

[2] Roman Szporluk, *Communism and Marxism: Karl Marx versus Friedrich List* (New York: Oxford University Press, 1988), Chapters 7–10, 12.

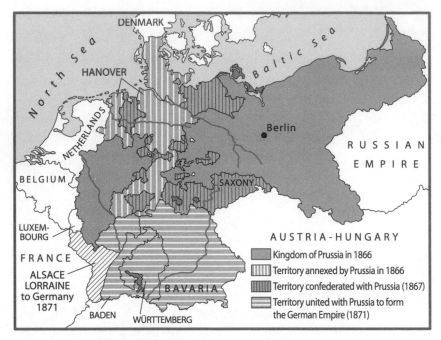

*Unification of Germany, 1866–71*

moil in 1848, German liberal professionals and intellectuals, pressing the
Prussian monarch to accept a partially democratic form of government,
began to adopt the typical nationalist argument that the culturally
defined nation ought to enjoy the right to popular self-rule. Thus, nationalism was in the air as a project of the urban middle classes and intellectuals when Bismarck was planning his series of lightning wars to unify the
German nation in a Prussian-led Reich.

This incipient nationalism still coexisted in an uncertain relationship to
liberal and monarchical ideas, and as yet had not spawned mass nationalist
organizations. Bismarck's wars of German unification reflect the nationalist tactics of a monarchical and aristocratic elite in anticipating the trends
of a coming era of rising mass participation in politics. However, in the
1860s, mass nationalism was at most an aspiration, not yet a reality.

Mass German nationalism played a more direct role in causing war in
1914. Though historians will debate the causes of World War I forever,
there is little dispute that Germany's aggressive policy toward France,
Britain, and Russia in the period after 1898 was the key that wound the
mainspring of conflict ever more tightly, until it was uncoiled in the
German military offensives of 1914. Despite rising economic prosperity

and a boom in foreign trade, Germany repeatedly picked fights with France over colonial issues, humiliated Russia in its Balkan confrontations with Germany's ally Austria, and initiated a naval arms race with Britain. Using war threats to try to break apart the encircling alliance that these policies provoked, Germany succeeded only in pulling the noose more tightly around its own neck. Fearing that the continuing rise of Russian military power would further shift the balance of power against Germany, the German General Staff took advantage of a Balkan dispute between Austria and Russia in August 1914 to attack its enemies in France and in the East (see maps on following page).[3]

This period of increasing belligerence corresponded closely with a rise in popular nationalism among the German middle classes. Over a million dues-paying members flocked into thousands of local branches of the Navy League, the Army League, the Pan-German League, and the Colonial Society.[4] All of these groups favored some form of German imperial expansion, which they justified by a variety of nationalist doctrines. Some claimed, for example, that all German speakers in Austria or Eastern Europe should be part of the German Empire, that Germany should conquer neighboring nations to spread its superior culture, or that all nations were inevitably locked in a struggle to the death for the survival of the fittest. Some of these groups attracted small farmers by promising them land for settlers in Eastern Europe or in overseas colonies. Other groups attracted big business and urban middle-class support with proposals for expansion of the German navy and commercial opportunities abroad.[5]

The views of these mass nationalist organizations often turned out to be more extreme than the views of the governmental bureaucracies and business groups that helped to create and finance them. For example, militant nationalist groups vilified the German government when it compromised with France in disputes over Morocco in 1905–06 and 1911. Likewise, the government lost nationalist votes in 1912, when it tried to rein in naval spending that was threatening to bankrupt the country. At the same time,

[3] Steven E. Miller, ed., *Military Strategy and the Origins of the First World War*, 2d ed. (Princeton: Princeton University Press, 1991).

[4] Geoff Eley, *Reshaping the German Right* (New Haven: Yale University Press, 1980), 102.

[5] Woodruff Smith, *The Ideological Origins of Nazi Imperialism* (New York: Oxford University Press, 1986).

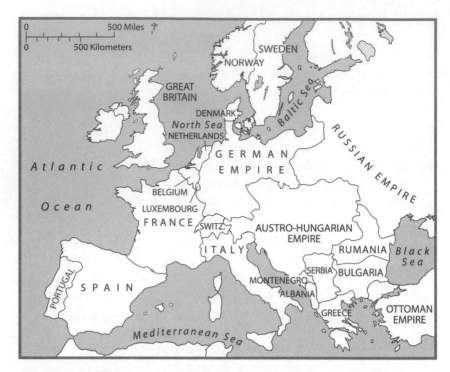

*Europe, 1914*

*Europe after the First World War, 1918*

the continued growth in the size of the working class made the socialists the largest party in the Reichstag by 1912. Thus, on the eve of World War I, Germany's ruling elites had an increased need to win the favor of the nationalist middle classes to stave off the threat from democratic socialism, just as the nationalists were demanding more belligerent foreign policies. The governing elites gambled that a victorious war would somehow extricate them from the political dilemma that they themselves had created.[6]

Germany was even more clearly the instigator of World War II in Europe. By the 1920s, Hitler was arguing that Germany needed to conquer a vast "living space" in Eastern Europe for Germany's "Aryan master race." During the 1930s, Hitler rearmed Germany and developed plans to carry out that goal. Britain and France declared war on Germany after Hitler's invasion of Poland in September 1939, but they sat passively on the defensive until the German army attacked France and Belgium in April 1940 (see map).

Popular German nationalism played a less direct role in Hitler's aggression than in the offensives of 1914. The Germans who voted for Hitler in 1932 were the same part of the electorate who had voted for various nationalist parties throughout the 1920s. Their ideas about the Darwinian competition among races and cultures had roots in the thinking of pre-1914 nationalist societies. Nonetheless, Hitler did not emphasize his plans for military conquest in the 1932 electoral campaign.[7] Once in power, Hitler's decisions to act on his aggressive agenda reflected his own internalization of a belligerent, nationalist worldview, not mass pressure from nationalist political movements.

In short, nationalism played a role in all five of Germany's aggressive wars between 1864 and 1945 (see Table 3.1, p. 101). Germany's ruling elites fought wars in the 1860s in order to unify a nation, which could serve as a popular basis for their continued rule. Once the elites had succeeded in promoting an enthusiastic mass nationalism by the turn of the century, they soon found their monstrous creation pushing them toward a great European war. Failing to learn the right lessons from Germany's

[6] Fritz Fischer, *War of Illusions* (New York: W. W. Norton, 1975).

[7] Ian Kershaw, "Ideology, Propaganda, and the Rise of the Nazi Party," in Peter Stachura, ed., *The Nazi Machtergreifung* (London: Allen & Unwin, 1983), 167; Eberhard Jäckel, *Hitler in History* (Hanover, NH: University Press of New England, 1984), 21, 34.

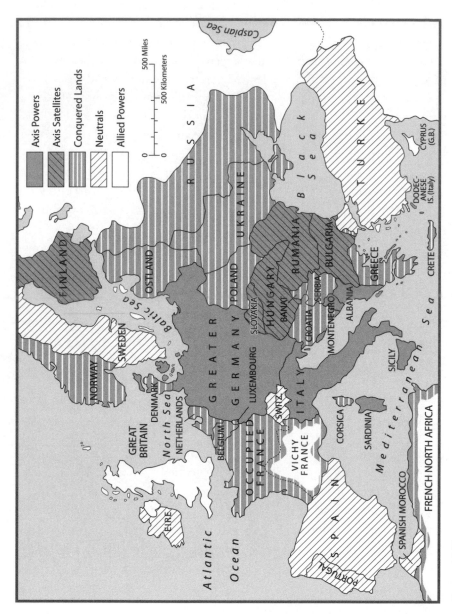

*Europe, 1942*

**Table 3.1 German Regimes and Foreign Conflicts, 1862–1945**

| Year | Regime | Leading Figures | Political System | Ruling Group | Foreign Conflicts |
|---|---|---|---|---|---|
| 1862–70 | Prussian monarchy | Minister President Bismarck* | Constitutional monarchy, limited suffrage, king-appointed ministers | Prussian aristocratic landowners; king | War with Denmark (1864), Austria (1866), and France (1870) |
| 1871–90 | German Empire | Chancellor Bismarck* | Constitutional monarchy, universal male suffrage, king-appointed ministers | Rise of "iron-and-rye" coalition: king, landowners, industry | Balance-of-power politics and crises, but no war |
| 1888–1918 | German Empire | Kaiser Wilhelm; various chancellors | Constitutional monarchy, universal male suffrage, king-appointed ministers | "Iron-and-rye" coalition; rise of mass nationalist pressure groups | Crises with France (1905, 1911) and Russia (1909); World War I (1914–18) |
| 1919–33 | Weimar Republic | Freely elected presidents and parliament | Constitutional democracy | Centrist coalitions, including Democratic Socialists, Nationalists, Catholics; Nazis (1932–33) | Germany disarmed by Versailles Treaty; France occupies Ruhr (1923–25); Locarno Treaty (1925) establishes cooperation with Western democracies |
| 1933–45 | German Empire | Hitler (Führer) | Dictatorship | Nazi Party | World War II (1939–45) |

*Otto Von Bismarck was minister president of Prussia before 1871 and chancellor of the German Empire after 1871.

defeat in World War I, grassroots nationalists once again pushed Germany toward war by installing one of their own, Adolf Hitler, in the seat of power in Berlin.

### Alternative Explanations for Germany's Wars and Nationalism

The connection between democratization and nationalist conflict in German history might be explained in several ways. In addition to my own explanation based on nationalist elite persuasion during the early phase of democratization, three potentially competing views also merit consideration: popular rivalries, industrialization as a force for political and cultural homogenization, and balance-of-power politics in the age of the mass army. None of these three alternative views suffices to explain Germany's nationalist conflicts, though the latter two help account for important aspects of the setting in which elite persuasion took place.

### *Popular rivalries*

Some scholars might expect long-standing popular cultural rivalries to explain why democratization, nationalism, and bloody conflict coincide in German history. Early nineteenth-century conceptions of "Germanness," like Herder's, took shape around ethnic rather than civic principles. This occurred in part because Germany existed as a common linguistic and cultural area well before the unification of the German state. Nonetheless, there were no ancient ethnic hatreds shaping the subsequent pattern of Germany's nationalist conflicts. Many of the rivalries of Germany's Prussian-dominated, middle-class Protestant nationalism were directed toward other German speakers: German socialists, German Catholics, and before 1866, German-speaking Austria. Although Poles and other Slavic peoples were the target of denigration, the English were admired. Throughout the nineteenth century, urban Jews such as Bismarck's banker and confidant Gerson von Bleichröder were well-integrated into German society.[8] Unlike Jews in the Russian Empire, those in Germany were not attacked in large-scale pogroms. Long-standing popular hatreds are implausible as an explanation for Germany's nationalist conflicts.

[8] Fritz Stern, *Gold and Iron* (New York: Knopf, 1977).

### Industrial homogenization

Theories like Ernest Gellner's that focus on the impact of industrialization have more to contribute to an understanding of German nationalism. The commercial and industrial revolution of the mid-nineteenth century created strong economic incentives to unify Germany's national market politically and culturally. These incentives were indeed part of the impetus behind Bismarck's wars of 1864, 1866, and 1870. Consequently, one might take the view that industrialization produced the drive for national unification, and that by promoting the growth of the middle and working classes, industrialization also fostered Germany's democratization. If so, democratization did not necessarily cause nationalism; perhaps they were just correlated in time because they were both caused by the rapid industrialization of the 1860s.

While this argument has some merit, it fails to explain the most dramatic period of mass-energized German nationalist conflict between 1890 and 1945. The unification of the national market was long since completed by the time Germany's popular nationalist movements arose in the late 1890s. To explain that, we need to know not just that Germany industrialized, but also how its late, abrupt industrialization shaped Germany's interest-group politics, which I explain later in this chapter.

### Military competition and the mass army

A third competing explanation is that Germany was especially war-prone not because of its nationalism per se, but because it occupied a particularly vulnerable position in the center of Europe. Stuck at the geographical fulcrum of the balance of power at a time when the relative strength of the great powers was shifting dramatically, even the most reasonable state with purely defensive motives might have found it necessary to resort frequently to war. Just as the Prussian king Frederick the Great (a monarchist, not a nationalist) had to fight preventive wars on multiple fronts with small professional armies in the vulnerable center of Europe in the eighteenth century, so too his German successors had to fight similar wars with mass armies in the nineteenth and twentieth centuries. It might be argued that, instead of nationalism causing the wars, war caused nationalism: in an era of million-man armies based on civilian reservists, the threat of war compelled the German state to promulgate nationalism as a means to secure a willing fighting force.[9]

The anarchical nature of international politics does make war a chronic danger, especially for vulnerable states. However, different states vary greatly in how they choose to play a similar strategic hand. For example, Bismarck followed a more moderate strategy than did later German leaders, who were caught in the grip of mass nationalism. Once Bismarck had achieved the objective of unifying Germany, he took advantage of Germany's position in the center of the balance-of-power system of five major states to make sure that Germany would always have two strong allies. By concluding conditional, defensive alliances that would come into force only if the ally was attacked, Bismarck was able to reassure potential enemies of his aim only to secure the status quo while retaining his flexibility of alignment.[10] The diplomacy of Bismarck's successors, however, became more rigid and belligerent, in part because of the rise of nationalist public opinion in Germany. Political leaders' efforts to rally domestic support through crisis showdowns and fleet-building made enemies simultaneously of France, Britain, and Russia, while the alliance with the German-speaking Austrians became unconditional. It was not that military rivalry created a nationalism-ridden garrison state, but more nearly the reverse. To understand how Germany wound up encircled and vulnerable, it is necessary to understand the nationalist bidding war touched off by the distinctive pattern of German democratization.

## Playing the Nationalist Card in German Democratization

Popular nationalism was conjured up by monarchical, aristocratic, and business elites in the years after the founding of Bismarck's Reich in 1871 as a way of maintaining their dominant position in the face of increasing demands for mass political participation, which industrialization accelerated. The ruling elite promoted exclusionary nationalism to divide potential supporters of democratic change into mutually hostile camps. These elites

---

[9] Barry Posen, "Nationalism, the Mass Army, and Military Power," *International Security*, 18:2 (Fall 1993), 80–124.

[10] Otto Pflanze, *Bismarck and the Development of Germany* (Princeton: Princeton University Press, 1971).

deployed the power of the state and their economic resources to set the political agenda and to shape the terms of public debate during Germany's initial period of democratization, but these same elites then became increasingly trapped by the implications of their own nationalist rhetoric.[11]

In presenting this interpretation of the rise of Germany nationalism and its role in causing the First World War, I first discuss Germany's pattern of late industrialization, the threat this posed to German elites, and the flaws in Germany's partially democratic institutions that allowed these elites to impose their agenda on mass politics. I then examine the consequences of this for coalition politics and for the promotion of nationalist ideas. Finally, I show how this political dynamic created enemies abroad and fostered war in 1914.

### Germany's late industrialization creates threats to elite interests

Germany's pattern of late industrialization left a legacy of powerful, inflexible elite interests that were inherently threatened by democratization. The huge capital investments needed for Germany's late, abrupt steel industrialization in the 1860s led to the development of centralized banking trusts and highly concentrated, large-scale heavy industry. The Prussian aristocratic landholders who staffed the Prussian state were largely left out of these industrial developments. They saw very few attractive economic prospects outside of their relatively inefficient agricultural holdings, and thus had a large stake in using state-backed protectionism and political repression to maintain their social position.[12] Thus, an aristocratic ruling class (with a shrinking agricultural base) and a business elite (concentrated in large-scale heavy industry) faced a growing and increasingly assertive working class, as well as a large peasant and artisan class still rooted in traditional ways. In this situation, Germany's unadaptable elites had interests that were sharply at odds with one another and with those of mass groups.

---

[11] For citations supporting this interpretation, see Wehler, *German Empire*, and Snyder, *Myths of Empire: Domestic Politics and International Ambition* (Ithaca: Cornell University Press, 1991), Chapter 3.

[12] In addition to Barrington Moore, *Social Origins of Dictatorship and Democracy* (Boston: Beacon, 1966), see David Spring, ed., *European Landed Elites in the Nineteenth Century* (Baltimore: Johns Hopkins University Press, 1977), and Robert Moeller, ed., *Peasants and Lords in Modern Germany* (Boston: Allen & Unwin, 1986).

To understand the political consequences of Germany's late, rapid economic development, it is helpful to contrast this pattern with Britain's earlier, gradual industrialization.[13] The accumulation of capital for Britain's textile industrialization before the 1840s had come from commercial agriculture and trade. This pattern of investment created an economically integrated aristocratic and commercial elite with mobile capital and little to fear from gradual democratization. British landowners were comparatively relaxed about the expansion of democratic rights: the relative mobility of their substantial commercial investments allowed many of them to accept the end of agricultural protection and to profit from a liberalizing, free-trading political alliance with the commercial middle classes.

Many of Germany's elite groups with an interest in retarding democratization also had a parochial interest in war, military preparation, empire, and economic protectionism. This is not accidental. When autocratic states start to democratize, many of the interests threatened by democratization are military. As Charles Tilly says, "war made the state and the state made war."[14] In early modern Europe (as in many more recent authoritarian states), military organizations occupied a privileged position in the state, which was built to serve their needs. Moreover, aristocracies were intertwined with military institutions, so democratization inherently challenged the vested social, economic, and bureaucratic interests of a ruling class that was at its core a military elite.[15] As a result, Germany's inflexible elites were willing to run great risks, including gambling on a nationalist foreign policy, to extricate themselves from their political dilemma.

### Weak democratic accountability, strong administrative institutions

Chancellor Otto von Bismarck realized that the new imperial German state created after the victory over France in 1870 would need a more

[13] Alexander Gerschenkron, *Economic Backwardness in Historical Perspective* (Cambridge: Belknap, 1962); Wehler, *German Empire*; Modris Eksteins, *The Limits of Reason: The German Democratic Press and the Collapse of Weimar Democracy* (London: Oxford University Press, 1975), 3–5.

[14] Charles Tilly, "Reflections on the History of European State-Making," in Tilly, ed., *The Formation of National States in Europe* (Princeton: Princeton University Press, 1975), 42.

[15] Joseph Schumpeter, *Imperialism and Social Classes* (New York: Kelly, 1950; orig. ed. 1919).

democratic system for electing its legislature than that of old Prussia. The formerly independent South and West German states, which joined Prussia's new empire, were reluctant to be ruled by decree from the Prussian capital of Berlin. Like the rising urban and middle classes throughout the new Reich, these areas wanted to have some say in the making of governmental policy. Consequently, some form of democratic representation was unavoidable, despite the dilemmas it posed for the old ruling elite.

Facing this kind of problem, some of Europe's other monarchical regimes had adopted systems of limited franchise, which gave the vote only to the upper classes and to middle-class property holders. However, Bismarck realized that this would have allowed Germany's emerging liberal parties to wield legislative power against the monarchical state. To finesse this problem, Bismarck boldly established a system of universal suffrage in the new German Reich, counting on safe rural and small-town districts, dominated by conservative local elites, to counterbalance the increasing votes of urban liberals and the working class.

The political system developed under Bismarck and his successors had many of the features of a democracy: competitive elections, universal male suffrage, large political parties with mass support, and some legislative control over the governmental budget. However, since government ministers were appointed by the kaiser rather than chosen by a majority coalition in the Reichstag, the unelected government had considerable freedom to use its administrative resources to set the political agenda. It did this by making deals directly with interest groups, withholding information from the legislature and the public, and using its power to initiate policy to shape the way issues would be defined during electoral campaigns.

The government's area of greatest constitutional freedom of action was in foreign and military affairs. Exploiting this free hand, it repeatedly trumped up foreign policy challenges on the eve of elections to boost vote totals for the ruling coalition. Lacking the right to scrutinize the details of military affairs, the Reichstag and hence the public were kept in the dark about internal studies showing that the war plans of the army and navy were inadequate to deal with the challenges that Germany's belligerent foreign policies were creating.[16] Thus, the government used its ability to

---

[16] Paul Kennedy, "Tirpitz, England, and the Second Navy Law of 1900: A Strategical Critique," *Militärgeschichtliche Mitteilungen* 2 (1970), 33–58; Jack Snyder,

initiate policy and monopolize crucial information to set Germany's public agenda on a nationalist course.

### Consequences for coalition politics and the promotion
### of nationalist ideas

Bismarck based his strategy of rule on the coalition of "iron and rye,"
which protected the economic interests and social power of heavy industrialists and aristocratic grain producers alike. In this arrangement, the
industrialists received protection against foreign manufactures, constraints on the socialists' ability to organize and strike, and under
Bismarck's successors, huge contracts for building a naval fleet. The aristocratic rye growers received high tariffs against foreign grain imports and
a continuation of their special tax exemption.

This coalition, based on governmental favoritism for elite economic
interests, naturally ran the risk of provoking opposition from a popular
democratic movement that might unite against it. To prevent this,
Bismarck launched an ideological war against groups that he labeled
"enemies of the Reich," especially the socialist workers and the South
German Catholics. In this way, Bismarck appealed to the Protestant
middle classes and farmers as the privileged core of the true German
nation, along with the iron-and-rye elites. This tactic succeeded in dividing the Protestant middle classes from those who might have been
potential allies in a broad, democratic coalition. Progressives dreamed of
a bloc extending from the liberal-democratic middle classes through the
moderately socialist working classes, but the government's use of the
nationalism issue prevented this by widening the gap dividing the middle class from the workers.[17] In the post-Bismarck period between 1890
and 1914, the iron-and-rye elites turned increasingly to militaristic
nationalist appeals to solidify their links with the middle classes.
Meanwhile, the rye-growing aristocrats organized a mass movement with
the support of small farmers to lobby in favor of high tariffs to keep out
foreign farm products.

---

*The Ideology of the Offensive: Military Decision Making and the Disasters of 1914*
(Ithaca: Cornell University Press, 1984), Chapters 4 and 5.

[17] Beverly Heckart, *From Bassermann to Bebel: The Grand Bloc's Quest for Reform in
the Kaiserreich, 1900–1914* (New Haven: Yale University Press, 1974).

For a time, this militarist-protectionist strategy worked extremely well for the kaiser-appointed governments of Bismarckian and Wilhelmine Germany, which faced the dilemma of winning budgetary approval from a Reichstag elected by universal suffrage. Especially effective was playing the nationalist card in election campaigns. Five times between the founding of the Reich and 1914 the government chose to contest elections on what it styled as "national" issues: the "culture struggle" against the Catholics in 1874, the campaign of 1878 tarring socialists as antinational, the campaigns to support bills strengthening the army in 1887 and 1893, and the so-called "Hottentot election" on German colonial policy in South West Africa in 1907. In each instance, the iron-and-rye governments claimed that the socialist, Catholic, or liberal opposition parties lacked sufficient commitment to the German nation to safeguard its national security and position of global power. Each time elections were fought on such "national" grounds, voter turnout increased and more progovernment candidates were elected, in part because conservative candidates got more votes overall and in part because coalitions of right-wing parties were more cohesive (see Table 3.2). Hidden financing of nationalist movements and publications by the navy and by industrial interests, combined with prosecutions of opposition voices under a restrictive press law, played an essential part in this strategy.[18]

Between elections, the government used its agenda-setting power in bargaining with special interest groups to sustain legislative support for its dubious foreign policies. For example, the government won the Catholic Center Party's backing for expanding the fleet by offering concessions on Catholic rights. The Center Party was not, however, offered cabinet positions. Such a move would have made the government more directly accountable to the party's rank-and-file voters, who were not in favor of expanding the fleet. Through these mechanisms, Germany's pattern of

[18] Brett Fairbairn, "Interpreting Wilhelmine Elections: National Issues, Fairness Issues, and Electoral Mobilization," in Larry Eugene Jones and James Retallack, eds., *Elections, Mass Politics, and Social Change in Modern Germany* (Cambridge: Cambridge University Press, 1992), 22–30; Robert J. Goldstein, *Political Repression in 19th Century Europe* (London: Croom Helm, 1983), 39; Dirk Stegmann, "Between Economic Interests and Radical Nationalism," in Larry Eugene Jones and James Retallack, eds., *Between Reform, Reaction, and Resistance: Studies in the History of German Conservatism from 1789 to 1945* (Providence: Berg, 1993), 173, 183; Geoff Eley, *Reshaping the German Right* (New Haven: Yale University Press, 1980), 140–47.

**Table 3.2  German "National" Elections, 1871–1912, and the Vote for the "Iron-and-Rye" Parties***

| | 1871 | 1874 | 1877 | 1878 | 1881 | 1884 | 1887 | 1890 | 1893 | 1898 | 1903 | 1907 | 1912 |
|---|---|---|---|---|---|---|---|---|---|---|---|---|---|
| *% Voter Turnout* | 51.0 | **61.2** | 60.6 | **63.4** | 56.3 | 60.6 | **77.5** | 71.6 | **72.5** | 68.1 | 76.1 | **84.7** | 84.9 |
| *Iron-and-Rye Seats* | 219 | **210** | 206 | **215** | 125 | 157 | **220** | 135 | **153** | 125 | 126 | **138** | 100 |
| *% Vote for Iron-and-Rye Parties* | 52.9 | **43.7** | 44.7 | **49.6** | 38.2 | 39.7 | **47.2** | 35.2 | **32.1** | 27.9 | 27.2 | **28.0** | 25.7 |

* The "iron-and-rye" parties, also called the *Kartell*, are the DKP (German Conservative Party), RP (Imperial Party), and NL (National Liberals). The Kartell parties contested the elections of 1874, 1878, 1887, 1893 and 1907 on "national" issues of culture, military power, or colonial policy.

Source: Brett Fairbairn, *Democracy in the Undemocratic State: The German Reichstag Elections of 1898 and 1903* (Toronto: University of Toronto Press, 1997), p. 48.

partial democracy and partial state autonomy created an opportunity for the ruling elite to set a nationalist agenda for foreign affairs that would sustain the iron-and-rye coalition.

The government's strategy of mixing interest-group politics with nationalism had the side effect of heightening divisions within its own camp. The conservative marriage of iron and rye superficially united the steel magnates of the West German Ruhr Valley with the landed aristocracy, which staffed the army's officer corps. However, iron and rye were loath to reconcile their mutually contradictory policies on a range of foreign and military issues. In the economic sphere, the East German aristocratic rye-growers insisted on high tariffs to keep out cheap Russian grain, while at the same time the industrialists wanted Russia to lower its tariffs on German manufactures. In the military sphere, the politically influential army sought a Europe-first strategy, building up the land army and limiting overseas commitments, whereas industrial interests insisted on a large navy and commercial expansion in the tropics. Meanwhile, the traditionally tax-exempt landowning aristocrats refused to pay taxes for the fleet desired by the steel magnates. The incompatibility of these interests made the policies of the iron-and-rye coalition incoherent. Germany wound up with plans for a big army, a costly navy, and nobody willing to pay for it.[19]

### Consequences for competitive mass mobilization

In a period of democratization, threatened elite groups have an overwhelming incentive to mobilize allies among the mass of people, but they wish to do so on their own terms, using whatever special resources these elites might still retain. These assets include wealth, monopolies of information, government patronage, organizational skills and networks, and the ability to use the control of traditional political institutions to shape the political agenda and to structure the terms of political bargains. In Germany before World War I, although elites could not rule without

[19] Eckart Kehr, *Economic Interest, Militarism, and Foreign Policy* (Berkeley: University of California Press, 1977); David D'Lugo and Ronald Rogowski, "The Anglo-German Naval Race and Comparative Constitutional 'Fitness'," in Richard Rosecrance and Arthur Stein, eds., *The Domestic Bases of Grand Strategy* (Ithaca: Cornell University Press, 1993), 65–95, esp. 81–83.

mass allies, they retained substantial tools to influence mass political choices. For example, Krupp Steel bankrolled mass nationalist and militarist leagues, which had chapters in every German town. And the German navy's unchallenged "expertise" in making strategic assessments meant that there were few credible voices to refute its claim that Britain would respond to an increasing German naval threat not with a naval arms competition but by seeking an alliance with Germany.[20]

This elite mobilization of mass groups took place in a highly competitive setting. Elites rallied mass support in order to win votes to neutralize mass threats. Nationalist leagues gave conservative elites a popular base to counterbalance the electoral weight of workers' movements. Elites also needed to mobilize mass support to counter other elite groups' successful efforts to attract popular allies. Thus, the Agrarian League gave aristocratic landowners a popular counterweight to the industrialist-backed Navy League.

These nationalist appeals succeeded among middle-class and rural target groups, despite the fact that the average German voter was not consistently pro-war or pro-empire. If Germany had had a fully developed set of democratic institutions, with an elected government directly accountable to public opinion, it is possible that party competition might have led to a moderation of German foreign policy. But given the way that Germany's partial democracy structured the competition of interest groups, the recruitment of mass allies served to magnify nationalist sentiment.

Social interests that were organized into mass parties shunned nationalism, imperialism, and militarism. The two largest mass parties, the Social Democrats and the Catholic Center Party, had no interest in a belligerent foreign policy. The working-class constituency of the Social Democrats was consistently skeptical about military and colonial projects. The Center Party backed the fleet not out of conviction, but as part of a bargain to reduce official discrimination against Catholics.[21]

In contrast, many Protestant middle-class and rural voters were recruited into politics by elite-led lobbying groups, not by broad-based

---

[20] Snyder, *Myths of Empire*, 103, 140–41, 205.

[21] Jonathan Steinberg, *Yesterday's Deterrent* (London: Macdonald, 1965), 190–91; David Blackbourn, *Populists and Patricians* (London: Allen & Unwin, 1987), 161–62, 190, 211.

political parties. Thus, their voices tended to reinforce the pattern of elite interests, not check them. The Agrarian League clamored for grain tariffs, the Navy League for a fleet, the Colonial Society for settler colonies abroad, the Pan-German League for the unification of all Germans in East Central Europe under Berlin's leadership, the Society for the Eastern Marches for farm land in Eastern Europe, and the Defense League for a bigger army (see Table 3.3, p. 114). In comparison, in countries where middle-class opinion has been articulated through an institutionalized two-party competition, as in twentieth-century Britain and the United States, public impact on foreign policy has mostly been more benign.

In the competition to mobilize mass support, the German elites' economic and administrative resources allowed them to affect the direction of mass participation in politics, but not to control its consequences. The imperative to compete for mass favor made it impossible for any single elite group to control the outcome of this process. Mass groups that gained access to politics through elite-supported nationalist organizations often tried to outbid their erstwhile elite sponsors. The Navy and Army Leagues took the popular ideology too literally and tried to use it for their own goals, pressing, for example, for an increase in the number of middle-class officers in an army that was still dominated by an aristocratic officer corps. They argued that if Germany really *were* surrounded by hostile neighbors, then it needed a much larger army, and its enlarged officer corps would have to include many more from the middle class. By 1911, German popular nationalist lobbies were in a position to claim that if Germany's foreign foes were really as threatening as the ruling elites had portrayed them, then the government had sold out German interests in reaching a compromise settlement of the dispute with France over the control of Morocco.[22]

Thus, playing the nationalist card became increasingly dangerous for the old elites. It threatened their social position, required tax increases that threatened their economic interests, and needlessly provoked foreign enemies. Nonetheless, most conservative elites saw little alternative but to keep playing this game, if they were to retain a base of middle-class support against the increasingly numerous working class (see Table 3.4, p. 115).

---

[22] Eley, *Reshaping the German Right*, Chapter 10; James Retallack, "The Road to Philippi: The Conservative Party and Bethmann Hollweg's 'Politics of the Diagonal,' 1909–1914," in Jones and Retallack, *Between Reform*, 286–87.

*From Voting to Violence*

### Table 3.3 Comparative Membership of Nationalist Pressure Groups in Germany, 1881–1914

| | Pan-German League | Navy League | Colonial Society | Society for the Eastern Marches | Society for Germandom Abroad | Defence League |
|---|---|---|---|---|---|---|
| 1881 | | | | | 1,345 | |
| 1887 | | | 14,838 | | | |
| 1891 | 21,000 | | 17,709 | | 36,000 | |
| 1893 | 5,000 | | 17,154 | | | |
| 1894 | 5,742 | | 16,264 | | | |
| 1895 | 7,715 | | 16,474 | 20,000 | 26,524 | |
| 1896 | 9,443 | | 17,901 | 18,500 | | |
| 1897 | 12,974 | | 21,252 | 9,400 | | |
| 1898 | 17,364 | 14,252 | 26,501 | | | |
| 1899 | 20,488 | 93,991 | 31,601 | | | |
| 1900 | 21,735 | 216,749 | 34,768 | 20,000 | 32,000 | |
| 1901 | 21,924 | 238,767 | 33,541 | | | |
| 1902 | | 236,793 | 32,161 | | | |
| 1903 | 19,068 | 233,173 | 31,482 | 29,300 | | |
| 1904 | 19,111 | 249,241 | 31,985 | | 34,774 | |
| 1905 | 18,618 | 275,272 | 32,159 | | | |
| 1906 | 18,445 | 315,420 | 32,787 | 40,500 | | |
| 1907 | | 324,372 | 36,956 | | | |
| 1908 | | 307,884 | 38,509 | | | |
| 1909 | | 296,172 | 38,928 | | | |
| 1910 | | 290,964 | 39,025 | 53,000 | 45,272 | |
| 1911 | | 297,788 | 39,134 | | | |
| 1912 | c.17,000 | 320,174 | 41,163 | | | 33,000 |
| 1913 | | 331,910 | 42,212 | | | 78,000 |
| 1914 | | 331,493 | 42,018 | 54,000 | 57,452 | 90,000 |

The following points should be noted:

- The Navy League also enjoyed a huge additional membership from organizations that were corporately affiliated with local branches. In 1899 this amounted to 152,890, more than doubling by 1900 and rising steadily to 675,168 by 1908, to reach a total of 776,613 in 1914. In aggregate terms this gave the League well over a million members.
- Both the Pan-Germans and the Colonial Society experienced striking gains in membership when campaigning on the naval issue between 1895 and 1900.
- The Navy League took a significant drop in membership as a result of the crisis in 1907–8.
- The turn away from "world policy" back to "continental policy" by the government after 1911 had no effect on the membership of the Colonial Society, which continued to rise.

Source: Geoff Eley, *Reshaping the German Right* (New Haven: Yale University Press, 1980), pp. 366–67.

**Table 3.4 Elite and Mass Alignments in Wilhelmine Germany, 1890–1914**

| | Socialist Ideology | Liberal Ideology | Centrist Ideology | Conservative Nationalist Ideology | |
|---|---|---|---|---|---|
| Governing Coalition | | | | Coalition of "iron and rye" | |
| Elites | Revolutionary intellectuals | Export-oriented industrialists | Catholics, especially South German | Agricultural aristocrats, king, army | Heavy industrialists, navy |
| Parties | Social Democrat | Progressive | Catholic Center | German Conservative | National Liberal |
| Mass Constituency | Industrial workers | Liberal middle class | Catholics | Farmers | Nationalist middle class |
| Mass Pressure Groups | Labor unions | Professional organizations | Catholic organizations | Agrarian League | Navy, Pan-German, Colonial, and Defense Leagues |

### *The vacuum of authority and nationalist mythmaking lead to conflicts abroad*

In late July 1914, the problem in Germany was not excessive authoritarian power at the center, but the opposite. As Europe's armies prepared to hurtle from their starting gates, Austrian leaders, perplexed by the contradictions between the German chancellor's policy and that of the German military, asked "Who rules in Berlin?"[23] As in many democratizing states, autocratic power was in decline vis-à-vis both the elite interest groups and mass groups, weakening the state's authority. Meanwhile, democratic institutions lacked the strength to take on the burden of integrating these contending interests and views. As a result, the weak central political leadership resorted to the same strategies as did the more parochial elite interests, using nationalist ideological appeals and special-interest payoffs to maintain its short-run viability, despite the long-run risks that these strategies might unleash.

Since the iron-and-rye coalition was cobbled together from contradictory bases of support, its leadership faced the problem of explaining away the self-contradictory aspects of its mutually incompatible policies. In foreign affairs, this meant sweeping tough tradeoffs under the rug, pretending that contradictory policies actually made sense or could not be avoided. As a consequence, German foreign policy became increasingly overcommitted, provoking too many enemies at the same time, while claiming that the resulting conflicts were due to other states' inherent hostility. For example, the hostile encirclement of Germany that resulted from the contradictory policies of the iron-and-rye coalition was explained away with two claims: first, that the hostility was inherent in the nature of Germany's opponents, German policy had done nothing to provoke it; and second, that the way to break apart the hostile coalition was to issue threats, not to make concessions that would require reversing the policies of the iron-and-rye coalition.[24] Once such myths became widespread in German thinking about international politics, designing effective national strategies became impossible. Nationalism was a doctrine well-suited to sustain these misconceptions.

---

[23] Gerhard Ritter, *The Sword and the Sceptre: The Problem of Militarism in Germany*, vol. 2 (Coral Gables: University of Miami Press, 1969), 257–63.

[24] Snyder, *Myths of Empire*, 85–89.

One of the simplest but most risky strategies for a hard-pressed regime in a democratizing country is to shore up its prestige at home by seeking victories abroad. Chancellor Johannes Miquel, who revitalized the iron-and-rye coalition at the turn of the century, argued that "successes in foreign policy would make a good impression in the Reichstag debates, and political divisions would thus be moderated."[25] Such prestige strategies made Germany's leadership highly sensitive to slights to its reputation. As Kaiser Wilhelm found out in confrontations with France and Britain over Morocco in 1905 and 1911, belligerent diplomacy is likely to produce not cheap victories but stiff foreign resistance and embarrassing defeats, which further complicate domestic governance. Like interest-group logrolling and strategic mythmaking, prestige strategies offer at best temporary relief from the political conundrums of democratization. The more the threatened elites rely on such expedients, the more likely they are to get caught up in an untenable spiral of posturing and overcommitment.

In short, elites in Germany's partially democratized state faced a strenuous political task. Fearing to permit full democratic accountability, they used nationalist appeals to divide the masses and then tried to piece together a heterogeneous coalition of elite and popular supporters in a context of weakly developed democratic institutions. Many of the measures that they adopted, such as belligerent prestige strategies, heightened the risk of conflicts with other nations.

## Selling Nationalism in Weimar Germany

Weimar Germany presents a challenge to those who prescribe democracy, open debate, and vigorous civil society as the antidote to nationalism and ethnic prejudice: Weimar Germany *had* all of these features, yet belligerent nationalism thrived. Its constitution established a free and fair electoral system based on proportional representation, the type of system that many advocate today to defuse nationalism. A high-quality, liberal press dominated Weimar's big-city newspaper markets. Record numbers of voluntary political clubs and civil society organizations formed. And yet one-

[25] J. C. G. Rohl, *Germany without Bismarck* (Berkeley: University of California Press, 1967), 250.

third of the electorate voted for Hitler's National Socialists in 1933. Were these voters simply duped, and if so, how?[26]

Racist, authoritarian nationalism triumphed at the end of the Weimar Republic not despite the democratization of political life but because of it. About one-third of the electorate had voted for right-wing nationalist parties throughout the Weimar period, most of which were led by big-business interests and traditional conservative elites (see Table 3.5). The late Weimar economic crisis convinced their middle-class constituencies that elite-led nationalist parties were indifferent to their plight. At that point, the dense network of grassroots voluntary organizations in small cities and towns turned massively to support a populist party that seemed to be one of their own, the Nazis (National Socialists). Although aspiring to assert popular sovereignty, these middle-class nationalists consciously turned their back on the Weimar form of democracy, which they associated with the defeat of Germany in 1918, the Versailles Treaty imposed by the victorious Western powers, the rise to power of the socialist class enemy, and the domination of middle-class party politics by elitist conservative parties. In place of Weimar democracy, middle-class voters became persuaded that the Nazis would create a new type of political system that would amalgamate Germany's plethora of middle-class, rural, and working-class interest groups in a structure that would somehow express the collective interest of the true German *Volk*, or nation.[27]

Where did the largely middle-class, Protestant, small-town and rural constituencies that voted for Hitler get the idea to define their interests in this way, and why did they think a vote for Hitler would advance those interests? One factor was the legacy of pre-1914 elite nationalist myth-making, which had deeply ingrained nationalism in the consciousness of the German middle classes.[28] This mindset enhanced the believability of

[26] This is the question posed by Richard Bessel, "The Formation and Dissolution of a German National Electorate," in Jones and Retallack, *Elections*, 399.

[27] Peter Fritzsche, "Weimar Populism and National Socialism in Local Perspective," in Jones and Retallack, *Elections*, 301–4; Mommsen, "Government without Parties," in Jones and Retallack, *Between Reform*, 359, 372; Bessel, "Formation," in Jones and Retallack, *Elections*, 404, 412–13.

[28] On the Wilhelmine origins of Nazi and other Weimar nationalist ideas, see Geoffrey Stoakes, *Hitler and the Quest for World Domination* (Leamington Spa, NH: Berg, 1986), and Woodruff Smith, *The Ideological Origins of Nazi Imperialism* (New York: Oxford University Press, 1986).

## Table 3.5 Weimar Republic: Percentage of the Vote Obtained by the Parties

| Year | Communist Party | Socialist Party | German Democratic Party | Center & Bavarian parties | German People's Party | Small Conservative & Regional parties | German National People's Party | Nazi Party | Not Voting |
|---|---|---|---|---|---|---|---|---|---|
| *1919* | 7.7 | 37.8 | 18.6 | 20.0 | 4.4 | 1.6 | 10.3 | | 17.3 |
| *1920* | 20.0 | 21.7 | 8.3 | 18.0 | 14.0 | 3.1 | 14.9 | | 21.6 |
| *1924* | 13.3 | 20.4 | 5.8 | 16.7 | 9.2 | 8.2 | 19.4 | 6.6 | 23.7 |
| *1924* * | 9.2 | 26.0 | 6.3 | 17.5 | 9.9 | 7.3 | 20.4 | 3.0 | 22.3 |
| *1928* | 10.7 | 29.8 | 5.0 | 15.2 | 8.6 | 13.0 | 14.3 | 2.6 | 25.5 |
| *1930* | 13.1 | 24.6 | 3.7 | 14.8 | 4.6 | 13.8 | 7.1 | 18.3 | 18.6 |
| *1932* | 14.3 | 21.6 | 1.1 | 15.7 | 1.1 | 3.0 | 6.0 | 37.1 | 16.5 |
| *1932* * | 17.0 | 20.3 | .9 | 15.1 | 2.0 | 3.5 | 8.5 | 33.0 | 20.0 |
| *1933* | 12.2 | 18.4 | .8 | 14.0 | 1.0 | 1.5 | 7.9 | 44.2 | 12.1 |

Shaded cells show which parties formed the governing coalition after an election.

* In 1924 and 1932, there were two elections.

Source: David Abraham, *The Collapse of the Weimar Republic: Political Economy and Crisis* (New York: Holmes & Meier, 1986), p. 23.

two myths that discredited the Weimar Republic, its dominant working-class parties, the Versailles Treaty, and the policy of cooperation with the democratic great powers. The first was the myth that Germany had had the World War forced upon it by a hostile encirclement of aggressive foes; the second was the myth that Germany had lost the war because of a socialist "stab in the back" on the home front. This way of thinking was powerfully reinforced in the Weimar period by a new wave of nationalist propaganda, much of it sponsored by the same big-business interests that had promoted it before World War I. As before the war, industrialists, big landowners, and conservative bureaucrats hoped that nationalism would provide a formula to maintain their leadership of the middle class and the rural population against the working class, and thus defend these elites' social and economic privileges.

Much of this pre-1914 pattern carried over into the Weimar period of 1918 to 1933, despite the democratization that followed Germany's defeat in World War I. Under the Weimar constitution, elections now determined who governed the country, and the socialists were normally one of the governing parties in the early Weimar era. In the brief period between the German defeat and the Versailles Treaty, even the conservative German National People's Party seemed to be heading in a more democratic direction. However, the international settlement and the recriminations over the alleged socialist "stab in the back" of the German war effort pushed bourgeois elites back toward pre-war Wilhelmine-style tactics.[29] As in the Wilhelmine system, people looked more and more to narrow pressure groups rather than broad-based parties to advance their interests.[30] Nationalism was the ideology used by these lobbying groups to justify their parochial concerns in terms of the broader public interest.

These conditions fostered a hot-house climate of middle-class nationalist opinion that the Nazis could exploit with their distinctive grassroots organizational tactics. Thus, despite its democratic political institutions, Weimar political discourse was shaped by partial media monopolies in

[29] Fritzsche, "Breakdown or Breakthrough," in Jones and Retallack, *Between Reform*, 299–328; Mommsen, "Government without Parties," in Jones and Retallack, *Between Reform*, 349–50.

[30] Bessel, "The Formation and Dissolution of a German National Electorate," in Jones and Retallack, *Elections*, 409–12.

the hands of elites threatened by democracy, and by the division of the public into segments that did not communicate with one another. Even a high-quality, liberal press that reached the majority of big-city readers was insufficient to create a functioning public sphere in the face of these deformations of the marketplace of ideas.

### Selling the nationalists' myth portfolio

In the wake of Germany's defeat in World War I, the country's nationalist elites struggled with the socialists to shape the historical memory of the German people. Shortly after the war, the new socialist government authorized the Marxist intellectual Karl Kautsky to publish a collection of diplomatic documents revealing that German officials bore much of the responsibility for embarking upon a war of aggression. But with the collapse of the socialist government, Kautsky's backing disappeared, and conservative circles in the foreign ministry moved to assert control over the publication of documents bearing on war guilt.

A huge historiographical bureaucracy was established, under the control of "patriotic" editors who systematically selected and outright falsified documents to whitewash the Wilhelmine leadership. The German official documents published by this bureaucracy were far more extensive than those published by the other countries that had fought in World War I. Consequently, the German-edited version of history became the standard source for scholarly work even in the United States, as well as the basis for propagandistic popular articles and school texts in Germany. Foreign Minister (and later Chancellor) Gustav Stresemann himself took an interest in the project, feeling that historiographical revelations of German war guilt "would render my entire Locarno policy [for reestablishing Germany's international standing] impossible."[31] Only a few of Germany's respected historians, like Hans Delbrück and Friedrich Meinecke, occasionally spoke out for the truth, but even they knowingly covered up some evidence of German aggression. Meinecke's tepid commitment to Weimar democracy was characteristic of Germany's well-established historians: "Democracy basically does not suit us," he said. "We became democrats because . . .

---

[31] Holger Herwig, "Clio Deceived: Patriotic Self-Censorship in Germany after the Great War," *International Security* 12:2 (Fall 1987), 35; see also 27.

there was no other way to preserve the popular unity and . . . aristocratic values."[32] Meanwhile, the left-wing historian Eckert Kehr, who really dug out the facts on the imperialist iron-and-rye coalition, was repeatedly denied academic positions and died in poverty at age thirty-one.[33]

The ending of the war was equally mythologized. In testimony before the entire Reichstag, Field Marshall von Hindenburg told the commission investigating the causes of the defeat that the heroic German officer corps had been "stabbed in the back" by pacifists and socialists. He charged that they had accepted Russian money, consciously sought to demoralize the troops, and fomented revolution on the home front. Hindenburg was never cross-examined, and the findings of the commission, which failed to support this view, were stamped secret.[34] Historians now agree that the conservatives' image of the "undefeated army" undermined on the home front is baseless: in the wake of mounting battlefield setbacks, a strike by German soldiers ended the war.[35]

German conservative publishers had a systematic plan for embellishing and disseminating these and other nationalist myths glorifying war. They commissioned works on the concept of "geopolitics," a strategic doctrine that provided a scientific-sounding rationale for conquest. Likewise, they subsidized theorists of racial purity and economic self-sufficiency. Publishers sympathetic to these new, radical, right-wing ideologies mapped out an activist agenda, suggesting topics to authors, offering prizes for essays on specific subjects, founding clubs and schools, and funding research by racist associations. By finding the most effective publicists to popularize these ideas, the publishing houses of the new right created a mass audience for the ideas of a fringe movement. Their war novels sold up to 300,000 copies, and even their anti-Jewish and anti-Versailles tracts could sell 100,000. The young Germans who flocked into Nazi SA units got their image of war from these novels, not from any actual experience in

[32] Fritz K. Ringer, *The Decline of the German Mandarins: The German Academic Community, 1890–1933* (Cambridge: Harvard University Press, 1969), 200–4, quotation at 203; see also Herwig, "Clio Deceived," 12–13.

[33] Pauline and Eugene Anderson, "Translators' Introduction," in Eckart Kehr, *Battleship Building and Party Politics in Germany 1894–1901* (Chicago: University of Chicago Press, 1973; orig. ed. 1930), xi–xxvii.

[34] Herwig, "Clio Deceived," 30–31.

[35] Richard Bessel, *Germany after the First World War* (Oxford: Clarendon, 1993), 263–64.

the trenches.[36] Eugen Diederichs and other publishers of such literature won honorary degrees and in turn lent legitimacy to the radical right.[37]

Once assembled, the nationalist ideology was disseminated on a mass basis through the newspapers and wire services owned or influenced by Alfred Hugenberg, the wartime chairman of the board of directors of Krupp Steel and during Weimar the chairman of the German National People's Party. Hugenberg's enterprises gave him influence over half of Germany's press, including almost all of its right-wing nationalist papers. Even so, Hugenberg could not stop the slide of middle-class nationalist voters from his party to the Nazis, so he allied with Hitler in 1931 and joined his government in 1933. "Without asserting that Hugenberg's press dominion destroyed the Weimar Republic," says historian Modris Eksteins, "one can say that it presented a major obstacle to the implantation of democratic, republican ideas amongst the German public."[38]

### Segmentation of Weimar media markets

The segmentation of the Weimar reading public stemmed in part from monopolies of supply, such as Hugenberg's domination via his wire service of the flow of news to the small-town press. However, even where competing views were available, the public divided itself into segments based on political sympathies that reflected the legacy of religious and class divisions sharpened by elite political strategies in the pre-1914 period. Once nationalism is firmly embedded in grassroots consciousness and social practices, even democratic institutions and a professionalized urban press, such as Weimar enjoyed, may be insufficient as antidotes to the continued sowing of nationalist myths.

By 1932, right-wing papers captured 38 percent of Germany's 30 million subscribers, compared with 28 percent for the left-wing and democratic press, 24 percent for nonpartisan papers, and 10 percent for the Catholic press.[39] Communist and Social Democratic papers "consisted

[36] Ibid., 259–60.

[37] Gary D. Stark, *Entrepreneurs of Ideology: Neoconservative Publishers in Germany, 1890–1933* (Chapel Hill: University of North Carolina Press, 1981), 18, 245.

[38] Eksteins, *Limits*, 78–81, quotation at 81; also Stegmann, "Between Economic Interests and Radical Nationalism," in Jones and Retallack, *Between Reform*, 183.

[39] Georges Castellan, *L'Allemagne de Weimar, 1918–1933* (Paris: Armand Colin, 1969), 255–66.

almost solely of tedious party news and polemical attacks on opponents,"
and were only read by the party faithful. Resolutely focused on its core
working-class constituency, the Social Democratic party bureaucracy
squelched any attempts to reach out to a broader audience through gen-
eral-interest reporting. Consequently, socialist workers typically read liberal or nonpartisan newspapers to learn the news.[40] Nazi newspapers had a
very small circulation. Even as Nazi vote totals were increasing ninefold in
1930, the readership of Nazi newspapers stayed around 100,000. Thus,
many Nazi voters continued to read liberal or mainstream nationalist
papers. The editor of a liberal paper in Baden, for example, estimated that
80 percent of his readers were voting Nazi, which gave him an economic
incentive to mute his criticisms.[41]

In the major urban areas, mass-circulation liberal dailies, often Jewish-
owned, were read by people across a wide spectrum of social classes and
political views. These broadly appealing papers were easy to read, offered
sports information and entertainment listings, and provided objective news
reporting at a low price.[42] Though they lacked Hugenberg's massive capital,
they were powerful enough to be plausibly characterized by their nationalist
competitors as effective manipulators of the public.[43] Though wary of
becoming too ideological for their heterogeneous readership and conservative advertisers, the liberal press found that taking a distinctly progressive
political line tended to enliven the paper and boost sales. Still, the liberal
papers adopted American-style journalistic credo and mottoes: "Divorce
the news from the views," and "Get it first but get it right."[44] In principle,
here was the German public sphere at its best. But in fact, a unified public
sphere in which Germany's segmented publics came together to discuss one
another's views did not exist. Though urban workers and Nazis both read
the liberal press for news of local events and activities, neither group
engaged the liberals or each other in real dialogue. Eksteins notes that "the
intense factionalism in German politics was carried over into the press, and
a large proportion of newspapers addressed themselves exclusively to specific, narrow groups in society." Germany had twice as many newspapers as

[40] Eksteins, *Limits*, 84.
[41] Ibid., 71, 248–49.
[42] Ibid., 14.
[43] Stark, *Entrepreneurs*, 193.
[44] Eksteins, *Limits*, 21, also 20, 75, 104, 160–75.

Britain at this time, reflecting a tailoring of individual media outlets to "deep-seated regional and local loyalties, cultural and religious diversity," and "the fragmentation of politics." As a result, the press was "not regarded as an independent element in the political process; it did not act as a check on government and administration and on the conscience of the political parties." Rather, these papers became "instruments of specific interests, as means of sectionalist propaganda, and as tools for biased pedagogy." Even the nonpartisan mass press was a weak tool for public discussion and evaluation; it gave de facto support to the status quo.[45]

On the demand side, the division of the marketplace of ideas into non-communicating segments was deeply embedded in Weimar social structure. Countless choral societies, drinking clubs, and veterans associations brought together middle-class townspeople of varied rank and wealth, but virtually none of the voluntary organizations brought workers and middle classes together. Patterns of residence and culture reinforced these divisions.[46] Thus, opinion and discourse in the different market segments proceeded on independent tracks. In Weimar's balkanized politics, the Nazis could increase their vote tenfold by unifying the nationalist camp and thus win the chancellorship despite persuading very few workers or liberals of the cogency of their views. Similarly, Erich Maria Remarque's classic antiwar novel, *All Quiet on the Western Front*, could become a bestseller in its market niche at the same time as Diederichs's war-glorifying pulp fiction was setting sales records in its segment of the market.[47] As Eksteins remarks, the liberal publishers "still assumed that even in an industrialized pluralistic society the only method of arriving at truth was by a free and noble competition of opinion in the open market. [But] the open market did not exist."[48]

The key to the Nazis' success was not brilliant persuasion in the realm of open debate.[49] Rather, Nazi success hinged on the penetration of a decisive market niche by word-of-mouth and the cultivation of a style

[45] Ibid., 14, 16, 28.

[46] Peter Fritzsche, *Rehearsals for Fascism: Populism and Political Mobilization in Weimar Germany* (New York: Oxford, 1990), 12, 75, 152, 166–68.

[47] Stark, *Entrepreneurs*, 151.

[48] Eksteins, *Limits*, 307.

[49] Richard Bessel, "The Rise of the NSDAP and the Myth of Nazi Propaganda," *Wiener Library Bulletin* 33 (1980), new series nos. 51, 52.

that appealed to targeted middle-class and small-town groups. The content of Nazi propaganda was little different from that of other nationalist groups. All such groups presented what Ian Kershaw characterizes as "an amalgam of phobias, resentments, and prejudice, coupled with vague expectations of a better future."[50] Dogma may have had an impact on the Nazi activists themselves, but not much on their audience.

Foreign policy doctrines played at most a background role in the Nazis' success. Their appeals to middle-class grievances focused more on the favoritism of the bourgeois parties for heavy industry than on the Versailles Treaty, the doctrine of territorial conquest of "living space," or the Nazi racial doctrine.[51] In the period of their greatest electoral successes, the Nazis soft-pedaled their aggressive foreign policy message and canceled the publication of Hitler's belligerent second book.[52] To the middle-class voter in late Weimar, nationalism connoted a popular, antisocialist domestic agenda more than it did a militaristic foreign policy. From the perspective of many Nazi voters, World War II was an unintended by-product of installing Hitler in power.

The Nazis were particularly good at linking their broader message to the narrow economic interests of middle-class and rural constituencies clamoring for subsidies, tax breaks, and governmental protection against inflation and other vagaries of the market. Like other right-wing nationalist groups, Nazis depended heavily on leaflets to disseminate propaganda. They targeted a third of these on specific occupational groups.[53] As David Blackbourn notes, "Demagogy worked where it went with the grain of particular experiences and interests."[54] The big bourgeois parties also adopted this strategy in an attempt to counter the plethora of small, special-issue parties, which attacked the traditional parties and the Weimar system as a whole for selling out the middle-class interest to big business and big labor.[55] Even rural farmwives organized as a nationalist pressure

[50] Ian Kershaw, "Ideology, Propaganda, and the Rise of the Nazi Party," in Stachura, ed., *The Nazi Machtergreifung*, 169

[51] Fritzsche, *Rehearsals*, 110–11; Kershaw, "Ideology," in Stachura, 167.

[52] Snyder, *Myths of Empire*, 106–7.

[53] Thomas Childers, "The Social Language of Politics in Germany: The Sociology of Political Discourse in the Weimar Republic," *American Historical Review* 95:2 (April 1990), 331–58, at 342.

[54] David Blackbourn, *Populists and Patricians*, 218–19.

[55] Childers, "Social Language," 352.

group, because they realized that this was the only way to be heard amid the self-seeking clamor of late Weimar politics.[56]

What distinguished the Nazis in appealing to shopkeepers, clerks, and small farmers was the effectiveness of their face-to-face propaganda in local political clubs.[57] In such settings, big businessmen and lawyers who dominated the leadership of the established bourgeois nationalist parties failed to attract young voters, who preferred the Nazis' style of forceful talk and decisive action.[58] The old local elites, such as the East German estate owners, continued to use right-wing populist appeals to rally support against labor and government policy, but increasingly the Nazis gained the benefit of this mobilization.[59] As the economic crisis discredited established institutions, the Nazis were able to convince middle-class and rural voters that the Nazis could advance their narrow, individual interests in a way that would be compatible with the greater national good.[60]

### Lessons of the Weimar media contests

The Weimar experience shows that nationalist mythmaking can flourish even in an electoral democracy with a professionalized press in big-city enclaves. Weimar elites, threatened by the rise of a democratic working class, promoted nationalist ideas as a means of attracting mass allies to a program that would be popular but not democratic. Lacking the authoritarian powers that had defended elite interests in the Wilhelmine era, Weimar elites depended even more heavily on ideological competition to defend their political position. Led by big-business interests, these nationalist elites used control over wire services and other sources of informa-

[56] Renate Bridenthal, "Organized Rural Women and the Conservative Mobilization of the German Countryside in the Weimar Republic," in Jones and Retallack, *Between Reform*, 375–405.

[57] Roger Chickering, "Political Mobilization and Associational Life: Some Thoughts on the National Socialist German Workers' Club," in Jones and Retallack, *Elections*, 315; Kershaw, "Ideology," in Stachura, 172; Pierre Birnbaum, *States and Collective Action* (Cambridge: Cambridge University Press, 1988), 39–41.

[58] Fritzsche, *Rehearsals*, 194–97; Kershaw, "Ideology," in Stachura, 170.

[59] Shelley Baranowski, "Convergence on the Right: Agrarian Elite Radicalism and Nazi Populism in Pomerania, 1928–33," in Jones and Retallack, *Between Reform*, 429–32; Fritzsche, *Rehearsals*, 114.

[60] Kershaw, "Ideology," in Stachura, 176–78.

tion to establish a partial media monopoly in small towns and rural areas. The Weimar nationalist elites were also able to exploit the legacy of Wilhelmine nationalist propaganda, which had helped to segment the German public and prime the middle classes for the nationalist messages. In the end, however, the Weimar elites found that the middle-class nationalism they had conjured up was impossible to control. The more forceful, activist line of the Nazis drew away their support, and Hitler became the ultimate beneficiary of their efforts.

The Weimar story is a cautionary tale showing how difficult it is to extirpate nationalism once it has become entrenched by elite mythmaking during the early phase of democratization. When nationalist ideas become ingrained in the mass consciousness and in social practices, free elections and party competition are more likely to fuel nationalist myth-making than check it. Likewise, an island of liberal, professionalized journalism is insufficient to create an effective marketplace of ideas if other segments of the community remain deaf to or isolated from its high-quality discourse. In conditions like those prevailing in the Weimar Republic, the vibrant civil society of a newly democratizing country is a factor that promotes, rather than mitigates, nationalist conflict.

# 4

## Varieties of Nationalism

*Civic Britain, Revolutionary France, and Ethnic Serbia*

T he distinctive trajectory a state follows toward democratization is crucial to forging the political identity of the nation. How the mass of
the population is included as active participants in politics stamps the
national character. Four distinct patterns, each bearing dramatically different implications for nationalist conflict, are illustrated by the classic
historical case of each type: counterrevolutionary Germany, civic Britain,
revolutionary France, and ethnic Serbia. Germany has been discussed in
the preceding chapter, and the three others will be examined in this one.
Among these cases, British civic nationalism produced the most prudent,
cost-conscious pattern of relations with other nations, though even
Britain was far from pacifist. The three other forms of nationalism were
more exclusionary at home and more reckless in their policies abroad.

Although ethnic nationalism has dominated the headlines in our own
times, all four types remain relevant to understanding future trends of
nationalist politics in democratizing countries. The revolutionary pattern
may illuminate contemporary developments in Iran, while some com-

mentators fear that the counterrevolutionary pattern may prefigure the future of China. Numerous post-Communist states continue to face a crossroads in choosing between civic and ethnic national identities. A close look at the four historical prototypes of these patterns sheds light on the distinctive causes as well as the consequences of these varieties of nationalism.

The four patterns are shaped by the interaction of two key causal variables: the adaptability of the interests of the groups playing the lead role in forming the nation, and the strength of participatory institutions at the moment when the masses enter politics (see Table 1.1 in Chapter 1 and Table 2.1 in Chapter 2). Wilhelmine and Weimar Germany demonstrate how the rivalry between declining old elites and rising challengers can promote counterrevolutionary nationalism when elites have unadaptable interests and when administrative institutions are stronger than democratic ones. Eighteenth- and nineteenth-century Britain exemplifies how civic nationalism emerges when elite interests are adaptable in the face of democratization and when liberal institutions develop before the era of universal suffrage. Revolutionary France shows how highly adaptable elites may seize upon revolutionary nationalism as a tool for political competition when state institutions suddenly collapse. Nineteenth-century Serbia illustrates how ethnic nationalism develops when elites tie themselves to an inflexible, exclusionary cultural identity in order to maintain popular legitimacy when political institutions are weak.

Despite their differences, the cases also illustrate a basic common theme. In all the cases, the development of nationalism coincided with an early phase of democratization. In every case, including to some extent the case of civic Britain, the immature nature of democratic political institutions gave elites the motive and the opportunity to promote nationalism as a way of defending their interests and establishing a popular basis for their rule. Though the resulting nationalisms varied substantially in the degree and kind of nationalist conflicts that they provoked, democratization in each case ushered in a phase of nationalist rivalry, which had lasting consequences for the development of the nation's identity. Proceeding chronologically, I begin with eighteenth-century Britain, history's earliest nationalism; then turn to revolutionary France, history's second nationalism; and finally conclude with nineteenth-century Serbia, a paradigmatic case of the development of nationalism at the periphery of a declining empire.

## British Civic Nationalism

British nationalism, which emerged during the eighteenth and nineteenth centuries, took the form of civic loyalty to the country's traditions of individual liberty and free speech, and to the state's representative institutions. While rooted in these liberal principles and practices, British identity is a full-blooded nationalism, not just an abstract political philosophy. The British public made willing sacrifices for the nation in the course of frequent wars, reveled in the presumed superiority of its distinctive national traits, glorified its heroes, and took for granted that legitimate rule must serve the popular national interest. Thus, Britain's increasing democratization went hand in hand with a rising imperial nationalism. Yet British civic nationalism avoided the degree of delusional mythmaking that embroiled the other varieties of nationalism in needlessly self-defeating wars against overwhelmingly powerful foes.

Thus, the story of British civic nationalism conveys a dual message. On the one hand, it illustrates the general rule that democratization and increases in freedom of the press often stimulate belligerent nationalism. Even in a relatively liberal setting, disenfranchised classes use nationalist appeals to gain access to the political process, and established elites co-opt nationalist ideology and turn it to their own ends. A heightened risk of war may be the unintended by-product of this posturing.

On the other hand, civic nationalism, whatever its flaws, is more prudent than the other varieties. The British case shows that civic nationalist principles create ideological constraints on the use of force against other liberal peoples, and that civic nationalisms are more sensitive to the costs of aggressive policies. The British example also supports the hypothesis that these benefits of civic nationalism are most likely to emerge under two conditions: first, when the elites who take the lead in forming the nation have flexible interests that are not greatly threatened by democratization, and second, when free speech and representative institutions are well established before the era of mass democracy.

### *War and nationalism in Great Britain*

Britain, like all of the great powers, repeatedly fought wars and used its military might to expand its sphere of economic and political influence during the eighteenth and nineteenth centuries (see map on facing page). Most notably, Britain seized French Canada in the Seven Years' War of 1756 to 1763, failed in its military effort to prevent the independence of its American colonies between 1776 and 1783, played a leading role in several of the coalitions that contained revolutionary France and finally defeated Napoleon in 1815, and joined with France in defeating Russia in the Crimean War of 1853–56. In the breathing spells between these major conflicts, Britain conquered India, coerced China, and repeatedly used its military power to shape political and economic outcomes almost everywhere around the globe. Thus, no one could claim that civic nationalism made Britain a pacific country.

Nonetheless, in contrast to more reckless great powers such as Germany, France, and Japan, Britain stands out as prudent and cost-conscious in its strategic choices. Except for the American War of Independence, Britain was always on the winning side in its major wars. It avoided fights that would have pitted it against a superior great-power coalition. It avoided heavy expenditures on a large peacetime army. Despite its far-flung colonial possessions, Britain generally avoided strategic overstretch by getting its colonies to pay for their own defense. And when miscalculations did lead it into a strategic dead end, as in the war with the American colonies, Britain's practice was to cut its losses and retrench.[1]

Britain's wars were expensive, but most of them were prudent investments. Though British commentators trembled at the size of the debt amassed during the Seven Years' War, for example, successful conquests of French Canada and in the tropics caused trade and customs receipts to expand rapidly during and after the war. A reliable system of finance meant that Britain could almost always borrow at low interest during wartime. The one time that credit did dry up (in the war against the American colonies), Britain prudently took that as the signal to make peace. Having learned the importance of avoiding financial overstretch in its imperial policy, the British government was still reducing its military expenditures as late as 1792, despite the dangers stirring in revolutionary

[1] Jack Snyder, *Myths of Empire* (Ithaca: Cornell University Press, 1991), Chapter 5; Paul Kennedy, *Strategy and Diplomacy* (London: Allen & Unwin, 1983); Miles Kahler, *Decolonization in Britain and France* (Princeton: Princeton University Press, 1984); for a more critical view, see Charles Kupchan, *The Vulnerability of Empire* (Ithaca: Cornell University Press, 1994).

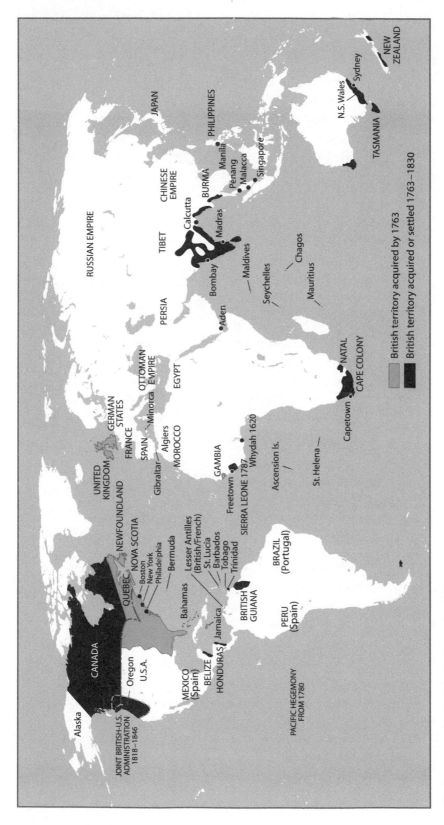

*The Expansion of the British Empire, 1763–1830*

Alaska

JOINT BRITISH-U.S.
ADMINISTRATION
1818–1846

CANADA

Oregon

U.S.A.

MEXICO
(Spain)

BELIZE

HONDURAS

Jamaica

Bahamas

QUEBEC

NOVA SCOTIA

Boston

New York

Philadelphia

Bermuda

NEWFOUNDLAND

Lesser Antilles
(British/French)

St. Lucia

Barbados

Tobago

Trinidad

BRITISH
GUIANA

PERU
(Spain)

BRAZIL
(Portugal)

PACIFIC HEGEMONY
FROM 1780

UNITED
KINGDOM

FRANCE

GERMAN
STATES

SPAIN

Minorca

Gibraltar

Algiers

MOROCCO

GAMBIA

Freetown

SIERRA LEONE 1787

Whydah 1620

Ascension Is.

St. Helena

OTTOMAN
EMPIRE

EGYPT

PERSIA

Aden

RUSSIAN EMPIRE

TIBET

CHINESE
EMPIRE

JAPAN

Bombay

Calcutta

Madras

Maldives

Seychelles

Mauritius

Chagos

Capetown

CAPE COLONY

NATAL

BURMA

PHILIPPINES

Manila

Penang

Malacca

Singapore

N.S. Wales

Sydney

TASMANIA

NEW
ZEALAND

British territory acquired by 1763

British territory acquired or settled 1763–1830

France.[2] In short, unlike those great powers whose nationalism was revolutionary or counterrevolutionary, Britain avoided irremediable overextension when its power was on the rise, just as it was relatively adept at managing its long, gradual decline in the twentieth century.

Popular national sentiment was a major force promoting the policy of British imperial expansion in the mid-eighteenth and mid-nineteenth centuries. Middle-class opinion, reflected in the increasingly free press of the eighteenth century, was a strong supporter of the use of military power to promote Britain's commercial interests abroad. William Pitt, the prime minister during the Seven Years' War, was a favorite of the urban trading classes. A century later, as the representation in Parliament of the urban middle classes began to increase, a similar middle-class constituency rallied around Prime Minister Palmerston's policy of confronting Russia in the Crimean War. Belligerent public opinion forced the British government to attack, despite Russian concessions that made war unnecessary in the eyes of most cabinet members.

However, public opinion also served in some ways to moderate the extent and targets of expansion. As Britain democratized, it increasingly showed a reluctance to take up arms against other liberal states. Even as early as the American War of Independence, those middle-class Britons who were most strongly committed to civic principles of government were the quickest to point out that the suppression of liberty in the colonies might pose dangers to British liberty at home. In the late nineteenth and early twentieth centuries, Britain astutely accommodated the rise of liberal America to replace it as the world's preeminent power. British taxpayers, though proud of their empire, used their electoral clout to force imperial statesmen to remain cost-conscious. In 1880, in the first modern political campaign based on a speaking tour before mass audiences, William Gladstone and his Liberal Party prevailed by criticizing tax increases needed to finance the Conservative Party's spendthrift colonial wars. Though the many victims of British imperialism will rightly reject a blanket characterization of British nationalism as benign, its imperial policies, viewed from the standpoint of Britain's national interests, were mostly prudent and moderate.

Moderation and realism also characterized the strategic thinking of

[2] Paul Kennedy, *Rise and Fall of the Great Powers* (New York: Random House, 1987), 81, 113, 121.

Britain's elites. Despite the chronic rivalry with France in the formative years of British nationalism, this was never reified in the form of an "ancient" ethnic hatred. As Palmerston put it, Britain has "eternal interests," but no "perpetual enemies" or "eternal allies."[3] Foreign Office doctrine held that Britain should throw its weight against any powerful state that threatened to overturn the European balance of power, regardless of historic or cultural considerations.[4]

In addition to being geopolitically prudent, British civic nationalism was also comparatively inclusive, especially in the period before the limits of the British identity were locked in by the era of democratization.[5] The British civic identity was of course built to a considerable extent upon the institutions and language of the English ethnic identity. After the 1707 Act of Union, however, Scots and Welsh integrated into those institutions and played a substantial role in the forging of the British empire and self-conception. Since the merger of these ethnic identities into a larger civic identity preceded the era of mass political participation, ethnicity was for the most part subsumed under the civic framework. Today, Scottish nationalists have been seeking some autonomy from the central government in London, including the right to levy taxes and independent representation in the institutions of the European Union. Yet for most Scots, these ethnonational goals are pursued within the context of a larger British civic identity that is taken for granted.

In contrast, the Irish identity, which was not integrated into the British civic identity before democratization, became politicized as a distinct ethnic nationalism. Ireland, unlike Scotland, was extensively colonized by a dominant class of English Protestant landlords, who were able to delay until 1800 the representation of Ireland in the British Parliament. At that point, some propertied indigenous Irish were allowed vote, but as Catholics, they were prohibited from running for parliamentary office until the Catholic Emancipation Act of 1829. Thus, during this period of early democratization in Ireland, the first Irish mass political movement

[3] Jasper Ridley, *Lord Palmerston* (London: Constable, 1970), 334.

[4] The classic statement of this policy is the 1907 Foreign Office memorandum by Eyre Crowe, reprinted in G. P. Gooch and Harold Temperley, *British Documents on the Origins of the War*, 1898–1914, vol. 3 (London: 1928).

[5] Linda Colley, *Britons: Forging the Nation 1707–1837* (New Haven: Yale University Press, 1992).

took shape under conditions of substantial ethnic political exclusion. The failure of Britain's later attempts to integrate Ireland into British democracy, culminating in violent conflict with Irish nationalists during and immediately after World War I, reflects the exclusionary ethnic origins of Irish popular nationalism, which were forged in part during early democratization. In this sense, Britain's belated and unfinished attempt to include Ireland in the British civic identity is the exception that proves the rule that civic nationalism mitigates ethnic conflict in multiethnic societies.[6]

In sum, British civic nationalism was an engine of imperial expansionism, tempered by a prudent cost-consciousness and moderated by a growing commonality of identity with other liberal states. It was also marked by an inclusionary stance toward groups like the Scots and Welsh, who were reasonably well assimilated to the civic identity before the era of democratization. What explains this distinctively civic outcome?

### Explanations for Britain's prudent, civic nationalism

#### 1. Strategic advantages
One possible explanation for Britain's distinctive pattern of assertive but prudently calculating behavior toward other nations might point to its strategic advantages as a commercially powerful island state. With a strong economy and a highly efficient system for financing its wars, Britain could afford the world's most powerful navy, which was able to deploy military forces at just the right time and place with maximum cost-effectiveness. Moreover, Britain's off-shore position allowed it to keep its standing army small, while its more exposed allies bore the brunt of the initial costs and risks of resisting aggressors. During the years between 1840 and 1870, Britain's position as the leader in the industrial revolution gave it a substantial military and economic edge over its rivals. These strategic advantages help explain why Britain was repeatedly tempted to use its military power to gain economic benefits around the globe, but

---

[6] Lawrence J. McCaffrey, *The Irish Question: Two Centuries of Conflict* (Lexington: University Press of Kentucky, 1995), Chapters 1, 2, and 7; Michael Hechter, *Internal Colonialism: The Celtic Fringe in British National Development, 1536–1966* (Berkeley: University of California Press, 1975), 72–73; K. Theodore Hoppen, *Elections, Politics, and Society in Ireland, 1832–1885* (Oxford: Clarendon, 1984).

also why Britain felt secure enough to avoid reckless provocations and to retrench, when necessary, from overcommitments. Britain had already staked out strong strategic and economic positions around the globe by the time its main European rivals caught up with its industrial power. Its lesser vulnerability meant that it rarely had to gamble everything on the defense of a indispensable position, but instead could cut costs and wait out adverse trends.

Even so, these strategic advantages do not fully explain Britain's distinctively prudent strategy. Britain retained its strategy of timely retrenchment from imperial overextension well past the point when its industrial and military superiority had been overtaken by its German rival. As Britain's vulnerability grew in the twentieth century, it did not become more reckless. On the contrary, it was assiduous in appeasing enough potential foes so that it would always remain in the stronger, more numerous alliance.[7] For example, as the strength of Germany's navy increased after the turn of the century, Britain patched up its colonial squabbles with other great powers, concluding strategic agreements with Japan in 1902, France in 1904, and Russia in 1907. In contrast, when Germany and Japan found themselves overextended, they became more aggressive, not more prudent. Whereas the ethnic, counterrevolutionary, and revolutionary nationalisms of other great powers spawned myths that reduced the realism of their strategic calculations, Britain's civic nationalism underpinned a prudent, flexibility in foreign affairs. Thus, Britain's prudence stemmed not simply from its strategic advantages, but from the fact that Britain made the most of its advantages whereas its rivals often squandered theirs. To explain this difference, it is necessary to examine more closely the pattern of flexible elite interests and the early development of liberal institutions that shaped a civic nationalism while Britain democratized.

## 2. Britain's phased democratization
Britain developed a relatively moderate, civic form of nationalism for two main reasons. First, its ruling elites were not highly threatened by the democratization of the country. Its dominant financial elite and commercialized aristocracy shared many economic interests with the urban middle class, including an interest in the use of military power to support

[7] Kennedy, *Strategy and Diplomacy*, Chapters 1 and 8.

trade and investment abroad. Second, civic institutions of representative government and free speech were already well established before the majority of the population was allowed to vote. In part this stemmed from the landed aristocracy's interest in asserting the rights of Parliament against the king. In part, it also reflected Britain's distinctive form of financing war through loans rather than mobilizing resources through large wartime tax increases and conscription. This kept popular political grievances low, so that demands for mass political participation developed only gradually, well after liberal institutions for managing that participation were firmly established. As a result, the motivation of elites to resort to more militant forms of nationalism was relatively low, and the political system's capacity to counteract nationalist mythmaking during the gradual transition to democracy was relatively high.

Nonetheless, moderate nationalism does not mean an absence of nationalism. Because financial and commercial elites shared with the middle class in port cities an interest in imperial expansionism, assertive nationalism was an attractive ideological platform that could unite elite and mass groups. As Britain's urban middle classes gradually took on a larger role in the nation's political life, old and new elites often used nationalist appeals to vie for their favor. In this sense, democratization was a two-edged sword in civic Britain, creating incentives to promote popular nationalism, yet also empowering middle-class (and later working-class) voters who would bear the costs if nationalism became reckless or took an illiberal turn.

The following sections show, first, how the distinctive British pattern of resource mobilization for war underpinned these developments; second, how flexible elite interests made common cause with middle-class interests in shaping British imperial nationalism; third, how an increasingly open press served as the catalyst for rising nationalist sentiment; and fourth, how civic ideals both energized and constrained British imperial nationalism.

### Popular Participation and Resource Mobilization for War

In the late seventeenth and early eighteenth century, Britain was becoming increasingly liberal in terms of civil rights, but decreasingly democratic in terms of the scope of its electoral suffrage. This bought time for the institutionalization of a British civic identity before the onset of the turbulent era of mass politics. A key reason for the gradual nature of British democratization was the state's ability to borrow funds for war from the London financial elite without laying additional direct taxes on the population.

The English Civil Wars of 1642–51 and the Glorious Revolution of 1688, pitting the Stuart monarchy against Parliament, were mainly struggles among elites. The enlistment of the popular classes in these conflicts was quite limited. The armies contending in the civil war were small, and no bureaucracies for raising and sustaining standing forces were created.[8] It is true that some scholars see precursors of popular British nationalism in these attempts by upwardly mobile commercial classes and an ambitious lower gentry to invoke the principle of popular sovereignty to claim equal status with more established elites.[9] Nevertheless, the outcome of the Glorious Revolution, which installed the German-speaking William of Orange as king in 1688, represented not the victory of the "nation" over the crown, but the ascendancy of the wealthiest stratum of the Whig faction of the landed aristocracy. After 1688, three-fourths of all agricultural land was owned by fewer than five thousand aristocrats and gentry, who constituted England's dominant social and political class.[10]

This era, called the "age of oligarchy," fostered the development of civil liberties, but it was not a period of democratization in other respects. Whig ideology tolerated relatively free speech, which was considered one of the aristocracy's ancient rights as free Englishmen vis-à-vis the crown. Parliament abolished press censorship in 1695.[11] Nonetheless, the electoral franchise was narrowed during the eighteenth century, not broad-

---

[8] Brian Downing, *The Military Revolution and Political Change* (Princeton: Princeton University Press, 1992), 168–79.

[9] Liah Greenfeld, *Nationalism: Five Roads to Modernity* (Cambridge: Harvard University Press, 1992), 72–74; Peter Furtado, "National Pride in Seventeenth-Century England," in Raphael Samuel, *Patriotism*, vol. I (London: Routledge, 1989), 44–56; Margot Finn, *After Chartism* (Cambridge: Cambridge University Press, 1993), 40; Christopher Hill, "A Bourgeois Revolution?" in J. G. A. Pocock, ed., *Three British Revolutions* (Princeton: Princeton University Press, 1980), 114.

[10] P. J. Cain and A. G. Hopkins, *British Imperialism*, vol. I, *Innovation and Expansion, 1688–1914* (New York: Longman, 1993), 58.

[11] Edmund S. Morgan, *Inventing the People: The Rise of Popular Sovereignty in England and America* (New York: W. W. Norton, 1988), 96–97, 102–6; Geoffrey Holmes and Daniel Szechi, *The Age of Oligarchy, 1722–1783* (London: Longman, 1993), 194–95.

ened. In 1715, 24 percent of adult males in England and Wales could vote; by 1831 only 14 percent could, as a result of tightened property restrictions. Even after the Reform Bill of 1832, only 18 percent could vote.[12] Thus, the Whig victory institutionalized free speech but delayed mass democracy.

Coinciding with the political ascendancy of the Whig oligarchy was a steep increase in the mobilization of resources for war. During the British internal struggles of the mid-seventeenth century, the powers of continental Europe were distracted by their own internecine Thirty Years' War. After 1688, however, the new British regime was constantly at war with the continental powers: from 1688 to 1697 in the Nine Years' War against France, and from 1701 to 1713 in the coalition war triggered by the dispute over the succession to the Spanish throne.[13] This constant warring required a sharp increase in military spending. Although governmental borrowing on private financial markets spread out these costs over time, tax rates did rise. Soon the British were taxed at a per capita rate twice that of the French. By the 1780s, Britain's per capita tax burden was 2.7 times that of France.[14]

Though the burden of war taxes is commonly held to be a cause of the French Revolution, the much higher British burden did not spur similar revolutionary demands for democratization. The Britons were richer, and thus better able to bear the tax burden. Moreover, Britain's superior financial methods raised resources more efficiently and less painfully. Britain financed its wars through borrowing in private capital markets at home and abroad, spending whatever was needed to win, and then repaying the loans gradually after the victory. When more military manpower was needed, soldiers could be hired abroad (e.g., the German Hessians who fought in the American Revolution) rather than conscripted at home.[15] Because the British crown was fiscally constrained by a Parliament in

[12] M. J. Daunton, *Progress and Poverty: An Economic and Social History of Britain 1700–1850* (Oxford: Oxford University Press, 1995), 482. Malproportioned districting further skewed electoral outcomes. In terms of votes cast, the Tories outpolled the Whigs in every election from 1722 to 1741, but the Whigs gained more seats in Parliament. Holmes and Szechi, *Age of Oligarchy*, 316.

[13] Downing, *Military Revolution*, 179–86.

[14] Daunton, *Progress*, 528; John Brewer, *The Sinews of Power: War, Money, and the English State, 1688–1783* (New York: Knopf, 1989), 89.

[15] Lawrence Stone, "Introduction," in Stone, ed., *An Imperial State at War: Britain from 1689 to 1815* (London: Routledge, 1994), 21–25.

which financial interests were strongly represented, creditors were confident that the government would pay back its loans.[16] Consequently, money was easy to raise at reasonable rates.

France was a hundred years behind Britain in the development of efficient, reliable capital markets, and thus could extract resources for war only through cumbersome direct taxation on agriculture.[17] British taxes, though steeper than those of the French, were less visible to the poor, because British taxes came in the form of customs duties, a tax on landowners, and an excise tax on large manufacturers.[18] British taxes were also more efficient: the cost of revenue collection in Britain was one-fourth that in France, where each link in the food chain of tax farmers and office purchasers took a bite out of the revenue.[19] In comparison to the French, British subjects felt less pain from war taxation, and they perceived more benefit from the wars they paid for.

Britons felt they were getting good value from this efficient system of war finance. The same financial mechanisms that funded the wars also financed the economic exploitation of those victories through investments in colonial settlement, export production, and overseas trade, which played an increasing role in the prosperity of the home economy. In 1750, North America, including the West Indies, absorbed 10 percent of Britain's woolen exports; by 1772–74, the figure had reached 30 percent.[20] Moreover, cost-conscious financiers of the empire insisted that areas of colonial expansion, such as India and North America, pay the price of their own defense. The resented Sugar and Stamp Acts were imposed on North American colonists after the victory over France in the Seven Years' War to defray the costs of patrolling the new conquests, suppressing the French settlers in Canada, and keeping the Indians and the

[16] Douglass North and Barry Weingast, "Constitutions and Commitment: The Evolution of Institutions Governing Public Choice in Seventeenth-Century England," *Journal of Economic History* 49:4 (1989), 803–32; Cain and Hopkins, *British Imperialism*, vol. I, 63–64.

[17] Cain and Hopkins, *British Imperialism*, vol. I, 64.

[18] Daunton, *Progress*, 528–29; Stone, "Introduction," *Imperial State at War*, 8.

[19] John Brewer, "The Eighteenth-Century British State," 64, and Thomas Ertman, "The *Sinews of Power* and European State-Building Theory," 33–51, both in Stone, *Imperial State at War*.

[20] Holmes and Szechi, *Age of Oligarchy*, 149–50; also 63–64. More generally, see Cain and Hopkins, *British Imperialism*, vol. I, 58.

settlers apart.[21] As it turned out, of course, this effort at close strategic accounting was a miscalculation. While Britain grew overextended in North America, European states resisted the expansion of British power, and the overtaxed American colonies seized the opportunity to fight and win their independence. Notwithstanding this setback, the British system for military and imperial finance—effective, prudent, cost-conscious—rebounded to prevail against the Napoleonic challenge and to build an even greater nineteenth-century empire on similar fiscal foundations.[22]

The efficient British system of war finance through private loans promoted the development of a moderate civic nationalism in two ways. First, it created a foundation for popular nationalism by winning wars at moderate cost and high benefit to all the commercial classes of society, whether aristocrats or commoners. Second, by spreading out the costs of military mobilization over time, it avoided provoking mass grievances that might have led to immediate demands for greater popular participation in politics. In conjunction with the Whig aristocracy's early support for free speech and a strong Parliament, this meant that democratic institutions were well developed before voting rights were extended to all social classes between 1832 and 1884. Given the firm foundation provided by well-established liberal institutions and flexible elite interests, the eventual expansion of suffrage produced a form of civic nationalism that, while it was occasionally belligerent, was more calculating and prudent than most other nationalisms.

### The Merging of Elite and Middle-Class Interests in British Nationalism
Both the aristocracy and the middle classes benefited from the imperial policy of the liberal state. The expansion of a commercial empire united

---

[21] Robert W. Tucker and David Hendrickson, *The Fall of the First British Empire* (Baltimore: Johns Hopkins University Press, 1982), 87–92, 191–94; Cain and Hopkins, *British Imperialism*, vol. I, 93–95.

[22] Brewer, *Sinews*, 177–78; Cain and Hopkins, *British Imperialism*, vol. I, 91; Paul Kennedy, *The Rise and Fall of British Naval Mastery* (London: Allen Lane, 1976), 116; H. M. Scott, *British Foreign Policy in the Age of the American Revolution* (Oxford: Oxford University Press, 1990); Daniel Baugh, "British Strategy in the First World War in the Context of Four Centuries: Blue Water versus Continental Commitment," in Daniel M. Masterson, ed., *Naval History: The Sixth Symposium of the US Naval Academy* (Wilmington, DE: 1987); Baugh, "Maritime Strength and Atlantic Commerce," in Stone, *Imperial State at War*, 205–6.

the old elites and the rising new ones. This had two effects on British foreign policy. On the one hand, it meant that increases in democratic participation promoted the development of an assertive nationalism. On the other hand, because widening participation did not pose an acute threat to the older elites, their motivation for reckless forms of nationalist myth-making, such as one finds in revolutionary or counterrevolutionary situations, was low. As a result, nationalism took a prudent and inclusive form.

Popular loyalty to the state, a key ingredient in nationalism, deepened during the eighteenth century because the state's policies provided benefits to a broad range of its citizens. By the beginning of the eighteenth century, one in five British families earned its livelihood from foreign trade. These trading interests benefited greatly from the state's role in waging military, colonial, and commercial competition with France. Britain's commerce with North America increased fourfold over the first half of the century. [23] To facilitate its international trade, the state also provided a host of domestic reforms, including a more stable currency, new roads and bridges to get goods to market, and standardized weights and measures.

The Scots as well as the English enjoyed the benefits of the inclusive British state. The 1707 Act of Union with Scotland eliminated internal customs duties. The Scots were further integrated into Britain by the disproportionately large role they played in staffing the military and administrative posts of the empire. One in four regimental officers in the middle of the eighteenth century was a Scot. [24]

The institutions of representative government played a central role in this expansion of inclusive state power in the early eighteenth century. Parliament began to meet routinely on an annual schedule in order to vote credits for the next year's military campaigns. Elections and parliamentary procedures became more regular, and party organization developed to coordinate both. [25] As Margot Finn puts it, "the institutions of the state ensured that nationalism in England [and Britain more generally] was not only an imagined community but a daily experience of common life." [26]

[23] Colley, *Britons*, 39, 56, 68.

[24] Ibid., 126.

[25] Downing, *Military Revolution*, 182–83; Geoffrey Holmes, *The Making of a Great Power: Late Stuart and Early Georgian Britain, 1660–1722* (London: Longman, 1993), Chapter 16, 257–65.

[26] Finn, *After Chartism*, 51.

The elite groups at the core of this system enjoyed the flexibility of mobile financial assets and diverse economic interests. The Whig aristocracy and London financial circles increasingly became merged into one class through their commercial dealings, common schooling at elite schools like Eton and Harrow, and intermarriage.[27] A career in the "City of London" financial world, unlike a career in industry, was seen as suitable for a gentleman. To obtain advantages in getting government contracts, these financiers bought representation in Parliament by purchasing sparsely populated rural "pocket boroughs," which would elect anyone picked by the local landholder.[28] The traditional aristocracy played a central role in both the financial and the military institutions that were the core of the new imperial system.[29] Linda Colley calls the Napoleonic Wars a "godsend" to the aristocracy, since their military role "gave them a purpose" in the social order.[30] More broadly, Britain's finance-based empire was a system of "gentlemanly capitalism" through which the old elite renewed itself while still trading on the traditional gentlemanly assets of social connections, prestige, and trustworthiness.[31] Thus, Britain's old elites were able to adapt to the challenges of modern state-building in the context of economic change and military competition.

Manufacturers and merchants, who were not at the core of the imperial elite, amassed smaller fortunes and were politically less powerful, in part because they were socially less compact and centralized.[32] Yet they too benefited from imperial expansion. The Seven Years' War brought huge profits to all sectors of the propertied middle classes, who gained government contracts, participated in the financing of war loans, and speculated

[27] Holmes and Szechi, *Age of Oligarchy*, 17; Cain and Hopkins, *British Imperialism*, vol. I, 25–32.

[28] Nicholas Rogers, *Whigs and Cities: Popular Politics in the Age of Walpole and Pitt* (Oxford: Clarendon, 1989), 18–19; Holmes and Szechi, *Age of Oligarchy*, 322.

[29] The beginning of this period, from 1690 to 1720, was marked by repeated disagreements between landed interests, who fretted about military costs, and moneyed interests, who sought an ambitious, commerce-promoting imperial policy. These disputes soon eased, however, as experience showed that both groups benefited from the financing of and profits from imperial conquests. Stone, "Introduction," *Imperial State at War*, 11.

[30] Colley, *Britons*, 178.

[31] Cain and Hopkins, *British Imperialism*, vol. I, 15, 26–27.

[32] Ibid., 40–41.

in buying shares in privateering ships. Insurance companies, rope makers, cheesemongers, warehousemen, linen drapers, and distillers directly profited from the provisioning of armies. And the victories provided expanded opportunities to sugar traders, slavers, and tobacco traders. Trade in Canadian fur, Senegal gum, and Chinese tea were all captured during the war.[33]

Later, when Britain's industrialization accelerated in the early nineteenth century, the commercialized landowning elites were well positioned to invest profitably in textile manufacturing and the international textile trade. This further reinforced the commonality of interests between the aristocracy and the industrial cities that were clamoring for democratic enfranchisement.[34]

Despite these common interests, conflicts over imperial issues did occasionally come between the more aristocratic financial circles and the rising commercial classes. High interest rates harmed traders and manufacturers, for example, who became financially overextended in their attempts to expand to meet wartime demand during the Seven Years' War.[35] These economic cleavages were reinforced by social barriers, as the financial elite distanced itself from the urban commercial classes, whose burgeoning clubs and civic associations were dominated by "middling trades and professions."[36] Overall, the regressive taxes and imperial expenditures of the eighteenth century primarily benefited bondholders in London, landowners, and overseas trading merchants. A thorough study of the distributional consequences of nineteenth-century British imperial expenditures finds that London financial interests were the big gainers, and domestically oriented businesses in the industrial Midlands cities of Birmingham, Manchester, and Leeds were the losers.[37]

In the long run, these rather mild divisions in the British elite helped to reinforce the British civic identity by highlighting the common interests of the London financial sector and the working class. By the late

[33] Rogers, *Whigs and Cities*, 111–13; more generally, Daunton, *Progress*, 543–44.

[34] Snyder, *Myths of Empire*, 190–91.

[35] Rogers, *Whigs and Cities*, 111; see also, 15–16.

[36] Ibid., 17.

[37] Cain and Hopkins, *British Imperialism*, vol. I, 74–75; Lance Davis and Robert Huttenback, *Mammon and the Pursuit of Empire: The Political Economy of British Imperialism, 1860–1912* (Cambridge: Cambridge University Press, 1986).

Victorian era, a strong political alliance developed between internationally oriented financiers of free trade in the City of London and working
classes favoring cheap food imports. Together, the workers and the
financiers effectively resisted the protectionist proposals of Midlands
manufacturers, who wanted to raise high tariff barriers against the impor-
tation of German industrial goods.[38] In this way, the democratization of
the Third Reform Bill of 1884, which added the bulk of the working class
to the electorate, protected rather than threatened the immediate interests
of Britain's core financial elite. Because the financiers had mobile assets
and flexible interests, they repeatedly found themselves able to adapt to
democratization based on moderate, civic nationalism. Unlike the pattern
in Wilhelmine Germany, the British ruling elite aligned itself in favor of
democratic inclusiveness and against narrow protectionism.

### Popular Nationalism and the Press

The urban middle classes were from the beginning a vocal constituency in
favor of an assertive imperial policy. Notwithstanding the shrinking proportion of the population eligible to vote in the eighteenth century, highly
literate urban classes actively debated foreign affairs in the press and lob-
bied the government on behalf of their views. In the 1740s, groups of
London tradesmen and artisans, bankrolled by the East India Company
and wealthy aristocrats, formed the Marine Society, the Troop Society, and
the Anti-Gallican Society, analogues respectively of the later German Navy
League, the German Army League, and the Pan-German Society.[39] While
prime minister during the Seven Years' War, William Pitt gained huge
popularity with the urban middle classes, both for his pursuit of colonial
expansion and for support of civil liberties, such as the 1758 bill extending
the right of *habeas corpus* to cases of naval impressment.[40]

Although the urban middle-class controlled few seats in Parliament,
their opinions were a powerful source of legitimacy in political competition. Governments ignored patriotic opinion at their own peril, in part

[38] Cain and Hopkins, *British Imperialism*, vol. I, 39.

[39] Kathleen Wilson, *The Sense of the People: Politics, Culture and Imperialism in
England, 1715–1785* (Cambridge: Cambridge University Press, 1995), 191; Colley,
*Britons*, 92.

[40] Rogers, *Whigs and Cities*, 114, also 4–5, 109–10; Kathleen Wilson, "Empire of
Virtue," in Stone, *Imperial State at War*, 150.

because of the increasing power of the press to shape the terms of elite debate. Admiral Edward Vernon, who against long odds captured a key Spanish colonial port in 1739, became a potent symbol of the failure of the allegedly penny-pinching Whig government to support its naval heroes. Ubiquitous Vernon cartoons, dinner plates, drinking songs, and editorials hastened the downfall of the Walpole ministry and set the stage for the age of Pitt's imperial populism.[41] The loss of the island of Minorca to Spain in 1756 exacted a similar cost in claims of governmental "effeminacy" and "treachery."[42] Thus, when Admiral Horatio Nelson used mass patriotic displays during the Napoleonic Wars to consolidate his authority in military and political circles, he was exploiting an already well-established tradition.[43]

The increasingly free press became the central vehicle for the expression of middle-class imperial sentiments and concerns. The lapsing of the press Licensing Act in 1695 produced a boom in the availability of foreign news, which filled more pages than domestic news.[44] A third of all magazines dealt exclusively with imperial and foreign affairs.[45] Continual warfare whetted popular appetites for foreign news.[46] At the same time, rising opportunities for profits abroad increased demand for information about foreign prices, stocks, bullion values, ships' goods lists, prizes taken by privateering ships, investments in American plantations, and foreign luxury goods.[47] The London press was consistently hawkish, taking a hard line on peace terms at the end of the Seven Years' War, for example. Reflecting London trading interests, the newspapers insisted that Britain should retain control over France's Caribbean colonies, whereas financial circles were inclined toward a less costly strategy of indirect control of commerce.[48]

The content of the press was shaped in part by the interests and sympathies of its middle-class readership, which ran strongly to political and imperial themes. However, content was also influenced by subsidies from

[41] Wilson, *Sense*, 142–55, 161.

[42] Ibid., 179–85, 338–39; Wilson, "Empire of Virtue," 146; Rogers, *Whigs and Cities*, 104, 108.

[43] Colley, *Britons*, 183.

[44] Holmes, *Making of a Great Power*, 245–46.

[45] Wilson, "Empire of Virtue," 134.

[46] Holmes and Szechi, *Age of Oligarchy*, 195; Colley, *Britons*, 100–1.

[47] Wilson, "Empire of Virtue," 134.

[48] Rogers, *Whigs and Cities*, 116.

a governmental Secret Service fund, which was not subject to detailed scrutiny by Parliament, and from wealthy private patrons.[49] Although there was no prepublication censorship, self-restraint in public discourse was encouraged by the 1702 sedition law and by the sense of decorum of the aspiring middle classes. For example, discussion guidelines in the 1770s at the Newcastle Philosophical Society for topics like the virtues of a republic versus limited monarchy prescribed "all the freedom of debate that is consistent with a decent attention to established opinion."[50]

Efforts to buy or suppress public opinion, which were never very successful, became even more difficult in the late eighteenth century when the number of nationwide-newspapers increased dramatically, as well as their availability due to postal improvements. The growth of advertising revenue and the independent sources of foreign news made control of the press difficult. As an 1830 London *Times* article explained, dismissing the danger that government subsidies might induce newspapers to suppress the reporting of opposition speeches, "one single newspaper reporting, and being known to report the speeches faithfully and impartially, would soon have more sale than all the other papers so shamefully bought up; and thus would be better paid than the ministers could afford to pay its tools."[51] This financial independence became further entrenched after the drastic reduction in the stamp tax in 1836.[52] As historian Arthur Aspinall states, "Newspapers now preferred, on the whole, to represent what they considered to be public opinion rather than the opinion of the government. It paid them to do so."[53]

Thus, the increased freedom of the press became a forceful vehicle advocating an assertive brand of civic nationalism. Nonetheless, the promulgation of nationalist ideas did not go unchallenged. Britain's free press constituted a marketplace of ideas that was competitive, integrated, and served by more and more professional journalists. As the next section

[49] David Harrison Stevens, *Party Politics and English Journalism, 1702–1742* (New York: Russell & Russell, 1916), 1, 79; Arthur Aspinall, *Politics and the Press, 1780–1850* (New York: Barnes and Noble, 1974), 66–67.

[50] Wilson, *Sense*, 68–69; Stevens, *Party Politics*, 12.

[51] The Times was earning 20,000 pounds annually at this time. Aspinall, *Politics and the Press*, 380, quoting *The Times*, July 3, 1830.

[52] Colley, *Britons*, 220; Robert J. Goldstein, *Political Repression in 19th Century Europe* (London: Croom Helm, 1983), 42.

[53] Aspinall, *Politics and the Press*, 380; also, 369–79.

shows, critics of imperial nationalism typically received a full hearing in the press when belligerent policies proved costly or threatened liberal principles.

### Civic Ideals in British Imperial Nationalism

British public opinion and its vehicle, the popular press, favored a strategy of militant empire-building not only for economic reasons, but also because an assertive civic nationalism helped to justify the role of the middle class in British politics. Yet this same civic nationalism led public opinion to balk at imperial adventures that seemed to undermine liberal principles. As a result, politicians of all stripes tried to exploit civic nationalist ideology as a tool of coalition politics during Britain's lengthy democratic transition.

Economic self-interest accounts for some of the mass enthusiasm for empire. It was not just financiers, traders, and industrialists who gained from empire but also the average consumer who was by the mid-eighteenth century accustomed to affordable imported tea, sugar, and tobacco.[54] Conversely, an aversion to excessive costs may also account for the public's occasional reluctance to sanction overcommitments. Yet economic interest did not always dominate middle-class thinking about empire. The civic ideals of British nationalism weighed heavily on these assessments, often in favor of militancy, but sometimes against it.

Popular imperialists in the eighteenth century devised an ideology in which traditional English liberty, popular representative government, and aggressive imperial nationalism were mutually supportive components. This ideology of civic nationalism was used as a tool to press middle-class interests against the haughty Whig elite. At the beginning of the century, the large urban districts returned Whigs to Parliament, but by the 1730s the urban middle class became alienated by limitations on suffrage, skewed districting, and financial scandals. They also resented Whig fiscal policy, which kept business credit tight, increased government patronage for Whig cronies, and made the collection of excise taxes harder to evade. In foreign affairs, urban constituencies chafed under the priority given to European balance-of-power maneuverings, which they felt came at the expense of commercially lucrative colonial expansion.[55] Radical publicists and politicians like John Wilkes linked these grievances in an integrated

[54] Wilson, "Empire of Virtue," 129.
[55] Rogers, *Whigs and Cities*, 5.

philosophy of liberal imperialism, which demanded *both* universal suffrage and a forceful mercantile diplomacy. Wilkes attacked the government over the purportedly weak peace treaty ending the Seven Years' War, for example, arguing that the sellout of British national interests by what he called a Frenchified, effeminate aristocracy was an inevitable consequence of the nonaccountability of the government to the people.[56] Wilkes's tendentious exploitation of nationalist themes inspired the Samuel Johnson mot: "patriotism is the last refuge of a scoundrel."[57]

Rhetorically, such liberal ideologues sought to package the middle class's interests in empire and democratization as constituting the national common good and to denigrate their elite opponents as self-seeking factions duped by foreign influences.[58] Voluntary patriotic societies argued that it was a "willingness to participate that marked out the true Briton," not rank or property.[59] Contributing toward collective action for the common good, whether through domestic charity or imperial conquest, became their criterion for nationalist virtue. Widespread personal and financial sacrifices during the Seven Years' War reinforced the idea that the people deserved more of a say in the governance of the state.[60] Meanwhile, the aristocratic elite was portrayed by socially resentful commoner intellectuals as treasonously swayed by French culture.[61] Ironically, however, among the commoners' motives for joining groups like the Naval Society was the opportunity to mingle with their social betters. Like the Catholic Center Party in Wilhelmine Germany, the middle classes calculated that supporting the fleet would impress the authorities and yield social and economic rewards.[62]

[56] Wilson, *Sense*, 213, also 189; Colley, *Britons*, 106–10; see also Rogers, *Whigs and Cities*, 123.

[57] Colley, *Britons*, 110.

[58] Ibid., 339–40; also, 5; Wilson, *Sense*, 157.

[59] Colley, *Britons*, 93–94.

[60] Wilson, *Sense*, 198. Of course, patriotic talk did not always lead to patriotic action. Nelson's example notwithstanding, British middle-class citizens took every opportunity to buy themselves out of military service obligations during the Napoleonic Wars, though the invasion scare of 1803 did serve as an impetus to a somewhat greater willingness to enlist. Colley, "The Reach of the State, the Appeal of the Nation," in Stone, *Imperial State at War*, 165–84; Colley, *Britons*, 295.

[61] Gerald Newman, *The Rise of English Nationalism: A Cultural History, 1740–1830* (New York: St. Martin's, 1987), esp. 123–27, 169.

[62] Colley, *Britons*, 92–93, 110.

As in so many other cases, the clamoring for increased mass political participation coincided with the rise of belligerent nationalism. Yet unlike many of those other nationalisms, British middle-class civic ideologists were distinctive in placing an absolute priority on the principle of individual civil liberty. As a result, it became increasingly difficult to justify imperialism directed toward other free peoples.

The war in the American colonies gave rise to a contradiction between the themes of imperial domination and popular self-government. Facing this contradiction squarely, Wilkes and most other democrats came down against the war. Wilkes argued that repression of democracy in the colonies was linked to tyranny at home, and he called for an end to the war and for representational reform in Britain.[63] The thinking of the Wilkites anticipates the theory of the democratic peace, that while liberal democrats may be imperialistic in their stance toward nondemocrats, liberal norms make them loath to attack a regime perceived to be democratic, lest they undermine their own legitimacy.[64]

Some democrats tried to argue against the war on commercial grounds, but most rejected this line of argument, insisting that the key issue was the maltreatment of a free people by a despotic power.[65] Antiwar views were especially strong among the colonial trading interests, which had always backed aggressive policies in previous struggles for imperial domination against the French and the Spanish.[66] Agitation and petitions against the war came disproportionately from the middles classes, shopkeepers, and artisans; they came least from titled gentlemen and professionals like doctors and lawyers. Attitudes toward the coercive state, not economic interest, drove these opinions.[67]

Challenged by these powerful doctrines, conservative elites of the Tory Party, like Edmund Burke, tried to co-opt the civic nationalist themes of liberty and popular sovereignty as principles guiding imperial strategy. Burke, the renowned spokesman for British conservatism, adopted

---

[63] Wilson, "Empire of Virtue," 151; Sidney Tarrow, *Power in Movement: Social Movements, Collective Action and Politics* (Cambridge: Cambridge University Press, 1994), 67–68.

[64] See the chapters by Michael Doyle and John Owen in Michael Brown et al., eds., *Debating the Democratic Peace* (Cambridge: MIT Press, 1966).

[65] Wilson, *Sense*, 417–18.

[66] Wilson, "Empire of Virtue," 151–52.

[67] Wilson, *Sense*, 270–72.

Wilkes's refrain, arguing that "No free country can keep another in slavery. The price they pay for it will be their own servitude."[68] Conservatives like Burke argued that continued leadership by Britain's traditional elites, not by radicals like Wilkes, would best conserve Britons' traditional liberties.[69] After the French Revolution reversed the class symbolism of the strategic rivalry with France, British conservatives were able to turn the tables on the middle-class radicals: now it was the radicals, not the aristocracy, who could be tagged as ideological stalking horses for the French arch foe.

Prime Minister Palmerston achieved an especially stunning success in co-opting civic nationalism to conservative ends on the eve of the Crimean War, reversing public opinion almost overnight. During the 1840s, Britain's first successful mass movement, Richard Cobden's Anti-Corn Law League, had favored free trade and pacifism. Workers and middle classes alike had joined in this popular movement. But the revolutionary upheavals that spread across Europe in 1848, including the militant Chartist workers' movement in Britain, scared the middle-class core of Cobden's constituency. As a result, the middle classes became available for a realignment with conservative elites against the further spread of democratic rights to the working class.

Civic nationalism provided the perfect ideological justification for this reversal of social alignments. Palmerston crystallized this change by proselytizing for a patrician view of the British citizen as a modern version of the citizen of imperial Rome (the *civis Romanus*), who would be deferential to authority at home but respected throughout the world and protected in his endeavors to trade and spread liberty by the might of the British fleet. This formula was civic, not ethnic: Palmerston propounded it in a speech justifying the blockade of a Greek harbor on behalf of the property claims of one Don Pacifico, a Gibraltar-born, Portuguese-speaking Jew who carried a British passport. Nationalistic middle-class democrats, led by John Roebuck, felt that Palmerston's version of a citizens' empire offered them a ticket to membership in an exclusive club that would be just democratic enough to give the middle class a cut of its ben-

---

[68] Ibid., 251, quoting *Debates in the House of Commons in the Year 1774, on the Bill for Making More Effectual Provision for the Government of Quebec*, ed. J. Wright (London: 1839; repr. 1966), ii–iv, 15–24.

[69] Newman, *Rise of English Nationalism*, 229; also 164, 230.

efits, but not so democratic that the middle class would be swamped by the growing working class.

Despite this realignment of the middle class with the aristocratic elite, tensions remained between these partners' conceptions of imperial civic nationalism. While Palmerston saw the Crimean War as a popular issue that could alleviate pressure for the expansion of the electoral franchise at home, Roebuck's adherents saw it as an opportunity to show the necessity of replacing aristocrats in military and imperial posts with more technically competent middle-class administrators.[70]

Palmerston's use of nationalist appeals as a substitute for true democratization, however reminiscent of Wilhelmine Germany, was symptomatic of only a passing phase of British nationalism. The more fundamental British pattern reflected a moderate civic nationalism, established on the foundation of strong representative and journalistic institutions, laid down by an elite with mobile capital, well before the era of mass mobilization for war. Though Britain conquered vast portions of the globe, it generally did so in a cost-conscious way: it appeased foes strategically, pulled back from overcommitments, and never placed its nationalism beyond the pale of rational discussion over the costs and benefits of imperial policies.[71] Though public opinion manipulated by elite demagogues figured in the origins of the Crimean War, the influence of the average voter more commonly played a moderating role on British strategic policy. Britain's first modern electoral campaign in 1880, featuring speaking tours aimed at mass audiences, was decided by William Gladstone's successful warnings to cost-conscious Scottish voters about the price of imperial overextension. In 1905, voters similarly rejected Joseph Chamberlain's call to replace free trade with a system of economic protectionism within an expanded empire.[72]

In short, the story of British civic nationalism embodies a two-sided lesson. On the one hand, this earliest case of modern, popular nationalism foreshadowed the subsequent tendency for democratization and increases freedom of the press to stimulate belligerent nationalism. Even in this rela-

[70] Snyder, *Myths of Empire*, 197–98; Olive Anderson, *A Liberal State at War*; see also Cain and Hopkins, *British Imperialism*, vol. I, 100.

[71] Kennedy, *Strategy and Diplomacy*, Chapters 1 and 8; for a more critical view, see Kupchan, *The Vulnerability of Empire*, Chapter 3.

[72] Snyder, *Myths of Empire*, 209–10.

tively liberal setting, middle classes used nationalist appeals to gain greater access to the political process, and established elites tried to co-opt nationalist ideology to their own ends. A heightened risk of war was a by-product of this posturing. On the other hand, British civic nationalism, whatever its other flaws, was more prudent and cost-conscious than the other varieties. Moreover, its civic nationalist principles created ideological constraints on the use of force against other liberal people.

These benefits of civic nationalism emerged for two main reasons: first, because the elites who took the lead in forming the nation had flexible interests that were not greatly threatened by democratization, and second, because free speech and representative institutions were well established before the era of mass democracy. In contrast, as the next section demonstrates, eighteenth-century France lacked such moderating institutions, and as a result its revolutionary nationalism triggered violence that engulfed all of Europe.

## French Revolutionary Nationalism

The wars of the French Revolution (1792–1802) and the Napoleonic Wars (1803–15) revealed for the first time in history the full potential of belligerent mass nationalism. This was hardly foreseeable at the beginning of the French Revolution in 1789, when the constituent assembly voted to renounce the use of military force in foreign affairs.[73] Yet within three years, France had declared war on Austria, to be followed shortly by war with Britain, the Netherlands, and Spain. Wars of expansion were waged almost ceaselessly by a parade of French postrevolutionary regimes: the republican Girondins in 1792–93, the guillotine-wielding Committee on Public Safety led by the revolutionary Jacobin faction in 1793–95, the somewhat more stable regime ruled by the Directory beginning in 1795, and regimes dominated by Napoleon after 1799. After two decades of nearly constant fighting against a series of coalitions of European states, the overextended French armies briefly occupied Moscow in 1812, only to collapse in defeat by 1814. French revolutionary nationalism extinguished itself in a last gasp at the Battle of Waterloo in 1815, and the pre-

[73] Jeremy Popkin, *Revolutionary News: The Press in France, 1789–1799* (Durham: Duke University Press, 1990), 153.

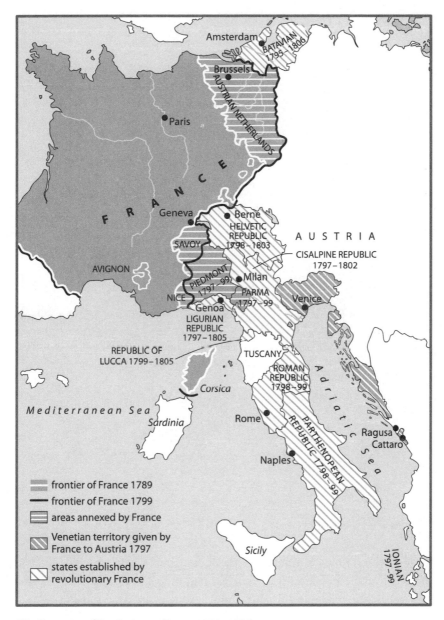

*The Expansion of Revolutionary France, 1789–1806*

revolutionary Bourbon dynasty returned to rule in Paris (see maps above and on the following page).

This nationalism was not ethnic. Citizenship was based on criteria of territorial residence and loyalty to French political principles, not on lan-

*Europe at the Height of Napoleon's Power*

guage or the ethnic culture of the Île de France. French nationalism also
differed from the British style of civic nationalism. The French variant
was collectivist, not individualist, and derived from participation in the
community, not from individual liberties. "In England," explains Liah
Greenfeld, "it was the liberty of the individuals who composed it that
made the nation free. In France, it was the liberty of the nation that constituted the freedom of the individuals."[74] Thus, nationalism in France
took the revolutionary form, basing its appeals for collective action on the

[74] Greenfeld, *Nationalism*, 167–68; also Beatrice Hyslop, *French Nationalism in*

defense of a political revolution that had brought to power a regime that governed in the name of the nation, and violently opposing those who were seen as trying to undo that change.

What accounts for this sudden outburst of self-defeating, revolutionary nationalist aggression? Like many subsequent instances of nationalist aggression, the French nationalism of the revolutionary wars coincided with early steps toward democratic elections and an avalanche of political verbiage from a newly free press. After the storming of the Bastille prison in 1789, the monarchy's relatively tight press censorship collapsed, as did state control of publications through regulation of the printers' guild. The number of newspapers exploded, from 60 in 1789 to over 500 in 1792 in Paris alone, where combined circulation could reach as high as 300,000.[75] With adult male literacy reaching 50 percent nationwide and over 90 percent in some districts in Paris, middle-class citizens of the new France read avidly and discussed what they read in ubiquitous political clubs. "Civil society" was at its most vibrant and spontaneous.[76] Journalists were among the leading political figures in the revolution, among them the leader of the war party in the assembly, Jacques-Pierre Brissot, a "hack writer and police spy in the 1780s" who used his control over a popular newspaper to assume leadership of the Girondins, one of the leading political factions opposing the king.[77] This uncontrolled hubbub of discourse did not, however, guarantee a full airing of major policy issues. Not one Paris newspaper voiced opposition when war was finally declared against monarchical Austria in April 1792.[78]

---

*1789 according to the General Cahiers* (New York: Octagon, 1968; orig. ed., New York: Columbia University Press, 1934), 98.

[75] Simon Schama, *Citizens* (New York: Knopf, 1992), 176–78, 525; Popkin, *Revolutionary News*, 32, 62, 82.

[76] Popkin, *Revolutionary News*, 24; Michael Kennedy, *The Jacobin Clubs in the French Revolution*, 2 vols. (Princeton: Princeton University Press, 1982 and 1988); Schama, *Citizens*, 180; Hugh Gough, *The Newspaper Press in the French Revolution* (London: Routledge, 1988), 214.

[77] Schama's phrase, *Citizens*, 582–83; see also Gary Kates, *The Cercle Social, the Girondins, and the French Revolution* (Princeton: Princeton University Press, 1985), 34; Popkin, *Revolutionary News*, 41.

[78] T. C. W. Blanning, *The Origins of the French Revolutionary Wars* (London: Longman, 1986), 113; see also Sydney Seymour Biro, *The German Policy of Revolutionary France*, vol. I (Cambridge: Harvard University Press, 1957), 62.

What made militant nationalism so attractive and persuasive in this era of burgeoning mass politics? Why was it part of every successful faction's program? Since the policy of war was costly, only intermittently success-ful, and ultimately disastrous for revolutionary France, why was it such a winner in political debates?

The lack of effective institutions to channel the explosion of mass poli-tics forced elites into an intense ideological competition for authority, according to the prevailing consensus of historians. In this war of ideas, the trump card was the scapegoating of enemies of the nation at home and abroad. Warhawks exploited flaws in the marketplace of ideas, which hindered an objective evaluation of these charges. Thus, the aftermath of the French Revolution illustrates the belligerent form that nationalism can take when political institutions have collapsed, press freedom is newly expanding, and opportunistic elites are willing to exploit any issue to win the favor of public opinion.

In the following sections, I first examine the political consequences of the collapse of French state institutions; second, explain why nationalist myths prevailed in public debate; and finally, show how Napoleon exploited the legacy of revolutionary nationalism.

### Filling the institutional vacuum

Whereas eighteenth-century Britain gestated liberal institutions inside the womb of its limited monarchy, the kings of eighteenth-century France were bent on achieving absolute power. To this end, the Bourbon mon-archs destroyed France's historic parliament and muzzled France's journal-ists. In Britain, when the masses started to play the decisive role in politics, a set of mature liberal institutions was ready to adapt to that pur-pose. In contrast, when the revolution swept away the Bourbon monar-chy, France lacked effective institutions, such as regularized electoral institutions, bureaucratic accountability to the legislature, effective legal protections of civil rights, and objective, independent news media, through which its citizens could participate in politics.

These differences are reflected in the way Britain and France mobi-lized resources for war. Britain was buffered from the demands of con-scription and direct taxation by its insular geography and greater borrowing power. Consequently, Britain's monarchs were able to meet the demands of international competition without abandoning traditional liberties and parliamentary institutions. The French monarchy, lacking such buffers, snuffed out France's ancient representative institutions in order to have a free hand imposing direct taxes on agriculture and therefore finance its costly wars.[79]

However, this system of absolute monarchy soon ran into a dead end. Under intensified financial pressure because of international setbacks, such as the defeat in the Seven Years' Wars, the French state attempted fiscal reform. But, this change was blocked by aristocrats and other beneficiaries of special privileges under the old regime.[80] With these elites divided and the peasantry growing surly under the weight of an unfair tax system, the monarchy finally acknowledged that it must establish a broader base of legitimacy for its efforts at resource extraction. Too late, the regime brought atrophied representative institutions out of mothballs. As Brian Downing remarks, "Revitalized local assemblies and the convocation of the first Estates-General since the early seventeenth century were unable to provide a stable political system upon which democracy could be built. None of these institutions had participated meaningfully in the eighteenth-century Bourbon state; they had no clear procedures, guidelines, or delineations of powers to provide coherent rule."[81]

As a result, after the collapse of the autocracy there was no fixed system for deciding who should rule and how policy should be made. The French elite was united against absolutism, but deeply split about what to put in its place. Thus, the king, the ministries, the deputies, the political clubs and factions, and a variety of freelancing political entrepreneurs all contended for power amid fluid institutions. Although there were elections for the assembly, the "average voter" did not provide a stable reference point for political authority: suffrage rules were constantly changing, there were no organized political parties, local issues dominated electoral campaigns, and changing circumstances rapidly left electoral promises outdated.[82] The Girondin regime's constitution of 1793 promised universal-suffrage elections for local officials, but after the rival Jacobins came to

[79] Downing, *Military Revolution*, Chapter 5.

[80] Theda Skocpol, *States and Social Revolutions* (Cambridge: Cambridge University Press, 1979), 60–64; François Furet, *Revolutionary France, 1770–1880* (Oxford: Blackwell, 1992), 11–13.

[81] Downing, *Military Revolution*, 135.

[82] Popkin, *Revolutionary News*, 4.

power, this went unfulfilled.[83] Lacking an institutionalized mandate, the contending factions reached out to urban popular groups via the press and the political clubs to create a mandate through ideological appeals.[84] With political power utterly insecure from one moment to the next, the factions had no choice but to view foreign policy almost entirely through a prism of short-run consequences for the ideological power struggle.[85]

The trump card then in this confused political struggle was to portray the integrity of one's opponent as being tainted by treasonous threats from enemies at home and abroad. Like most nationalisms, French popular nationalism asserted the right of the people to rule themselves in their own state. But since stable democratic rule was far from institutionalized, who truly represented the nation was always in doubt. Ernest Renan's famous characterization of nationalism as a "daily plebiscite" to win the loyalty of the people was never more true than at this juncture of the French Revolution.[86] In these circumstances, one dramatic way to establish popular credentials was to take the vanguard in the fight against the nation's enemies. Factions that played this card won; factions that did not play it lost.[87] "If the Girondins, from late 1791, were the most eloquent advocates of war with the Austrian Emperor," says historian François Furet, "it was because they were convinced that it was the only way they could come to power."[88]

In relations with foreign states, this strategy had the advantage of being a self-fulfilling prophecy: treating neighboring regimes as enemies tends to make them so. And in domestic politics, this strategy put the onus on the opponents to prove their loyalty. In revolutionary France, the right to self-rule was seen as a collective right, an emanation of what Rousseau

[83] Vivien Schmidt, *Democratizing France: The Political and Administrative History of Decentralization* (Cambridge: Cambridge University Press, 1990), 12–25.

[84] François Furet, *Interpreting the French Revolution* (Cambridge: Cambridge University Press, 1981), 49; Skocpol, *States and Social Revolutions*, 65–66.

[85] This interpretation is advanced most clearly by Furet, *Interpreting*, 47, 53–56, but the detailed diplomatic histories by Blanning and by Paul Schroeder, *The Transformation of European Politics, 1763–1848* (Oxford: Clarendon, 1994), also invoke this argument.

[86] Quoted in E. J. Hobsbawm, *Nations and Nationalism since 1780* (Cambridge: Cambridge University Press, 1990), 88.

[87] Schroeder, *Transformation*, 126; also Blanning, *Origins*, 106, 111–12.

[88] Furet, *Interpreting*, 65; also 47, 53–55.

had called "the general will." The concept of a loyal opposition to the general will threatened the prevailing ideology of national self-rule, so any disagreement could potentially be portrayed as treasonous.[89] As Brissot himself put it, "We need great acts of treason; therein lies our salvation."[90]

### Selling nationalist myths

This rhetorical competition in the institutional vacuum explains why the factions had an incentive to sell belligerent nationalist myths, but why was the public so willing to buy them? The reason was not a revolutionary zeal for conquest, nor misperceptions inherent in revolutionary ideology, but rather the warhawks' domination of a press that acted as an amplifier of opinions rather than as a medium of debate. As historian Georges Michon put it, "The activity of the press was decisive in the psychological preparation for war."[91]

At the outset of the revolution, French citizens were not eager for military adventures. On the contrary, between 1789 and 1791, France was totally self-absorbed. The notion of spreading the revolution by the force of bayonets was scarcely present in French debates until after international conflicts had already arisen.[92] Delegates to the assembly commonly described themselves as nationalists, but by this they meant proponents not of belligerence abroad, but of popular sovereignty at home and effective national government.[93] "All power emanates from the nation, and can only be exercised for its welfare," the delegates intoned. "The States-General is the organ of the will of the nation."[94] Policies that were self-described as nationalist included the national standardization of laws,

[89] Popkin, *Revolutionary News*, 115.

[90] Furet, *Interpreting*, 66, quoting Jacobin Club speech, December 30, 1791; also 127.

[91] Georges Michon, *Le Rôle de la presse en 1791–1792: La Déclaration de Pillnitz et la Guerre* (Paris: A. Nizet & M. Bastard, 1941), 5.

[92] Frank L. Kidner, "The Girondists and the 'Propaganda War' of 1792: A Re-Evaluation of French Revolutionary Foreign Policy from 1791 to 1793," (Princeton University: Ph.D. dissertation in modern history, 1971), 100.

[93] Hyslop, *French Nationalism*, 203–8, 214; Frances Acomb, *Anglophobia in France, 1763–1789: An Essay in the History of Constitutionalism and Nationalism* (Durham: Duke University Press, 1950), 52–55, 61.

[94] Hyslop, *French Nationalism*, 65.

weights, and measures, the elimination of tariffs on internal trade, and uniform taxation without respect to class privileges.[95]

From the very beginning of the revolution, nationalist arguments, though not warlike, drew sharp distinctions between friends and foes of the nation, internal and external. At home, revolutionary nationalism sharpened class differences. For example, the premier pamphleteer of the revolution, Abbé Sieyès, argued that the French nobility had cut itself off from the privileges of citizenship in the nation by seeking special class privileges.[96] Revolutionary nationalism similarly sharpened perceptions of differences from neighboring states. Though initial debates on the design of governmental institutions showed some willingness to borrow from the experiences of other states, the nationalist climate required that republicans find French precedents for their authority, lest they be labeled Anglophile.[97] Though proponents of free trade within French borders, nationalist delegates argued for protectionism toward foreign states, claiming that "buying French" would serve as an antidote to domestic economic depression.[98] Moreover, the stirrings of popular sovereignty gave rise to the notion of French superiority and a vague sense of mission to spread this innovation abroad.[99] Thus, French revolutionary nationalism sharpened political differences both at home and abroad, though the revolution was not at first overtly warlike.[100]

Nor is it true that war was forced upon France by hostile autocratic states seeking to snuff out political change. Modern diplomatic histories agree, rather, that Austria's king Leopold hoped to avoid conflict with revolutionary France because war would divert his energies from his more immediate rivalry with autocratic Prussia. By 1791, French émigré aristocrats, including members of the French royal family and Leopold's own in-laws, were organizing opposition to the revolution from bases in France's monarchical neighbors and pressing Leopold to back their cause.

---

[95] Ibid., 52–56, 78, 130–34.

[96] Furet, *Interpreting*, 47–48.

[97] Hyslop, *French Nationalism*, 169–74; Acomb, *Anglophobia*, 14.

[98] Ibid., 134, 168–69.

[99] Ibid., 169–74.

[100] For a very nuanced discussion of the way that drawing national boundaries inexorably sharpened these distinctions, see Rogers Brubaker, *Citizenship and Nationhood in France and Germany* (Cambridge: Harvard University Press, 1992), 43–48.

To mollify these groups, Leopold issued a vague declaration in favor of restoring the full powers of the French king. The French press initially reacted with a yawn to Leopold's declaration. They correctly saw his statement as intending to buy time, not to provoke conflict.[101] Shortly, however, warhawks like Brissot were able to portray the declaration as an affront to French popular sovereignty and an interference in revolutionary France's internal struggle against perfidious aristocratic plotters.[102]

It is also untrue that all French revolutionaries had a psychological predisposition to overrate the hostility of their foreign foes and underrate their power.[103] Maximilien de Robespierre, the chief voice of the Jacobin faction on the eve of the conflict with Austria in 1792, argued correctly that war would fuel inflation, that the French army was unprepared to fight, and that "armed missionaries are loved by no one."[104] He also pointed out the contradictions in the Girondin image of the adversary: "Do not tell us sometimes that all the Princes of Europe will remain indifferent spectators to our dealings, and sometimes that we will overthrow the governments of all these princes."[105] Brissot himself acknowledged that his arguments were driven as much by domestic tactics as by his true perceptions of the situation abroad: "Rome always followed a policy more or less similar," he told the assembly. "When threatened by some domestic storm, the Senate launched a war far away from Italy, and as a result of this salutary diversion, achieved peace at home and victories abroad."[106] Despite such admissions, French revolutionaries were convinced by Girondin arguments that revolution would be easy to spread to Belgium, that further revolutionary bandwagons would follow, that this would restore faith in

[101] Blanning, *Origins*, 86–88; Schroeder, *Transformation*; Michon, *Rôle de la presse*, 9–11.

[102] Schama, *Citizens*, 590–91; Biro, *German Policy*, vol. I, 62.

[103] Stressing the perceptual biases of both the revolutionaries and the status quo states are Stephen Walt, *Revolution and War* (Ithaca: Cornell University Press, 1996), Chapter 3; and Blanning, *Origins*, 108–16, 123, 152.

[104] Biro, *German Policy*, vol. I, 63.

[105] Kidner, "The Girondists and the 'Propaganda War' of 1792," 91.

[106] Blanning, *Origins*, 106. More generally on the domestic motivations of Brissot's war rhetoric, see Eloise Ellery, *Brissot de Warville* (Boston: Houghton and Mifflin, 1915), 253; Biro, I, *German Policy*, vol. 46; Schroeder, *Transformation*, 94–95; Blanning, *Origins*, 98–100; Kidner, "The Girondists and the 'Propaganda War' of 1792," 85; Michon, *Rôle de la presse*, 65.

France's shaky currency, that war would pay for itself, that there were military advantages to striking first, and that war was inevitable anyway.[107]

In this setting where all factions were working hard to manipulate French opinion, why did the war-mongering tactics of the Girondins prevail? A major reason is that Girondin newspapers enjoyed a much greater circulation than those of Robespierre's antiwar faction, even before Brissot took up the war theme. "How is it that such a negligible man [as Brissot] can do so much harm to the public good?" asked a speaker at the Jacobin Club in November 1792. "It is because he has a newspaper, and . . . his friends have newspapers . . . and . . . command all the loudest trumpets, and have momentarily perverted public opinion."[108]

The warhawks' advantage was reinforced by the two-pronged instrument of subsidies to the pro-war press and suppression of the opposition. The Girondin press received secret subsidies from the Ministry of Interior, which sought to counter the Jacobin radicals, and from Foreign Minister Dumouriez, who wanted upbeat propaganda to cheer troops in depressing straits. He also paid for phony stories alleging collusion between Jacobins and royalists, which succeeded in instigating the assembly to mount treason proceedings against both.[109]

In their contest to influence French opinion, Brissot and the Girondin warhawks were initially far more effective than Robespierre, partly because of the appeal of their message, partly because the media they controlled magnified their voice, and partly because their belligerence created a self-fulfilling prophecy. Brissot's initial speeches on a possible war with Austria made a great impression on the assembly. They appealed in particular to uncommitted delegates, neither pro-monarchical nor ultraradical, who were struck by the danger of a hostile encirclement and by the call to French glory. The wider public, however, was somewhat slower to

---

[107] In addition to Walt and Blanning cited above, see Michael Kennedy, *The Jacobin Clubs in the French Revolution*, vol. II, *The Middle Years*, 127; Biro, *German Policy*, vol. I, 114; Kidner, "The Girondists and the 'Propaganda War' of 1792," 86; H. A. Goetz-Bernstein, *La Politique extérieure de Brissot et des Girondins* (Paris: Hachette, 1912), 39.

[108] Gough, *Newspaper Press*, 112, n29, citing F.-A. Aulard, ed., *La Société des Jacobins*, 6 vols. (Paris: 1789–95); also Gough, 92. In historian Georges Michon's view, this "explains why the magnificent resistance of Robespierre and that of some moderates like Dupont de Nemours had no effect." Michon, *La Rôle de la presse*, 5.

[109] Gough, *Newspaper Press*, 85–86, 90.

pick up the war theme. The Jacobin Club debated both sides of the issue, and as late as January 1792, several Paris newspapers were backing Robespierre.[110] Where the strategy of persuasion was slow to work, however, the tactics of accusation helped to make the war cry a self-fulfilling prophecy. In order to deflect Brissot's charges of treason, King Louis and his ministers threatened to attack the small German states harboring French émigrés. Louis's virtual ultimatum in December 1791 triggered vague Austrian deterrent threats, which provided further ammunition for Brissot's belligerent speeches and newspaper campaign.[111] In this kind of superheated political environment, the political elite paid little attention to the balanced, well-informed opinions of antiwar experts like the international law professor who sat as a delegate to the assembly.[112]

Between December 1791 and April 1792, the bandwagon for war gathered momentum even in the Jacobin faction. In 154 local Jacobin clubs throughout France, where politically minded middle-class radicals met to discuss contemporary events, 141 clubs expressed an opinion (in straw votes) favoring war, 3 favored peace, and 12 were uncertain or divided. In club after club, Brissot's arguments for war that had been repeated constantly in the press were parroted back and amplified: victory is certain, only war can foil the antidemocratic plot, and the rest of Brissot's litany.[113] By the declaration of war in April, pro-war opinion in the assembly, the clubs, and the press was overwhelming.

One reason that the press acted as a megaphone of ill-founded assertions was that journalists lacked a strong news reporting ethic. Most journalists were young, well-educated, and bourgeois, attracted by a combination of the prospect of fame, relatively high pay, and ideological zeal.[114] Much of the newspaper's content was not news but opinions of the writers, or opinions, insults, interruptions, and droning of the speakers in the assembly, a spectacle that "shattered the optimistic belief that unlimited public debate would lead to a reasoned consensus," says historian Jeremy Popkin.[115] As a result, hard news was sometimes very scarce, and

---

[110] Biro, *German Policy*, vol. I, 46, 53; Schama, *Citizens*, 593.
[111] Blanning, *Origins*, 101.
[112] Ellery, *Brissot*, 242.
[113] Kennedy, *Jacobin Clubs*, vol. II, *Middle Years*, 129–30.
[114] Popkin, *Revolutionary News*, 28–29, 41–47.
[115] Ibid., 123.

consequently rumors ran wild, especially in the provinces. In the "Great Fear" of 1789, for example, spontaneous false reports of brigands hired by aristocrats, linking up with foreign armies headed by émigrés, spread throughout much of the country overnight, triggering peasant attacks on landlords' manors.[116] Even in Paris, wild rumors had powerful political effects. The fall of Robespierre, for example, was orchestrated through a rumor, manufactured by his enemies on the Committee of Public Safety, that he intended to marry Louis XVI's daughter and proclaim himself king. The conspirators, fearing that Robespierre was about to order their execution, started the rumor through newspapers and pamphlets, but it spread largely by word-of-mouth.[117]

Readers were as much to blame as journalists for the poor quality of the press. Most readers chose their newspaper by its political orientation. Only a minority were looking for objective information from the press, choosing to read an accurate newspaper even if they disagreed with its editorial line.[118] Hard facts were not the most highly prized commodity in this marketplace of ideas.

In this setting, volatile public moods were crucial to political outcomes. While public opinion was not initially warlike, it rapidly became so when fortuitous catalysts, such as the machinations of treasonous émigrés, were exploited by powerful voices in the media. On this and other issues, press campaigns succeeded only when they captured the moment in a way that resonated with the public mood. For example, a concerted campaign by agitators in the fringe press to depose Louis in July and August 1792 succeeded despite resistance from the mainstream press.[119] Thus, the press could not manipulate specific outcomes whenever it chose to do so. Rather, according to historian Jeremy Popkin, it served to "produce an atmosphere of tension and expectation that made an explosion of some sort inevitable," and then catalyzed the explosion when the

---

[116] Georges Lefebvre, *The Great Fear of 1789* (New York: Pantheon, 1973), esp. 66; Schama, *Citizens*, 429–31; Christopher Todd, *Political Bias, Censorship and the Dissolution of the "Official" Press in Eighteenth-Century France* (Lewiston, NY: Edwin Mellen, 1991), 147.

[117] Bronislaw Baczko, *Ending the Terror* (Cambridge: Cambridge University Press, 1989), 3, 16–17.

[118] Popkin, *Revolutionary News*, 88–89.

[119] Ibid., 136–38, 142.

time was opportune.[120] In this way, the flaws in the newly freed press magnified the potential for nationalist conflict that was inherent in the revolutionary situation.

### Napoleon's counterrevolutionary nationalism

Napoleon made French revolutionary nationalism routine and harnessed it to the purposes of the rebuilt French state. After the revolution had destroyed the institutional basis of authority, nationalism played a large role in the reconstruction of state power. When the inefficient old regime collapsed, political entrepreneurs from Brissot to Napoleon struggled to build a new state capable of mobilizing collective action to meet modern military and economic challenges. All of them used nationalist ideology to overcome this institutional deficit. Nationalism, tied to conspiracy theories linking purported domestic traitors with foreign foes, was used to do away with factional rivals and to motivate military enlistment in the new mass army.[121] It was not just that a politically conscious nation demanded to have a state, but to some extent it was also the converse: "We must have a nation for such a grand undertaking" as the revitalization of French state power, exclaimed one enthusiast, "and the Nation will be born."[122]

Napoleon's use of nationalism to reinforce his rule echoed the tactics of Brissot. Like Brissot, Napoleon had to co-opt nationalist fervor and link it to domestic threats in order to prop up his rule. When Napoleon came to power, France was already weary from a decade of war, which had yielded mixed results. To reforge nationalism as a tool of legitimation, Napoleon mounted a systematic public relations campaign accusing the British of backing rebels in the Vendée region.

However, in place of a free, spontaneously nationalist press, Napoleon substituted the orchestrated debates and nationalist rhetoric of a tightly

[120] Ibid., 142; also Gough, *Newspaper Press*, 233.

[121] Barry Posen, "Nationalism, the Mass Army, and Military Power," *International Security*, 18:2 (Fall 1993), 80–124; John Lynn, *The Bayonets of the Republic* (Urbana: University of Illinois Press, 1984); Jean-Paul Berthaud, *The Army of the French Revolution* (Princeton: Princeton University Press, 1988).

[122] Greenfeld, *Nationalism*, 167, quoting a statement by Phillippe Grouvelle in 1789.

controlled press. In lieu of genuine, revolutionary mass patriotism, Napoleon demobilized authentic mass participation and substituted for it the "symbols, ritual, and propaganda of a highly generalized French nationalism," as Theda Skocpol puts it.[123] Whereas Brissot used the more dangerous live virus of nationalism promoted by a free press, Napoleon closed all but thirteen Paris papers and administered a controlled dose of vaccine.[124]

Napoleon's tactics were the culmination of a pattern that had been set in motion during the revolutionary period, when press freedom expanded, civil society burgeoned, and "government" amounted to a cacophony of warring factions. Idealists who ushered in the French Revolution, such as Abbé Emmanuel Sieyès, the publicist of the rights of the middle class, soon became disabused of the view that truth would rise to the top in an open marketplace of ideas and would point the way toward the brotherhood of man. Learning that this was a perverse market in which the bad ideas drove out the good, the revolutionaries cast about for ways to regulate the volatile market by subsidies, taxes, repression, and ultimately remonopolization.[125] These ex post facto attempts to regulate the passions of the revolution suppressed its democratic character and manipulated its nationalism to serve the ends of the state. In other words, as the state's administrative institutions became stronger, revolutionary nationalism was transformed into its counterrevolutionary variant.

At the outset of the revolution, men like the journalist Brissot invoked nationalism not to defend some vested interest, but rather to ride a wave that had washed away entrenched interests and made them fluid. In this sense, their revolutionary nationalism was the antithesis of the counter-revolutionary nationalism of the Wilhelmine German elites. Soon, how-ever, under Sieyès and the Directory, and especially under Napoleon, French nationalism was co-opted by the very interests that the revolution-ary wars had created: the revolutionary army and the militarized economy that depended on never-ending spoils of new conquests to remain finan-cially solvent. At this point, the rhetoric of popular nationalism was

---

[123] Skocpol, *States and Social Revolutions*, 195.

[124] Robert Holtman, *Napoleonic Propaganda* (Baton Rouge: Louisiana State University Press, 1950), 1–11; Popkin, *Revolutionary News*, 177.

[125] On the press policies of the Directory, see Popkin, *Revolutionary News*, 38, 174–76.

deployed to rationalize what had become a counterrevolutionary autoc-racy.[126] This new, strengthened state was indeed effective at resource mobilization for international competition, but it was brought down by the side effects that went along with it—the imperial nationalist ideology that legitimated it, the insatiability of its military economy, and the type of leader produced by such a system.[127]

Turning now to the development of nineteenth-century Serbian nationalism, there too the weaknesses of the state during the early phase of democratization shaped the character of the nation. However, since the politicians were building Serbia's nation-state under different constraints than were their French revolutionary counterparts, the Serbian nation took a different, ethnic form.

## Serbian Ethnic Nationalism, 1840–1914

Emblematic of the revival of aggressive ethnonationalism in the contem-porary period, Serbia's history also offers a revealing paradigm of the eth-nic form of nationalism in the nineteenth century. In this form of nationalism, leaders base their collective appeals on common culture, lan-guage, religion, shared historical experience, and/or the myth of shared kinship, and they use these criteria to include or exclude members from the national group. The development of this ethnic form of nationalism in nineteenth-century Serbia is deeply paradoxical in ways that illuminate the subtleties of ethnic nationalism in our own era.

As in Western Europe, the state created nationalism, not the reverse. Facing a weakly organized and backward society, the Serbian state molded the political consciousness of the Serbian people to fit its purposes. Yet the state itself was weak in comparison to the difficult tasks it faced. Some of these tasks were strategic. Wedged between the Austrian and Ottoman empires and surrounded by a host of smaller aspiring states, the ruling Obrenovic dynasty had to secure the loyalty of its population quickly in

[126] Furet, *Revolutionary France*, 155, 162, 213; Schroeder, *Transformation*, 138; on nationalist rhetoric used to justify parochial resource-grabbing, see also Ted W. Magardant, *Urban Rivalries in the French Revolution* (Princeton: Princeton University Press, 1992).

[127] Skocpol, *States and Social Revolutions*, 195.

order to safeguard the state's independence.[128] At the same time, the state had to strengthen itself against dynastic rivals at home. Given the institutional weakness of the state and the urgency of these tasks, civic nationalism was an infeasible solution. The Serbian government consequently promoted an ethnic form of nationalism, which was a culturally accessible tool for mobilizing mass political support. This conjunction of state-building and mass politics produced an explosive form of nationalism that was one of the catalysts for Balkan wars in 1877, 1885, 1912, 1913, and most devastatingly in 1914 (see map).

### *Cultural nationalism as a tool of state-building*

Serbia achieved a status of virtual independence from the Ottoman Empire through a series of revolts and negotiations between 1804 and 1830. The decline of Ottoman Turkish power left the empire unable to support or control its own armies and officials in the imperial periphery. At the same time, rising Austrian demand for Serbian pigs, which thrived on acorns in Serbia's vast oak forests, gave Serbia a lucrative alternative to integration with the Ottoman economy. Reacting to both disorder and opportunity, Serbian merchants seeking to establish better conditions for pig exports to Austria organized peasant rebellions to eject Ottoman authorities and landowners in 1804 and more successfully in 1815.[129]

Almost all modern scholars deny that this rebellion was motivated by Serbian nationalism. The rebelling peasants sought ownership of their own land and relief from arbitrary taxation. Smaller-scale pig merchants sought a decentralized system that would give them local autonomy, whereas the rival leaders of the two largest merchant dynasties, Karageorge and Milos Obrenovic, vied to establish a more centralized system with themselves as the new overlords of the region. It is true that the Ottoman Turks were

---

[128] On this paradox of the late-developing state that exerts a strong despotic power vis-à-vis its society yet is too weak to establish effective institutions to promote the development of a self-regulating society, see Kiren Chaudhry, "The Myths of the Market and the Common History of Late Developers," *Politics and Society* 21:3 (September 1993), 245–74.

[129] Daniel Chirot and Karen Barkey, "States in Search of Legitimacy: Was There Nationalism in the Balkans of the Early Nineteenth Century?" *International Journal of Comparative Sociology* 24:1–2 (1983), 30–46; see also Gale Stokes, "The Absence of Nationalism in Serbian Politics before 1840," *Canadian Review of Studies in Nationalism* 4:1 (Fall 1976), 77–90.

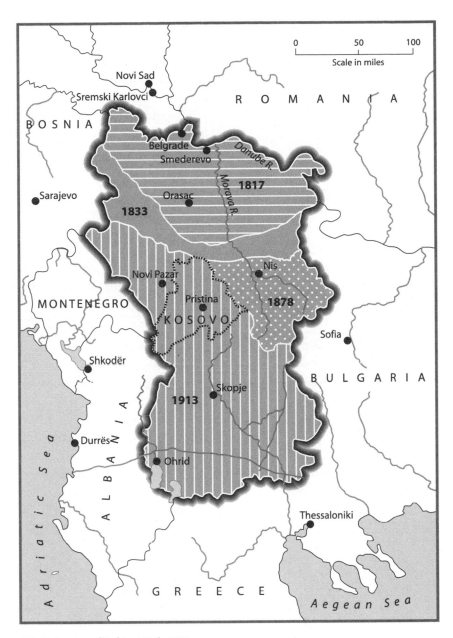

*The Expansion of Serbia, 1804–1913*

viewed as alien oppressors, but before about 1840 this grievance was not conceptualized in national terms. Though the Turks were Muslim and the Serbs Orthodox Christians, cultural and ethnic differences were more complex than that. For example, among the most hated Ottoman elites were the janissary troops, Christian babies who had been kidnapped and raised by the Ottomans as a separate military caste. Serb leaders also lived in a Turkified manner, and they culturally aspired to the status of favored, autonomous lords loosely integrated at the margins of the Ottoman system. In addition, some Muslim merchants, no less inconvenienced than the Serbs by the chaos of Ottoman decline, fought alongside Karageorge for Serbian autonomy.[130]

After the expulsion of Ottoman officialdom, Serbia had no traditional aristocratic or bureaucratic elite of its own. The local elite were the rich peasants and traders. Thus, the dynasties of Karageorge and then in 1815 of Milos Obrenovic ruled with very little state apparatus over a highly undifferentiated society of illiterate peasants. Thus, Milos confronted the problem of establishing his rule in an institutional vacuum, in the face of competition from two empires (Ottoman and Austrian), a rival dynasty, and local notables, and he drew on a population with minimal organizational experience. In an attempt during the 1830s to better institutionalize the rule of the Obrenovic dynasty, Milos brought in educated Serbs from Austrian lands to staff government bureaucracies and schools.

The first glimmerings of truly national goals and consciousness came only with these efforts to build a modern Serbian state in the 1830s. At this time, Milos sought to gain popular support among the peasantry by reviving the tradition of the *skupstina,* a mass outdoor assembly of armed men from a clan or locality. This served as the basis for periodic popular assemblies to ratify the ruler's decisions. At this stage, the peasantry typically aligned with Milos and the bureaucracy against the local notables, who sometimes spouted Western-style constitutionalist doctrine against absolutist rule, but in these early years mainly sought to impose a local patriarchy. Thus, a populist alliance between the central state and the peasantry began to take shape.[131]

Nationalism was the natural ideology to cement this alliance. Throughout the nineteenth and early twentieth centuries, the Serbian state used the public school system, which it controlled, to inculcate the historical lesson that only a strong, unified state could protect the Serbian

[130] Barbara Jelavich, *History of the Balkans* (Cambridge: Cambridge University Press, 1983).

[131] Charles Jelavich and Barbara Jelavich, *The Establishment of the Balkan National States, 1804–1920* (Seattle: University of Washington Press, 1977), 56, 60.

nation from foreign domination.[132] Nationalism was an advantageous ideology for Serbia's state-building elites in part because it helped to assert
central authority over local elites. It also helped to rationalize steep taxes
to support hugely expensive railroad projects and military programs,
which fed the growth of the state bureaucracy and provided a steady flow
of cash for kickback schemes.[133] In addition, popular nationalism helped
mobilize eager manpower for the state's repeated wars through the universal conscription law of 1861.[134]

### The weakness of democratic institutions

This nationalism took an ethnic form in part because civic-territorial
institutions were too transient and disordered to serve as a stable basis for
popular loyalty. The Karageorgevic and Obrenovic dynasties lacked any
firm basis of legitimacy. As parvenu pig merchants, they could claim no
historic right to rule. Moreover, the Obrenovic rulers in particular were
corrupt playboys, shamelessly using tax increases to fund gambling debts.
The final downfall of the Obrenovic dynasty came in 1903, when King
Alexander married his mother's lady-in-waiting, an older widow who had
sold her favors to men and tried to use false pregnancies to trick them
into marriage. Alexander and his wife had no children, and fears that her
drunken, wastrel brother would inherit the throne triggered a military
coup, which put the Karageorgevic dynasty back in power.[135] The legitimacy of Peter Karageorgevic stemmed from two factors, first that he was
not an Obrenovic, and second that he was a patriot who had fought as a
volunteer in the 1875 Bosnian Serb uprising against Ottoman rule. Thus,
far from being an alternative to ethnic nationalism, dynastic legitimacy
came increasingly to depend on it (see Table 4.1).

Nor could civic principles serve as an effective alternative to ethnic
legitimacy. Serbia had comparatively democratic constitutions, but

---

[132] Charles Jelavich, *South Slav Nationalism: Textbooks and Yugoslav Union before 1914*
(Columbus: Ohio State University Press, 1990), 191; Michael Petrovich, *A History of
Modern Serbia, 1804–1918* (New York: Harcourt Brace Jovanovich, 1976), 583–84.

[133] Stokes, "Social Origins," in Chirot, 236–37; Jelavich, *History of the Balkans*, vol. 1,
379–80; Jelavich and Jelavich, *Establishment*, 141.

[134] Jelavich and Jelavich, *Establishment*, 65.

[135] Petrovich, *History of Modern Serbia*, 504–5, also 371.

**Table 4.1 Government and Expansion of Serbia, 1817–1914**

| Year | Ruler/Dynasty[1] | Constitution | War | Territorial Gain |
|---|---|---|---|---|
| 1817–39 | Prince Milos Obrenovic | "Turkish" Constitution of 1838 promulgated by Ottomans divides power between Serb king and council of oligarchs | Rebellion and internal struggles (1804–17) | State founded in northern Serbia under Ottoman sovereignty; middle Serbia seized from Ottomans (1833) |
| 1839 | Milan Obrenovic | | | |
| 1839–42 | Michael Obrenovic | | | |
| 1842–58 | Alexander Karageorgevic | | | |
| 1860–68 | Michael Obrenovic | | | |
| 1868–82 | Milan Obrenovic | Constitution of 1869 establishes partially elected national assembly | Serbia defeats Ottoman Turkey (1877) | Southern Serbia annexed (1878) |
| 1882–89 | King Milan I Obrenovic | Constitution of 1888 increases power of elected assembly | Serbia attacks Bulgaria, but loses (1885) | No change |
| 1889–1903 | Alexander I Obrenovic | Constitution of 1901, minor changes | | |

| 1903–21 | Peter I Karageorgevic | Constitution of 1903, assembly gains budget power | Serbia and Balkan League attack and defeat Turkey (1912); Bulgaria attacks Serbia and coalition, but loses (1913); Austria invades Serbia to start World War I (1914) | Serbia gains Kosovo and Macedonia (1913) |

[1] Before 1882, the monarch is called prince, after 1882, king.

because democratic procedure was often violated, liberal civic principles were a thin basis for rallying loyalty to the state. As early as 1869, all tax-payers, including the bulk of the peasantry, could vote.[136] Political parties recruited electoral support from all sectors in society, but elections were often rigged.[137] Western-sounding laws existed, but the rule of law did not: government ministries instructed judges not to apply them literally and to make rulings instead "according to conscience and conviction and with a regard for popular justice and customs."[138] The political system became more democratic under the short-lived Constitution of 1888, which established the secret ballot, banned emergency rule by the execu-tive branch, gave the elected assembly power over the budget, and barred censorship of the press. In 1889, the Radical Party, a populist nationalist movement led by Nikola Pasic, came to power through a relatively free and fair election. Far from consolidating rule by law, however, the Radical victory was taken as a signal that the law and order imposed by more but-toned-down regimes was a thing of the past. Banditry, arson, political murders, and riots increased, even under the eye of the police. Losing some support in the 1893 elections, the Radicals were maneuvered out of power when the king revoked the 1888 Constitution.[139] Thus, politics was populist, but not institutionalized in a way that might root civic loy-alty in effective democratic practices.

In the Serbian context, liberalism was not an alternative to ethnic nationalism, but a promoter of it. Self-styled liberals were among the most committed ethnic nationalists. For example, the "Patriot King" Peter Karageorgevic, known for his militant support of Serb ethnic causes, was also the translator of John Stuart Mill's *On Liberty* into Serbo-Croatian. The more democratic the party and the more popular its appeal, the more belligerent was its nationalism.

Liberal militants often prevailed in public debate, despite the dubious-ness of their arguments. For example, the Liberal Party defeated the Conservative Party in the 1875 elections on the strength of its vociferous clamoring for Serbian support of the popular Bosnian uprising against the

---

[136] Ibid., 367; Gale Stokes, *Legitimacy through Liberalism: Vladimir Jovanovic and the Transformation of Serbian Politics* (Seattle: University of Washington Press, 1975).

[137] Jelavich and Jelavich, *Establishment*, 190.

[138] Petrovich, *History of Modern Serbia*, 402.

[139] Ibid., 441, 448–50, 460.

Ottomans. In contrast, conservative proponents of a more prudent style of power politics, including the reigning monarch Milan Obrenovic, were wary of triggering an Austrian military occupation of Bosnia, but the monarch's caution was swept aside. "Serbia had been nurtured for so long on a bellicose romantic nationalism that not much was needed to arouse the nation," says historian Michael Petrovich. Two thousand Belgrade volunteers, primed by nationalist poetry readings at public rallies, signed up within days to fight in the Bosnian resistance movement.[140] Reinforcing emotional appeals with the usual panoply of strategic arguments, Liberal interventionists claimed that Austria's rival Russia would deter Austrian countermoves against the Serbs. They also predicted that all Balkan Christians would join the Serbian side, that war would counter the internal threats from Serbia's socialists and restore internal unity, that the economy required military expansion, and that military expenditure would spur economic growth. Finally, the Liberals also contended that Serbia would get no spoils if it refused to fight. In fact, none of these liberal nationalist assertions were borne out. When Russia attacked the Ottoman army in the Balkans in 1877, the Serbian military intervened against Ottoman forces, which were already reeling from a Russian offensive. Serbia's efforts failed to impress the great powers. All the territory occupied by Serb forces had to be ceded to Bulgaria. Austria occupied Bosnia. Inside Serbia, the intervention failed to stem Liberal criticism of Milan's government, which was vilified as incompetent in its pursuit of national goals.[141]

Seeing that militant nationalism worked as a potent rhetorical tool for the Liberal Party, Milan tried to adapt nationalism as a popular basis for a government dominated by conservative parties, but the attempt again miscarried. On the heels of an electoral setback in 1883, Milan saw an opportunity for nationalist posturing when in 1885 Bulgaria annexed Rumelia, a formerly Ottoman region populated by Bulgarians. Though Serbia had no claim to Rumelia, Milan argued that the increase in Bulgaria's size would upset the balance of power to Serbia's disadvantage. Consequently, he insisted, Bulgaria should cede some territory to Serbia as compensation. Rebuffed, Milan sent the Serbian army into a disastrous offensive inside Bulgarian territory. This stratagem worked no better in domestic politics than it did on the battlefield. Serbs could mount little

---

[140] Ibid., 381–82, 536.
[141] Ibid., 384, 392, 394–95.

enthusiasm for a war against fraternal Slavs, from whom they felt little
ethnic differentiation. Radicals and liberals wanted compensation from
the Ottomans, not war against Bulgaria.[142] Thus, nationalist manipula-
tions were attempted, but their effectiveness was constrained by the
underlying sympathies and enthusiasms of the people.

### The weakness of media institutions

Like party politics, journalism was freewheeling but poorly institutionalized, contentious, and unprofessional. The reading public was intensely
interested in politics; by 1904 Belgrade alone supported seventy-two newspapers. Only one, however, the newly established *Politika*, was a truly professional paper, not tied to any party and offering news, features, reports
from foreign correspondents and wire services, and a sports section.
Virtually all of the other newspapers were bitterly polemical mouthpieces
for political parties, substituting personal attacks for real news reports.[143]
This press, especially the populist Radical organs, was stridently nationalistic. In the wake of the Austrian annexation of Bosnia-Herzegovina in 1908
and the Austro-Serbian import tariff "war" (the so-called Pig War) of
1906–11, much of this ire was trained on Vienna. In 1914, following the
assassination of Austrian archduke Franz Ferdinand in Bosnia by a Serbian
nationalist, Austria's ultimatum insisted that the Serbian government
clamp down on anti-Austrian diatribes in the Serbian press and on the
teaching of militant nationalism in Serbian public schools.[144] The Carnegie
Commission, examining the origins of the Balkan Wars of 1912 and 1913,
laid a great deal of the blame on strident nationalist propaganda in the
press and from official institutions.[145] Leon Trotsky, later famous as a
Russian Bolshevik leader but then a war correspondent in the Balkans,

[142] Jelavich and Jelavich, *Establishment*, 188–89; Petrovich, *History of Modern Serbia*,
430–31.

[143] Petrovich, *History of Modern Serbia*, 585–86. This situation remained unchanged in
interwar Yugoslavia. See Joseph Rothschild, *East Central Europe Between the Two World Wars*
(Seattle: University of Washington Press, 1974), 237, 277.

[144] Petrovich, *History of Modern Serbia*, 492–93, 614; Jelavich, *History of the Balkans*, vol.
II, 33.

[145] Carnegie Endowment for International Peace, *The Other Balkan Wars* (Washington,
DC: CEIP, 1993), reprinting CEIP, *Report of the International Commission to Inquire into
the Causes and Conduct of the Balkan Wars* (Washington, DC: CEIP, 1914), 19, 50–51.

reported that "agitation for war—never mind with whom: Austria, Bulgaria, Turkey, even the Concert of Europe—has furnished the uniform political keynote of the entire 'independent' press of Belgrade."[146]

In short, Serbian institutions created outlets for mass political energies and pluralistic debate, but they did not provide a stable framework for democratic politics or the coherent assessment of public arguments. In this setting, loyalties could not attach themselves to civic processes as a basis for nationalism. Rather, civic and state institutions, such as dynasties, parties, and newspapers, gained legitimacy by cloaking themselves in the mantle of an extra-institutional loyalty to the Serbian ethnic group. As Petrovich puts it, a weak but modernizing bureaucratic state grafted on elements of pre-modern "folk democracy" to legitimize its rule in an era of mass politics.[147]

### The state made the ethnic nation

This ethnic loyalty, though based on a putative common language, culture, and history, was not primordial and fixed. On the contrary, its content was to some degree constructed and changeable. This can be seen by the evolution of Serbian nationalism in Serbian school textbooks and by its contrasting development in the Croatian part of the Austro-Hungarian Empire.

Initially, Serbian nationalist literature focused on highly romanticized accounts of the glorious medieval Serb kingdom and historic struggles against the Turks.[148] Later, such texts shifted to defining Serbian identity vis-à-vis other South Slav peoples. Typically, this involved attempts to define stateless Slavs still under Ottoman rule as Serbs, while differentiating rival state-building groups as non-nationals. Thus, Macedonians and even Bosnian Muslims were said to be Serbs, but Bulgarians were portrayed as outsiders who were trying to Bulgarize Serbs residing in their state.

The treatment of Croats varied with political circumstances. At first, they tended to be treated as Catholic Serbs, a peripheral offshoot of the ethnic family tree. However, Croatians' generally favorable view of Austria's assertion of rights to Bosnia in 1878 placed them in the category

---

[146] Leon Trotsky, *The War Correspondence of Leon Trotsky: The Balkan Wars, 1912–1913* (New York: Monad, 1980).

[147] Petrovich, *History of Modern Serbia*, 443.

[148] Ibid., 511–13.

of rivals, who were sometimes left off the list of South Slav peoples. In the years immediately before World War I, however, Serbian premier Nikola Pasic was convinced that the central contest would be to determine who would take the lead in unifying the South Slavs in the wake of the collapse of the Ottoman and Austrian Empires. Consequently, Serb literature once again began to treat Croatians as a consanguinary, but secondary Serbian offshoot. Meanwhile, in Croatia, the Austrian governors played a different game, treating Serbian and Croatian culture as distinct but equally worthy. This helped the Serb minority resist assimilation by the Croat majority, and thus won the Serbs as an ally against the Croats' attempts to oppose Austrian rule.[149]

In short, while it is true that the Serbian state relied increasingly on Serbian ethnicity as the basis for its legitimacy, it is also true that the state played a central role in eliciting and defining that ethnic consciousness. As in Western Europe, the state made the nation, but it did so under different constraints and thus made a different product.

These patterns of nineteenth-century Balkan ethnic nationalism seem remarkably familiar in the late twentieth century. This is because some of the same conditions that created Balkan ethnic nationalism in the first place—in particular the collapse of empire and the unleashing of mass politics in multiethnic societies that lack integrative institutions—have been recreated by the collapse of communism. Of course, history never plays itself out exactly the same way twice. Social conditions and historical memories are now sufficiently different to play distinct variations on these historical themes of ethnic nationalism. In this contemporary setting, a number of post-Communist states seem poised to choose between ethnic and civic forms of nationalism. Before turning to a discussion of these cases in the next chapter, it will be helpful to take stock of what the four historical cases show about the factors that are likely to shape these contemporary choices.

## Comparisons, Contrasts, and Causes

The single most important take-home point from the case studies of Germany, Britain, France, and Serbia is one that they hold in common:

[149] Jelavich, *South Slav*, 15, 17–19, 39, 91, 137, 143, 158–59.

in each of these prototypical cases, increasing democracy and increasing freedom of the press gave rise to popular nationalism that resulted in violent conflicts with other nations. In none of these cases was this nationalism or the conflicts it spawned due simply to a long-standing popular cultural rivalry, nor to military necessity. Rather, new or old elites (and often both) used nationalist appeals to attract popular allies in the initial phase of democratization, when institutions regulating political participation were still in their infancy.

In each of these cases, elites promoted nationalism to protect their interests at a time when they increasingly needed mass support to establish effective rule. Nationalism fostered loyalty to the state they ruled, or hoped to rule. It provided an ideology that was popular yet did not subject the elites to full democratic accountability, and it provided the legitimacy lacking in weak administrative or participatory institutions.

People adopted nationalism because they thought it would serve their interests. Sometimes they shared with elites a common interest in the use of force against other nations; sometimes they only thought they did, because they received biased information and analysis from sources controlled by nationalist elites. Often elites used their control over the political agenda to prevent mass groups from gaining access to the political process unless they accepted nationalist terms of debate.

Violent conflicts with other nations were often side effects, sometimes intended, sometimes unintended, of these domestic political interactions between elites and the peoples they ruled. Elites often found themselves trapped in their own nationalist rhetoric, having to act out the ideology they had promoted lest they lose credibility in the eyes of the public, and hence risk losing their power and position.

### Variations across the four varieties of nationalism

Apart from these common themes, the four cases vary in their type of nationalism and their pattern of nationalist conflict. Britain's civic nationalism reflected the adaptability of its elite to democracy and the development of its representative and journalistic institutions before the era of mass suffrage. Civic Britain was no less war-prone than the others, yet it was the most prudent in entering only the fights that it could win and profit from. Revolutionary French nationalism reflected the collapse of the state, which created an incentive for opportunistic new elites to use ideology that exploited nationalist themes and substituted for missing political institutions. Germany's counterrevolutionary nationalism reflected the ability of old elites threatened by democratization to exploit the combination of strong administrative institutions and weak democratic ones to restructure politics in their favor around nationalist themes. These French and German nationalisms were neither limited nor prudent, because their ruling elites' open-ended domestic need for nationalist militancy compensated for institutional weaknesses, in the former case, and staved off social change, in the latter. Serbian ethnic nationalism reflected the need of its weak state to exploit and lock in cultural cleavages as a basis of legitimate rule. Ethnic Serbia was imprudent in its wars, yet it was limited in its objectives by its cultural definition of the nation, which sometimes made it more difficult to whip up support for fighting other Slavs.

Because of the importance of ethnic nationalism in the next chapter on the post-Communist states, let me recapitulate what features this ethnic form shares with the other types, and what distinguishes it from them. Ethnic nationalism arises, like civic nationalism, in eras of expanding democratic political participation, but it does so in conditions where the weakness of representative and deliberative institutions makes civic loyalty infeasible. By default, then, loyalty attaches to the least common denominator, mass culture. Like revolutionary nationalism, ethnic nationalism arises in an institutional vacuum, but in the revolutionary case, political action converges around the re-establishment of temporarily collapsed state institutions, whereas in ethnic nationalism, actions converge on the appropriation of cultural themes to lend legitimacy to the task of building a wholly new state. Like counterrevolutionary nationalism, ethnic nationalism entails mythmaking by hard-pressed ruling elites who are trying to exploit popular nationalism in order to retain power in turbulent conditions of rising political participation. However, in the counterrevolutionary case, those elites command powerful administrative or economic institutions that inflexibly determine their interests and provide leverage over mass groups. In the ethnic case, in contrast, elites command weaker institutional levers, and instead rule by exploiting mass cultural themes. In the ethnic pattern, the tactics of ruling elites become inflexible when they succeed in locking mass political identities into a particular cultural frame.

Though each of the four cases generally corresponded to one of the four main types of nationalism, some of the cases were in minor respects hybrids of two of the types. The value of the fourfold typology is not primarily to pigeonhole each case into one of four mutually exclusive categories. Rather, the typologies reveal different causal dynamics, which may be present in various mixes in actual cases.

In mid-Victorian Britain, for example, Prime Minister Palmerston's nationalism mixed civic themes with counterrevolutionary purposes. Representing elite interests that wanted to slow if not stop democratization after the working-class disturbances of 1848, Palmerston tried to equate British civic nationalism with opposition to autocrats abroad, combined with lower-class deference to the established semiliberal order at home. In another permutation, French nationalism in 1789 was both revolutionary and civic in its principles. However, precisely because of the difficulty of creating a functioning civic polity in a revolutionary institutional vacuum, this combination proved unstable. Administrative institutions, especially the army, turned out to be easier to build than strong representative ones, and French nationalism under Napoleon Bonaparte's military dictatorship evolved from a civic-revolutionary to a pseudocivic counterrevolutionary type.

Hybrids between ethnic and counterrevolutionary patterns are also common. In the contemporary period, for example, Serbia under Slobodan Milosevic has become both ethnic and counterrevolutionary. Entrenched elite interests in the Serbian Communist Party and the Serb-dominated army found ethnic mobilization a promising tactic for surviving an era of partial democratization, in light of the long-established character of ethnic cleavages and the weakness of civic institutions. Thus, fomenting ethnic nationalism helped them achieve their counterrevolutionary ends of holding onto power as the old regime collapsed.

The prevalence of such hybrid cases suggests that one of the attractions of nationalism as a political doctrine is its ambiguity and plasticity. When political institutions are weak and fragmented social interests are strongly opposed, political entrepreneurs need to find an ideology that holds out the prospect of being all things to all people. Politicians find nationalism attractive partly for the same reason that scholars find it hard to define. Thus, hybrid nationalisms often reflect the attempt to serve the narrow interests of ethnic groups or elite cartels, while also seeming to serve the broader public interest.

### Can the conditions causing civic nationalism be replicated?

Among the four cases discussed in the past two chapters, Britain's comparatively prudent and inclusive form of nationalism stands out as the one most worthy of emulation. What light do these historical cases shed on the conditions that have been favorable to the emergence of strong civic institutions and mobile elite interests? Were the conditions that fostered British and other Western civic nationalisms historically unique, or can they be replicated elsewhere? Can potential ethnic conflicts be steered toward civic outcomes, if their causes are better understood? A full answer to these policy questions must wait until the concluding chapter. However, because the feasibility of fostering civic nationalism in multi-ethnic states looms as a key issue in the next chapter on post-Communist nationalism, it will be timely to reflect on what the historical cases suggest about the conditions that permit the development of civic nationalism.

At first glance, the historical patterns seem to imply at best mixed prospects for the development of civic nationalism in the new democracies of the future. But closer scrutiny suggests that the application of the right incentives early in the democratization process may in some cases be able to alter the trajectory of a state's nationalism toward a civic outcome.

The British case suggests that one factor favoring the development of civic nationalism is a comparatively high per capita income and a large middle class. The Weimar case shows, however, that this is not a guarantee of a stable civic outcome. In any case, few contemporary nondemocracies are likely candidates for a wealthy transition in the near future.

The historical cases suggest, furthermore, that the state's strategic vulnerability and form of military resource mobilization affects the character of its nationalism. Civic nationalism is especially likely to develop in international settings where security competition from other states creates an incentive to mobilize popular support, but where geographical buffers keep the intensity of that competition to a moderate level. Examples include Britain, protected by its off-shore location, and Switzerland, protected by its mountainous geography. Such buffers permit successful defense without the creation of large standing armies or the arrogation of power in the hands of an absolutist garrison state. In these conditions, war can be financed by loans floated on private capital markets, thus fostering the development of mobile assets among powerful elites rather than by centralized bureaucracies for the extraction of direct taxes. Social and economic power remains dispersed in private hands, so the state must work through representative institutions to gain access to resources for national defense.[150] Therefore, insofar as the U.S. hegemony promotes military security and liberal economic reform in states undergoing transitions to democracy, contemporary conditions should be conducive for the development of civic nationalism.

The British case also suggests that civic nationalism is more likely when the predemocratic elite has economic interests in common with the rising middle and working classes. In the British case, this dovetailing of interests emerged naturally through the pattern of early textile industrialization. It remains to be seen whether the spontaneous workings of capitalist development in contemporary Russia and China will approximate this British pattern, or whether they will more closely resemble the German pattern, where democracy threatened elite economic interests. Once the causal mechanism is understood, however, it may be possible for the international community to design economic incentives to ease the pain of potentially dangerous elites during democratic transitions.

Most worrisome, the British case suggests that civic nationalism may require the perfection of liberal institutions for elites before democracy can be made available for the masses. Britain enjoyed a long dress rehearsal for democracy, during which everyone enjoyed the right of free speech, but only the rich got to vote. Apart from Britain itself and Britain's colonies, such arrangements have been rare in history, and they have been even more rare in recent times. Many future democratizing states will lack well-developed legal, party, and journalistic institutions because the autocrats that rule them now will prevent their development until it is too late. One of the main dilemmas for proponents of democracy assistance is to figure out how to do in two years what Britain did in two hundred, and like Britain, how to do it in the right sequence.

Finally, however, there is one area where an analysis of the historical cases should engender unexpected optimism about fostering civic nationalism in future democratic transitions. The most common explanation of the origins of civic and ethnic nationalism stresses the different timing of state formation in Western and Eastern Europe. These standard accounts exaggerate the differences between early-forming civic states and later-forming ethnic ones. As a consequence, they overestimate the inevitability of ethnic nationalism in the latter cases.

---

[150] Downing, *Military Revolution*, Chapters 7–9.

Conventional wisdom claims that West European civic-territorial nationalism arose where a strong, centralized state emerged long before the masses began to play role in politics. Thus, popular ethnic or cultural differences were stamped out before they became politicized. The state homogenized language and popular culture through mass education and military service and by creating uniform political institutions and an integrated economic market. Consequently, the nation took the shape of the institutions of the state, and citizenship meant becoming an equal participant in those institutions. As Eugen Weber put it, the state turned "peasants into Frenchmen," despite the original cultural diversity of the peoples inhabiting the territory of France.[151]

In contrast, according to this simple but misleading schema, East European ethnic nationalism emerged where popular national consciousness preceded the creation of modern states. Peoples became politically aware while still entrapped in weak, archaic, imperial institutional forms. In an institutional vacuum, these peoples mobilized politically around their cultural identities or cultural institutions, which were the only usable instruments for mobilization to create an effective modern state. As Clifford Geertz puts it, "in modernizing societies, where the tradition of civil politics is weak and where the technical requirements for an effective welfare government are poorly understood, primordial attachments [are] widely acclaimed as preferred bases for the demarcation of autonomous political units."[152] Whereas in the West the nation took the shape of the already established state, in the East the state allegedly sought to take the shape of the already conscious nation.[153] Because ethnic groups lived interspersed, each had to subjugate, expel, or assimilate the others in order to achieve its goal of a state serving the aims of the nation. As a result, the his-

---

[151] Eugen Weber, *Peasants into Frenchmen* (Stanford: Stanford University Press, 1976).

[152] Clifford Geertz, "Primordial Sentiments and Civil Politics in the New States," in Geertz, ed., *Old Societies and New States* (New York: Free Press of Glencoe, 1963), 110.

[153] See especially Hans Kohn, *The Idea of Nationalism* (New York: Macmillan, 1961; orig. ed., 1944), 329; Anthony Smith, *The Ethnic Origins of Nations* (Oxford: Blackwell, 1986), 131–37; Anthony Smith, "Ethnic Identity and Territorial Nationalism in Comparative Perspective," in Alexander Motyl, ed., *Thinking Theoretically about Soviet Nationalities* (New York: Columbia University Press, 1992), 45–66; and for variations on this theme, Brubaker, *Citizenship and Nationhood*, 4; Gellner, "Nationalism in the Vacuum," in Motyl, ed., *Thinking Theoretically*, 243–54; Ernest Gellner, *Thought and Change* (London: Weidenfeld and Nicolson, 1964), 147–78; Ernest Gellner, *Nations*

tory of the twentieth century in Eastern Europe and the Balkans is one of the eventual unmixing of peoples, since most of the states have become ethnically more homogeneous, mainly as a result of World Wars I and II.[154]

However, the Serbian case shows that reality is not quite so simple as this. In fact, even in the Eastern pattern, the sovereign state or its forerunner often preceded the crystallization of political consciousness among the ethnic group that later formed the core of the nation. Serbia, for example, obtained a status tantamount to sovereignty in the 1830s, following a series of revolts and negotiations in which pig traders bargained with Ottoman overlords for the right to become the region's new pashas. These struggles, in which Ottomanized Christian rebels often aligned with local Muslim merchants, had little national character. Serbian nationalism appeared only later, when Western-influenced Serbian bureaucrats and intellectuals, trying to strengthen and rationalize the Serbian state, used their control over police, elections, investments, and education to break the power of traditional local elites.[155] The builders of nationalism were not primarily the bearers of traditional culture, such as peasants or old aristocrats, but officials, lawyers, and intellectuals—those modernizing circles that Austria's reactionary Count Metternich called the troublemakers.[156] In this sense, the genesis of Eastern nationalism was not quite as different from that of Western nationalism as the schematic version of the story would suggest.

The divergence between the civic and ethnic types was caused not so much by the sequence of the formation of the state and the nation as by the time that elapsed between the two, and consequently, by the strength

*and Nationalism* (Ithaca: Cornell University Press, 1983), 99–101; John Plamenatz, "Two Types of Nationalism," in Eugene Kamenka, ed., *Nationalism: The Nature and Evolution of an Idea* (New York: St. Martin's, 1976). This standard story can be expressed in terms of my two variables of institutional strength and the adaptability of interests. In the Western civic pattern, political institutions are strong, and pre-politicized group identities are adaptable; in the Eastern ethnic pattern, political institutions are weak, and already-politicized group identities are comparatively fixed.

[154] Rogers Brubaker, *Nationalism Reframed* (Cambridge: Cambridge University Press, 1996), Chapter 6.

[155] Daniel Chirot and Karen Barkey, "States in Search of Legitimacy," 34–35; Jelavich, *History of the Balkans*, vol. 1, 379–80; Gale Stokes, "Social Origins of East European Politics," in Daniel Chirot, ed., *The Origins of Backwardness in Eastern Europe* (Berkeley: University of California Press, 1989), 236–37.

[156] Rupert Emerson, *From Nation to Empire* (Boston: Beacon, 1960), 194–95.

of the state during the transition to mass politics. In the West, absolutist states had two centuries to consolidate themselves before the era of mass nationalism, whereas in the East, states had no sooner achieved a degree of independence when they faced the need for mass military mobilization, economic development, and electoral legitimation.[157] Whereas France had the institutional power to transform its polyglot peasants into Frenchmen, the East European states had to appeal to them in whatever terms were at hand, working within existing cultural categories. It is not that Serb, Croat, and Muslim already existed as fixed political categories, but that given the state's institutional limitations, these cultural categories were eas-ier to politicize than were civic-territorial categories like Yugoslav.[158]

This differs only in timing and degree from the experience of the West. Even in France, civic institutions for the expression of popular grievances were largely lacking until the mid-nineteenth century, and consequently popular contention before that time was generally vented through com-munal village channels, not political parties, trade unions, and voluntary associations.[159] Much of the Balkans is still at that stage.[160]

This does not mean that it will be easy to promote civic identities in contemporary cases of late-state formation, such as Ukraine, Belarus, or Kazakhstan. It does imply, however, that the task is not impossible. Unless ethnic identities were already firmly implanted by a predecessor state during an earlier era of partial democratization, the new state elites may have considerable latitude for choice. As we will see in the next chap-ter, post-Communist elites have differed greatly in the style of national-ism that they have chosen to promote.

[157] Stokes, "Social Origins," in Chirot, *Backwardness*, 236, discussing the case of Serbia.

[158] Even Kohn argues that, because of the backwardness of East European society, Eastern nationalists had to politicize culture through education and propaganda, not just tap a political sentiment that was already present. Kohn, *Idea of Nationalism*, 330.

[159] Pierre Birnbaum, *States and Collective Action* (Cambridge: Cambridge University Press, 1988), 33, citing Charles, Louise, and Richard Tilly, *The Rebellious Century: 1830–1930* (Cambridge: Harvard University Press, 1979).

[160] For a recent Romanian example, see Katherine Verdery, *National Ideology under Socialism: Identity and Cultural Politics in Ceausescu's Romania* (Berkeley: University of California Press, 1991), 130–31; also 83–87.

# 5

## Nationalism amid the Ruins

## of Communism

The collapse of communism brought partial democratization to most of the newly independent states and regimes. It also brought a rise in nationalism in many of the post-Communist states. In the former Yugoslavia and in the Caucasus, including the Chechen region inside the Russian Federation, ethnic groups and new states claiming to act on their behalf fought extremely costly wars, which uprooted millions of refugees and killed hundreds of thousands of combatants and civilians.[1] Even some of the instigators of aggressive nationalism paid a heavy price, suffering political ignominy or indictment as war criminals. What accounts

[1] The war in Bosnia uprooted 2,500,000 and, according to some estimates, may have killed as many as 200,000. In Croatia, 320,000 were displaced and perhaps as many as 25,000 killed. In Azerbaijan, these figures were 1,700,000 and 55,000; in Georgia, 475,000 and 17,500; in Tajikistan (which as I explain below was not a nationalist war by my definition), 320,000 and 70,000; and Moldova, 105,000 and 1,000. The war in Chechnya displaced 400,000. See Michael E. Brown, *The International Dimensions of Internal Conflict* (Cambridge: MIT Press, 1996), 4–6.

for this counterproductive nationalist violence in some post-Communist states? Conversely, what explains the success of many other post-Communist states in avoiding ethnic strife?

Democratization played a central role in this outbreak of costly nationalism. All of the warring post-Communist states have experimented with elections and pluralistic politics except for Tajikistan, whose civil war was not by my definition fueled by nationalism. Some of these states carried out elections that the international community deemed free and fair, and all experienced at least a temporary increase in freedom of the press.[2] However, none of these warring states can be called a successfully consolidated democracy except for Slovenia, which was briefly involved at the periphery of the Yugoslav conflict. The most thoroughly consolidated democracies—the Czech Republic, Poland, and Hungary—did not experience any rise in belligerent nationalism. Other relatively successful democracies—Estonia and Latvia—were founded on discriminatory ethnonational principles, yet they have avoided conflict with their ethnic minorities. In short, successful democratization dampened nationalism, whereas partial democratization in some cases promoted it.

I begin by briefly considering some leading explanations for post-Communist nationalist violence and then sketch my own explanation based on democratization and elite persuasion. I test my argument first by examining the three major arenas of post-Communist nationalist conflict—the former Yugoslavia, the conflict between Armenians and Azerbaijan over the disputed province of Nagorno-Karabakh, and the Russian military attacks on the Chechens. In all of these cases, the earliest phase of democratization played a role in promoting nationalist-inspired bloodshed. Then I turn to a briefer discussion of some other post-Communist cases where there was no democratization, only moderate nationalism, or no violent

[2] According to Freedom House, for example, the democracy index improved for Armenia in 1992 and again in 1993, for Georgia in 1992 and 1995, for Russia in 1991, for Yugoslavia in 1988, for Croatia and Slovenia upon independence in 1991 and subsequently, and for Moldova in 1991 and 1994. Civil liberties improved for Armenia in 1992, Yugoslavia in 1989, Russia in 1991, and Croatia in 1995. According to this ranking, Azerbaijan shows increase in freedom in neither index from the USSR 1990 baseline since independence in 1991, but that baseline already reflects an improved position compared to the late 1980s. Tajikistan's rankings became steadily worse after independence. See Adrian Karatnycky, ed., *Freedom in the World* (NY: Freedom House, 1996 and previous editions).

conflict. I show that these variations in the pattern of nationalist conflict are explained by differences in the conditions in which the early phase of the political transition took place: i.e., differences in the level and historical timing of the state's economic development, in the nature of the challenge to elite interests, and in the institutional legacy from communism. Thus, the same three factors that shaped nationalist outcomes in the four historical cases analyzed in the previous chapters were likewise central to the patterns of nationalist war or peace in the post-Communist states. I conclude by comparing the relative propensity for violent conflict of the civic and ethnic forms of post-Communist nationalism (see maps on following pages).

## Competing Explanations for Post-Communist Nationalist Violence

Both scholars and the broader public have extensively debated the causes of the surge in nationalist and ethnic conflict in the post-Communist world. Long-standing popular rivalries, intermingled ethnic residential patterns, and military insecurity resulting from the collapse of empire have all been advanced as purported causes of these conflicts.[3] While such factors certainly played a role in shaping some of these conflicts, each factor by itself does a poor job of explaining why some post-Communist states suffered from nationalist violence, whereas others did not. Past experience of popular ethnic rivalry, intermingled demography, and military insecurity led to nationalist conflict only when the character of popular politics in these newly democratizing states fostered it.

### Long-standing popular rivalries

The most common explanation for post-Communist ethnic conflicts offered in the American press blames ancient hatreds between ethnic groups that were unfettered by the collapse of Communist power. This view errs mainly in overpredicting post-Communist conflict. It is true that there are historical precedents for all of the contemporary conflicts in the former Yugoslavia, Transcaucasia, and Chechnya. Past rivalries and slaughters left a legacy of

[3] Van Evera, "Hypotheses on Nationalism and War," *International Security* 18:4 (Spring 1994), 26–33, provides an excellent list of factors.

*Russia and the Former Soviet Union*

distrust and fear that played a role in escalating the post-Communist violence in these regions. However, there are also historical precedents for
bloody animosity between almost every other imaginable pair of nations in
central Eurasia, yet Hungarians are not fighting Romanians, Estonians and
Ukrainians are not fighting Russians, Bulgarians are not fighting Turks, and
so forth. Conversely, Georgians fought the Ossetian minority despite the

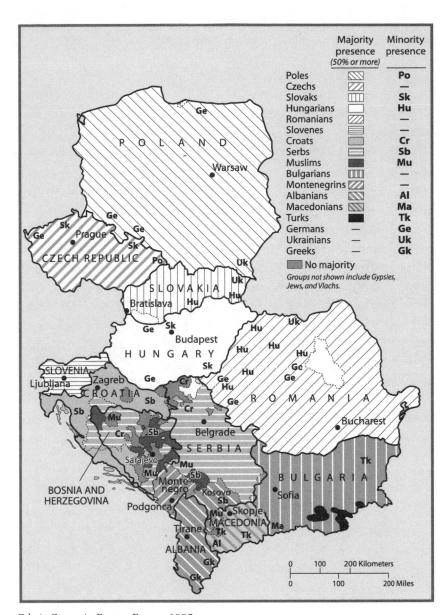

Legend:

| | Majority presence (50% or more) | Minority presence |
|---|---|---|
| Poles | (diagonal crosshatch) | **Po** |
| Czechs | (diagonal lines) | — |
| Slovaks | (vertical lines) | **Sk** |
| Hungarians | (blank) | **Hu** |
| Romanians | (diagonal lines) | — |
| Slovenes | (horizontal lines) | — |
| Croats | (light gray) | **Cr** |
| Serbs | (light gray lines) | **Sb** |
| Muslims | (black) | **Mu** |
| Bulgarians | (vertical lines) | — |
| Montenegrins | (diagonal lines) | — |
| Albanians | (diagonal lines) | **Al** |
| Macedonians | (diagonal lines) | **Ma** |
| Turks | (black) | **Tk** |
| Germans | — | **Ge** |
| Ukrainians | — | **Uk** |
| Greeks | — | **Gk** |

(gray) No majority

*Groups not shown include Gypsies, Jews, and Vlachs.*

*Ethnic Groups in Eastern Europe, 1995*

fact that grassroots cultural animosity seems to be very low: nearly half of Ossetian marriages are with Georgian partners.[4] While popular rivalries were

[4] George Khutsishvili and Neil MacFarlane, "Ethnic Conflict in Georgia," manuscript, 16.

not irrelevant to the mobilization of ethnic conflict in the post-Communist states, they were neither necessary nor sufficient for it, and their presence or strength does not correlate convincingly with the outcomes.

## Demography

Likewise, demography by itself explains little of the variance in post-Soviet outcomes. For example, the situation of ethnically homogeneous Hungary with respect to the Hungarian enclave in Romanian Transylvania mirrors that of homogeneous Armenia facing the Karabakh enclave in Azerbaijan, yet in the first case, the two states signed a treaty recognizing borders and minority rights, whereas the latter pair of nations fought a war. Nor do demographic proportions provide a satisfying explanation for variations in ethnic rivalry. Latvian and Estonian ethnic nationalists claim, for example, that the precariousness of their ethnic majorities compels them to limit the civil rights of the large Russian-speaking minority, whereas Lithuanians can treat their handful of Russians as equals, simply because there are so few of them. But the nearly equal size of the Russian and Kazakh communities in Kazakhstan seems to have had the opposite effect: the Kazakh government is prudently solicitous of Russian concerns. In cases in which political dynamics trigger a rise in exclusionary ethnic nationalism, an intermingled residence pattern will increase the likelihood of violent conflict, but without some other factor to strike the political spark, mixed demographic patterns do not in themselves cause violence.

## Military imbalances and insecurity

Some argue that the collapse of communism has created fertile conditions for nationalist conflict by removing the imperial enforcement of order, by heightening uncertainty about the security of borders, and by creating fluctuations in the balance of power between nations.[5] As always in relations between nations in conditions of anarchy, security fears and the balance of military force surely weigh on the minds of political actors. However, similar strategic conditions can provoke opposite responses,

---

[5] Barry Posen, "The Security Dilemma and Ethnic Conflict," *Survival* 35:1 (Spring 1993), 27–47.

depending on the ideological or political prism through which these conditions are viewed. For example, the prudent decisions of Ukrainians and Kazakhs to shy away from open confrontation with Russians were to some extent colored by the threat of Russian military might looming across the border, yet similar military conditions did not keep the Georgians from provoking a reckless conflict with the Russians' long-standing client nationality, the Ossetians. Thus, to understand the impact of military factors on the likelihood of nationalist conflict, it is necessary to know not only the strategic setting but also the domestic political situation.

## Nationalist elite persuasion and the pattern of democratization

I argue that variations in the intensity of post-Communist nationalist violence were shaped by differences in the post-Communist states' patterns of democratization. Different political conditions in the immediate aftermath of communism created different motives and opportunities for nationalist persuasion and thus affected the type of nationalism that emerged. These patterns were influenced by (1) the state's degree and timing of economic development, (2) the degree to which democratization threatened elite interests, and (3) the nature of its political institutions during the transition.

### The Timing of Economic Development

The first step in understanding these patterns of nationalist war and peace is to place the post-Communist states into three categories according to their trajectories of economic development: early, late, and extremely late development. One group of states developed early, relative to the other states of this region. These include Poland, the Czech Republic, Hungary, Estonia, Latvia, and Slovenia. By the 1920s, their populations had achieved high levels of mass literacy or had begun to shift in large numbers into nonagricultural employment. In the 1930s, a number of these countries did experience nationalist movements, but this was at a very early phase of their democratization and in a destabilizing international context sandwiched between Hitler's Germany and Stalin's Russia. The further development in the Communist era of a highly educated, urban, white-collar class consolidated the underlying social preconditions for democracy in these countries, though communism itself was not democratic. When communism collapsed, these countries' educated work forces had the skills needed to make democratic and market institutions work,[6] and the people replaced communism through democratic popular movements or "roundtable" negotiations among nascent parties, trade unions, and civic groups. This led to the relatively quick consolidation of civic politics, or in the cases of Latvia and Estonia, to a comparatively moderate form of ethnic politics that creates the possibility for compromise with and eventual inclusion of the Russian minority in civic life. Except for Slovenia's brief war of independence against the Yugoslav army, none of these states experienced ethnic violence in the post-Communist period. Thus, relatively early economic development produced moderate nationalism and little if any nationalist violence.

At the other end of the spectrum are the extremely late developers. These include the Central Asian states of Turkmenistan, Uzbekistan, Tajikistan, and (with some qualifications) Kazakhstan and Kyrgyzstan. These states have low per capita income and high levels of employment in agriculture. Their populations achieved literacy relatively late. For the most part, they lacked effective mass movements, had sham elections and a muzzled press, expressed a tepid official nationalism, and experienced little if any nationalist conflict in the aftermath of communism's collapse. Like Western Europe before the eighteenth century, they are at a prenational stage, where the masses are not yet sufficiently mobilized into political life to sustain a coherent nationalist movement. Tajikistan is the only extremely late developer to undergo a major violent conflict. However, this resulted not from nationalism or ethnicity, but rather from the collapse of the authoritarian state. The resulting situation of anarchy produced civil strife among a variety of local social groups, few if any of which can legitimately be called ethnic or nationalist.[7] In short,

[6] Herbert Kitschelt, "A Silent Revolution in Europe?" in Jack Hayward and Edward C. Page, *Governing the New Europe* (Cambridge: Polity Press, 1995), 141–45, 148. For a similar conceptualization contrasting northern and southern Italy, see Robert Putnam, *Making Democracy Work* (Princeton: Princeton University Press, 1993). See also Vladimir Tismaneanu, *Reinventing Politics: Eastern Europe from Stalin to Havel* (New York: Free Press, 1992). On the role of engineers, mid-level managers, teachers, lawyers, and agronomists in the Estonian independence movement, see Anatol Lieven, *The Baltic Revolution* (New Haven: Yale University Press, 1993), 226. On nationalism in the 1930s, see Joseph Rothschild, *East Central Europe between the Two World Wars* (Seattle: University of Washington Press, 1974).

[7] Barnett Rubin, "Russian Hegemony and State Breakdown in the Periphery," in

extremely late development produced no nationalism and no nationalist conflict.

Between the early and the extremely late developers are the late developers. These include Russia, Ukraine, Slovakia, the Balkan states (the former Yugoslavia, Romania, Bulgaria, and Albania), and the Caucasus (Armenia, Georgia, and Azerbaijan). These states generally lie between the early developers and the Central Asian states in the timing of their move out of peasant agriculture and the emergence of a literate, middle-class population. For example, in 1897 the literacy rate was three times lower in Russia than in the Baltic states, but three times higher in Russia than in Central Asia.[8] Employment in the late developing states was still about 80 percent agricultural in the 1920s, as compared with 65 percent in Poland, 51 percent in Hungary, and 25 percent in Czechoslovakia (even though its Slovak part was mainly agricultural).[9] Despite subsequent Communist industrialization and educational campaigns, these late developers generally continued to lag behind the relatively early developers in per capita income and in the development of a sophisticated middle-class society.[10] In the Caucasus, education and industrialization increased to relatively high levels under communism, but clannish social patterns characteristic of pre-modern society remained strongly entrenched. Thus, these late-developing

---

Barnett Rubin and Jack Snyder, eds., *Post-Soviet Political Order: Conflict and State-Building* (London: Routledge, 1998), Chapter 7.

[8] David Laitin, *Identity in Formation* (Ithaca: Cornell University Press, 1998), 64.

[9] Herbert Kitschelt, "Formation of Party Cleavages in Post-Communist Democracies," *Party Politics* 1:4 (1995), 456.

[10] The white-collar sector of the Soviet workforce in 1979 by nationality was Estonian and Georgian, 32 percent; Russian and Armenian, 31; Latvian and Kazakh, 28; Lithuanian, 27; Azerbaijani, Ukrainian, and Belorussian, 23; Kirgiz, 20; Uzbek, 18; Turkmen, 16; Tajik and Moldavian, 15. Robert J. Kaiser, *The Geography of Nationalism in Russia and the USSR* (Princeton: Princeton University Press, 1994), Table 5.12, p. 237. See also Table 5.13, p. 239. Note, however, that Daniel Treisman, "Russia's 'Ethnic Revival': The Separatist Activism of Regional Leaders in a Postcommunist Order," *World Politics* 49:2 (January 1997), 212–49, esp. 232, finds that education levels and other attributes of modernity fail to correlate with separatist movements within the Russian Republic. For data on per capita income, see World Bank, *Social Indicators of Development* (Baltimore: Johns Hopkins University Press, 1995). On the correlation between the strength of civil society and the nature of the transition in Eastern Europe, see David Stark and Laszlo Brust, *Postsocialist Pathways* (Cambridge: Cambridge University Press, 1998), 16.

societies were still at a transitional stage, where rapid consolidation of civic politics was impossible. This created the potential for the politics of nationalist mythmaking (see Tables 5.1 and 5.2, pp. 200–202).

In the former Yugoslavia and the Caucasus, these late developers experienced wars fueled by nationalism; in other late developers, nationalism was more controlled and conflict was minimal. These contrasting outcomes were shaped by two factors that I discuss next: (1) the pattern of threats to elite interests and (2) the institutional legacy of the Communist period.

**Threats to Elites**

In the cases of warring nationalisms in late-developing states, such as the former Yugoslavia, elites faced rising demands for mass political participation or the impending likelihood of it. Typically, elites in these cases were divided among themselves, faced strong challenges from opposition groups, and therefore had a strong incentive to find popular allies to prevail in the political struggle. Under these conditions, nationalism—usually ethnic, but sometimes civic—was an attractive instrument to mobilize mass support and to demobilize support for opponents. The old Communist elite groups threatened by political and economic change, as well as the political entrepreneurs trying to ride those changes into power, struggled to dominate the marketplace of ideas and to purvey nationalist myths that would serve these purposes.

In contrast, nationalism was more moderate in those late-developing states, such as Ukraine, where former Communists encountered weaker elite and mass opposition in the early stages of the transition.[11] These states faced poorly developed civil societies that, without the aid of state bureaucracy, lacked the capacity to organize collective action. In these cases, old elites adopted a moderate brand of nationalism that was designed not to shape a mass movement but to lay a popular veneer over a superficially reformed Communist state. The former Communist elites in these states typically sought to limit democratic competition, hindered freedom of the press, and slowly introduced market reforms in such a way

---

[11] Tim Snyder and Milada Vachudova, "Are Transitions Transitory? Two Types of Political Change in Eastern Europe Since 1989," *East European Politics and Societies* 11:1 (Winter 1997), 1–35, esp. 6; see also Valerie Bunce, *Subversive Institutions: The Design and Destruction of Socialism and the State* (Cambridge: Cambridge University Press, 1999), and Stark and Bruszt, *Postsocialist Pathways*, 18.

that the elites could convert their bureaucratic power into private property. In some cases (e.g., Slovakia under Vladimir Meciar and Romania under Ion Iliescu), former Communists adopted the rhetoric of ethnic nationalism and included some fringe ethnic nationalist groups in their political coalitions. In other cases (notably Ukraine), nationalism took a more civic cast. But in both the civic and ethnic patterns, the intensity of nationalist mobilization and nationalist conflict remained low. Since mass opposition groups remained relatively inert and disorganized, the old elites concluded that stirring them up with intense nationalist appeals would be unnecessary and counterproductive.

**Institutional Variations**

The legacy of Communist institutions also affected the pattern of nationalist politics in the post-Communist transition. Institutions for democratic participation and public debate were weak or absent everywhere in the Communist world. The early developers, such as the Czech Republic, had relatively sophisticated societies that could create workable democratic institutions. In most of the extremely late developers, there was no transition to democratic politics at all. In the late developers, however, the gap between rising political participation and the weakness of democratic institutions created the potential for an intensification of nationalism. How this potential played itself out depended in part on the administrative institutions inherited from the Communist period and on differences in the way that groups were organized to take part in politics. Especially important for the trajectory of nationalism and nationalist conflict are the different legacies of (1) ethnically segmented federal states versus unitary states, (2) states at the former imperial center of a multinational conglomeration versus those at the periphery, and (3) bureaucratic versus patronage-based systems of administration.

*Ethnofederalism.* Three Communist states were organized on ethnofederal lines: the Soviet Union, Yugoslavia, and Czechoslovakia. They were composed of ethnically titled republics that had statelike administrative structures staffed by elites who were able to promote the language and culture of their titular ethnic group. All three states broke up along ethnofederal boundaries when communism collapsed.[12] Violent ethnic conflict occurred in two of these cases, the former Soviet Union and the

---

[12] Bunce, *Subversive Institutions*, 110–12, 136–40.

**Table 5.1 Selected Indicators of Development in Eastern Europe and the USSR: Pre–WWII and 1950–70**

| | Pre–WWII | 1950 | 1960 | 1970 |
|---|---|---|---|---|
| ***Illiterates*** *(percent of total population)* | | | | |
| Bulgaria | 31.5% (1934) | | (10.7%)[a] | |
| Czechoslovakia | 4.1% (1930) | | | |
| Hungary | 9.0% (1930) | | 3.8% | 2.4% |
| Poland | 23.1% (1931) | 5.8% | 2.7% | |
| Romania | 42.9% (1930) | 23.1% | | |
| USSR | 43.4% (1926) | | 1.5% | 0.3% |
| Yugoslavia | 44.6% (1931) | 25.4% | 21.0% | 15.1% |
| ***Infant Mortality*** *(rates per thousand live births)* | | | | |
| Bulgaria | 147 (1935) | 94.5 | 45.1 | 27.3 |
| Czechoslovakia | 130 (1935) | 77.7 | 23.5 | 22.1 |
| Hungary | 157 (1935) | 85.7 | 47.6 | 35.9 |
| Poland | 137 (1935) | 111.2 | 54.8 | 33.4 |
| Romania | 182 (1935) | 116.7 | 74.6 | 49.4 |
| USSR | 181 (1926) | 80.7 | 35.3 | 24.7 |
| Yugoslavia | 153 (1935) | 118.4 | 87.7 | 55.5 |

**Agricultural Population** *(active earners and dependents in agriculture as percent of total population)*

| | | | | |
|---|---|---|---|---|
| Bulgaria | 73.2% (1934) | | 45.2% | |
| Czechoslovakia | 34.7% (1930) | 24.9% | 19.3% | 13.2% |
| Hungary | 51.9% (1930) | 49.3% | 34.8% | 22.8% |
| Poland | 60.0% (1931) | 46.4% | 37.8% | 29.8% |
| Romania | 72.3% (1930) | | | (45.1%)[b] |
| USSR | 77.5% (1926) | | | 22.8% |
| Yugoslavia | 76.6% (1931) | | 49.6% | 38.2% |

**Urbanization** *(population in urban areas 20,000 and over as percent of total population)*

| | | | | |
|---|---|---|---|---|
| Bulgaria | 12.1% (1934) | | (29.1%)[c] | 39.7% |
| Czechoslovakia | 16.6% (1930) | 23.6% | 25.3% | 31.1% |
| Hungary | 29.1% (1930) | 34.3% | 37.0% | |
| Poland | 17.0% (1931) | 25.6% | 31.8% | 37.3% |
| Romania | 13.4% (1930) | 17.1% | 19.6% | 28.4% |
| USSR | 12.0% (1926) | | 35.6% | 44.3% |
| Yugoslavia | | | 18.8% | 26.0% |

[a] Average of 1956 and 1965 figures
[b] 1966 figure
[c] Average of 1956 and 1965 figures

Note: Where figures are not given, reliable information was not available.
Source: Paul S. Shoup, *The East European and Soviet Data Handbook: Political, Social, and Developmental Indicators, 1945–1975* (New York: Columbia University Press, 1981), p. 382.

### Table 5.2 Literacy Rates* in the Former Soviet Union, 1897–1939

| | *Percent* | | |
|---|---|---|---|
| *Territorial Unit* | *1897* | *1926* | *1939* |
| Soviet Union | 28.4** | 56.6 | 87.4 |
| Russian Republic | 29.6[†] | 60.9 | 89.7 |
| Ukraine | 27.9 | 63.6 | 88.2 |
| Belorussia | 32.0 | 59.7 | 80.8 |
| Uzbekistan | 3.6 | 11.6 | 78.7 |
| Kazakhstan | 8.1 | 25.2 | 83.6 |
| Georgia | 23.6 | 53.0 | 89.3 |
| Azerbaijan | 9.2 | 28.2 | 82.8 |
| Lithuania | 54.2 | | 76.7 |
| Moldavia[‡] | 22.2 | | 45.9 |
| Latvia | 79.7 | | 92.7 |
| Kyrgyzstan | 3.1 | 16.5 | 79.8 |
| Tajikistan | 2.3 | 3.8 | 82.8 |
| Armenia | 9.2 | 38.7 | 83.9 |
| Turkmenistan | 7.8 | 14.0 | 77.7 |
| Estonia | 96.2 | | 98.6 |

* Percent of population between nine and forty-nine years old
** Since the Soviet Union was founded only in 1922, this is the figure for the Tsarist Russian Empire as a whole.
[†] Figure for Russian region of the Tsarist Empire
[‡] Now Moldova; before 1939, Bessarabia
Note: Some caution must be exercised in interpreting the literacy data, since the criteria used to establish whether or not a person was literate changed over time. For example, while in 1897 a person was considered literate if he or she claimed the ability to read, in 1926 literacy was based on the respondent's ability to sign his or her last name.
Source: Robert J. Kaiser, *The Geography of Nationalism in Russia and the USSR* (Princeton: Princeton University Press, 1994), p. 130.

former Yugoslavia. All other former Communist states had unitary forms of administration, where minority ethnic groups did not have statelike republics. None of these unitary states broke up, and none experienced ethnic violence. While ethnofederalism does not always produce ethnic violence in late-developing, transitional societies, it does create strong incentives for their elites to mobilize mass support around ethnic themes. When other factors are favorable for intense nationalist mobilization, the legacy of ethnofederalism heightens the likelihood of conflict.

***Imperial centers.*** Two post-Communist states (Russia and Serbia) were the former "imperial" centers of their erstwhile multinational states (the Soviet Union and Yugoslavia). As such, they inherited much of the military power of the former empires and were the headquarters for the remnants of imperial bureaucracies and economic networks. This left an institutional and ideological legacy that loaded the dice in favor of using military force against nations formerly under their domination.[13] As part of their domestic strategy for consolidating a political hold over the old imperial core, nationalist or neo-imperialist politicians faced the temptation of using force in areas of their breakaway empire. The availability of these military forces creates a heightened possibility of nationalist conflict but does not make it inevitable. While Serbia, for example, used the remnants of the Yugoslav army against several of the other former Yugoslav nations, Russia has done so principally in the case of Chechnya (which was not a "union republic" in the Soviet ethnofederal system, but rather a semi-autonomous region within the Russian Federal Republic). These former imperial centers, like Germany earlier in this century, embarked on their transition to democracy with strong administrative institutions, including the military, but weak democratic ones—a combination that has proved conducive to aggressive nationalism.

***Patronage politics.*** A final institutional factor is the difference between successor states that inherited a legacy of legalistic bureaucratic administration under communism and those that were dominated by informal patronage networks. While formal administrative institutions were roughly the same across the post-Communist states, these institutions operated differently in practice. In the early developers, like the Czech Republic, the German Democratic Republic (East Germany), and the Baltics, economic administration tended to be more impersonal and bureaucratic.[14] In the Caucasus, in contrast, the economy was organized around clannish networks linking patrons and clients in ways that depended more on local ties than on bureaucratic lines of authority. When the Soviet Union began to unravel, the Baltics and the Caucasus

[13] Alexander Motyl, "After Empire: Competing Discourses and Inter-State Conflict in Post-Imperial Eastern Europe," in Rubin and Snyder, *Post-Soviet Political Order*, 14–33; see also Bunce, *Subversive Institutions*, 117-20.

[14] Kitschelt, "Formation of Party Cleavages in Post-Communist Democracies," 455; for a related point, see Laitin, *Identity in Formation*, 66–67.

both experienced large mass political movements in favor of national independence and popular self-rule. This reflected the relatively high levels of education and urbanization in both regions. However, the organization of these mass movements differed from one another, reflecting the regions' different patterns of organized collective action left over from the Communist and pre-Communist periods. In the Baltic, mass politics quickly took shape along Western legal and civic lines.[15] In the Caucasus, mass politics was hijacked by clans and established patronage networks whose rivalrous interests turned out to be irreconcilable with democratic processes. Civic politics requires the subordination of self-interest to the rule of law and the acceptance of electoral defeat as a tolerable, temporary disadvantage. These notions were alien to the clannish competitors in the Caucasus, who exploited popular mobilization and elections as mere instruments to seize and plunder the state.[16] Immoderate appeals to ethnic nationalism proved to be attractive weapons in this factional rivalry.

### Nationalist Mythmaking and the Yugoslav Breakup

Between the breakup of Yugoslavia in 1991 and the signing of the 1995 Dayton Accord providing for the stationing of NATO troops in Bosnia, armed conflict and atrocities claimed some 200,000 lives in the former Yugoslavia and displaced over 2,500,000 people.[17] The expulsion of ethnic Albanians from Serbian-controlled Kosovo in 1999 caused thousands more deaths and hundreds of thousands more refugees. All sides suffered in cycles of aggression and retaliation, and all sides engaged in strategies that seem to have been self-defeating. For example, Croatian fears of a potentially traitorous Serbian internal minority led to the introduction in 1991 of Croat police into Serbian villages in Croatia's border regions, which acted as a self-fulfilling prophecy, provoking an alliance between those Serbs and the adjacent Serbian state. Serbs in Croatia and Bosnia perpetrated violent expulsions and massacres against Croats and Bosnian Muslims, actions that

---

[15] Gale Stokes, *Three Eras of Political Change in Eastern Europe* (New York: Oxford University Press, 1997), 179–80.

[16] For a similar analysis in the Latin American context, see Guillermo O'Donnell, "Illusions about Consolidation," *Journal of Democracy* 7:2 (April 1996), 34–51.

[17] Brown, *International Dimensions*, 4–6.

*The Former Yugoslavia, 1999*

were paid back in kind by Croats and Muslims after international military aid to Serbia's victims and an international economic blockade of Serbia eventually turned the military balance in Croatia and Bosnia against the Serbs. The 1999 war over Kosovo likewise proved costly to all sides. Ethnic Albanians fighting for Kosovo's freedom from Serbian rule provoked the Serbs into an escalating campaign of atrocities against Albanian residents, which in turn triggered a massive NATO bombing campaign against Serbia, including attacks on its capital, Belgrade. This was countered by a Serb campaign to force a substantial portion of the Albanians to leave Kosovo for Albania or Macedonia. All the former Yugoslav peoples paid dearly for this upsurge of nationalist violence

This outcome occurred in circumstances that, according to commonly accepted liberal theory, should have been quite promising. The power of the central Yugoslav state and the Yugoslav Communist Party was evaporating by the 1980s, giving rise to a more pluralistic political environment in most of the federal republics. Political and economic decentralization, which are widely advocated liberal prescriptions for authoritarian multiethnic societies, had been accelerating since the 1960s. At the time of the breakup, the central Yugoslav government was advocating thorough market reforms along lines approved by Western lending agencies. Bureaucratic representation for all ethnic groups, rights for ethnic minorities to veto legislation, and resource transfers from richer to poorer ethnic groups and regions were standard practices.[18] As power was devolving to the various republics, politics was also becoming more competitive within the republics. By 1990, eighty-six political parties had formed, six of them in Serbia.[19] Ruling groups in all of the republics were facing open electoral competition from parties that ranged from ultranationalist to liberal. According to Freedom House, civil liberties and freedom of speech, though still far from perfect, had improved somewhat on the eve of the breakup.[20] During the 1980s, although journalists and intellectuals might still suffer for deviating from the views of the powerful, some of them were able to seize opportunities to take those risks. Socially, the enforced ethnic tolerance of the Communist years had created an integrated, secular, urban culture in which the rate of interethnic marriages reached as high as one-third among some groups. In short, according to standard liberal prescriptions, Yugoslavia should have been well positioned for peaceful democratization.

In fact, however, this combination of incipient democratization and political decentralization contributed to the rise of aggressive nationalism and led to the derailment of liberal reform. Impending democratization threatened the position of the Communist elite, giving them an incentive to reposition themselves at the head of popular nationalist movements. At the same time, the ethnofederal character of Yugoslavia's institutions gave these elites administrative resources to shape events and public debates in ways that sharpened ethnic cleavages. The historical legacy of Serbian and Croatian nationalism laid a groundwork for these developments, and

[18] Sabrina Ramet, *Nationalism and Federalism in Yugoslavia, 1962–1991,* 2d ed. (Bloomington: Indiana University Press, 1992), 36.

[19] Ramet, *Nationalism and Federalism,* 234.

[20] Raymond Gastil (and later R. Bruce McColm), ed., *Freedom in the World* (New York: Freedom House, 1988–89), 411–12 in the 1988 yearbook, 272–74 in 1989–90.

security fears occasioned by the collapse of the Yugoslav state further heightened ethnic tensions. Nonetheless, these factors would probably not have been sufficient to trigger violent ethnic conflict, apart from the persuasion campaigns of ethnofederal elites.

The following sections discuss, first, the historical legacies that created a propensity for conflict; second, the causes and consequences of Yugoslav ethnofederalism; third, Milosevic's nationalist strategy in response to threats facing Communist elites in the mid-1980s; and finally, his use of the media to sell this strategy.

### Historical legacies: Early democratization, late economic development

As the last chapter discussed, Serbia's long experience as an independent democratizing state before World War I stamped the political identity of the Serbian people in the mold of ethnic nationalism. When the Versailles Treaty united Serbia, Croatia, Bosnia, Macedonia, and Montenegro to create Yugoslavia after World War I, Serbs continued to think of themselves as a distinct nation heading a multiethnic state. Tension over the Serbs' preference for greater centralization under their own predominance and the Croats' desire for greater local autonomy was a common theme in Yugoslav politics from the democratic regime of the 1920s through the Communist regime after World War II. Thus, Serbia's distinct national identity, forged during the nineteenth century, was persistent, yet this distinct identity was compatible with integration into a broader South Slav identity on Serbian terms. This historical legacy helped to set the stage for the violent conflict of 1991 but did not in itself determine it.

Another historical factor that primed Yugoslavia for nationalist conflict was its relatively late economic development. Peasant agriculture dominated the Yugoslav economy until well into the Communist era. Whereas a few urbanized areas of Yugoslavia were cosmopolitan and civic in their orientation by the late 1980s, the large rural areas were bastions of support for ethnic nationalism and authoritarianism, just as they had been in the years leading up to World War II.[21] Because the early phase of democ-

---

[21] Laitin, *Identity in Formation*, 13; see also Aleksa Djilas, *The Contested Country: Yugoslav Unity and Communist Revolution 1919–1953* (Cambridge: Harvard University Press, 1991), 103–27, on the rural base of support for the Ustashe from the 1920s through World War II.

ratization preceded economic development in Serbia, mass politics arrived without the sophisticated middle class needed to sustain a civic outcome. Serbia reversed the developmental sequence that led to Britain's civic outcome, and as a result, the country was primed for rivalrous ethnic nationalism.

A final historical legacy was the ethnic slaughter that took place during World War II. When the Nazis invaded Yugoslavia, they installed in power a Croatian regime run by the Ustashe fascist party. This group had had a relatively small following among rural Croats before the war and lacked the active support of most Croats. In order to rally Croats to the fascist regime, the Ustashe arbitrarily attacked Serb villagers, who retaliated against neighboring Croats, polarizing ethnic relations and driving the Croats into the arms of the fascist state.[22] The horrific atrocities perpetrated by and against all ethnic groups at this time left a legacy of fear and distrust, which provided a backdrop for the nationalist mythmaking of the late 1980s. Nonetheless, the fairly high level of ethnic intermarriage among urban Yugoslavs during the Communist period suggests that many were able to focus blame for these killings on fascists and on the violent times, rather than generalizing blame on all members of other ethnic groups.

Thus, it would be misleading to argue that incipient democratization caused ethnic conflict in the early 1990s simply because of deep-seated hatreds and historically unreconcilable demands for national self-rule on the part of Yugoslavia's constituent ethnic groups. Historical legacies created the conditions from which conflict could emerge, but the institutional context of ethnofederalism and the mythmaking of opportunistic elites were required to activate this latent potential.

### Ethnofederal institutions: Empowering the nationalists

Another factor loading the dice in favor of ethnic conflict was the radically decentralized ethnofederal structure of the Yugoslav state. Except for multiethnic Bosnia, each of the other republics—Serbia, Croatia, Slovenia, and Macedonia—was dominated by the majority ethnic group whose name it bore. Within Serbia, this ethnofederal logic was formally recapitulated by the semi-autonomous regions of Kosovo, with its Albanian majority, and Voivodina, with its heavy concentration of Hungarians. A

---

[22] Djilas, *Contested Country*, 122.

rotating, eight-person presidency composed of representatives from the various republics oversaw cooperation among these units. Communist Yugoslavia's founder, Marshall Josip Tito, was the ninth (and permanent) member of the presidency until his death in 1980.

Although Communist Yugoslavia had always had an ethnofederal state, the decentralizing reforms of the 1960s and early 1970s sharply increased the power of the ethnic republics. Two-thirds of the federal budget went to the army, but most other tasks were devolved to the republics.[23] By the early 1980s, the relationship among the republics was already being compared to an anarchic balance-of-power system.[24] The central state was entirely lacking in economic, representative, or media institutions to accommodate or co-opt pressures for expanded political participation that developed later in the 1980s. The first elections took place in the ethnic republics for republic-level officials and served to legitimate further the devolution of power.[25]

In this balkanized structure, the Yugoslav army, disproportionately commanded by Serb officers, remained the one strong institution that was committed to the central state. However, its comparative advantage was in violence, not in democratic participation. Moreover, many of its high command shared the Serb vision of a centralized Yugoslavia, unified under Serb and army leadership. Thus, the army was useless as a tool for holding the federation together through democratic reform, but it was highly useful as an instrument for supporting ethnic Serbs stranded in Croatia and Bosnia.

But was this institutional pattern an independent cause of the conflict, or had ethnofederal institutions been created precisely because fearful, rivalrous ethnic nationalists had insisted on creating those institutions in the first place? In part, ethnofederal arrangements did reflect prior nationalist feelings. In 1943, the League of Communists promised a federal constitution as a way of attracting wary nationalities to the common cause of ousting the Nazi-supported regime.[26] The further devolution of power to

---

[23] Susan Woodward, *Balkan Tragedy* (Washington, DC: Brookings, 1995), 39.

[24] Ramet, *Nationalism and Federalism*, Chapters 1 and 2.

[25] Juan Linz and Alfred Stepan, "Political Identities and Electoral Sequences: Spain the Soviet Union, and Yugoslavia," *Daedalus* 121:2 (Spring 1992), 123–40; Jim Seroka and Vukasin Pavlovic, eds., *The Tragedy of Yugoslavia: The Failure of Democratic Transformation* (Armonk, NY: M. E. Sharpe, 1992).

[26] Woodward, *Balkan Tragedy*, 30.

the republics in the 1960s and 1970s, however, can only partly be ascribed to ethnic rivalry per se. The more important motive was the need to revive the moribund economy through decentralizing, market-oriented reforms. In particular, the wealthier regions, Croatia and Slovenia, sought to diminish the central government's uneconomical investments in the less developed regions. These decentralizing changes were favored not only by nationalists in the more advanced republics, but also by those whom some Western analysts call "liberals"—people who sought the adoption of profitability criteria for investments, greater pluralism within the Communist party, and a more open society with greater respect for human rights. For liberals and their allies, including party leader Tito, the weakening of the central state and the fueling of nationalism was an unintended consequence of federalism, not its objective. [27] The institutions, not simply the underlying nationalistic preferences of some of the political actors, played an independent role in shaping the outcome.

### Challenges facing the post-Tito elites and their nationalist responses

After Tito's death in 1980, politicians began to maneuver in search of new bases of support in the increasingly decentralized system. This coincided with a period of growing economic crisis. By 1985–86, annual inflation stood at 50 percent. Unemployment reached 20 percent outside of Slovenia and Croatia, creating what has been described as a "revolutionary situation." [28] This crisis heightened incentives for an intensification of nationalism in several ways.

By the 1980s, most of Yugoslavia's elites accepted that a solution to the economic impasse would require further devolution of central authority, marketization, and local initiative. Even Milosevic, as president of the bank of Serbia in 1983–1985, argued for market-oriented policies. [29] This economic decentralization further strengthened the ethnic republics at the expense of the central state. Reinforcing this trend, the economic cri-

[27] Ramet, *Nationalism and Federalism*, 83–84.

[28] Woodward, *Balkan Tragedy*, 73; see also Branka Magas, *The Destruction of Yugoslavia* (London: Verso, 1993), 53.

[29] Mihailo Crnobrnja, *The Yugoslav Drama* (Montreal: McGill-Queen's University Press, 1994), 84–85; see also Magas, *Destruction of Yugoslavia*, 166.

sis disproportionately disrupted trade between republics and made the control of local economic resources more crucial.[30]

Despite general agreement on market-oriented solutions, the varieties of market reform that Serbia preferred differed from those preferred by Croatia and Slovenia. The latter two were better adapted to attempt a strategy of economic liberalization and acceptance of the strict conditions imposed by the International Monetary Fund. The Serb economy, in contrast, was more tied to an uncompetitive metallurgical sector and East-bloc trade on the Danube.[31] Although Yugoslavia's president promoted liberalization, the central government commanded so few resources that the commitment to meet IMF targets could be made only by the true power centers, the republics. But some of them, including Serbia, were unwilling to meet these targets.[32] As a result, the economic crisis continued, and power further devolved to the ethnic republics.

Though hard pressed by the dilemmas of economic reform and the need to attract support in a more open political system, Communist elites were able to exploit the increasing powers of the ethnic republics in devising strategies for political survival.[33] Milosevic was especially astute. By the early 1980s, he had already served loyally under pragmatic, moderate Serbian party leaders like Ivan Stambolic, the head of the Serb government from 1980 to 1982 and president of Serbia in 1986. In the new circumstances, however, Milosevic saw that the nationalism issue could be exploited to reconcile popular politics with continued authoritarian leadership, while also presenting a chance to

[30] Woodward, *Balkan Tragedy*, Chapter 3.

[31] Ibid., 29.

[32] On the IMF's role, see Woodward, *Balkan Tragedy*, Chapter 3; Magas, *Destruction of Yugoslavia*, 96–99.

[33] Woodward, *Balkan Tragedy*, 15. Sabrina Ramet, likewise, places the rise of eth-nonationalist conflict in the context of collapsing authoritarian institutions and the rise of mass politics: "As the 1980s wore on, it became clear that the fragmentation of power engineered by Tito's quasi-confederal but one-party framework was producing institutional weakness and political chaos. Chaos, of course, creates maneuvering room and uncertainty—which give the sense of freedom. And this inevitably opened the door to greater political participation by large numbers of citizens, as one could predict on the basis of Samuel P. Huntington's classic work on political order." Ramet, *Nationalism and Federalism*, 214.

push aside less nimble leaders like Stambolic, who shunned nationalist rhetoric.[34]

A 1986 "Memorandum on the Position of Serbia in Yugoslavia," signed by many prestigious members of the Serbian Academy of Sciences, provided the formula for a nationalist pseudodemocracy that would play into Milosevic's hands. Decrying the constraints placed on Serbia by the constitutional rights accorded to non-Serbs in the Serbian provinces of Kosovo and Voivodina, the memorandum called for a new constitution to provide for the sovereignty and self-determination of "the Serbian people," defined in terms of the ethnic nation, not in terms of democratic participation by individuals.[35] Elite groups, including Communist-era parliamentarians and intellectuals, jumped on the nationalist bandwagon, and Milosevic replaced Stambolic in April 1987.[36]

Milosevic's trumpeting of wrongs done to Serbs in Kosovo proved especially popular with people who had previously taken no part in the political process, especially older, rural, less-educated Serbs. These constituencies, who voted heavily for Milosevic's party in the 1990 Serbian elections, perceived little potential gain from market-oriented, westernizing, liberalizing reforms.[37] Milosevic succeeded, says Veljko Vujacic, by "giving free rein to mass activity, and thereby satisfying the aspirations for political participation of an audience disgusted with the ineffectiveness of institutions."[38]

Even so, Milosevic was not the most extreme nationalist competing in the elections. Other parties campaigned on platforms of abolishing entirely the autonomy of the Voivodina and Kosovo regions.[39] In Croatia, likewise, the campaign leading up to the April 1990 election featured an explosion of nationalist rhetoric. Surveys recorded a large increase in ethnic tension between Serbs and Croats during those months.[40] The nationalist strategy served not only to mobilize a base of popular support for

[34] Magas, *Destruction of Yugoslavia*, 194–97.

[35] Crnobrnja, *The Yugoslav Drama*, 98.

[36] Woodward, *Balkan Tragedy*, 92–93; Magas, *Destruction of Yugoslavia*, 198.

[37] Lenard J. Cohen, *Broken Bonds: The Disintegration of Yugoslavia* (Boulder, CO: Westview, 1993), 157; Woodward, *Balkan Tragedy*, 93.

[38] Veljko Vujacic, "Serbian Nationalism, Slobodan Milosevic and the Origins of the Yugoslav War," *Harriman Review* 8:4 (December 1995), 31.

[39] Ramet, *Nationalism and Federalism*, 235.

[40] Lenard Cohen, "Embattled Democracy," in Karen Dawisha and Bruce Parrott,

threatened elites of the erstwhile one-party state, but also to demobilize support for their liberal foes. Whereas opponents of the Communist regimes of Czechoslovakia and Hungary rallied effectively in the streets and in political committees, in Serbia the atmosphere of ethnic resentment made it easier to silence opponents of the regime as traitors to the Serb people.[41]

Less than six months after the first democratic elections, the country was at war.[42] Slovenia and Croatia, failing to win Serbian agreement to their demands for greater autonomy, declared independence. The Serb-dominated Yugoslav army used force in an unsuccessful attempt to prevent this. In response, Serbs in Croatia's border regions planned a referendum on autonomy from Croatia, so the new Croatian state moved to supplant local police forces in Serb villages.[43] These Serbs, provided military materiel by Milosevic and the Yugoslav army, battled to create their own state along Croatia's southern perimeter.

### Targeting the segmented media market

Nationalist manipulation of the mass media played a central role in creating a climate for ethnic conflict. The story of how this was accomplished provides a good illustration of the interplay among three factors: the rising political participation, the partial opening of public debate, and the ethnofederal segmentation of Yugoslav institutions.

Liberal nongovernmental organizations like Human Rights Watch typically stress only one side of this story: they show how government officials in the republics of Serbia and Croatia used their near monopoly control of the news media to fuel their publics' ethnic prejudices, mobilizing a popular nationalist constituency to support their rule while discrediting more liberal opponents.[44] However, the media monopoly merely

---

eds., *Politics, Power, and the Struggle for Democracy in South-East Europe* (Cambridge: Cambridge University Press, 1997), 80.

[41] V. P. Gagnon, "Ethnic Conflict as Demobilizer: The Case of Serbia" (Cornell University, Institute for European Studies Working Paper no. 96.1, May 1966).

[42] Woodward, *Balkan Tragedy*, 17; see also Bogdan Denitch, *Ethnic Nationalism: The Tragic Death of Yugoslavia* (Minneapolis: University of Minnesota Press, 1994), 42–48.

[43] Cohen, "Embattled Democracy," 82.

[44] Human Rights Watch, *Slaughter among Neighbors: The Political Origins of*

gave elites in the republics the means to sell nationalist myths. The motive and the opportunity were created by the Serbian elite's fear of democratization, by the unevenness of journalistic standards, and by the plausibility of these myths to the ethnically segmented target audiences. Under these highly imperfect conditions of public discourse, the weakening of the central Yugoslav state created a potential opening for increased political pluralism. This threatened the oligarchs who ruled the republics and also created an opportunity for political entrepreneurs—including politicians, journalists, and intellectuals—to exploit their media power in the competition for mass support.

### The Ethnic Republics Gain Control over Television

Control over television had been dispersed to the republics in the 1960s and 1970s, under the theory that a federalist devolution of power would dampen underlying ethnic tensions. This turned out to be a grave mistake. By 1989, when Yugoslav prime minister Ante Markovic finally embarked on the creation of an all-Yugoslav television network, it was already too little, too late.

In 1987, Milosevic exploited his power as head of the Serbian Central Committee of the League of Communists to mount a systematic campaign on the Serbian state television monopoly to convince the Serbian people that Serbs residing in Kosovo province, the historic cradle of Serbdom, were suffering discrimination, repression, and rape at the hands of the Albanian majority there. He chose the television correspondent reporting to Belgrade from Pristina, the capital of Kosovo, and personally phoned the station almost daily to tell the editors what stories to highlight.[45] After Milosevic's April 1987 speech in Kosovo, Belgrade TV showed the local Albanian police clubbing people in the Serbian crowd and Milosevic saying, "From now on, no one has the right to beat you," but the coverage left out pictures

---

*Communal Violence* (New Haven: Yale University Press, 1995), 121–23. The following section on the Yugoslav media is adapted from Jack Snyder and Karen Ballentine, "Nationalism and the Marketplace of Ideas," *International Security* 21:2 (Fall 1996), 25–30.

[45] Mark Thompson, *Forging War: The Media in Serbia, Croatia and Bosnia-Hercegovina* (London: Article 19, International Center Against Censorship, May 1994), 20; Zdenka Milivojevic, "The Media in Serbia from 1985 to 1994," in Dusan Janjic, ed., *Serbia Between the Past and the Future* (Belgrade: Institute of Social Sciences, 1995), 168–69.

of the crowd stoning the police.[46] Exploiting the wave of nationalist sentiment touched off by this media campaign, Milosevic used the Kosovo issue not only as a pretext to purge anti-Milosevic journalists, charging them with issuing "one-sided and untrue reports," but also to consolidate conservative domination in party circles in Belgrade. Thus, as power devolved from the center in the post-Tito period, nationalist media manipulation became the heart of Milosevic's successful strategy for defeating liberal reformers in the scramble for mass and elite support.

Milosevic never achieved an absolute monopoly over the Serb media, but he controlled its commanding heights, the state television station and Belgrade's three major daily newspapers. An independent TV station and the semi-independent *Borba* newspaper were prevented by low wattage and limited newsprint from reaching beyond the Belgrade suburbs into Milosevic's stronghold in rural Serbia.[47]

Because of Yugoslavia's decentralized federal structure, republic television stations were totally independent of the central government but were monopolized by the republican Communist parties. The Yugoslav media, like most other aspects of Yugoslav life, had become by the 1980s "an alliance of regional oligarchies."[48] Republic television would not even show Yugoslav prime minister Markovic's speeches. To combat this, Markovic established an all-Yugoslav network, Yutel, in 1989. However, the central government's financial limitations, themselves a consequence of Yugoslavia's federal structure, left Yutel dependent on army surplus equipment and the sufferance of local broadcasters. After only four months on the air, Croatia pulled the plug on Yutel over a sensitive story on Slavonia, and most other republics followed suit. As the *coup de grace*, Serbian nationalist thugs trashed Yutel's Belgrade office.[49] Thus, the abil-

---

[46] Velko Vujacic, "Serbian Nationalism, Slobodan Milosevic and the Origins of the Yugoslav War," 29; Thompson, *Forging War*, 20.

[47] V. P. Gagnon, "Ethnic Nationalism and International Conflict: The Case of Serbia," *International Security* 19:3 (Winter 1994/95), 130–66; Woodward, *Balkan Tragedy*, 99, 230–32, 293; Magas, *The Destruction of Yugoslavia*, 3–76; Thompson, *Forging War*, 56, 65–66, 114–16, 124.

[48] Thompson, *Forging War*, 6–7, 16.

[49] Ibid., 38–43; Woodward, *Balkan Tragedy*, 230. In Croatia, only 600,000 people out of 10 million obtained the news from media not controlled by the government, according to a survey conducted by Miklos Biro, "Is Anybody Out There?" *War Report*, No. 39 (February/March 1996), 17.

ity of republican government leaders to manipulate the mass media
reflected the collapse of the multinational Yugoslav state.

### Journalists and Intellectuals Disseminate Nationalist Myths

The nationalist slant of the media cannot be blamed entirely on the governments of the republics. Journalists and scholars also played the ethnic card,
in some cases well before Milosevic. Many Serbian intellectuals were
obsessed with the Albanian threat in Kosovo even before Milosevic began
his media campaign on the issue. The 1986 memorandum by prominent
members of the Serbian Academy of Sciences, which charged that a "genocide" was being perpetrated against Serbs in Kosovo, was initially con-
demned by the Serbian Central Committee under Stambolic. These
intellectuals saw the Kosovo issue as vehicle for breaking down Communist
limitations on intellectual freedom and for press "liberalization."[50] By
speaking out forcefully on a potentially popular issue that the republic government was trying to ignore, these public intellectuals could establish a
niche for themselves as bold practitioners of a seemingly more open style of
popular discourse about politics. This reflected the necessity for all Yugoslav
elites to reposition themselves on a new foundation of ideological legitimacy in the context of the waning centralized Communist authority. In
this setting, the professional journalistic community split, some choosing
the nationalist route and energetically aiding Milosevic's seizure of power,
some resisting it and ultimately being forced out.[51]

Mark Thompson of the journalism nongovernmental organization
"Article 19," though generally a strong partisan of Yugoslavia's independent
journalists, describes the Milosevic takeover in the fall of 1987 as "a collusion among Serbia's Communist politicians, its bureaucracy, its intellectual
class, and its news media."[52] Indeed, the Serbian author and head of the
Democratic Party of Serbia, Jovan Raskovic, admitted that "it is not surprising that a situation of total hatred and paranoia is developing in this coun-

---

[50] Milivojevic, "The Media in Serbia," 164; Thompson, *Forging War*, 54; Laura
Silber and Allan Little, *Yugoslavia: Death of a Nation* (New York: TV Books, 1996),
33; see also Magas, *Destruction*, 49–76.

[51] Gagnon, "Ethnic Nationalism and International Conflict: The Case of Serbia,"
145–52; Vujacic, "Serbian Nationalism," 30; Thompson, *Forging War*, 23–24,
52–53.

[52] Thompson, *Forging War*, 55.

try. . . . I feel myself responsible, because I prepared this war, although not with military preparations. Had I not provoked this emotional tension within the Serbian people, nothing would have happened. My party and I myself have set fire to the fuse of Serbian nationalism, not only in Croatia, but everywhere else, particularly in Bosnia-Hercegovina."[53]

Thus, organized forces in "civil society," no less than in government, saw the benefits of exploiting media power to promote nationalist myths. They were sometimes even willing to conspire explicitly with their ethnic arch foe to accomplish it. For example, after Serb, Croat, and Muslim nationalist parties emerged as the winners of Bosnia's 1991 elections, the three nationalist camps tried to collude by dividing up the assets of Bosnia's ethnically integrated television service among themselves, while excluding the moderate parties of their respective ethnic groups.[54]

### Popular Demand for Nationalist Propaganda

The success of media propaganda depended both on monopoly of supply and also on the nature of demand, including the plausibility of the message in light of consumers' predispositions. Some propaganda campaigns were strikingly successful. For example, in northern Bosnia the Serbs enjoyed a six-month period of television monopoly, which they used to prime their population for the 1992 campaign of "ethnic cleansing" by repeatedly charging that Muslims were plotting to establish an Islamic fundamentalist state. Later, Serbs guarding prison camps accused their Muslim captives of precisely the charges that had been reiterated on the news. Similarly, as a result of Serb propaganda, 38 percent of Belgrade residents in a July 1992 poll thought that it was the Muslim-Croat forces who had recently been shelling the Bosnian capital of Sarajevo, versus only 20 percent who knew it was the Serbs.[55] However, viewers refused to swallow every lie whole. When the popular nationalist Vuk Draskovic

[53] Quoted in Jacques Rupnik, "The Reawakening of European Nationalisms," *Social Research* 63:1 (Spring 1996), 58–59. Thanks to Karen Ballentine for pointing out this quotation.

[54] Thompson, *Forging War*, 221–24; Woodward, *Balkan Tragedy*, 230.

[55] Changes in media content were also used successfully to shift opinion in favor of peace. On April 9, 1993, 70 percent of Serbian respondents said they opposed the Vance-Owen peace plan, but on April 27, after a reversal of policy by the Serbian government and media, only 20 percent opposed it and 39 percent were in favor. Thompson, *Forging War*, 127–28, 209, 264.

mounted a mass antiwar rally in March 1991, the government-controlled media's attempts to portray him as in league with the Croats and Albanians fizzled as too implausible. The following year, only 8 percent of Serbian respondents thought that state TV kept them "well informed," versus 43 percent for the independent media.[56]

Thus, the impact of the supply of nationalist propaganda must be assessed in light of the demand for it. As the premier student of the media campaign Mark Thompson puts it, "People's bedrock attitude toward the wars in Croatia and Bosnia are not created by the state media; rather, the media play variations upon those attitudes, which derive from other sources (national history, family background, education, oral culture). Media did not inject their audiences with anti-Muslim prejudice or exploitable fear of Croatian nationalism. The prejudice and fear were widespread, latently at least; there was a predisposition to believe 'news' which elicited and exploited the prejudice; without the media, however, Serbia's leaders could not have obtained public consent and approval of its nationalist politics."[57]

The importance of underlying predispositions is demonstrated by the antithetical propaganda strategies that Milosevic tailored for the Serbs and that President Franjo Tudjman of Croatia adopted for his audience. Belgrade TV portrayed the Serbs as always on the defensive, the perennial victims of every battle. Dead Serbs were favored imagery. This was thought to strike the right chord in a people who glorify a defeat at the hands of the Turks half a millennium ago in the battle of Kosovo. In contrast, Croatian government propaganda directives told Croatian TV to soft-pedal defeats, never show footage of destroyed Croat towns, and "always finish such reports with optimistic declarations and avowals."[58] It was feared that Croats, lacking as firm a tradition of statehood as the Serbs had, might simply give up hope if they knew the true odds they faced.

---

[56] Thompson, *Forging War*, 73–75, 127–29. Nonetheless, even independent media found itself caught in the self-fulfilling prophecies generated by nationalist mythmaking. As Serbian journalist Stojan Cerovic said in May 1992, "Anybody who explains the truth can do so only at his own cost. Reality sounds like the blackest anti-Serbian propaganda, and anyone who describes it will frighten people and turn them against him" (Thompson, *op. cit.*, 129). For a dissenting view which stresses the limited success of appeals to Serbian nationalism, see V. P. Gagnon, "Ethnic Conflict as Demobilizer."

[57] Thompson, *Forging War*, 127–28.

[58] Ibid., 105–11, quotation at 161.

### The State's Role in Structuring the Marketplace of Ideas

What lessons emerge from this story of nationalist media hijacking? What was lacking in this case were strong central state institutions to promote a professional, unbiased, pan-Yugoslav mass media. To establish conditions for better public discourse, the central state needed to be made stronger, not weaker. Thus, the limitation of central state power over media, a prescription that liberal nongovernmental organizations commonly suggest, actually exacerbated nationalist mythmaking in this case. Federalism, that standard remedy for constraining state exploitation of ethnic minorities, was one of the main problems. Ethnic powersharing, which is often prescribed as a complement to federalism, also caused trouble. In the Bosnian media, for example, the practice of allotting equal time for each group's biases made the evening news a series of stories with different slants. Meanwhile, the true story of the Yugoslav army's role in the attacks on Sarajevo, for example, was suppressed because it would have upset the Serbs.[59] What was needed was not a media expressing three different biases, but a professional one reporting the facts. Moreover, providing piecemeal subsidies to individual newspapers in the capital city, as the International Federation of Journalists did for the newspaper *Borba,* failed to go to the heart of the problem, because the backbone of support for nationalism lay in the Serb countryside, where Milosevic's media monopoly was uncontested.

Finally, the typical proposal of NGOs like Human Rights Watch to maximize freedom of speech would have also been a dubious remedy in this climate. In Serbia, even pro-democratic elites have been inclined to exploit the population's predispositions to ethnic anxiety. For example, Zoran Djindjic, the leader of pro-democracy protests after Milosevic invalidated local election results in November 1996, criticized Milosevic for abandoning the Krajina Serbs in the face of a Croatian attack. "The reasons Serbs in their history have lost battles, from Kosovo to November 17 of this year," Djindjic added, "is because our opponents waited until they could crush us while we slept."[60] He dismissed the qualms of his more liberal allies over the exploitation of nationalist rhetoric, insisting that "if we want to build a popular movement, we must use nationalism to do it. Our primary goal is to reform the economy and push Yugoslavia into Western

[59] Ibid., 225, 229–31.
[60] Chris Hedges, "Serb Leader's Foes Persist, Hoping He Will Blink First," *New York Times,* December 10, 1996, A8.

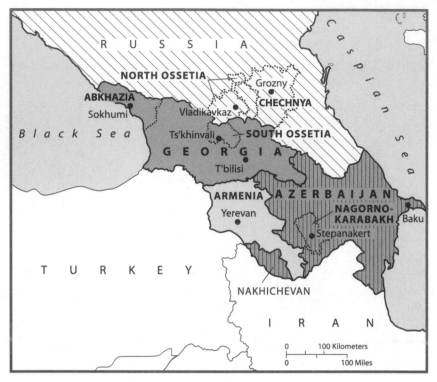

*The Caucasus Region*

Europe, but we cannot rally popular support around an economic program. This is why we are building our movement on Serbian nationalism."
His estranged antinationalist adviser Dragoljub Micunovic reported that
"Djindjic said that if I wanted to pursue morality I was better off in a
church."[61] Thus, in the face of such overwhelming incentives to resort to
nationalist rhetoric, free speech can become part of the problem.

## Mass Politics and War in the Caucasus

Each of the three post-Soviet states of the Caucasus—Armenia, Azerbaijan,
and Georgia—went through a phase of democratization after the Soviet
collapse. Each held at least one election that international observers credited

[61] Chris Hedges, "Ambitious Serb Takes on His Less Telegenic Twin," *New York
Times*, December 1, 1996, 18.

as being reasonably fair.[62] In each country, too, a mass nationalist movement was a significant political force.

This popular energy helped to fuel ethnic wars in Georgia and between Armenians and Azerbaijani that were extremely costly for each of these Caucasian nations. In Georgia, the democratically elected ethnonationalist government's conflicts with Ossetian and Abkhazian minorities created a pretext for Russian military intervention, which squabbling Georgian factions lacked the cohesion to resist. The conflicts in Georgia had by 1996 displaced 475,000 people and killed 17,500, many of them ethnic Georgians.[63] The war over Nagorno-Karabakh, the Armenian enclave inside Azerbaijan, had by 1996 produced 1,700,000 refugees and killed 55,000.[64] Armenian forces occupied a third of Azerbaijan's territory; in turn, an Azerbaijani-Turkish embargo helped cut Armenian gross national product in half. Armenia, lacking oil to generate electricity, faced the agonizing dilemma of whether to destroy a unique lake to produce hydroelectricity or instead to restart a nuclear power plant that had been mothballed as utterly unsafe; they wound up doing both. Corrupt clans and organized crime profited on each side, sharply skewing the distribution of wealth to the benefit of the few, while the mass publics that had been so enthusiastic for the ethnonational aims that fueled the conflict bore the brunt of the costs.[65] By January 1996, 18 percent of the "victorious" but impoverished Armenian people had emigrated to Russia or the West.[66]

[62] For a balanced discussion of these cases, see James Lee Ray, *Democracy and International Conflict* (Columbia: University of South Carolina Press, 1995), 122–24. On Armenia, see the Commission on Security and Cooperation in Europe, *Report on Armenia's Parliamentary Election and Constitutional Referendum*, (Washington, DC: U.S. Government, July 1995), and idem., *Report on Armenia's Presidential Elections, March 16 and 30, 1998* (June 1998). On the extent of irregularities in the 1992 Azerbaijani presidential election, see Thomas Goltz, *Requiem for a Would-Be Republic: The Rise and Demise of the Former Soviet Republic of Azerbaijan, a Personal Account of the Years 1991–1993* (Istanbul: Isis, 1994), 271–85. On Georgia, see Irakli Tsereteli, "Georgia: Country Update. Seeking Stability under Shevardnadze," *Transition* (July 26, 1996), 42–45.

[63] Brown, ed., *International Dimensions*, 4–5.

[64] Ibid.

[65] Nora Dudwick, "Political Transformations in Postcommunist Armenia: Images and Realities," in Karen Dawisha and Bruce Parrott, eds., *Conflict, Cleavage and Change in Central Asia and the Caucasus* (Cambridge: Cambridge University Press, 1997), 69–109; Goltz, *Requiem*, Chapter 15.

[66] Dudwick, "Political Transformations," 82.

### Demands for participation outstrip the capacity of political institutions

Of all the post-Communist states, the three states of the Caucasus had the largest gaps between high levels of mass political participation and underdeveloped political institutions.[67] Under these conditions, nationalist mobilization in the streets and on the battlefield became the most effective method for mass groups to play a role in the political process, and the defense of the nation became the accepted cover for the pursuit of corrupt activities.[68] Of the three, the Armenians' grassroots institutions for organizing collective action were the best developed, and consequently they had the greatest success in generating resources for the war effort and maintaining military cohesion. However, these institutions, grounded in kinship and patronage networks, worked at cross purposes with the development of a law-governed, democratically elected, bureaucratic state. They helped Armenia to win the war but not to develop civic nationalism or to consolidate its shaky democracy.[69]

The Soviet institutional legacy left the peoples of the Caucasus with the worst of both worlds: politics were organized around ethnicity, yet there were no meaningful institutions for democratic participation along ethnic or any other lines. The Soviet policy of "nativization" placed a premium on ethnic identity in the social and political organization of the region. In each federal republic (named after its principal ethnic group), education policies, language policies, and bureaucratic staffing favored the development of an ethnically conscious elite. This reflected not only the Bolsheviks' inability in the 1920s to impose a centralized Russified identity but also their preference for ethnic identities as an alternative to pan-Turk or Islamic identities, which posed more of a threat to Bolshevik hegemony.[70]

To be sure, politicized ethnic identities had begun to form among the

[67] Explicitly invoking Huntington in this respect is Mark Saroyan, "Beyond the Nation-State: Culture and Ethnic Politics in Soviet Transcaucasia," in Ronald Suny, ed., *Transcaucasia: Nationalism, and Social Change*, 2d ed. (Ann Arbor: University of Michigan Press, 1996), 426. See also Suny, "On the Road to Independence: Cultural Cohesion and Ethnic Revival in a Multinational Society," in Suny, *Transcaucasia*, 2d ed., 377–400.

[68] Dudwick, "Political Transformations," 79–81, 99.

[69] Ibid., 89–91, 98–99.

[70] David Laitin, Roger Petersen, and John Slocum, "Language and the State:

peoples of the Caucasus before the Soviet period. Although the very concept of "Armenia" was unknown to the mass of rural Armenians during
much of the nineteenth century, it was propounded by the Armenian
middle-class intelligentsia as a means of mobilizing resistance against the
Turkish massacres of 1894–96.[71] The 1905 Russian Revolution further
opened up space for mass political organization by the Armenian nationalist Dashnak Party in the Russian-ruled Transcaucasus, which included
what is now called Azerbaijan. The "Armenian-Tatar War" of 1905, triggered by seasonal migrations through the Nagorno-Karabakh region, was
won by the more modernized, more nationally conscious Armenians,
spearheaded by the Dashnaks. The Armenian identity was strongly reinforced as a political concept by the mass expulsion and slaughter of
Armenians in Turkey during World War I.

Armenia's brief period from 1918 to 1920 as an independent state,
ruled by the democratically elected Dashnak Party, also helped to lock in
Armenian national consciousness. After the collapse of the Russian
empire, the Dashnaks were chosen to govern the newly independent
Armenian state in 1918 in multiparty elections based on a system or pro-
portional representation and universal suffrage without regard to sex or
religion. Beset by impoverished refugees from Turkish military advances,
and governing more through the authority of popular nationalism than
through the niceties of democratic procedure, the Dashnaks and the
Armenian Republic were ousted by Soviet forces in 1920.[72] The Dashnak
Party maintained its organizational cohesion in the diaspora, and since
the collapse of Soviet power in 1991, the Dashnaks have again played a
role in shaping popular nationalism in contemporary Armenia. Arguably,

---

Russia and the Soviet Union in Comparative Perspective," in Alexander Motyl,
*Thinking Theoretically about Soviet Nationalities* (New York: Columbia University
Press, 1992), 144–49.

[71] Ronald Suny, *The Revenge of the Past: Nationalism, Revolution, and the Collapse
of the Soviet Union* (Stanford: Stanford University Press, 1993), 72; Nora Dudwick,
"Armenia: The Nation Awakens," in Ian Bremmer and Ray Taras, eds., *Nations and
Politics in the Soviet Successor States* (Cambridge: Cambridge University Press, 1993),
264.

[72] Richard G. Hovanisian, "Caucasian Armenia between Imperial and Soviet Rule:
The Interlude of National Independence," in Suny, *Transcaucasia*, 2d ed., 264–67,
citing Richard Hovanisian, "Dimensions of Democracy and Authority in Caucasian
Armenia," *The Russian Review* 33 (January 1974), 37–49.

the Armenian people's tribulations in the early twentieth century had a lasting impact on the formation and institutionalization of their national consciousness, in part because these events coincided with Armenia's initial period of democratic mobilization.

Turkish-speaking, Shiite Muslim Azeris were much slower to develop a distinct national consciousness. Baku, Azerbaijan's major city, industrialized rapidly in the late nineteenth century with the development of the Caspian Sea oil fields. Ruled by Russia, Baku's economy was run by Christian Armenian entrepreneurs, while unskilled Muslims served as its laborers. Lines of rivalry were conceptualized first in terms of social class and religious differences, occasionally in terms of the broader Armenian-Turkish conflict, and only rarely in terms of a distinctive Azeri ethnicity. Even the term Azeri was not a common designation. The Armenians' foes in the "Armenian-Tatar War" of 1905 were people who would nowadays be called Azeris.[73]

In Georgia, the development of national consciousness may be neatly periodized: cultural awareness in the 1830s, the initial formulation by intellectuals of a political concept of the nation in the 1860s, and the creation of a mass constituency for Georgian nationalism in 1918, in the form of the Georgian Menshevik socialist movement.[74]

These incipient national identities were solidified along ethnic lines through Soviet-era policies. Stalin's creation of the federal republics helped to institutionalize these ethnic identities, especially the weakly developed Azeri identity, and gave their elites a stake in advancing them as political categories. In the three Caucasian republics, as elsewhere in the Soviet Union, every individual's passport specified an ethnically defined "nationality." Career prospects were better for nationals in their titular republic, so over time many people migrated to their homeland.[75]

[73] Tadeusz Swietochowski, *Russia and Azerbaijan* (New York: Columbia University Press, 1995), 34–41, see also 21–29, 51–62; Suny, *Revenge of the Past*, 79–81; Audrey Altstadt, *The Azerbaijani Turks: Power and Identity under Russian Rule* (Stanford: Hoover, 1992), 42–43; Swietochowski, *Russian Azerbaijan 1905–1920: The Shaping of National Identity in a Muslim Community* (Cambridge: Cambridge University Press, 1985).

[74] Stephen F. Jones, "Old Ghosts and New Chains: Ethnicity and Memory in the Georgian Republic," in Rubie S. Watson, ed., *Memory, History, and Opposition under State Socialism* (Santa Fe: School of American Research Press, 1994), 155, applying a three-stage typology advanced by Miroslav Hroch

[75] Suny, *Revenge*, 102–6, 110.

The most ethnically homogeneous of all Soviet republics, the Republic of Armenia was 88 percent ethnic Armenian in 1959; by 1989 it was over 93 percent Armenian. In 1959, 56 percent of Soviet Armenians lived in the Armenian republic; by 1989 that proportion had grown to 67 percent. Over the same period, Georgia went from 64 percent to 70 percent ethnic Georgian; Azerbaijan from 67 to 83 percent Azeri.[76] The population of the Sumgait slum district near Baku, the site of anti-Armenian pogroms in 1988, was swelled in the late 1940s by Azeri refugees expelled from their villages in Armenia.[77] Thus, the Soviet form of federalism heightened the importance of ethnic identity and directed post-Soviet mass collective action into ethnic channels.

While the Soviet legacy left behind an ethnicized bureaucracy and a culturally aware local elite, it did nothing to develop an institutional framework for popular political participation. In comparison to the democratic infrastructure left behind in some British colonies, for example, there was no legacy of pluralistic party politics, competitive elections, meaningful parliamentary representation, or professional journalism. When Soviet power collapsed in the center, the stage was therefore set for the mobilization of mass politics animated by ethnic concerns, but there were no effective democratic channels to express or reconcile these concerns.

In the Baltic republics of the USSR (Estonia, Latvia, and Lithuania), this institutional void was relatively easily filled, due to the region's significantly longer history of mass literacy and their familiarity with impersonal forms of legal, bureaucratic, and political organization. In these Baltic states, mass "popular fronts" leading national independence movements quickly gave way to organized political parties. European-style democratic and market institutions were readily improvised, and journalists aspired toward Western standards.[78]

By 1988, intellectuals leading the opposition against Soviet rule in the Caucasus began consciously to copy the Baltic popular fronts, with varying

---

[76] Kaiser, *Geography of Nationalism*, Tables 4.1 and 4.3, pp. 161, 174, also pp. 124–35; Philip Roeder, "Soviet Federalism and Ethnic Mobilization," *World Politics* 43:2 (January 1991), 196–232; Rogers Brubaker, *Nationalism Reframed* (Cambridge: Cambridge University Press, 1996), Chapter 2. To some extent, these figures may reflect differential birthrates as well as migration.

[77] Altstadt, *Azerbaijani Turks*, 197.

[78] Lieven, *Baltic Revolution*, Chapters 8 and 9.

consequences, depending on the local setting. In the comparatively educated, urbanized, and industrialized republics of Armenia and Georgia, the
independence movement mounted orderly mass demonstrations, and the
transition from rule by Communist apparatchiks to elected nationalist leaders was accomplished virtually by consensus.[79] In Azerbaijan, in contrast,
mass demonstrations tended to degenerate into mob violence, directed in
particular toward Armenian neighborhoods in Baku. Notwithstanding
these differences, an underlying similarity—the interaction of mass nationalism and weak democratic institutions with corrupt, clannish, patronage
politics—provided a permissive setting for belligerent ethnic nationalism in
all the states of the Caucasus.

### Azeri mass nationalism and the politics of corruption

Mass politics in Azerbaijan, demographically and economically balanced
between its urban industrial sector and traditional agriculture, was
strongly influenced by over 165,000 rural Azeri refugees who crowded
into Baku in the late 1980s after being expelled from Armenia or
Armenian-dominated areas of Nagorno-Karabakh. Though the Azeri
nationalist movement was in large part spontaneously triggered by these
grassroots grievances, Azeri intellectuals quickly moved to position themselves at the head of this movement, organizing the Azerbaijani Popular
Front. By November 1988, nationalists had taken control of the

---

[79] Georgians and Armenians had the highest proportion of individuals with higher
education among all the Soviet nationalities (for urban Georgians, 231 per 1,000 in
1979; for urban Armenians, 151; for urban Azeris, 128). See Kaiser, *Geography of
Nationalism*, Table 5.9, p. 229. In 1975, national income per capita in Armenia stood
at 83 percent of the USSR average, 76 percent in Georgia, and 65 percent in
Azerbaijan. For industrial production, Armenia stood at 88 percent, Georgia at 61,
Azerbaijan at 56. For per capita consumption, Georgia stood at 90 percent, Armenia
at 84, and Azerbaijan at 67. Georgia leads among the three in number of doctors.
Gertrude Schroeder, "Transcaucasia since Stalin: The Economic Dimension," Suny,
ed., *Transcaucasia: Nationalism and Social Change*, 1st ed., (Ann Arbor: University of
Michigan, 1983), Tables 1 and 2, pp. 399, 401, 409, 411; Ronald Suny, *Looking
toward Ararat: Armenia in Modern History* (Bloomington: Indiana University Press,
1993), 183–84. Schroeder's chapter in Suny, ed., *Transcaucasia*, 2d ed. (1996), 473,
shows that Azerbaijan had narrowed some of these gaps by 1990, for example, in
medical personnel.

Azerbaijani press, engaging in continuous polemics with Armenia over the Karabakh issue, despite the rather passive attitude of Azerbaijan's Communist government.[80]

Mass energies in Azerbaijan were initially directed more toward the immediate issue of rivalry with Armenia, such as the formation of committees organizing relief for Karabakh refugees, than toward restructuring the Azeri state. Whereas elections in Armenia and Georgia quickly turned Communist officials out of office, the party bosses won the rigged 1990 elections in Azerbaijan, with the popular front winning less than ten percent of the seats.[81] However, the seizure of state power soon became the central issue in Azerbaijani popular politics as well.

After Azerbaijan declared its independent statehood in 1991, the regime of ex-Communist Ayaz Mutalibov still failed to reach out for mass support in addressing the refugee crisis and refused even to take steps to create a standing army to compete with the Armenian militia forces in Karabakh. Four defense ministers serving an average of one month each produced only a five-hundred-man army. No sooner were units formed than Mutalibov disbanded them as being under the influence of opponents to his regime.[82]

By 1992, leaders of the popular front were finally able to force Mutalibov from office on the grounds that the failure to generate military power and a rationalized tax base to support it was crippling the ability of the Azeri nation to defend itself against the Armenian foe. (This recapitulated the pattern that Charles Tilly described in early modern Europe, in which war and the need for military mobilization demanded a harnessing of the forces of popular nationalism to strengthen the state.)[83] Riding this issue and proclaiming a platform of ethnonational solidarity with Turkey, Abulfez Elchibey, the scholarly founder of the popular front and a self-styled democrat, was chosen as president in elections that were considered

[80] Stuart Kaufman, *The Symbolic Politics of Ethnic War: Elites, Masses, and Ethnic Violence in Post-Communist Europe* (Ithaca: Cornell University Press, forthcoming).

[81] Swietochowski, *Russia and Azerbaijan*, 195–99, 210–11; Altstadt, *Azerbaijani Turks*, 201, 204–5. On Armenia and Georgia, see Dudwick, "Armenia: The Nation Awakens," 261–87, and Stephen Jones, "Georgia: A Failed Democratic Transition," 288–312, both in Bremmer and Taras, *Nations and Politics*.

[82] Swietochowski, *Russia and Azerbaijan*, 218–19.

[83] Charles Tilly, *Coercion, Capital, and European States* (Cambridge: Blackwell, 1990).

reasonably free and fair, if occasionally a bit absurd. One of Elchibey's most effective rivals was an unknown crackpot whose popularity surged in the polls after he promised free butter for everyone. During Elchibey's election campaign, Thomas Goltz remarked that "the level of censorship was nil—but so was the level of responsible reporting."[84]

Elchibey's regime, despite his nation-building rhetoric and electoral mandate, was utterly incapable of institutionalizing nationalist collective action, let alone procedural democracy. No less than under the Communist administration, government officials were corrupt from top to bottom. Efficiency and the national good meant nothing; the only incentive that spurred action was the opportunity for a kickback. For example, Azerbaijan could have funded a substantial military effort by utilizing the natural gas that was a by-product of its own oil refining, rather than flaring off the gas and buying it from Central Asia. To tap this wasted resource, Pennzoil, a partner in the Azerbaijani oil consortium, provided natural gas compressors free of charge. But since they were free, there was no kickback on the contract; and because there was no incentive to get them off the boat, the compressors sat rusting away.[85]

In the military area, the problem was the same. Azeri armed forces continued to be largely privately organized militias operating on the "for profit" principle.[86] Commanders kept the dead bodies of their soldiers under refrigeration in order to continue drawing their combat pay. When possible, they sold the bodies at extortionary rates to family members who wanted to provide proper Muslim burials.[87] Money appropriated for field hospitals went into officers' pockets. Consequently, care of combat casualties was abysmal, morale suffered, and desertion rates were high. To compensate for this, press gangs trawled the Baku slums to conscript on sight all men of military age. Lower-class and refugee elements who had been Elchibey's core of support became disgruntled.[88] As a result, the self-described democrat Elchibey had to ban bad news and repress complainers more than the Communist Mutalibov ever did.[89]

---

[84] Goltz, *Requiem*, 271, 273–74; Swietochowski, *Russia and Azerbaijan*, 220.

[85] Goltz, *Requiem*, 335–36.

[86] Robin Bhatty, Columbia University, dissertation in progress.

[87] Goltz, *Requiem*, 5; Robin Bhatty, personal communication.

[88] Elizabeth Fuller, "Azerbaijan's June Revolution," *RFE/RL [Radio Free Europe/Radio Liberty] Research Report* 2:32 (August 13, 1993), 24–29.

[89] Goltz, *Requiem*, 33–34.

Military forces were used not to fight Armenians but to provide muscle against contending Azeri factions. Though proclaiming national solidarity, the Azeri government, intellectuals, and regional clans were consumed with self-serving resource extraction and mutual distrust. As an Azeri analyst explained, "inter-clan conflicts" rooted in a "feudal-tribal concept" led to "regional confrontations," and "the government's irrational cadre selection policy" produced dissatisfaction among intellectuals.[90] Finally, Elchibey was overthrown by a regional military commander who invited the old Communist-era party chief, Heidar Aliev, to assume power. Thereafter, elections were once again rigged, and corruption was at least better organized.[91]

In short, despite high levels of mass involvement in politics, Azerbaijan lacked the institutional channels to sustain a coherent nationalist movement, let alone a democratic state. Incipient democratization initially led to a burst of popular mobilization against the national arch foe, but this energy was soon dissipated by the corrupt patronage networks that still dominated Azeri politics and society.

### Armenian mass nationalism and clan-based mobilization

On the surface, Armenian national collective action could not have been more different from that of the Azeris. Bolstered by the formative memory of the genocide at the hands of the Turks, inspired by the precedent of the 1918 democratic republic, institutionalized in the diaspora by the Dashnak organization, and experienced in military organization through the development of an armed force based in Lebanon, Armenian nationalists seized independence with an already highly developed national consciousness. Fighting for one's nation was a well-established social norm enforced by informal instruments for monitoring and sanctioning those who shirked their duty to the nation. The Armenian Christian church constituted a ready-made surveillance network in every village, with the local priests who allocated food aid keeping tabs on which young men

---

[90] Hikmet Sabiroghlu, "Problem No. 1," *Baku Azadlyg*, October 15, 1994, 5, repr. in *Foreign Broadcast Information Service [FBIS] Report: Central Eurasia*, FBIS-USR-94-130, December 1, 1994, 98–99.

[91] Commission on Security and Cooperation in Europe, *Report on Azerbaijan's November 1995 Parliamentary Election* (Washington, DC: US GPO, January 1996).

were fighting and which were not.[92] Civil society was nationalist and highly organized.

Nonetheless, the social institutions underlying Armenian collective action reveal some strong similarities to those of patronage-ridden Azerbaijan.[93] In both cases, the clan basis of social organization channeled nationalism in nondemocratic directions. Military force on the Armenian side, no less than among the Azeris, was organized in the form of free-lance militias.[94] The fighting in Nagorno-Karabakh, though promoted by the mass-based nationalist Karabakh Committee in Armenia proper, was actually touched off by local militias and mafia-type organizations.[95]

In Armenia proper, political parties degenerated into thinly veiled disguises for patronage-seeking clans. Though the 1991 election came close to being free and fair, practices in the 1995 elections were more ham-handed: the leader of the main opposition "party," controlled by a rival clan to that of the incumbent president, Levon Ter-Petrossian, was jailed and barred from running. In the 1996 presidential election, international observers and Armenians alike concluded that Ter-Petrossian simply stole the election through irregularities at the polls.[96]

Officeholding was mainly valued as an opportunity to dispense patronage. Clans supported the ruling coalition only if they got to control the patronage of a valuable government ministry. Until President Ter-Petrossian's ouster in February 1998, his brother Telman was known as the richest man in Armenia. Formerly a high Communist official, he controlled government contracts and oversaw the commission on the privatization of industry.[97] Thus, the strong informal organizations of Armenian

[92] Nora Dudwick, "Nagorno-Karabakh and the Politics of Sovereignty," in Suny, *Transcaucasia*, 2d ed., 427–40; Dudwick, "Political Transformations," 98–99; Robin Bhatty, personal communication, July 9, 1996.

[93] Suny, "On the Road to Independence: Cultural Cohesion and Ethnic Revival in a Multinational Society," in Suny, *Transcaucasia*, 2d ed., 380–81.

[94] Robin Bhatty, personal communication; Ara Tatevosyan, "Nagorno-Karabakh's New Army of 'Iron Will and Discipline,' " *Transition* (August 9, 1996), 20–23.

[95] Stuart Kaufman, "An 'International' Theory of Inter-Ethnic War," *Review of International Studies* 22 (1966), 164.

[96] Steve LeVine, "Armenia Chief Faces Protests Over Election," *New York Times*, September 24, 1996, A6.

[97] Dudwick, "Political Transformations," 90–91; Dudwick, "The Mirage of Democracy: A Study of Post-Communist Transition in Armenia" (paper prepared for

civil society were oriented not toward pluralistic representation and debate but toward small-group mobilization for parochial gain. In this setting, notes Peter Rutland, the "ability to win in elections was less important than the ability to control the streets, to organise relief, and to run a military campaign."[98]

Nationalist discourse served as ideological cover for this corruption of democratic politics. [99] Though elections were patently stolen and state assets stripped, the government could still claim to rule on behalf of the people as long as it prevailed in the struggle against the Azeri arch foe. The government monopoly over television and radio was a useful vehicle for disseminating this message in a country where only 3 percent of the population could afford to buy a daily newspaper.[100]

In part because the Armenian people were subjected to a one-sided nationalist discourse in the postindependence period, nationalist appeals served as trump cards in the factional contest for government patronage. No one, not even the president, could survive surrendering the nationalist high ground to a competing faction. President Ter-Petrossian faced this dilemma when he came to understand that Armenia's unbending militancy in the conflict with Azerbaijan was provoking a dangerous coalition of opponents, which threatened the country as well as his flow of patronage. Not only was Armenia's economy being strangled by the continuing Azerbaijani blockade, but international donors were beginning to see Armenians, who occupied a third of Azerbaijan's territory, as unjust aggressors. Despite the efforts of Armenian-American lobbying groups, U.S. oil companies with interests in Caspian oil development were gaining ground in their attempts to convince Congress to eliminate sanctions against Azerbaijan. In November 1997, Ter-Petrossian summed up these dangers in a remarkable speech. He warned that unless the Karabakh dispute were settled soon through a compromise, Azerbaijan's growing oil wealth could allow it to overwhelm Armenia in the

---

a workshop on post-Communist democratization, School of Advanced International Studies, Johns Hopkins University, November 16–17, 1995), 28.

[98] Peter Rutland, "Democracy and Nationalism in Armenia," *Europe-Asia Studies* 46:5 (1994), 857; see also Dudwick, "Armenia," in Bremmer and Taras, *Nations and Politics*, 276.

[99] Dudwick, "Political Transformations," 80–81, 99; Dudwick, "The Mirage of Democracy," 41.

[100] Dudwick, "Political Transformations," 101.

not too distant future.[101] This realistic strategy put Ter-Petrossian at a fatal disadvantage. One of the reasons that he could not afford a fair election in 1996 was that the opposition had already gained popularity by charging him with "treason" and "capitulation" on the Karabakh issue.[102] As Ter-Petrossian moved even further outside the militant nationalist consensus, competing factions saw an opportunity to break his hold on power and patronage, forcing his resignation in February 1998. Relatively fair democratic elections in March 1998 chose as Armenia's new president the hawkish former leader of the Karabakh Armenians, Robert Kocharian.

### Georgia: States within the state

Georgia faced similar difficulties in its post-Communist transition. Like Armenia, it enjoyed a relatively high level of education and a well-developed national consciousness when the Soviet Union collapsed. In its first election in May 1991, the anti-Communist dissident nationalist writer Zviad Gamsakhurdia won the presidency with 87 percent of the vote. However, the ability to hold an election did not make Georgia a functioning state, let alone a democracy. Gamsakhurdia's regime quickly collapsed into warfare among various factions based on loyalties to particular regions or warlords—all of them ethnic Georgians. Following Gamsakhurdia's ouster, a military council invited the Soviet-era party boss, Eduard Shevardnadze, to form a new government. Free and fair elections were held in 1992 and again in 1995. Nonetheless, Georgia's "democracy" rested not on a firm foundation of democratic institutions but on Shevardnadze's mastery of a personalistic network of patron-client relations and on the good relations he had fostered with the West during his earlier tenure as the Soviet foreign minister.[103]

---

[101] Levon Ter-Petrossian, "War or Peace? Time for Thoughtfulness," *Hayastani Hanrapetutiun*, November 1, 1998. I am grateful to Robin Bhatty for providing this translation and related materials. See also Commission on Security and Cooperation in Europe, *Report on Armenia's Presidential Election, March 16 and 30*, 1998, 5–6.

[102] Edward W. Walker, "No Peace, No War in the Caucasus: Secessionist Conflicts in Chechnya, Abkhazia and Nagorno-Karabakh" (Harvard University Kennedy School of Government: Strengthening Democratic Institutions Project, February 1998), 40.

[103] S. Neil MacFarlane, "Democratization, Nationalism and Regional Security in

Although Georgia succeeded in holding free and fair elections, it lacked the strong institutions that would have been needed to integrate the demands of its various ethnic minorities into a process of democratic compromise. In this democratizing environment, the legacy of Soviet ethnofederal institutions helped to politicize incompatible ethnic claims. The Soviets had created an Autonomous Region inside Georgia for the Ossetian minority and an Autonomous Republic, complete with its own parliament, for the Abkhazians. In 1989, the Ossetians constituted only 3 percent of Georgia's population, the Abkhaz only 1.8 percent. The Abkhaz were less than a fifth of the population even in their own autonomous region, which included Russians and Armenians as well as Georgians.[104]

These ethnically titled jurisdictions were soon locked in violent struggles. Georgians were eager to establish an exclusive ethnic identity for their new state. The newly elected Gamsakhurdia sought to strip South Ossetia's status as an autonomous region and pressed for the Ossetians to "return" to their homeland north of the border with Russia. When Georgia's factions relapsed into civil conflict, the Abkhaz succeeded in attracting Russian military support for their efforts to expel ethnic Georgians from their Autonomous Republic and to declare Abkhazia an independent state.

It would be an exaggeration to blame Georgia's ethnic conflicts entirely on the dynamics associated with democratization. Georgian national identity was well established before its 1991 elections. Moreover, the conflicts that followed the Soviet collapse were driven in part by anarchical conditions that pitted groups of all kinds, not just ethnic groups, against each other. Likewise, the intervention of the Russian military, eager to retain a toehold in the region despite the Soviet withdrawal, also fomented conflict. Even so, the dynamics of democratization also played their part in heightening nationalist conflict. In a setting that was structured perversely by the legacy of ethnofederalism, politicians tried to use

---

the Southern Caucasus," *Government and Opposition* 32:3 (Summer 1997), 399–420, esp. 406. This article provides a balanced, subtle evaluation of arguments linking democratization and war, as applied to the cases of Armenia and Azerbaijan, as well as Georgia.

[104] Jones, "Georgia," 289.

nationalist appeals to channel the rising levels of political participation that overwhelmed the capacity of weak political institutions. To integrate ethnic groups on the basis of pluralistic compromise, strong democratic institutions are needed. In contrast, Georgia's democracy, based on old-style patron-client ties and intermittent elections, was inadequate as a tool of ethnic integration, even at its best under Shevardnadze. At its worst, under Gamsakhurdia, it was highly divisive.[105]

### Late development and flawed democracy in the Caucasus

In summary, the belligerent nationalist movements of the Caucasus reflected its intermediate place in the spectrum of social and political development. Nationalist popular movements developed differently in the post-Soviet periphery depending on the historical timing of their development of literacy and of their professionalized middle class, and on their familiarity with legal and bureaucratic relationships not based on personal favoritism. In the Baltics, where these characteristics developed relatively early, mass nationalist movements quickly became institutionalized in democratic structures. At the other extreme, in Central Asia, where these characteristics are still only weakly developed among the largely rural indigenous population, no strong mass movements emerged. Politics remained dominated by clans, patronage networks, and repressive bureaucratic institutions, including the remnants of the Soviet army.

The states of the Caucasus lay in the nationalist danger zone in between. More literate, industrialized, and urbanized than Central Asia, the peoples of the Caucasus had the capacity to conceive of themselves as nations and to organize national movements. However, they lacked the organizational resources of the Balts for democratic forms of collective action. Governments in the Caucasus, no matter how free and fair the elections that chose them, operated not on the basis of the rule of law but through corrupt, personalized patron-client ties. Thus, the Caucasian states had reached that nationalism-prone stage where a high demand for mass political participation overwhelms inadequate institutional channels. In this setting, nationalism was harnessed to the parochial concerns

---

[105] MacFarlane, "Democratization, Nationalism and Regional Security in the Southern Caucasus," 413–19.

of patronage-hungry clans, mass groups demanding access to power, and state elites justifying the repression of opponents.[106] Compared to other post-Soviet states, the three Caucasian states were especially primed to undergo the traumas of incomplete democratization and nationalism.

## Media Wars in Post-Communist Russia

Nationalism and democratization are also intertwined in Russia's war against the separatist regime in the northern Caucasus region of Chechnya, which claimed about 35,000 lives between December 1994 and August 1996.[107] In this case, the competitive dynamic of mass pluralistic politics was both a stimulus to belligerent Russian nationalism and a check on its excesses. On the one hand, rising mass participation in a context of weak democratic institutions gave Russian demagogues like Vladimir Zhirinovsky a chance to win votes by his nationalist appeals and thus put pressure on moderates like Russian president Boris Yeltsin to respond in kind. On the other hand, key elite groups having a stake in good relations with the West were able to use the electoral process and the mass media to make common cause with voters weary of the burdens of empire. As a result, the mobilization of popular Russian nationalism was limited, despite the weakness of representative and journalistic institutions in Russia's transitional democracy.[108]

Russian president Boris Yeltsin embarked on the military intervention in Chechnya in a misguided attempt to save his regime in the face of plummeting popularity and rising Russian nationalism. In the December 1993 parliamentary elections, the party of the extreme Russian nationalist

[106] See esp. Karen Peabody O'Brien, "Patterns of Modernization and Mobilization: Nationalism and Political Patronage in Transcaucasia and Central Asia," Columbia University dissertation in progress, for a related analysis.

[107] For this estimate, see Gail Lapidus, "Contested Sovereignty: The Tragedy of Chechnya," *International Security* 23:1 (Summer 1998), 6 (fn 3). General Aleksandr Lebed, in estimates supported by some Western human rights groups, put the toll of the Chechen War at 80,000 killed and 240,000 wounded. Michael R. Gordon, "Chechnya Toll Is Far Higher, 80,000 Dead, Lebed Asserts," *New York Times*, September 4, 1996, A3.

[108] Michael McFaul, "A Precarious Peace: Domestic Politics in the Making of Russian Foreign Policy," *International Security* 22:3 (Winter 1997–98), 5–35.

Vladimir Zhirinovsky exploited working-class anxieties over economic reform to win a quarter of the seats. Frustrated by perceived slights to the status of Russians in the newly independent states of the so-called near abroad and by claims of autonomy by non-Russian minorities within the Russian Federation itself, Russian politicians and commentators uniformly dropped the cooperative internationalist rhetoric of the Gorbachev era, replacing it with increasingly surly assertions of what they termed the Russian national interest. Meanwhile, by the fall of 1994, polls showed that 70 percent of Russians were dissatisfied with the president's performance. Increasingly unable to assert his authority over a hostile parliament, recalcitrant regions, stubborn bureaucracies, and disaffected public opinion, Yeltsin saw a military crackdown on Chechen pretensions to sovereign independence as a popular way to demonstrate his ability to act decisively in the face of the deadlock of democracy. Pundits in the Russian press cheekily asserted that Yeltsin was recapitulating the strategy of a tsarist minister who, on the eve of the Russo-Japanese War (and the 1905 Russian Revolution), reputedly said, "What we need is a short, victorious war to stem the tide of revolution."[109] As Michael McFaul has concluded, "Yeltsin did not order his troops into Chechnya to save the Russian Federation. He moved against Chechnya to save his presidency."[110]

This strategy was as counterproductive for Yeltsin as it had been for the tsar's ministers. Public opinion and independent media applied strong brakes to Yeltsin's war policy. Independent television coverage revealed the costs and futility of the war, and because of it, Yeltsin's popularity fell still further. Instead of outbidding Yeltsin's nationalist stance toward the Chechens, most of his political rivals sought to win popularity by opposing the war. Even the nationalistic retired general Aleksandr Lebed, co-opted as Yeltsin's national security czar after winning 15 percent of the

[109] Though the quotation is often attributed to Interior Minister Viacheslav Plehve, Richard Pipes, *The Russian Revolution* (New York: Knopf, 1990), 12, and Abraham Ascher, *The Revolution of 1905* (Stanford: Stanford University Press, 1988), 44, show that it was actually former finance minister Sergei Witte, not Plehve, who held to this view.

[110] Michael McFaul, "Eurasia Letter: [Russian] Politics after Chechnya," *Foreign Policy* 99 (Summer 1995), 151. On the electoral setting, see Stephen White, Richard Rose, and Ian McAllister, *How Russia Votes* (Chatham, NJ: Chatham House, 1997), Chapters 6–12.

vote in the first round of the 1996 presidential election, tried to position himself as the popular successor to the ailing Yeltsin by negotiating an end to the hostilities on terms favorable to the Chechens.

Despite the public dissatisfaction over the Chechen war, nationalism and ethnic intolerance remained background themes of political discourse in democratizing Russia. Thus, Russia's fragile democratic institutions could be mobilized in crisis against imperial excesses, but they were less effective in scrutinizing nationalist mythmaking on a day-to-day basis.

### Institutions and interests of democratizing Russia

This ambivalent relationship between democratization and Russian nationalism was shaped by the legacy of the Soviet system and by the mixed configuration of elite interests that emerged from its collapse. A number of Soviet legacies—imperial elite interests, the weakness of democratic institutions, and the habit of imperial thinking—worked in favor of a form of nationalism that envisioned the reassertion of Russian control over the territory of the Soviet Union. These legacies were counterbalanced, however, by the emergence of political and economic elites with a stake in good relations with the developed capitalist world, which required moderation abroad and some degree of democracy at home.

Like the other newly independent states, the Russian Federation was formed from the detritus of empire, but it differed in inheriting the core of the empire and the broken remains of its central institutions. Whereas the legacy of the Soviet nativization policy loaded the dice in favor of ethnic nationalist mobilization in the former USSR's non-Russian republics, Russia inherited imperial infrastructure, interests, and outlooks. The Soviet army, though depleted by drastic budget cuts, was inherited largely intact by Russia, except for some units devolving to Ukraine and some erstwhile bases left behind in the near abroad. Just as Serbia inherited the bulk of a Yugoslav army with a mainly Serb officer corps and a centralizing outlook, so too the Russian army retained a good deal of its Soviet imperial ethos and leadership.[111] Russian army units continued to carry

---

[111] Thomas Nichols, *The Sacred Cause: Civil-Military Conflict over Soviet National Security, 1917–1992* (Ithaca: Cornell University Press, 1993); for qualifications, see Deborah Yarsike and Theodore Gerber, "The Political Views of Russian Field Grade Officers," *Post-Soviet Affairs* 12:2 (April-June 1996), 155–80.

out the mission of guarding parts of the outer frontier of Soviet Central Asia, and they supported the Abkhaz separatist movement in Georgia and the so-called Transdniestr Republic in Moldova.[112]

In the economic sphere, the imperial legacy also shaped options and outlooks. Russian energy pipelines continued to serve the near abroad. Hard-pressed industrial suppliers looked to restore ties to their former markets in the Soviet periphery. Neo-Communists, trying to turn back the clock in the face of market changes, ran for office on the platform of reestablishing trade with the former empire as a substitute for trade with the West.

Another legacy was an imperial mindset. Whereas the Soviet nativization policy had institutionalized ethnic identities in the non-Russian republics, imperial habits had been inculcated in the Russian core.[113] Not only neo-Communists like presidential candidate Gennadi Zyuganov and conservatives like former vice president Aleksandr Rutskoi, but even liberal democrats like St. Petersburg mayor Anatolii Sobchak and Independent Television director Igor Malashenko considered Ukrainian independence unnatural and untenable over the long run. According to one well-designed 1993 opinion survey, imperial views ran stronger among elites than among the general populace, while Russian ethnic solidarity was a more salient concern for the broader public. Fifty-six percent of the foreign policy elite (but only 34 percent of the public) were inclined to "send military aid if asked to aid a country of the former Soviet Union." Seventy-seven percent of the elite (but only 57 percent of the public) agreed that the "national interests of Russia extend beyond its current territory." At the same time, 81 percent of the public (but only 69 percent of the elite) thought that Russia should take unspecified means to "defend the interests of Russians abroad."[114]

Another legacy of the authoritarian Soviet empire, this one shared with the periphery, was the weakness of Russian representative institutions. Political parties, apart from the Communists, began as elite cabals, not grassroots organizations. Yeltsin refused to start or join one. Constitutional

---

[112] John Lepingwell, "The Russian Military and Security Policy in the 'Near Abroad'," *Survival* 36:3 (Autumn 1994), 70–92.

[113] Motyl, "After Empire," in Rubin and Snyder, *Post-Soviet Political Order*, 14–33.

[114] William Zimmerman, "Markets, Democracy, and Russian Foreign Policy," *Post-Soviet Affairs* 10 (April–June 1994), 102–26 at 115.

crisis was routine, as bureaucracies, regions, and the parliament ignored presidential decrees, while parliament passed bills to no effect. Yeltsin attacked the parliament building with tanks, presented a draft constitution featuring a strong presidency for a yes/no referendum, and called the 1993 election of a new parliament on short notice. The 1995 parliamentary elections, won by the Communists and their allies, were carried out in a less arbitrary fashion. But the 1996 presidential election was marred by the incumbent's virtual monopoly over television, threats from Yeltsin's entourage to cancel the election at the last minute, and the Communist candidate's failure to mount even the most minimal campaign during the runoff. Though political parties and civil organizations were becoming better established, Russia's electoral politics still teetered on an unstable foundation of haphazard institutions.[115]

These post-Soviet legacies could have made Russia ripe for nationalist mythmaking. However, Russian opponents of nationalist demagogy enjoyed substantial countervailing advantages. The Soviet system was brought down by elite reformers who surrounded Gorbachev and later Yeltsin; they used their government positions to open public debate and increase political participation. In Serbia, by contrast, the transformation of communism was carried out by elites who had not supported free speech and democratization and thus were in greater need of invoking nationalism as a substitute for democracy. Moreover, both Gorbachev and Yeltsin consistently spoke out for civic conceptions of Soviet or Russian identity. At the historic center of an imperial system, not a nation-state, Russians never developed an exclusive ethnic identity.[116] In contrast, Serbia was an ethnonational state before it became the core of a multiethnic mini-empire, and consequently it had established ethnic myths that could be restored when the multiethnic Yugoslav project unraveled.

Many members of Russia's Soviet-era elite adapted well to the post-Soviet setting of partial democracy and economic privatization. The two most powerful economic interests in the new Russia were the banking sec-

---

[115] Steven Fish, *Democracy from Scratch: Opposition and Regime in the New Russian Revolution* (Princeton: Princeton University Press, 1995); White et al., *How Russia Votes*, 251. On the analogy between Russia's and Weimar's weak parties, see Stephen Hanson and Jeffrey Kopstein, "The Weimar/Russia Comparison," *Post-Soviet Affairs* 13:3 (1997), esp. 276–77.

[116] Laitin, *Identity in Formation*, Chapter 11.

tor and the oil and gas industry, which was largely staffed by nimble holdovers from the Communist era. Russian prime minister Viktor Chernomyrdin's background was in the natural gas industry. Both the banking and energy sectors had a major stake in maintaining good relations with their clients abroad and with international lending institutions. Thus, these cartels had little reason to thwart Russia's system of limited democracy or to flirt with excessive imperial nationalism. They played no role in pressing for a military solution in Chechnya. On the contrary, their considerable financial and bureaucratic influence acted as a force for moderation in state policy and in the content of the news media that they owned.[117]

As a result of this complex legacy, democratizing Russia became a breeding ground for all four dynamics of nationalism: counterrevolutionary, revolutionary, ethnic, and civic. In the counterrevolutionary mode, the heads of Kremlin's military and security bureaucracies (called the "power ministries") constituted a "party of war," which tried to secure their own organizational and career interests through a lightning victory over the Chechen separatists. The entrenched interests of these elites and their organizations were threatened by the chaotic conditions of Russia's poorly institutionalized democracy, and thus they sought to reestablish their authority on the popular but nondemocratic basis of a neo-imperial Russian nationalism. A successful war, using bureaucratic might to cut through the tangles of democratic politics, held out the prospect of more funds for the military, greater prestige for the intelligence bureaucracy, and a new lease on life for hard-pressed officials overseeing these security services.[118]

In the revolutionary mode, Yeltsin calculated that the growing vacuum of institutional authority could be filled only by forceful action legitimated by a popular idea. That idea was nationalism.[119] A victory over the breakaway Chechens would show that Russia could act decisively to defend its national interest and, at the same time, create a strong precedent for unilateral presidential action on a crucial national issue. Thus, it could set the stage for state-building and economic transformation under centralized presidential rule. Moreover, dramatic action in Chechnya

---

[117] McFaul, "Precarious Peace," 24–28.

[118] McFaul, "Eurasia Letter," 154.

[119] On Yeltsin and the radical reformers as revolutionaries, see Motyl, "After Empire," in Rubin and Snyder, *Post-Soviet Political Order*, 24–25.

could have appeal under the banners of both ethnic and civic national-ism: ethnic, because Chechnya's substantial Russian minority would be protected from domination by ethnic Chechens whom Yeltsin demonized as congenital terrorists; and civic, because the civic principle of the unity of multiethnic Russia would be upheld against the principle of ethnic secessionism.

Thus, all political forces were jumping on the nationalist bandwagon to some degree on the eve of the Chechen War. Even Yeltsin's notoriously pro-Western foreign minister, Andrei Kozyrev, began to speak of Russia's right to use force in the near abroad. A 1995 survey showed that liberal and nationalist attitudes were positively correlated with each other.[120] One victim of this trend, Yeltsin's nationalities adviser, Galina Starovoitova, warned that "one cannot exclude the possibility of [a fascist period] in Russia. We can see too many parallels between Russia's current situation and that of Germany after the Versailles Treaty. A great nation is humili-ated, [and] many of its nationals live outside the country's borders. The disintegration of an empire [has taken place] at a time when many people still have an imperialist mentality. . . . All this [is happening] at a time of economic crisis."[121]

Yet despite Yeltsin's attempt to profit from the nationalist trend by using military force against the Chechen separatists, a nationalist wave of support never materialized. The Russian army performed execrably in Chechnya, bombing the Russian-inhabited capital city to destruction yet failing to defeat the Chechen forces. Russian public opinion rebelled against the costs of the war, which were graphically portrayed in the inde-pendent media. In the midst of the 1996 presidential electoral campaign, Yeltsin promised to settle the unpopular war. He recruited General Lebed, a major critic of the war, to preside over that policy change. Should democratization and free speech therefore be seen as an antidote to belligerent nationalism rather than its cause? Not entirely.

[120] Bear Braumoeller, "Deadly Doves: Liberal Nationalism and the Democratic Peace in the Soviet Successor States," *International Studies Quarterly* 41:3 (September 1997), 375–402.

[121] *Ekho Moskvy*, October 14, 1992, as quoted by Vera Tolz, "Russia: Westernizers Continue to Challenge National Patriots," *Radio Free Europe/Radio Liberty Research Report* 1:49 (December 11, 1992), 3. On Starovoitova, see John Dunlop, "Gathering the Russian Lands," in Bremmer, ed., *Nationalism Explained* (forthcoming).

## Nationalism and Russia's marketplace of ideas

At first glance, the outcome of the Chechen War seems to validate unconstrained free speech and democratic accountability as an antidote to the state's nationalist excesses.[122] The deeper lesson, however, is less sanguine: in Russia's poorly institutionalized marketplace of ideas, pluralistic debate is at best a haphazard check on nationalist mythmaking. Driven by opportunistic rivalry, nationalists, Communists, and "liberals" alike drifted toward a neo-imperial discourse, which the media did not evaluate rigorously. As the editor of *Nezavisimaya Gazeta*, Vitaly Tretyakov, remarked: "Freedom of expression and freedom of speech do exist in Russia today. But this is not because of President Boris Yeltsin's struggle for democracy. It is because all the groups fighting for power find it beneficial and profitable to use the media as a weapon against their opponents. They need freedom of speech to destroy their opponents."[123] Insofar as nationalist mythmaking can sometimes be an effective weapon in this struggle, there is no guarantee that pluralistic debate without strong regulatory norms and institutions will check nationalist mythmaking rather than feed it.

### The Television War

The invasion of Chechnya was Russia's first "television war"—the first time that the Russian public had access to competing views of such events as they unfolded. Western commentators praised Russia's independent and state-run media for actively criticizing official policy and successfully resisting government efforts at censorship during the conflict.[124] Not only

[122] The following section on Russian media is adapted from Karen Ballentine and Jack Snyder, "Nationalism and the Marketplace of Ideas" (manuscript, May 1996), a longer version of the fall 1996 *International Security* article with the same title. The original version of this section was researched and written by Ballentine.

[123] Vitaly Tretyakov, "Political Threats to a Free Press in Russia," *Demokratizatsiya* 2:4 (Fall 1994), 621.

[124] Ellen Mickiewicz and Dee Reid, "Russian TV's Freedom Fighters," *New York Times*, January 21, 1995, 15; Paul Goble, "Chechnya and its Consequences: A Preliminary Report," *Post-Soviet Affairs* 11(1995), 25; Robert Orttung, "A Painful Price," *Transition* (March 15, 1995), 3. For a more mixed evaluation see Nina Bachkatov and Andrew Wilson, "Fallout from Chechnya," *The World Today* (May 1995), 93–94.

did journalists prove adept at exposing the falsity of official versions of events in Chechnya, they also served notice to the Yeltsin administration of the overwhelming lack of popular support for its conduct: widely disseminated polling revealed that as early as February 1995, 71 percent of Russians opposed the war.[125] Popular opinion gave high marks to the media's performance during the conflict, particularly the critical role played by Independent Television (NTV) in compelling state broadcasters to provide more accurate information.[126]

However, subsequent developments suggest that the media's successes in Chechnya may be far from self-sustaining. Yeltsin's government reacted to its public relations setbacks by reasserting its monopoly over state television, selectively harassing influential opposition media, and restricting media access to the war zone.[127] Yeltsin's presidential guard led an attack on the offices of NTV's parent company in retaliation for its Chechnya coverage.[128] Given the struggling financial condition of the media, economic manipulation proved an even more effective method of muzzling the press. Russia's premier liberal daily, *Nezavisimaya Gazeta*, was forced to suspend publication after a concerted effort of government harassment that included punitive taxes, manipulation of newsprint supply, and intimidation of potential investors.[129] The Duma, where a Zhirinovsky-sponsored draft law to nationalize all media failed by only twenty-eight votes, offered little protection against presidential assaults on media independence.[130] When Chechen forces seized hostages inside Russia in January 1996, restricted media access made it hard to check government claims that Chechen terrorists had provoked a punitive attack by execut-

---

[125] McFaul, "Eurasia Letter," 151.

[126] Michael Haney, "Russia's First Televised War: Public Opinion on the Chechen Crisis," *Transition* (April 14, 1995), 6–8.

[127] *Segodnya*, September 1, 1995, 1, repr. in *Current Digest of the Post-Soviet Press* (CDPSP), XLVII: 27 (1995), 16. Before the June 1996 elections, Yeltsin fired Oleg Poptsov, the head of Russian television, for his negative programming on Chechnya. See Michael Gordon, "Yeltsin's Ouster of TV Chief Stirs Storm," *New York Times*, February 18, 1996, 10. Note also, Shannon Peters Talbott, "Early Chechen Coverage Tests Print Journalists' Independence," *Transition* (August 9, 1996), 48–51.

[128] Julia Wishnevsky, "Manipulation, Mayhem and Murder," *Transition* (February 15, 1996), 40.

[129] Ibid., 38; Tretyakov, "Political Threats to a Free Press in Russia," 619–20.

[130] Laura Belin, "High Stakes at Ostankino TV," *Transition* (April 28, 1996), 8.

ing their hostages.[131] This combination of tactics succeeded in breaking the unanimity of media opposition. Even some liberal newspapers endorsed the harsh methods of the assault on the hostage-holders and the restricted media coverage of terrorist actions.[132] Media criticized the authorities less for disregarding civilian hostages' welfare than for failing to prevent the terrorists' escape.[133]

### Weak Journalistic Norms

Compounding the effect of these attacks on media independence was the media itself, which suffered from low journalistic standards and narrow partisanship. Despite improved methods of investigative reporting and a nascent ethic of media professionalism under glasnost, Soviet-era journalistic habits of conflating hard news and editorial opinion, as well as a casual reliance on unverified sources, continued to impair the development of Western-style journalistic objectivity.[134] Checks on political mythmaking remained weak and inconsistent, the result more of factional battles in a highly segmented and partisan media than of burgeoning civic norms of open and accurate debate.[135]

[131] *Nezavisimaya Gazeta,* January 20, 1996, 3, repr. in CDPSP, XLVII:3 (1996), 25–26.

[132] *Segodnya* ran a front-page feature by Pavel Felgengauer that was particularly supportive of the government. *Kommersant* was more critical but acknowledged that the media restrictions were necessary to combat terrorism. Repr. in CDPSP, XLVII:3 (1996), 8. NTV war coverage became more cautious in response to Kremlin pressure and public sympathies for Russian soldiers at the front. *New York Times*, March 5, 1995, 4Y.

[133] There were a few voices, most notably Sergei Kovalev, who lamented this neglect of civilians as well as the new tendency even of segments of the liberal press to focus solely on Chechen terrorism. *Moskovskiye Novosti* 1, January 1–14, 1996, 5, repr. in CDPSP, XLVII:2 (1996), 9–10.

[134] For background, see Laura Belin, "Wrestling Political and Financial Repression," *Transition* (October 6, 1995), 59–63; Ellen Mickiewicz, *Split Signals: Television and Politics in The Soviet Union* (New York: Oxford University Press, 1988); Linda Jensen, "The Press and Power in The Russian Federation," *Journal of International Affairs* 47:1 (Summer 1993), 101–2; Elena Androunas, *Soviet Media in Transition: Structural and Economic Alternatives* (Westport, CT: Praeger, 1993); and Jennifer Turpin, *Reinventing the Soviet Self: Media and Social Change in the Former Soviet Union* (Westport, CT: Praeger, 1995).

[135] Victor Davidoff, head of an independent news agency, argues that only the bal-

Journalists and other public opinion-makers failed to scrutinize historical and nationalist myths effectively.[136] Election coverage in both 1993 and 1995 lacked in-depth interviews and analysis.[137] Liberal attacks on nationalist mythmaking were as crudely polemical and self-serving as was the mythmaking itself. Just as often, however, mythmaking went unopposed in the name of journalistic neutrality.[138] Zhirinovsky's television appearances during the 1993 Duma election showed both tendencies at work. Under new rules for campaign coverage, which dictated strict impartiality, journalists were prevented from engaging even the most tendentious of Zhirinovsky's claims. By allowing Zhirinovsky free rein, state television officials acted on the misguided presumption that his antics would prove self-defeating. Journalistic neutrality, however, was observed only selectively. While foreclosing the possibility of rational exchange, it did not prevent state television from bracketing Zhirinovsky's appearances with crude antifascist propaganda films, a none-too-subtle signal that viewers should equate Zhirinovsky with Hitler. Despite (or perhaps because of) the media's dubious tactics, Zhirinovsky's popularity increased after these televised appearances.[139]

During the 1996 presidential campaign, the Communist candidate Zyuganov routinely misrepresented history, understating for example the number of Russians that Stalin's policies had killed. On the rare occasions when such fictions were challenged, Zyuganov's spokesperson invoked "poetic license."[140] It is little wonder that free speech, discredited by cavalier disregard of the truth, finished dead last in a 1993 survey of

---

ance of power between contending elites makes press freedom possible. "Regional Press Fights Political Control," *Transition* (October 6, 1996), 65; see also Vitaly Tretyakov, "Political Threats to the Free Press in Russia," 621.

[136] Astrid Tuminez, "Russian Nationalism and the National Interest in Russian Foreign Policy," in Celeste Wallander, ed., *The Sources of Russian Foreign Policy after the Cold War* (Boulder, CO: Westview, 1996), 52–54.

[137] White et al., *How Russia Votes*, 118, 213.

[138] Ibid., 118.

[139] Ellen Mickiewicz and Andrei Richter, "Television Campaigning and Elections in the Soviet Union and Post-Soviet Russia," in Ellen Mickiewicz and David Swanson, eds., *Politics, Media, and Modern Democracy* (Westport, CT: Praeger, 1996), Chapter 6, esp. 21.

[140] David Remnick, "The Threat of Zyuganov," *New York Review of Books* 43:9 (May 23, 1996), 45–51, at 48.

Russians' political priorities.[141] Only one-fifth of Russians said they trusted the mass media.[142]

## A Segmented Media Market

As in Weimar Germany, Russia's print media became segmented along regional and ideological lines at the time of the Chechen War. Very few mass circulation papers served an integrated marketplace. Under financial duress, the regional readership of Moscow dailies fell precipitously.[143] While state television and NTV broadcasts provided some compensation, the Russian public outside of Moscow found themselves ever more isolated from national news and debates.[144]

Further reinforcing the segmented nature of political discourse was the Communist mobilization of support, which relied heavily on local grassroots organizing, not on open media debate. Blocked by Yeltsin from television advertising, the Communists, like the Nazis on the eve of the collapse of the Weimar Republic, concentrated instead on handbills and pamphlets. This strategy proved highly effective in the 1995 Duma elections. Prime Minister Chernomyrdin's party, Our Home Is Russia, was the heaviest spender on television advertising, yet it fared poorly in the vote. The Communists' strategy of local political mobilization was less effective, however, in the 1996 presidential race. Despite the local party infrastructure that the Communists had inherited from the Soviet era, Russia had nothing comparable to the dense network of illiberal organizations in civil society that facilitated the Nazis' success in late Weimar.[145] Thus, the Communists could not tap into local networks that would out-

[141] Stephen Whitefield and Geoffrey Evans, "The Russian Election of 1993: Public Opinion and the Transition Experience," *Post-Soviet Affairs* 10 (1994), 38–60 at 51.

[142] White et al., *How Russia Votes*, 214.

[143] By 1992, *Pravda*'s circulation had declined to 600,000 from a peak of 10.5 million in 1985, and by 1996 it went out of business entirely. In all, the major Moscow-based newspapers suffered a decline of 18 million readers by 1992, and lost even more thereafter. Ellen Mickiewicz, "The Political Economy of Media Democratisation," in David Lane, ed., *Russia in Transition: Politics, Privatisation, and Inequality* (New York: Longman, 1995), 160. For a survey of diverse segments in the print media, see Belin, "Wrestling," 60–62.

[144] Most local papers are weak in providing coverage of federation-wide issues. See "Regional Press Fights Political Control," *Transition* (October 6, 1996), 64.

[145] Jack Snyder, "Russia: Responses to Relative Decline," in T. V. Paul and John

weigh the impact of Yeltsin's television monopoly in the 1996 election.[146]

Also aggravating the segmentation of the market was the fact that few media sources routinely provided either balanced, objective coverage of diverse political viewpoints or unbiased evaluations of major political parties. On this score, the liberal media were scarcely less partisan than their nationalist or Communist competitors.[147] Typically, Russian newspapers and broadcast media espoused the ideological and political program of particular factions and transmitted this bias uncritically to an already converted audience.[148] Instead of serving as a public-interest mediator of the diverse voices of Russian society or as a neutral arena of political contestation, the media behaved as interested parties to this contest.[149] For example, Igor Malashenko, the head of Russia's principal "independent" TV network, NTV, served simultaneously as Yeltsin's media adviser during the 1996 presidential campaign.

The segmented nature of Russia's political discourse facilitated the marketing of nationalist ideas to its hard-core constituencies. So-called national-patriots like Alexander Prokhanov, Alexander Sterligov, and Sergei Baburin devoted their efforts to mobilizing niche constituents: disgruntled army personnel, unemployed workers, disillusioned youth, and the rank-and-file remnants of the Communist Party of the Soviet Union. Newspapers such as *Zavtra*, *Nash Sovremennik*, and *Sovetskaya Rossiya* and a host of more obscure pamphlets provide an undiluted diet of nationalist and neo-imperialist polemics to their targeted readerships.[150]

---

Hall, eds., *International Order and the Future of World Politics* (Cambridge: Cambridge University Press, 1999).

[146] Some argue, however, that his revival in the polls preceded his major media campaign. See Daniel Treisman, "Why Yeltsin Won," *Foreign Affairs* 75:5 (September/October 1996), 64–77, esp. 65.

[147] Newspapers such as *Segodnya* and *Kommersant* came closest, but their coverage was still heavily biased. *Segodnya*, for example, was consistently pro-Yavlinsky and anti-Yeltsin. And all liberal papers were ideologically anti-Communist. See Bachkatov and Wilson, "Fallout from Chechnya," 93, and Belin, "Wrestling," 62.

[148] Laurie Wilson, "Communication and Russia: Evolving Media in a Changing Society," *The Social Science Journal* 32:1 (1995), 113.

[149] Belin, "Wrestling," 60. On the climate of oppositionalism and its effects on the development of "civil society," see Richard Rose, "Postcommunism and the Problem of Trust," *Journal of Democracy* 5:3 (July, 1994), 18–30.

[150] Belin, "Wrestling," 61; Belin, "Ultranationalist Parties Follow Disparate Paths,"

In the aftermath of the 1993 campaign, politicians of virtually every stripe took up nationalist or neo-imperialist themes.[151] What journalistic Sergei Kovalev described as a "wave of soft, emotional, tasteless, ceremonial patriotism" became the primary discourse of every faction.[152] Although the vote for Zhirinovsky's misnamed Liberal Democratic Party slipped to 11 percent in the 1995 Duma elections, the Communists increased their share of the popular vote to 22 percent by co-opting populist nationalism, thus refashioning the traditional basis of Communist support to appeal to voters beyond the party rank-and-file.[153] Alongside pledges to restore worker's councils and renationalize property, the Communists' Duma election platform also included a commitment to the restoration of the Soviet Union—a promise that was quickly followed by a Communist-led Duma vote to invalidate the dissolution of the USSR.[154] The revamped Communist Party relied as heavily on neo-imperialist nostalgics as on economic appeals.[155]

## Mixed Impact on Public Opinion

Such elite appeals to nationalist and imperial sentiment had a variable impact on Russia's volatile public opinion. Nationalist mythmaking was least successful when confronted by sustained public scrutiny in a diversi-

---

*Transition* (June 23, 1995), 8–12; Alexander Yanov, *Weimar Russia* (New York: Slovo Publishing, 1994). Official proscriptions on hate propaganda and fascist activity have not prevented these groups from freely disseminating their views. See Robert Orttung, "A Politically Tinged Fight Against Extremism," *Transition* (June 23, 1995), 2–6.

[151] Tuminez, "Russian Nationalism," 52.

[152] Sergei Kovalev, "On the New Russia," *The New York Review of Books*, 43:7 (April 18, 1996), 10.

[153] On Zyuganov's hard-line nationalist credentials, see Remnick, "The Threat of Zyuganov," 45–51; Tuminez, *Russian Nationalism*, 50–51; Adrian Karatnycky, "The Real Zyuganov," *New York Times*, March 5, 1996, A23; Alexander Yanov, *Weimar Russia*, 216–22; Alessandra Stanley, "Russian Communist Aims for Wide Appeal," *New York Times*, March 15, 1996, A9.

[154] Michael Specter, "Russia's Parliament Denounces Soviet Union's Break-Up," *New York Times*, March 16, 1996, 3.

[155] Alexander Tsipko, "Why Zyuganov's Party Could Win the December Elections," *Nezavisimaya Gazeta*, November 9, 1995, 5, repr. in CDPSP, XLVII:45 (1995), 4–5; for an alternative view, see Boris Kagarlitsky, "The Russian Parliamentary Elections," *The New Left Review* 215 (January/February 1996), 117–28, esp. 119.

fied and integrated media environment. At the outset of the war in Chechnya, for example, when Russia-wide television coverage was both extensive and critical, polls indicated an overwhelming popular rejection of the official reasons advanced for the invasion.[156] Despite pervasive negative Russian perceptions of the Chechens, most Russians believed that the invasion was motivated more by the self-interest of Russia's elite than by any objective threat that Chechen separatism posed to Russia.[157]

However, the more amorphous expression of nationalist or neo-imperialist themes, which the media had not resisted, did find popular resonance. Though Russians continued to oppose the war in Chechnya, the percent of Russians expressing a general hostility to foreigners rose from 7 percent in 1989 to 50 percent by 1995. Among Russian youth, where residual norms of Soviet internationalism were weakest, the figure was 70 percent.[158] Neo-imperialist sympathies were even more widespread. For example, in 1995, 72 percent of Russians supported the claim that "Russia has a unique path," 70 percent viewed the collapse of the USSR as both regrettable and harmful, and 81 percent favored the re-establishment of Russia's great power status.[159]

Despite the media's successes in exposing the truth about government policies in the Chechen War, Russia's marketplace of ideas remained vulnerable to nationalist mythmaking during the early years of Russian democratization. Pluralistic media rivalry scored only intermittent successes in checking attempts at nationalist demagoguery, whether by the government or its opponents.

In the period since the Chechen War, nationalist mobilization has remained relatively weak in Russia, but this cannot be credited as a success of media pluralism. On the contrary, television and other key media have become increasingly concentrated in a few hands. But fortunately the financial and business cartels that dominate the media understand that their international operations and domestic position could be dis-

---

[156] Mickiewicz and Reid, "Russian TV's Freedom Fighters," 15.

[157] "The Status of Chechnya," *Segodnya*, July 18, 1996, 3, repr. in CDPSP, XLVII:30 (1995), 13–14.

[158] According to the same measures, politicians were substantially more intolerant than the average Russian. See *Izvestiya*, July 4, 1995, 2, repr. in CDPSP, XLVII:28 (1995), 15.

[159] "Who Are Russians More Dissatisfied With?" *Izvestiya*, October 13, 1995, 6, repr. in CDPSP, XLVII:41 (1995), 15.

rupted by a popular nationalist movement. Consequently, as in the Chechen War, these media have had no incentive to play the nationalist card. In the long run, however, self-serving business interests are weak reeds upon which to base the moderation of public discourse in a democratic great power. For a well-functioning marketplace of ideas capable of combating dangerous nationalist myths, it is not enough that journalists do the bidding of pacific bankers: they must also cultivate an evaluative capacity based on norms of reasoned public discourse, toleration of competing views, and respect for evidence.

## Comparing Post-Communist Nationalisms

Patterns of democratization make an important contribution to explaining which post-Communist states experienced nationalist conflict and which did not. In the wake of the collapse of communism, wars broke out only in the former Yugoslavia, the Caucasus (including Russian Chechnya), Tajikistan, and on a lesser scale the Transdniester region of Moldova. The pathologies of incipient democratization played a central role in the nationalist conflicts in Yugoslav and the Caucasus. The Tajik struggle was not fueled primarily by nationalism, as defined for the purposes of this study, and the classification of the Transdniester conflict is ambiguous, so after a brief discussion, these will be set aside. Other states were free of large-scale nationalist fighting, either because they quickly consolidated full-fledged democracy (such as Poland, Hungary, and the Czech Republic), or because elites could accommodate limited pressure for mass political participation without resorting to extreme appeals to nationalism (such as Ukraine).

### *Non-nationalist wars*

The war in Tajikistan was not primarily a war of nationalism, in the sense of a political movement demanding sovereignty in order to preserve and advance the interests of a culturally or historically distinct people. Rather, the cleavages in the civil war, which began in 1992, were based more on local patronage groups than on ethnicity or nationality. As Matthew Evangelista succinctly summarizes the "extremely complicated situation, the war pitted stalwarts of the old Soviet *nomenklatura* [officialdom], supported by an array of organized criminals largely drawn from the province of Kulob, plus Tajikistan's ethnic Uzbek minority, against a loose coalition of Muslims, democrats, nationalists, and residents of the Gharm and Pamir regions that have long been Kulob's rivals."[160] Indeed, most of these "Muslims, democrats, and nationalists" had simply adopted ideological labels to thinly disguise the true nature of their clannish, resource-extracting groups.[161] Like all of the conflicts examined in this chapter, the war in Tajikistan reflected the rivalry of contentious groups in the anarchical post-Communist setting, but by my definition it was not mainly a nationalist conflict.

Likewise, the character of the Moldovan conflict is unusually complex. The Dniester Republic in Moldova has been called "a living museum of the old USSR," dominated by local military commanders and rust-belt industrialists who sought in 1991 to detach this largely Russian- and Ukrainian-populated region from Romanian-speaking Moldova. Despite its self-evidently ethnic aspects, however, officials on both sides of the dispute denied that the root of the conflict was primarily ethnic. The Dniestrians' ideology was not nationalism, but nostalgia for the Soviet empire.[162] Russians in other regions of Moldova, who outnumbered the Dniestrian Russians, did not support the breakaway republic. Among the Romanian-speaking Moldovans, however, a case can be made that their political movement was indeed ethnonational, and that the early stages of Moldova's democratization heightened the conflict with the Dniestrian Slavs. Elements of the Moldovan popular front proposed unification with Romania, and the newly elected Moldovan parliament further provoked the Dniestrians by designating Romanian as Moldova's sole official language. Thus, the complex Moldovan case has elements that fit the predicted link between democratic transition and a heightened risk of nationalist conflict. However, because the undemocratic elites of the Dniestrian military-industrial complex espoused an ideology that was

[160] Matthew Evangelista, "Historical Legacies and the Politics of Intervention in the Former Soviet Union," in Brown, *International Dimensions*, 123.

[161] Rubin, "Russian Hegemony and State Breakdown in the Periphery," in Rubin and Snyder, *Post-Soviet Political Order*, Chapter 7.

[162] Evangelista, "Historical Legacies," in Brown, 113–14. See also Julian Duplain, "Chisinau's and Tiraspol's Faltering Quest for Accord," 10–13, and Dan Ionescu, "Media in the 'Dniester Moldovan Republic': A Communist Memento," *Transition* (October 20, 1995).

explicitly antinationalist, and because they played a key role in fomenting the most violent phase of the conflict in 1991–92, it remains somewhat ambiguous whether this should be classified as a nationalist conflict.[163]

Setting Tajikistan and Moldova aside, then, what explains why nationalist conflict occurred in some post-Communist states but not in others?

### *Transitions from communism without nationalist conflict*

Violent nationalist conflict was virtually absent in states that quickly consolidated a stable democratic regime: Poland, Czech Republic, Hungary, the Baltics, and Slovenia.[164] These states were relatively early developers of mass literacy and a nonagricultural middle class, and thus the skills needed for democratic participation were widespread. At the other end of the spectrum, nationalism did not play a central role in extremely late developing societies of Central Asia, where mass participation had not become a regular feature of political life. Between these two extremes, moderately late developing societies did experience an intensification of nationalism during their post-Communist transitions. In these cases, elites had the motive and the opportunity to use nationalist rhetoric to evade full democratic accountability. Whether this led to violent conflict depended more specifically on the nature of the threats to elite interests and on the legacy of Communist-era institutions. Nationalist violence happened only where popular opposition to ruling elites was strong, where ethnofederal institutions channeled political activity along ethnic lines (USSR and Yugoslavia), where the core state of a multinational empire retained military predominance (USSR and Yugoslavia), or where democratic participation followed the lines of traditional patron-client relationships (the Caucasus). Where those conditions did not occur, elites employed milder forms of nationalism (usually ethnic, but sometimes civic) in an effort to cloak semi-authoritarian rule in popular garb and to

[163] On the elite-mass dynamic in Moldovan politics and on the difficulty of classifying Dniestrian identity, see Stuart Kaufman, "Spiraling to Ethnic War: Elites, Masses, and Moscow in Moldova's Civil War," *International Security* 21:2 (Fall 1996), 108–38.

[164] Milada Anna Vachudova, "Peaceful Transformations in East Central Europe," in Brown, *International Dimensions*, 70, 76. These states, along with Bulgaria, are the only post-Communist states having a Freedom House ranking of 2 or better on both political freedoms and civil liberties for 1995–96. Karatnycky, *Freedom in the World.*

keep a weak opposition demobilized (Romania, Bulgaria, Slovakia, and Ukraine); there, violent conflict did not result.

Where democracy was quickly and thoroughly consolidated, nationalism was very moderate, sometimes even in the face of provocation. For example, the nascent Hungarian democracy watched with relative equanimity as, next door in Romanian Transylvania, Romanian nationalists incited peasants to use scythes to attack members of the Hungarian minority. When nationalists in the ruling party of Hungary tried to whip up a belligerent response, their popularity sank.[165] The voters of Poland, Hungary, and Lithuania, even when disgruntled by economic setbacks, turned not to authoritarian nationalists but to market-oriented, social-democratic neo-Communists.

At the other end of the spectrum are the Central Asian states, where mass groups did not organize to play a sustained political role during the transition from communism. At the bottom of the scale in industrialization, educational attainment, and skills needed to sustain mass collective action on a national scale, states like Turkmenistan and Uzbekistan stayed under the heel of Communist-era cliques, or else broke up into anarchical small-group conflicts like Tajikistan. Where the doctrine of nationalism has appeared in such states, as in Uzbekistan, it is a formula initiated from the top down, not an active ideology of mass mobilization. Kazakhstan and Kyrgyzstan are not at the extreme end of this spectrum, but over time they are drifting toward it. In the immediate post-Communist transition these states experimented with limited forms of democratic representation, some civil liberties, and limited press pluralism, but subsequently curtailed even those limited freedoms. In Kazakhstan, President Nursultan Nazarbaev assumed heightened dictatorial powers after parliamentary elections and press commentary exacerbated ethnic jealousies between Kazakhs and Russians.[166] Thus, in these cases, nationalist movements failed to develop either because these populations lacked the social resources to sustain them, or because coercive ruling elites prevented their development, or for a combination of both

---

[165] Patrick O'Neil, "Revolution from Within: Institutional Analysis, Transitions from Authoritarianism, and the Case of Hungary," *World Politics* 48:4 (July 1996), 579–604.

[166] On the media factor, see Bhavna Dave, "Cracks Emerge in Kazakhstan's Government Monopoly," *Transition* (October 6, 1995), 73–75.

reasons. This shows that nationalist bidding wars and competitive mobilization of mass allies are not the preferred strategies of elites threatened by democratization; rather, the more attractive option is outright repression, when that is feasible.

In some late-developing cases, nationalism did play a significant role in the politics of the post-Communist transition, but it remained more moderate than in the violent cases of the former Yugoslavia and the Caucasus. This occurred, for example, where the fall of communism was accomplished without a sustained mass movement, yet where the level of social development made some degree of mass political participation unavoidable. Romania exemplifies this pattern, which is marked by fairly low levels of administrative organization and education, a large agricultural sector, an uncompetitive industrial sector, and a history of peasant nationalism in the period before the Communist regime. I will elaborate on three of the moderate nationalisms: those of Romania, Slovakia, and the Ukraine.[167]

## Romania

After the overthrow of Romania's Communist dictator, Nicolae Ceausescu, the neo-Communist government of Ion Iliescu sought to base its legitimacy on a combination of socialism, nationalism, and a limited form of state-dominated electoral democracy. For the most part, the neo-Communist elite sought to avoid the disruptive consequences, both internally and internationally, of fomenting a mass nationalist movement. Continuing to stress socialist themes like the social safety net and the protection of threatened economic sectors from unrestrained market competition, their aim was to depoliticize the masses, not to mobilize them.

The Iliescu regime, though restrained in its own nationalism, sometimes included in its ruling coalition extreme nationalist parties, which carved out an entrenched position in a few constituencies. Taking advan-

---

[167] Kitschelt, "A Silent Revolution," 145, 148; Vachudova, "Peaceful Transformations," in Brown, *International Dimensions*, 70. Bulgaria is in some respects a similar case. Juan Linz and Alfred Stepan, *Problems of Democratic Transition and Consolidation* (Baltimore: Johns Hopkins University Press, 1996), 342–43, noted that Bulgaria "overperformed" relative to its apparent social capital and institutional preparation for democracy. After 1996, however, endemic economic crisis, leading to political instability, placed Bulgaria about where the Kitschelt, Vachudova, and Linz-Stepan approaches would have predicted it.

tage of the low level of professionalism of the press in Romania, these extreme nationalists have had no trouble finding media outlets for their divisive nationalist commentary.[168] Arguably, this not only put the civil rights of minorities in jeopardy but also created a climate in which democratic rights in general could be constrained. Such a climate was useful to the Iliescu government when it deployed miners to break up antiregime protests by the democratic opposition, and when government henchmen staged anti-Hungarian pogroms in Transylvania, bussing scythe-toting Romanian thugs into Hungarian villages. Opinion polls indicate the manipulated character of much of Transylvania's ethnic rivalries. They show that Romanians in Transylvania view Hungarians more favorably than do Romanians in other regions where there are no Hungarians.[169] Through such tactics, the regime dominated by former Communists in Romania based its legitimacy on ethnic rather than civic criteria.

Further progress along Romania's trajectory of democratization, however, reduced the level of ethnic tension. The 1996 defeat of the Iliescu regime by the more liberal, market-oriented Constantinescu led to improved relations with the West and with Hungary, and it held out the prospect of better regulated relations between the ethnic communities based on civic principles. Nonetheless, simultaneous setbacks to democratization and market reform in neighboring Bulgaria suggest that such trends are hardly irreversible in societies where the necessary political skills are scarce.

### Slovakia

Slovakia is another case where former Communists employed nationalist rhetoric, but nationalist violence was absent. A largely rural region until the Communists promoted its industrialization after World War II, Slovakia fits the profile of a late developer. As in Romania and Bulgaria,

[168] Thomas Carothers, *Assessing Democracy Assistance: The Case of Romania* (Washington, DC: Carnegie Endowment for International Peace, 1966), 80–89; for a parallel analysis of Slovakia, see Owen Johnson, "Failing Democracy: Journalists, the Mass Media and the Dissolution of Czechoslovakia," paper prepared for the Conference on Czechoslovakia's Dissolution, Charles University, Prague, June 1996.

[169] Sandra Pralong, "Romanian Nationalism—Double Problem, Double Talk?" in John Micgiel, *State and Nation Building in East Central Europe: Contemporary Perspectives* (New York: Columbia University, Institute on East Central Europe, 1996), 90, citing an opinion poll by the Institutul de Marketing si Sondaje, quoted in *Balkan Report* 29, October-November 1994.

the liberal democratic opposition was too weak to dislodge Slovakia's former Communists from power in the first elections after 1989. Former Communist Vladimir Meciar, elected to head the Slovak government after the fall of the Czechoslovak Communist regime, exploited the ethnofederal system to increase Slovakia's autonomy from the reformist government in Prague. This was popular not only with those who sought a vehicle for Slovak national self-expression but also with subsidized heavy industrial interests who wanted to be buffered from Prague's market-oriented policies. Though polls showed that most Slovaks, and possibly even Meciar, wanted to stay within a loosely confederal "Czecho-Slovakia," Czech prime minister Vaclav Klaus called the Slovaks' bluff and forced independence upon them.

After briefly losing his parliamentary majority to a more liberal coalition, Meciar regained the prime ministership on the strength of effective media appeals to nationalist pride and the sanctity of the social safety net, aimed at a coalition composed of older voters, ethnic Slovaks in the rural north, directors of heavy industry, and some industrial workers. Back in office, Meciar sought to gerrymander electoral districts to curtail parliamentary representation of Slovakia's Hungarian minority and thus strengthen the electoral margins of the neo-Communist ruling party. Meciar's high-handed practices in parliament neutralized the influence of the democratic opposition on key committees, despite its substantial representation in terms of seats.[170] In the view of the democratic opposition to Meciar, his suppression of the Hungarian language created a climate in which other forms of speech could be curtailed.[171] By warning against the danger of Hungarian secession, Meciar justified strict measures to keep Slovaks united under his rule. State-owned broadcast media were reduced to cheerleading for the Meciar government. Thus, Meciar sought to use

[170] John Gould and Sona Szomolányi, "Bridging the Chasm in Slovakia," *Transition* (November 1997), 70–76; John Gould and Sona Szomolányi, "Elite Fragmentation, Industry and the Prospects for Democracy in Slovakia: Insights from New Elite Theory," in Sona Szomolányi and John Gould, eds., *Slovakia: Problems of Democratic Consolidation and the Struggle for the Rules of the Game* (New York: Columbia International Affairs On-Line at www.ciaonet.org, 1998).

[171] Miroslav Kusý, "The State of Human and Minority Rights in Slovakia," in Sona Szomolányi and John A. Gould, eds., *Problems of Democratic Consolidation in Slovakia: The Struggle for the Rules of the Game* (Bratislava: Slovak Political Science Association, Friedrich Ebert Foundation, 1997).

nationalism not to whip up a belligerent mass movement but to consolidate a coalition of conservative interests and to stymie liberal opponents.

In the long run, however, Meciar found that this game of restrained nationalist mythmaking and political demobilization could not be sustained. His regime was voted out of office in September 1998 by a grand coalition of opposition parties supported by trade unions, independent media, parts of the Catholic Church, and nongovernmental organizations. Despite the panoply of economic and bureaucratic levers that Meciar used to induce much of the media to toe his line, he was unable to stifle the opposition's message, in part because Slovak society is relatively well endowed with liberal civil-society groups and independent intellectuals who are well connected to Western nongovernmental organizations.[172] For example, when Meciar's government sought to adopt a new school history textbook lauding the Nazi-era, anti-Semitic Slovak collaborationist regime, liberal critics were able to spark a firestorm of international criticism. Ironically, the textbook had been funded by an inept European Union democratization project.[173]

## Ukraine

Ukraine shares with Bulgaria, Romania, and Slovakia some of the characteristics that produced moderate variants of nationalism but not much nationalist violence. Ukraine's former Communist elite oversaw the country's assertion of independence from the USSR and prevailed in the first elections. A mass nationalist movement appeared only in Ukraine's most western districts. The Ukrainian-speaking population, which remains heavily rural, lacks the skills or traditions of statehood to facilitate the mobilization of a mass ethnonationalist movement. In the industrialized and urban areas of central and eastern Ukraine, Ukrainian ethnicity is insufficiently distinct from the culture of the large Russian-speaking minority to serve as a mass political catalyst.[174] Moreover, any political

[172] Timothy Garton Ash, "The Puzzle of Central Europe," *The New York Review of Books* (March 18, 1999), 18–23; Mary Kaldor and Ivan Vejvoda, "Democratization in East and Central European Countries," *International Affairs* 73:1 (January 1997), 59–82, esp. 80.

[173] Peter S. Green, "School Text Glorifies Slovakia's Role as a Nazi Puppet," *International Herald Tribune*, August 13, 1997, 5.

[174] For a vivid discussion of these linguistic and cultural nuances, see Laitin, *Identity in Formation*, esp. 144–51.

strategy based on mobilizing Ukrainian speakers against Russian speakers would have risked driving Ukraine's Russian minority into the arms of nationalist politicians in Moscow.

In these circumstances, Ukrainian former Communist elites, led by President Leonid Kravchuk, found it expedient to use a moderate form of civic-territorial Ukrainian nationalism to consolidate their control over state power. Instead of harping on ethnic themes, Ukrainian state leaders stressed the trappings of sovereignty such as Ukrainian nuclear weapons, the Black Sea fleet based in Ukrainian Crimea, and the severing of some trade ties with Russia. Ukrainian was adopted as the language of state, but Russian, Hungarian, and other minorities could receive public education in those tongues.

Even this moderate degree of nationalism turned out to be counterproductive. The economic costs of placing the symbolism of national sovereignty ahead of rational economic policy undermined this strategy. Soon, both the elite and public opinion recognized the need for improved relations with Moscow. At this turning point, Kravchuk was defeated for re-election by his former prime minister Leonid Kuchma, another gray former-Communist bureaucrat who had to brush up on his rusty Ukrainian to give speeches in public. Especially in rural areas, the neo-Communist elite maintained strong control over local political organizations and thus managed to reconcile a reasonably high degree of procedural democracy and moderate civic nationalism with their continued rule.[175]

Paradoxically, one reason for the stability of Ukraine's democracy has been its dearth of civil society organizations and the lack of an active mass role in politics. Only one in ten Ukrainians report much interest in politics, and only one in a hundred is a member of a political party.[176] Though most Ukrainians do vote, they lack a more active commitment to participation in the life of the nation. According to one Ukraine-wide May 1997 survey, nationalist feeling runs so low that 44 percent of the 2,000 Ukrainian citizens polled said they would support merging their state sovereignty into the Russian-Belarusian union.[177] Ukrainian elites have thus

---

[175] Jane Perlez, "On Ukraine Capitalist Path, Clique Mans Roadblocks," *New York Times*, October 18, 1996, A17.

[176] José Casanova, "Ethno-linguistic and Religious Pluralism and Democratic Construction in Ukraine," in Rubin and Snyder, *Post-Soviet Political Order*, 81–103.

[177] RFE/RL Newsline, No. 74, Part II, July 16, 1997.

faced fewer of the popular pressures that destabilize other democratizing regimes and consequently had less need to mobilize support through belligerent nationalist doctrines.

### Civic versus Ethnic Nationalism and the Violence of Post-Communist Transitions

The former Yugoslavia and the Caucasus were the sites of the bloodiest nationalist conflicts among the post-Communist democratizing states. In these regions, the ethnic form of nationalism prevailed. Conversely, the East Central European states of Poland, the Czech Republic, and Hungary experienced the smoothest and least violent transitions to post-Communist democracy. Though each of these three states has a distinct ethnic character, their constitutions also embody many of the features of civic democracy. Thus, ethnic nationalism produced the most intense conflicts, but when ethnicity was tempered by civic features, conflict was avoided. This pattern echoes the results of the four historical case studies presented in earlier chapters: civic Britain was the most prudent in its conflicts with other nations, though even Britain became embroiled in an intractable conflict when it pursued an ethnically exclusionary policy in Ireland.

The Russian case, however, suggests a qualification to this pattern of comparatively prudent civic outcomes. The form of Russian nationalism propounded by Boris Yeltsin is distinctly civic rather than ethnic, in that it promises equal civic rights for all citizens of the Russian Federation, regardless of ethnicity. And yet Yeltsin's civic Russia fought a large-scale war against the Chechen ethnic separatists. This raises the question of whether civic nationalism has a moderating effect only in states that, unlike Russia, have the well-developed political institutions that are needed to consolidate civic democracy fully. If so, this would impose sharp limits on the feasibility of civic nationalism as an antidote to ethnic conflict in transitional states. To address this question, it is necessary to look at a broader range of post-Communist cases.

Political scientist Ian Bremmer has made the most systematic attempt to rank the post-Communist states on the civic-ethnic dimension.[178] He

---

[178] For a classification of the post-Communist states' nationalisms according to civic and ethnic types, and variations within these, see Ian Bremmer, "Understanding

notes that none of these states embodies what he calls an "individualistic civic" nationalism of the British or American type. However, he classifies several states in the "collectivistic civic" category, meaning that the state promotes a national language and a national identity, but it does not discriminate based on culture in granting the benefits of citizenship. Based on his examination of the states' constitutions and laws, he includes Hungary, Poland, Slovenia, Russia, and Macedonia in that category.[179] (He does not rank Ukraine, which would be included in this group.) Lithuania is on the borderline between the civic and ethnic categories, and the Czech Republic ranks as the most civic of the ethnic states.

Categorized in the mid-1990s as "assimilative ethnic states" (states which try to induce or compel minorities to adopt the language and identity of the majority culture) are Romania, Slovakia, Estonia, Latvia, Bulgaria, and the Central Asian states. Serbia is categorized as an exclusionary ethnic state, which discriminates against and refuses to assimilate minorities. (Bremmer does not discuss the three states of the Caucasus, but they should probably be included in the exclusionary group [see Table 5.3, pp. 262–64].)

Some of these states fit the pattern that would be expected from the theory presented in Chapter 2 and in the historical cases presented in Chapter 4. Hungary and Poland, for example, are comparatively civic states that consolidated democracy quickly and haven't experienced any nationalist conflict. Conversely, Serbia and the Caucasian states are ethnically exclusionary, use popular nationalism as a substitute for true democracy, and have undergone intense ethnic bloodshed. In between lie states whose nationalism is ethnic, but much less exclusionary, and are not involved in violent conflict. All of this conforms to the expected.

However, some of the post-Communist civic states do not fit the theoretically expected pattern. In Britain, the historical legacy of liberal institutions made civic nationalism possible. In contrast, despite the extreme weakness of such institutions in Russia, Ukraine, and Macedonia, their

---

Nationalism in the Postcommunist States," in Bremmer, ed., *Understanding Nationalism* (an uncompleted book manuscript).

[179] On the applicability of the civic category to Macedonia, see Steven L. Burg, "Nationalism and Civic Identity: Ethnic Models for Macedonia and Kosovo," in Barnett R. Rubin, *Cases and Strategies for Preventive Action* (New York: Century Foundation Press, 1998), 23–46.

state elites promoted civic identities. In all three of these cases, state elites feared that ethnic forms of nationalist mobilization would cause intractable conflicts and undermine their ability to rule. In these circumstances of weakly institutionalized semidemocratic politics, it was civic identity that had the advantage of dividing people the least and mobilizing them the least.

In a somewhat similar case, President Nazarbayev of Kazakhstan also sought to establish the post-Communist national identity on an inclusive territorial basis rather than an exclusionary ethnic one. However, after Kazakhstan's initial parliamentary elections polarized the Russian and Kazakh ethnic groups, Nazarbayev curtailed civic politics in order to prevent ethnic mobilization. His subsequent policies have tipped toward a controlled favoritism for the Kazakh ethnic group.[180]

In comparison with the successfully consolidated civic democracies, these weakly institutionalized civic states seem more at risk for violent nationalist conflict. Russia has already fought a war with nationalist overtones in Chechnya. Kazakhstan's ruler had no confidence that civic democracy would be a barrier to conflict. The outcome in Macedonia seems at best uncertain. Nonetheless, it would be hard to argue that any of these states would be less war-prone if they moved further away from the civic form of nationalism. Russia's civic institutions helped it learn at least some of the right lessons from the Chechen War. Moreover, despite discrimination against Russian speakers in Estonia and Latvia, the nationalist backlash in civic Russia has been limited. Based on this evidence, it seems plausible to argue that the promotion of the civic form of nationalism is warranted even when the institutional preconditions for its full success are lacking.

---

[180] Laitin, *Identity in Formation*, 98–99, 285–88, 359–60.

**Table 5.3 Timing of Economic Development, Democratization, and Nationalist Outcomes in Post-Communist States**

| Timing of Development | Country | Institutional Legacies | | | Democratization | | Nationalist Outcomes | | |
| --- | --- | --- | --- | --- | --- | --- | --- | --- | --- |
| | | Ethno-federal History | Imperial Center | Clan Patronage | Began Transition | Consolidated | Type of Nationalism[1] | Intensity of Nationalism[2] | Nationalist Violence |
| Earlier | Czech Republic | ✓ | | | ✓ | ✓ | Borderline civic/ethnic | Low | Low |
| | Estonia | ✓ | | | ✓ | ✓ | Assimilative ethnic | High | Low |
| | Hungary | | ✓ | | ✓ | ✓ | Civic | Low | Low |
| | Latvia | ✓ | | | ✓ | ✓ | Assimilative ethnic | High | Low |
| | Lithuania | ✓ | | | ✓ | ✓ | Borderline civic/ethnic | Low | Low |
| | Poland | | ✓ | | ✓ | ✓ | Civic | Low | Low |
| | Slovenia | ✓ | | | ✓ | ✓ | Civic | Low | Low since independence |
| Later | Armenia | ✓ | | ✓ | ✓ | | Exclusionary ethnic* | High | High |
| | Azerbaijan | ✓ | | ✓ | ✓ | | Exclusionary ethnic* | Varied to high | High |

| | | Type | | |
|---|---|---|---|---|
| **Later** | Bulgaria ✓ | Assimilative ethnic | Moderate to low | Low |
| | Croatia ✓ | Exclusionary ethnic* | High | High |
| | Georgia ✓ ✓ | Exclusionary ethnic* | High | High |
| | Macedonia ✓ | Civic | Varied to low | Low |
| | Moldova ✓ | Varied* | Varied | Some nationalist violence |
| | Romania ✓ | Assimilative ethnic | Varied | Fairly low |
| | Russia ✓ ✓ | Civic | Varied to low | Varied, low to high |
| | Serbia ✓ ✓ | Exclusionary ethnic | High | High |
| | Slovakia ✓ | Assimilative ethnic | Varied | Low |
| | Ukraine ✓ | Civic* | Low | Low |
| **Very late** | Kazakhstan (✓)[3] ✓ | Civic territorial to assimilative ethnic | Low | Low |

**Table 5.3 Timing of Economic Development, Democratization, and Nationalist Outcomes in Post-Communist States**

| Timing of Development | Country | Institutional Legacies | | | Democratization | | Nationalist Outcomes | | |
|---|---|---|---|---|---|---|---|---|---|
| | | Ethno-federal History | Impe-rial Center | Clan Patron-age | Began Trans-ition | Consoli-dated | Type of Nationalism[1] | Intensity of Nationalism[2] | Nationalist Violence |
| **Very late** | Kyrgyzstan | ✓ | | ✓ | (✓) | | Civic territorial to assimilative ethnic | Low | Low |
| | Uzbekistan | ✓ | | ✓ | | | Assimilative ethnic | Low | Low |
| | Tajikistan | ✓ | | ✓ | | | Assimilative ethnic | Low | Non-nationalist civil war |
| | Turkmenistan | ✓ | | ✓ | | | Assimilative ethnic | Low | Low |

[1] Coding scheme and initial codings prepared by Ian Bremmer, "Understanding Nationalism in the Post-Communist States" (manuscript). * indicates coding provided or updated by Jack Snyder. Croatia recoded in light of "ethnic cleansing" of Serbs in 1995 military operations. Kazakhstan and Kyrgyzstan are coded as changing from civic to ethnic over the course of the 1990s.

[2] Reflects elite persuasion efforts and popular mobilization. This column is intended as a rough summary of the more nuanced discussions in this chapter. "Moderate" means between low and high; "varied" means that some time periods or some actors manifested more intense nationalism than did others.

[3] (✓) indicates weak value of the variable.

# 6

# Nationalism and Democracy in

# the Developing World

Ethnic conflict has risen to the top of the international agenda in part because of its resurgence in a number of the collapsed Communist states. In much of the developing world, however, ethnic conflict is not new; rather, it has been endemic in the postcolonial period. A comprehensive survey by Ted Robert Gurr identified thirty-seven protracted ethnic civil wars between 1945 and 1989, all of them in the developing world, and another forty-two shorter-term ethnic rebellions, all but four in developing countries.[1] Moreover, some conflicts that were perhaps misleadingly defined as ideological during the cold war, such as the Angolan civil war, now drag on as struggles between groups that are constituted largely along ethnic lines.[2]

---

[1] Ted Robert Gurr, *Minorities at Risk* (Washington, DC: US Institute of Peace, 1993), 99.

[2] On the characteristics of ideological and ethnic conflicts, see Chaim Kaufmann, "Intervention in Ethnic and Ideological Civil Wars," *Security Studies* 6:1 (Autumn 1996), 62–103.

This pattern of conflict is exactly what would be expected in light of the theoretical propositions advanced in previous chapters. The peoples of the developing world, many of whom emerged from colonial status less than half a century ago, are struggling to build states that can deal effectively with the challenges of military security, economic growth, and popular participation in politics. Starting from weak institutional foundations and a legacy of arbitrary colonial boundaries, state-builders have not found it easy to mobilize unified nations around their efforts. The congruence between the nation and the state remains problematic in much of the developing world. As a result, the task of national—often ethnonational—mobilization will remain on the agenda until this problem is resolved.

In the developing world today, the problems of state-building and national mobilization are tightly intertwined with the process of democratization. Rupert Emerson's classic 1960 analysis of postcolonial nationalism held that nationalism arises out of "deep-running social ferment and change which disrupt the old order of society and speed the processes of social mobilization [and] democratization."[3] As Emerson points out, popular nationalism in developing countries is a two-edged sword:[4] it can be a force to rally diverse communities and social interests to the common cause of building an effective political framework for joint action, but it can also be divisive when popular energies of one group are mobilized at the expense of others.

Which of these outcomes will prevail depends on which groups take the lead in mobilizing the nation and in what institutional setting this occurs. Democratization in the developing world, as in other settings, is most likely to stimulate nationalist conflict when elites are threatened by rapid political change and when the expansion of political participation precedes the formation of strong civic institutions. Thus, democratization under the helm of the conciliatory Nelson Mandela dampened ethnic conflict in the context of South Africa's well-developed civic institutions, whereas it led to ethnic slaughter amid the institutional desert and fears of blood vengeance in Burundi.

Conventional wisdom, particularly in the United States, has been slow to grasp this contingent nature of the consequences of democratization in developing countries. During the early years of the cold war, American

[3] Rupert Emerson, *From Empire to Nation* (Boston: Beacon, 1960), 215.
[4] Ibid., 213–14, 378.

liberals often believed, in Robert Packenham's phrase, that "all good things go together"—i.e., that decolonization, economic development, rising literacy, and vigorous political debate would automatically bring liberal, capitalist democracy—whereas in fact these social processes often increased support for radical, illiberal political movements.[5] Similarly, in the post–cold war period, nongovernmental global advocacy groups, still believing that all good things go together, commonly argue that the promotion of democracy, free speech, and a vigorous civil society undermines belligerent nationalism and ethnic conflict in the developing world. A 1995 report by Human Rights Watch, for example, contended that in ten of the hottest contemporary ethnic conflicts, manipulative governments had fomented the ethnic rivalry as a way to forestall declining popularity or to pursue strategies of divide-and-rule. "Dictatorship offers the ideal condition for playing the 'communal [i.e., ethnic] card,' " the report argued, because "official control of information makes public opinion highly manipulable."[6] Moreover, because "conditions for polarization along communal lines are less propitious in a society where public debate is encouraged," where past human rights abuses are vigorously prosecuted, and where there is "free participation in a broad range of voluntary and public associations," the report asserted that the cure is "vigorous civic debate" in a "well developed civil society."[7]

In fact, however, the reverse is often the case. Almost all of the cases of violent conflict in the Human Rights Watch report—Sri Lanka, India, South Africa, Lebanon, Israel, Romania, the former Yugoslavia, Russia, Armenia, and Azerbaijan—had recently held openly contested elections where powerful opposition groups were more nationalist than the government.[8] Indeed, most of the instigators of ethnic conflict in the cases stud-

[5] Robert A. Packenham, *Liberal America and the Third World* (Princeton: Princeton University Press, 1973), 123–29.

[6] Human Rights Watch, *Playing the "Communal Card"* (New York: Human Rights Watch, April 1995), viii, xiv, repr. as *Slaughter among Neighbors: The Political Origins of Communal Violence* (New Haven: Yale University Press, 1995).

[7] Human Rights Watch, *Playing the "Communal Card"*, xiv, xvii. For a more nuanced NGO view, see Bruce Allyn and Steven Wilkinson, *Guidelines for Journalists Covering Ethnic Conflict* (Cambridge: Conflict Management Working Paper, January 1994).

[8] Thus, the Indian Congress government was outflanked by the nationalist Bharatiya Janata Party, the Israeli Labor government by Likud, South Africa's De Klerk government by irreconcilable Afrikaners, Romania's Iliescu government by the

ied by Human Rights Watch, such as the Hindu fundamentalist Bharatiya Janata Party (BJP) and the Armenian Karabakh Committee, *are* "civil society," that is, voluntary grassroots organizations not created by the state.[9] Moreover, according to Freedom House, civil liberties, which include freedom of speech, had improved in Rwanda and Burundi shortly before the recent outbreaks of massive ethnic violence there.[10]

In short, promoting unconditional freedom of public debate in newly democratizing societies is likely in many circumstances to make the problem worse.[11] Many newly democratizing Third World states lack institu-

---

anti-Hungarian nationalist party, the Sri Lankan government by grassroots Buddhist organizations, Serbia's Slobodan Milosevic by Vojislav Seselj, the Syrian-backed Lebanese government by leaders of the various ethnic groups, Russian president Boris Yeltsin by Vladimir Zhirinovsky, the moderate Armenian government of Levon Ter-Petrossian by the nationalist Dashnaks, and the inert Azerbaijani government of Ayaz Mutalibov by the ethnopopulist Abulfez Elchibey. Human Rights Watch's own study often acknowledges this but blames the governments for weakly resisting these pressures. *Playing the "Communal Card,"* 28.

[9] The BJP is part of civil society, insofar as it is a mass social movement; insofar as it is a political party, however, it is part of what Linz and Stepan call "political society." In either case, it began as an opposition group, which gained a role in governing the central state only after its electoral successes in 1997 and 1998. For the distinction between civil and political society, see Juan Linz and Alfred Stepan, *Problems of Democratic Transition and Consolidation* (Baltimore: Johns Hopkins University Press, 1996). On the dual character of the BJP as both social movement and party, see Christophe Jaffrelot, *The Hindu Nationalist Movement in India* (New York: Columbia University Press, 1996). On the origins of the Karabakh Committee in civil society, see Nora Dudwick, "Political Transformations in Postcommunist Armenia," in Karen Dawisha and Bruce Parrott, eds., *Conflict, Cleavage, and Change in Central Asia and the Caucasus* (Cambridge: Cambridge University Press, 1997), 76–79. Some theorists define civil society in such a way as to exclude voluntary groups that reject principles of human rights, equality, moderation, and compromise. If so, however, the link between a strong civil society and social harmony would become virtually tautological, rendering the concept meaningless. For further discussion of the concept, see Craig Calhoun, "Civil Society and the Public Sphere," *Public Culture* 5:2 (Winter 1993), 267–80.

[10] See Freedom House, *Freedom in the World* (New York: Greenwood Press, annual yearbooks for 1991–94).

[11] R. H. Coase, "The Market for Goods and the Market for Ideas," *American Economic Review* 64:2 (May 1974), 384–91, argues that imperfect markets for ideas are in no less need of regulation than imperfect markets for goods. On the benefits of gag rules in ethnically or religiously divided societies undergoing democratization, see

tions to break up governmental and nongovernmental information monopolies, to professionalize journalism, and to create common public forums where people with diverse ideas can engage one another under the scrutiny of well-informed observers. In the absence of such institutions, an increase in the freedom of speech can create an opening for nationalist mythmakers to hijack public discourse. Well-intended policies designed to promote democracy and free speech in the developing world can, as in the cases of Rwanda and Burundi, contribute to disastrous consequences for the very people whom humanitarians are seeking to help. Assessing the likely consequences of the international community's policies toward the developing world requires a more clear-eyed conception of the causes of nationalism and its relationship to increased democratic political participation.

In this chapter, I first show how different paths to democratization in developing countries can lead to each of the four types of nationalism (civic, ethnic, revolutionary, and counterrevolutionary) and to the distinctive patterns of nationalist conflict associated with each. I then discuss a few especially revealing cases in somewhat more detail. A comparison between Sri Lanka and Malaysia shows how incipient democratization can fuel ethnic bloodshed, and how the truncation of democracy can sometimes avert it. In India, the race between rising mass political participation and incipient democratic institutions was not so unequal, and although its track record is mixed, India's experience can help illuminate the conditions under which successful democratic transitions may dampen ethnic rivalry. Rwanda and Burundi are hard cases that, on first glance, may not seem to support my argument but upon closer examination do indeed show that rising pluralism can lead to, rather than dampen, ethnic rivalry. Finally, I explain why nationalist conflict has not occurred in a number of other democratizing countries in the developing world.

## Democratization and Nationalist Trajectories in the Developing World

Pressures for increased mass political participation in developing countries may lead to nationalist conflict through any of three main paths dis-

Stephen Holmes, *Passions and Constraint: On the Theory of Liberal Democracy* (Chicago: University of Chicago, 1995), Chapter 7, esp. 206–13.

cussed in earlier chapters: the "German" or counterrevolutionary pattern, the "Serbian" or ethnonationalist pattern, and the "French" or revolutionary pattern. A fourth, the civic path, is generally part of the solution rather than a problem, but even civic nationalisms may sometimes conflict with the aspirations of ethnic groups and lead to violence.

In the counterrevolutionary pattern, an authoritarian regime whose power is slipping tries to mobilize popular support for its continued rule by fomenting popular sentiment against foreign rivals. Authoritarian regimes in the developing world may succeed for a time in holding together an elite coalition of military factions, traditional landowning elites, or concentrated industrial interests. But when rising state subsidies to these interests cause the economic policies to collapse, internal divisions within the ruling clique create incentives for some elite factions to reach out for mass support. While liberal democratic or class-based revolutionary appeals are possible, it is more natural for most authoritarian elites, especially military ones, to attempt to appeal to the masses through nationalist populism by invoking an external threat to the nation. This strategy may also be used by rising challengers who are competing for a combination of elite and mass support in a partially liberalizing or democratizing setting.

The classic example is the Argentine invasion of the British-owned Falkland Islands in 1982. The ruthless Argentine military junta led by General Videla, its popularity waning due to the failure of its economic policies, transferred power in 1981 to the more pluralistic regime of General Roberto Viola, who permitted labor unions and opposition political parties to organize openly. Viola also allowed a dramatic increase in the freedom of the press. However, since liberal journalists had earlier been removed by Videla's regime, the more open discourse was dominated by nationalist voices supporting the Argentine government's claims on the islands and clamoring for their seizure. A faction of hard-line officers led by General Leopoldo Galtieri saw both dangers and opportunities in this fluid political situation. Fearing prosecution for crimes committed during Videla's "dirty war" against opponents of the military regime, they seized power in the hope of bolstering the military's popularity through a nationalist prestige strategy centered on the conquest of the islands.[12]

---

[12] Jack Levy and Lily Vakili, "Diversionary Action by Authoritarian Regimes," in Manus Midlarsky, ed., *The Internationalization of Communal Strife* (London:

In the ethnonationalist pattern, political entrepreneurs who want to gain mass support to seize or strengthen state power find that traditional cultural networks based on a common religion or language provide convenient channels to mobilize backers. When this occurs, democratization becomes an occasion for cultural groups to use elections to seize the levers of state power and the economic spoils of office-holding.[13] When masses no longer defer to the authority of elites, back-scratching bargains between elites of different cultural groups may break down, as they nearly did in Malaysia in 1969.[14] As politics becomes more democratic, elites of the majority culture may mobilize their coethnics in an attempt to grab jobs held by members of a minority culture, as in Sri Lanka in the 1950s. In some cases, democratization may threaten to tip the balance of political power away from well-armed, well-organized, privileged, and hated cultural minorities, like the Tutsi of Burundi, in favor of the cultural majority, in this case the Hutu. This may create overwhelming incentives for the minority to instigate preventive violence to forestall democratic change. For all these reasons, in culturally plural societies where the integrative power of the state is weak, elections often become a census rather

---

Routledge, 1992), 118–46, esp. 130–31; David Pion-Berlin, "The Fall of Military Rule in Argentina: 1976–1983," *Journal of Interamerican Studies and World Affairs* 27 (October 1985), 382–407. Another instance is Chile's role as an instigator of the War of the Pacific against Peru and Bolivia in 1879 (the so-called "guano war" over nitrate deposits), discussed in Edward D. Mansfield and Jack Snyder, "Democratic Transitions, Institutional Strength, and War," forthcoming. Other examples that have been analyzed in roughly similar terms include Nasser's risky strategy on the eve of the 1967 Arab-Israeli War, Sadat's decision for war in October 1973, Bhutto's policy leading to the 1971 Indo-Pakistani War, the 1974 Turkish invasion of Cyprus, and a series of border skirmishes between Peru and Ecuador, most recently in 1995. See, for example, Sumit Ganguly, "War and Conflict between India and Pakistan: Revisiting the Pacifying Power of Democracy," in Miriam Fendius Elman, ed., *Paths to Peace: Is Democracy the Answer?* (Cambridge: MIT Press, 1997), 267–300; James Lee Ray, *Democracy and International Conflict* (Columbia: University of South Carolina Press, 1995), 120–22.

[13] Crawford Young, *The Politics of Cultural Pluralism* (Madison: University of Wisconsin Press, 1976), 158; Mahmoud Mamdani, *Citizen and Subject: Contemporary Africa and the Legacy of Late Colonialism* (Princeton: Princeton University Press, 1996), 300.

[14] Milton Esman, *Ethnic Politics* (Ithaca: Cornell University Press, 1994), 73; see Arend Lijphart, *Democracy in Plural Societies* (New Haven: Yale University Press, 1977), on the necessity for deference to elites in consociational powersharing schemes.

than an opportunity for civic deliberation. When this happens, democratization is a likely trigger to ethnonational rivalry.

Where violent surges of mass political participation suddenly topple authoritarian states, revolutionary nationalism remains a potent cause of international conflict. In the classic French case and in more recent examples, the nationalist character of the revolutionary violence is often intermingled with class-based ideological rhetoric, as in the case of the *contra* war in Nicaragua, or sometimes with religious fundamentalist rhetoric, as in the Iranian revolution. For example, Mark Juergensmeyer has argued that today's religious fundamentalist movements in the developing world are the functional equivalents of the secular nationalist movements of the 1950s and 1960s: both are attempts to mobilize popular support for strengthening the state's woefully inadequate capacity to deal with the problems of development. In these cases, violence is often instigated not only through the turbulent domestic politics of the revolutionary state, but also by the fearful reactions of counterrevolutionary neighboring states. For instance, the Iran-Iraq war of 1980, which came on the heels of the Islamic revolution in Iran, began with Iraqi president Saddam Hussein's decision to attack Iran, which had been militarily weakened in the course of the revolution. His motive was in part to take preventive action against the religious nationalist Shiite Islamic ideology, which had the potential to inspire Iraq's large Shiite minority to rebel and induce militant volunteers in Iran to mount a holy war to support the Iraqi minority.[15]

Finally, even civic nationalisms, such as India's, may sometimes give rise to conflict with the ethnic or religious nationalisms of minority groups, such as the Sikhs of the Punjab or the Muslims of Kashmir, that seek political autonomy from the secular central state. Ironically, ethnic nationalist majority groups may, at least occasionally, be more willing to resolve problems with ethnic minorities by simply letting them secede. In the case of the Malaysian Federation, for example, the peaceful secession of largely Chinese Singapore was facilitated by Malaysia's move toward a more ethnic Malay (and less multicultural) definition of national identity.[16] Moreover,

---

[15] Mark Juergensmeyer, *The New Cold War? Religious Nationalism Confronts the Secular State* (Berkeley: University of California Press, 1993); on the propensity of such revolutionary states for international conflict, see Stephen Walt, *Revolution and War* (Ithaca: Cornell University Press, 1996).

[16] Sumit Ganguly, "Ethnic Politics and Political Quiescence in Malaysia and

civic nationalism in developing countries may sometimes unite domestic ethnic groups in order to fight outsiders. In a recent case of this type, the Eritrean People's Liberation Front forged an enduring civic identity to unite eight ethnolinguistic groups that included equal numbers of Christians and Muslims, and to win independence from the Ethiopian Marxist-Leninist regime. This Eritrean civic nationalism helped dampen rivalries within Eritrea, but it has continued to exacerbate relations with Ethiopia. In 1998–99, Eritrea and Ethiopia, both newly democratizing states, fought a border war that produced thousands of casualties.[17] Thus, while civic nationalisms may help to reconcile the political aims of diverse ethnic minorities, they come with no guarantee against the risk of violence.

While democratization may foster nationalisms of all four kinds in the developing world, ethnic conflicts occupy an especially significant place on the contemporary agenda. Consequently, I examine a few cases of ethnic violence in greater detail, beginning with those of Sri Lanka and Malaysia. Often the subject of paired comparison because of their similar characteristics but contrasting experiences with ethnic strife, these cases are paradigmatic of the dangers of democratization in multiethnic societies.

## Sri Lanka and Malaysia: Opposite Twins

Sri Lanka and Malaysia constitute a favorite paired comparison for students of ethnic conflict. In particular, political scientist Donald Horowitz touts these cases as crucial evidence in support of his approach to resolving ethnic rivalry by using electoral rules to create incentives for cross-ethnic coalitions. In both of these countries, British constitutional

Singapore," in Michael E. Brown and Sumit Ganguly, eds., *Government Policies and Ethnic Relations in Asia and the Pacific* (Cambridge: MIT Press, 1997), 233–72.

[17] Arlo Devlin-Brown, "Eritrea Offers Key Lessons in Nation-Building," *Christian Science Monitor*, June 18, 1996, 18; James McKinley, "Eritrea: African Success Story Being Written," *New York Times*, April 30, 1996, A1; James McKinley, "Eritrea-Ethiopia War: Unwanted but Unchecked," *New York Times*, June 12, 1998, A3; "President Says Eritrea Is Ready to Discuss Border," *New York Times*, June 15, 1998, A7; Ruth Iyob, *The Eritrean Struggle for Independence: Domination, Resistance, and Nationalism, 1941–1995* (New York: Cambridge University Press, 1995); Ruth Iyob, "The Eritrean Experiment: A Cautious Pragmatism?" *Journal of Modern African Studies* 35:4 (December 1997), 647–73.

commissions established systems of ethnic powersharing and mass democratization in the waning years of colonial rule. Indeed, Sri Lanka (called Ceylon under British rule) was the first Asian democracy to enjoy universal suffrage.

As Horowitz remarks, given their starting points at each state's independence (Sri Lanka in 1948 and Malaysia in 1957), a betting man would surely have picked Sri Lanka as the more likely to succeed in dampening ethnic tensions. In Malaysia, the Chinese and Indian minorities were recent immigrants, while the Hindu Tamil minority in Sri Lanka had coexisted with the Buddhist Sinhalese majority for centuries. Malays had more reason to envy the dramatic economic success of the Chinese minority than the Sinhalese had to resent the more modestly successful Sri Lanka Tamils. Moreover, a Chinese-led post-1945 Communist insurgency left Malays doubting the loyalty of a large segment of the Chinese community. The dice seemed loaded in favor of a better outcome in Sri Lanka.[18] In fact, the outcome was the reverse: ethnic violence has been nearly absent from Malaysia since some 800 died in a postelection riot in Kuala Lumpur in 1969, whereas over 36,000 have been killed and over 1,200,000 displaced from their homes by ethnic violence in Sri Lanka.[19]

What accounts for this surprising difference in outcomes? Horowitz claims that it stems from different incentives for the formation of political coalitions in the two electoral systems. In Malaysia, he notes, a centrist coalition competing in ethnically heterogeneous electoral districts wins by drawing votes from both major ethnic groups. In Sri Lanka, Tamil districts are both fewer and more homogeneous, and thus rarely significant in determining who governs. Consequently, says Horowitz, Sinhalese parties usually pay attention only to the interests of Sinhalese voters. This description, though superficially accurate, fails to capture the underlying causal difference between the two political systems.

Malaysian political coalitions avoid the promotion of ethnic conflict not because democratic politics works better in Malaysia, but because democracy has been sharply curtailed there since 1969. By 1969, Malaysian democracy was rapidly heading toward the same dangerous pattern of

---

[18] Donald Horowitz, "Making Moderation Pay," in Joseph Montville, ed., *Conflict and Peacemaking in Multiethnic Societies* (New York: Lexington, 1991), 459.

[19] Michael E. Brown, *International Dimensions of Internal Conflict* (Cambridge: MIT Press, 1996), 6.

polarization and ethnic outbidding that Sri Lanka was experiencing. This was reversed only when Malaysian politicians revoked the British-sponsored constitution after the 1969 riots, replacing it with one that banned public discussion of ethnic relations and handed the government the tools it needed to manipulate electoral outcomes. The result was more peaceful relations between Malays and Chinese. In contrast, a 1978 electoral reform in Sri Lanka, designed using the principles Horowitz prescribes to award extra seats to Sinhalese and Tamil politicians who attract votes from the opposite ethnic group, was followed by intensified ethnic conflict.[20]

The fundamental difference was not the type of democracy but the *degree* of democracy in the two countries. Malaysia, which had less violence, also had less democracy. Armed with decisive powers after 1969, the government enforced a lopsided compromise that discriminated massively in favor of ethnic Malays in education and state employment, while it also created favorable economic conditions for Chinese-owned private enterprises. In contrast, Sri Lankan governments, whether socialist or laissez-faire, were beholden to Sinhalese constituents who repeatedly punished leaders if they compromised with moderate Tamil politicians. Whereas the autonomous Malaysian government tightly controlled opposition politicians and newspaper editorial offices, power was less centralized in Sri Lanka. Because Sri Lanka's ruling parties lacked an effective grassroots organization, they depended on local elites, such as the fiercely sectarian village Buddhist monks, to appeal to rural Sinhalese voters. The point is not simply that Sri Lanka had too much democracy but that electoral mobilization was in the hands of exactly the wrong groups in society—those whose interests were tied to a narrow ethnic identity.[21]

### Sri Lanka: The dangers of democratization

In Sri Lanka (see map), as in Malaysia, the British had fostered the development of a small, English-educated, elite of cosmopolitan officials. This elite tended to favor the inclusive civic identity of "Ceylonese," an identity based on loyalty to the governmental system that Britain had established in the colony of Ceylon, rather than on the exclusive ethnic identities of

[20] Horowitz, "Making Moderation Pay," 463.
[21] Dennis Austin, *Democracy and Violence in India and Sri Lanka* (New York: Council on Foreign Relations, 1995), esp. 66, 83.

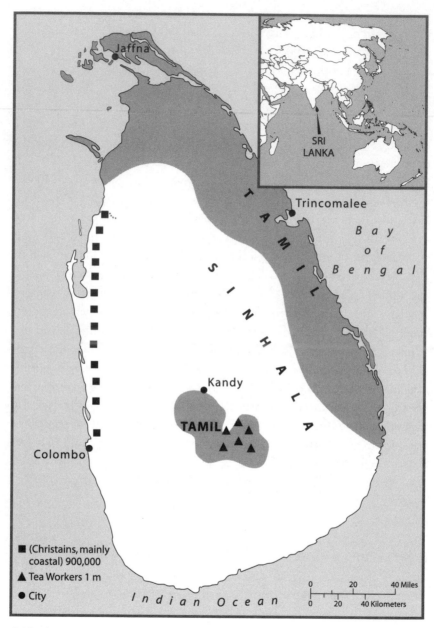

*Sri Lanka*

Sinhalese or Tamil.[22] In part because of the success of Christian missionary activities in the Tamil-populated Jaffna region, Tamils constituted a dis-

---

[22] K. N. O. Dharmadasa, *Language, Religion, and Ethnic Assertiveness: The Growth*

proportionate share of that elite. Fewer Sinhalese learned English, because the powerful Buddhist priesthood had blocked British interference with the traditional monopoly of temple schools to educate lay children.[23]

High-level British-trained native officials never sunk deep roots into local communities and failed to attract a popular following. Before 1931, local government boards, which did have strong grassroots ties, were strictly administrative, not participatory, and could largely be ignored by the elite English-speaking bureaucrats. Ceylon's main representative body, the State Council, was elected under an old powersharing system that restricted suffrage and reserved a proportion of the seats for Tamils. Thus, the cosmopolitan Ceylonese elite was reluctant and ill-prepared when, in 1931, the Donoughmore Commission introduced universal suffrage while still under British colonial rule.[24]

Despite growing populist ferment, the old cosmopolitan elite managed to prevail in elections to form the first two postindependence governments in 1947 and 1952. Soon, however, the Sinhalese rebellion against knowledge of the English language as a requirement for government employment began to gather force. Sinhalese teachers and Buddhist monks also wanted to exclude Tamil as an official language, arguing that language parity would somehow allow the large Tamil population of South India to swamp Sinhalese culture. Particularly active were radical monks in the less wealthy temples. They resented the influence of Western culture and administrative practices, which deprived them of their traditional role as the link between the state and the villages.[25] These monks experimented with socialist rhetoric in the late 1940s, but by the mid-1950s they found that nationalist populist themes were a more effective vehicle for expressing their demands.

---

*of Sinhalese Nationalism in Sri Lanka* (Ann Arbor: University of Michigan Press, 1992), 225–26, 254.

[23] S. J. Tambiah, *Sri Lanka: Ethnic Fratricide and the Dismantling of Democracy* (Chicago: University of Chicago Press, 1986), 65–66, 79, 155.

[24] Urmila Phadnis, *Religion and Politics in Sri Lanka* (New Delhi: Manohar, 1976), 159; Chelvadurai Manogaran, *Ethnic Conflict and Reconciliation in Sri Lanka* (Honolulu: University of Hawaii, 1987), 8; Tambiah, *Sri Lanka*, 108–9; James Manor, "The Failure of Political Integration in Sri Lanka (Ceylon)," *Journal of Commonwealth and Comparative Politics* 17:1 (March 1979), 23; Dharmadasa, *Language*, 227.

[25] Tambiah, *Sri Lanka*, 8, 20; Phadnis, *Religion and Politics*, 74.

Given the competitive incentives of universal-suffrage elections, even a secular, cosmopolitan, Oxford-educated politician such as Solomon Bandaranaike found it expedient to tap into this popular movement. Perceiving an opportunity to gain power in the 1956 elections, the Buddhist political organization offered to support Bandaranaike's challenge to the ruling United National Party (UNP), if he agreed to campaign on the platform of "Sinhala only" as the official language of state. This marriage of convenience served, moreover, to consolidate the ideological shift of the Buddhist movement from socialism to ethnonationalism.[26]

The monks were indispensable to Bandaranaike because of their unique organizational network at the grassroots level. The colonial infrastructure of centralized administration, modern courts, English-educated civil servants, and political parties floated on top of the traditional village organization, where the authority of the village headman and the local monk remained untouched. The monks had an unmatched ability to drum up votes for national candidates who supported their views. Through word-of-mouth, by playing a central role at local political meetings, and by distributing election leaflets, local monks delivered "vote banks" on behalf of Bandaranaike and the ethnically divisive policy of "Sinhala only." The secular press spoke out against the monks' role as political organizers in the villages, but this had little impact at the grassroots. Besides, the clergy started their own newspapers to rebut the mainstream press.[27]

Although Bandaranaike owed his electoral victory to the support of the militant Buddhist organization, once in power he negotiated a pact with Tamil leaders to establish Tamil as the language of administration in Tamil-majority provinces of the northeast and to allow local authorities to block Sinhalese immigration into their regions. These concessions triggered anti-Tamil rioting in the capital city of Colombo. Bandaranaike gave up his plan to gain legislative approval of the pact, declared an emergency, and implemented the main features of the agreement by decree.[28]

---

[26] Phadnis, *Religion and Politics*, 183–87; Austin, *Democracy and Violence*, 66; Dharmadasa, *Language*, 296–97, 300; Tambiah, *Sri Lanka*, 69–71.

[27] Phadnis, *Religion and Politics*, 73–74, 160, 164–65, 185–86; Manor, "The Failure of Political Integration in Sri Lanka (Ceylon)," 21–22; Dharmadasa, *Language*, 314.

[28] W. Howard Wriggins, *Ceylon: Dilemmas of a New Nation* (Princeton: Princeton University Press, 1960), 268–70; Phadnis, *Religion and Politics*, 272.

Buddhists, claiming that the pact would "lead to the total annihilation of the Sinhalese race," only intensified their resistance.[29]

After a monk assassinated Bandaranaike in 1959, the Buddhist militant organizations became increasingly seen as partisan extremists who had lost their moral and political authority.[30] Nonetheless, the pattern of electoral outbidding was by then firmly established. Not only the monks but even the hitherto moderate Sinhalese United National Party of Junius Jayawardene attacked Bandaranaike's powersharing agreement with the Tamils, trying to outflank him in appealing to Sinhala intransigence.[31] This pattern was repeated on several subsequent occasions when the party in power sought agreement with the Tamil minority, and the opposition responded with demagogic attacks to wreck the agreement. In preparation for the 1965 elections, Bandaranaike's widow, who had become prime minister, sought to attract Tamil votes by proposing to revive the 1958 pact. The UNP, opposing this, outpolled Bandaranaike's party, yet they lacked a majority and ironically had to sign a similar pact with the Tamils in order to govern.[32]

This elite-negotiated pact, like a later one in 1977, disintegrated under populist pressure spurred by a flagging economy, 20 percent unemployment, and disaffected Sinhala youth. As competition for government jobs and agricultural land intensified, ethnic rioting broke out in the capital, in market towns among transient unemployed youth, and in new Sinhalese settlements in Tamil-majority regions.[33] The intermittent powersharing efforts of Bandaranaike and Jayawardene, both more moderate than key elements of their mass Sinhalese constituency, repeatedly foundered under the exigencies of mass electoral competition.[34] The mass press, facing similar demand incentives, likewise adopted an opportunistic strategy of ethnic outbidding. In 1964, for example, a press commis-

---

[29] Stanley J. Tambiah, *Buddhism Betrayed? Religion, Politics, and Violence in Sri Lanka* (Chicago: University of Chicago Press, 1992), 50.

[30] Dharmadasa, *Language*, 314; Phadnis, *Religion and Politics*, 275; see also Tambiah, *Sri Lanka*, 58–59.

[31] Tambiah, *Buddhism Betrayed?*, 48–49.

[32] Manogaran, *Ethnic Conflict and Reconciliation in Sri Lanka*, 53–55.

[33] Tambiah, *Sri Lanka*, 13–15, 34–35, 38, 48–52, 55–56.

[34] Austin, *Democracy and Violence*, 70–71; A. Jeyaratnam Wilson, *S. J. V. Chelvanayakam and the Crisis of Sri Lankan Tamil Nationalism, 1947–1977* (Honolulu: University of Hawaii Press, 1994), 89.

sion charged that Tamil- and Sinhala-language newspapers owned by the same media conglomerate were sowing ethnic hatred against each other in their respective communities.[35]

The Sri Lankan case suggests that once the pattern of ethnic mobilization and populist outbidding is established, it is hard to undo. Even seemingly good strategies and good intentions produced repeated failures. Attempts to implement elite powersharing pacts in the face of an ethnically divided electorate were futile. Revamping the electoral system in 1977 to reward candidates who appealed across ethnic lines also failed to break the spiral of conflict.[36] By that time, groups had developed the habit of rioting in the streets against policies that they disliked, so conflict was fueled regardless of electoral incentives. None of this means that democracy per se is incompatible with ethnic harmony in Sri Lanka or elsewhere. It does suggest, however, that the process of democratization can veer in a reckless direction unless it is started out on firm, straight rails. Universal suffrage is dangerous in an ethnically divided society where integrative political parties are poorly institutionalized at the mass level, and where the religious or cultural networks of traditional society are decisive for mobilizing grassroots voters. Sri Lankans would have been better served if the rails had been laid straight, before the train of democratization had left the station.

### Malaysia: The advantages of authoritarianism

Malaysia (see map) achieved independence from Britain in 1957, a decade after Sri Lanka. In many respects, the two started out on similar trajectories. As in Sri Lanka, the British brokered an agreement for a democratic constitution, which was underpinned by a powersharing accord between cosmopolitan, English-speaking elites from the Malayan and Chinese communities. Again as in Sri Lanka, mass electoral competition began to undermine the powersharing accord during the first decade after independence as nationalist parties in both major ethnic groups began to draw

---

[35] John Lent, *Newspapers in Asia* (Hong Kong: Heinemann Asia, 1982), 524.

[36] Horowitz, "Making Moderation Pay," 463. For a good overview of the development of the conflict that includes information about the more recent period, see Amita Shatri, "Government Policy and the Ethnic Crisis in Sri Lanka," in Brown and Ganguly, *Government Policies and Ethnic Relations in Asia and the Pacific*, 129–64.

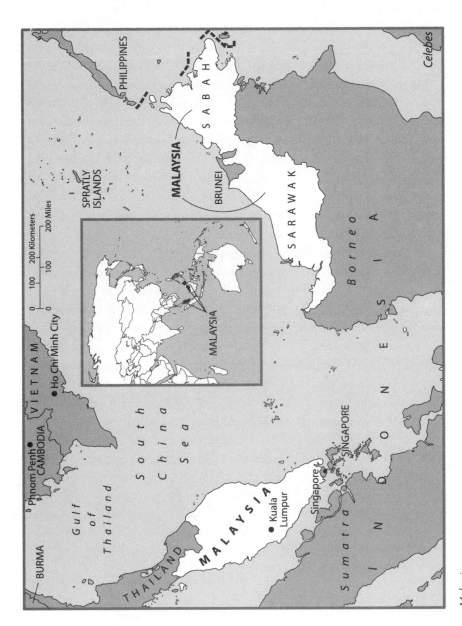

*Malaysia*

votes away from the centrist, cross-ethnic alliance. Interethnic harmony was restored only after democracy was truncated through a suspension of the liberal constitution following the 1969 postelectoral riots.[37]

During the early years of the cold war, an armed rebellion mounted by the Chinese-dominated Malaysian Communist Party had left all Chinese politically suspect. As a result, the Chinese business elites faced difficulties in organizing politically on their own. Moreover, wealthy Chinese found that their interests often coincided more closely with those of Malayan bureaucratic elites than they did with working-class Chinese. As a result, the main Chinese party, the Malaysian Chinese Association (MCA), combined with the Malayan elite party, the United Malays' National Organisation (UMNO), to form a coalition known as the Alliance, for the purpose of contesting the Kuala Lumpur city elections in 1952. This arrangement was reinforced by the British, who made ethnic cooperation a precondition of eventual independence.[38]

The cross-ethnic coalition agreement held firm for the first two postindependence elections. In 1959, the Alliance won 52 percent of the vote in free and fair elections and, because of the magnifying effects of single-member districts, 74 out of 104 seats in parliament. In 1964, the Alliance benefited from the rallying effect induced by military threats from Indonesia and increased its margin of victory.[39]

By 1969, however, the powersharing formula of the Alliance was coming under intense challenge by a second generation of political elites, more ethnically oriented and less cosmopolitan than the founders of the independent Malaysian state.[40] The Alliance continued to campaign on what in retrospect sounds like an extraordinarily reasonable platform. Alliance politicians offered programs to rectify the economic disadvantages of impoverished, ill-educated Malayans, though they justified these

[37] Gordon P. Means, *Malaysian Politics: The Second Generation* (Singapore: Oxford University Press, 1991), Chapter 1; Muthiah Alagappa, "Contestation and Crisis," in Alagappa, ed., *Political Legitimacy in Southeast Asia* (Stanford: Stanford University Press, 1995), 63–64.

[38] Stanley S. Bedlington, *Malaysia and Singapore: The Building of New States* (Ithaca: Cornell University Press, 1978), 85–87.

[39] Karl von Vorys, *Democracy without Consensus: Communalism and Political Stability in Malaysia* (Princeton: Princeton University Press, 1975), 249, 297.

[40] Gordon P. Means, *Malaysian Politics*, 2d ed. (London: Hodder and Stoughton, 1976), 448, citing Stephanie Neuman.

policies in terms of their need to develop agriculture, not in terms of ethnic favoritism. Malay was to become the "sole" official language, but other languages could be used for official business as needed. The Chinese would continue to benefit from a liberal policy on granting citizenship. The ideology propounded by the Alliance was one of Malaysian civic-territorial nationalism, not Malayan ethnic nationalism.[41]

This seemingly reasonable formula began to wear thin, however, in the troubled economic context of 1969. Both the Malays and the Chinese had grounds for complaint against the elitist Alliance, whose supporters came disproportionately from upper-income groups of both ethnicities.[42] By 1969, Malays' per capita income remained less than half that of non-Malays. Malays owned only one and a half percent of the capital assets of limited companies in western Malaysia. Opposition Malay parties believed that the solution should be a massive program of employing Malays in new state-sector industries.[43] Yet they saw that the Malay political power needed to accomplish this was receding because the Alliance's liberal citizenship policies were swelling the ranks of Chinese nationalist voters.[44] "Racial harmony is only skin deep," the manifesto of the Malay opposition party concluded. "Ninety percent of the nation's wealth is still in the hands of non-Malays."[45]

At the same time, Chinese economic grievances were rising. A devaluation of the British pound sterling harmed Chinese business interests. Because the Alliance was hard pressed by the Malay opposition in the intense 1969 parliamentary election campaign, it refused to compensate those who suffered financial losses as a result of the devaluation. This gave added ammunition to the Chinese opposition parties. In a perverse form of interethnic elite collusion, Malay nationalist and Chinese nationalist parties agreed not to divide the opposition vote and so refrained from running candidates in districts where the opposite ethnic group held the majority. The Alliance gained only 49 percent of the popular vote, though it retained a majority of the seats in parliament. Despite this "victory," the Alliance government saw itself eventually heading down a slip-

---

[41] von Vorys, *Democracy without Consensus*, 268.

[42] Means, *Malaysian Politics*, 2d ed., 426–27.

[43] Ibid., 410.

[44] Bedlington, *Malaysia and Singapore*, 146.

[45] von Vorys, *Democracy without Consensus*, 271.

pery slope toward ethnic polarization and ultimate electoral defeat. When riots broke out in Kuala Lumpur between Chinese and Malays in the ethnically polarized atmosphere after this tense election, the government declared an emergency and suspended the constitution.[46]

The government then began to pursue a two-pronged strategy of truncating democracy while implementing a technocratic policy designed to maximize economic growth and increase educational and employment opportunities for ethnic Malays. Heavy government investments would modernize rural areas where Malays were the majority. According to this formula, which was codified in the Second Malaysia Plan of 1971, Chinese businesses could continue to enrich themselves, but national symbolism and government-backed affirmative action would strongly favor Malays. Inflammatory ethnic appeals were made illegal. Political coalitions were arranged through backroom bargaining and patronage deals, rather than open contestation.[47] In the jargon of social science, the Alliance instituted an "ethnic control regime" based on a combination of repression and side-payments to some of the losers.[48]

This strategy was so successful that by 1973 even the nationalist opposition parties had been co-opted into the ruling Alliance, which controlled 80 percent of the seats in parliament. Under this system of sharp limitations on free speech and truncated democratic rights, Malaysia has enjoyed three decades of extraordinary economic growth without serious ethnic violence, with the Alliance unassailably in power.[49]

A key factor in this success is the power of Malaysian state administrators over society. Malaysia had a long tradition of effective central bureaucracy, a powerful tool that Alliance politicians could use to coerce or buy off

[46] Bedlington, *Malaysia and Singapore*, 145–48, also 116.

[47] Means, *Malaysian Politics*, 2d ed., 439; von Vorys, *Democracy without Consensus*, 394–412; Bedlington, *Malaysia and Singapore*, 116.

[48] D. Rumley, "Political Geography of Control of Minorities," *Tijdschrift voor Economische in Sociale Geographie* 84:1 (1993); Ian Lustick, "Stability in Deeply Divided Societies: Consociationalism versus Control," *World Politics* 31:3 (April 1979), 325–44.

[49] Bedlington, *Malaysia and Singapore*, 152; William Case, "Malaysia: Aspects and Audiences of Legitimacy," in Alagappa, *Political Legitimacy*, 75–76, 79–80, 106; Ganguly, "Ethnic Politics and Political Quiescence in Malaysia and Singapore," in Brown and Ganguly, *Government Policies and Ethnic Relations in Asia and the Pacific*, 233–72.

opponents under the Second Malaysia Plan.[50] The co-optive powers held by the state under the revised 1971 constitution included the ability to distribute patronage to cooperative opposition politicians, the distribution of central tax revenues to cooperative localities, and the parceling out of economic development projects. Political opposition was further reduced by revoking the citizenship or legal right of residency of 181,000 non-Malays.[51] The immediate repression of the rioting was facilitated by the loyalty and efficiency of the Malay-dominated military and police.[52] Moreover, under the new system, the state was equally ruthless in repressing unruly gangs among all ethnic groups, including Malays. Sarawak ranger units formed of Iban tribesmen were brought in from the Malaysian part of Borneo to repress opposition in Malay areas.[53]

Finally, the state had strong powers to bar ethnonationalist messages from the media. A 1971 constitutional amendment made it a crime even for legislators to discuss ethnically sensitive questions about Malay-language dominance, citizenship, or the constitutionally mandated "special position" of Malays as the original "sons of the soil" of the country. Ownership and staff of the mass media were "Malaysianized" in the 1970s. This assertion of state authority over the press was legitimized in part by a policy begun under the British, who had required newspapers to apply for annual licenses and had threatened seditious newspapers with closure. After 1969, the police kept close tabs on the opposition press. Even as recently as 1987, the main Chinese newspaper was closed down for a year after it protested the policy of having Malay principals administer Chinese schools. As a result, says Gordon Means, Malaysian journalists had become "cautious, timid, and frequently servile."[54] A degree of academic freedom was allowed, but only for boring, small-circulation scholarly journals that had no impact on a wider audience.[55]

[50] Milton Esman, *Administration and Development in Malaysia: Institution Building and Reform in a Plural Society* (Ithaca: Cornell University Press, 1972).

[51] Means, *Malaysian Politics*, 2d ed., 400, 404.

[52] Bedlington, *Malaysia and Singapore*, 166–67.

[53] von Vorys, *Democracy without Consensus*, 348.

[54] Means, *Malaysian Politics: The Second Generation*, 137–40; Bedlington, *Malaysia and Singapore*, 150; Jon Vanden Heuvel, *The Unfolding Lotus: East Asia's Changing Media* (New York: Columbia University, Freedom Forum Media Studies Center, 1993), 146–62; von Vorys, *Democracy without Consensus*, 429.

[55] Means, *Malaysian Politics: The Second Generation*, 140–41.

What is the long-run prognosis for this strategy of controlling ethnic conflict by truncating democracy in a rapidly developing society and economy? One criticism of the Alliance regime of Mahathir bin Mohamed is that it has done little to prepare for a transition to a more open form of democratic participation. Instead, it has relied on the continued viability of the strategy of repression and the rapid economic growth that benefits all constituencies. It is a "paradox," Means argues, that the post-1969 formula, which was meant to defuse ethnicity as an issue in Malaysian politics, has in fact led to "the perpetuation of ethnic divisions in law, in institutions, and in public policy," turning "subjective identities" into far more rigid, exclusionary categories, especially through the favoritism shown to ethnic Malays. As an antidote, he urges switching to a policy of affirmative action for disadvantaged Malays based on nonethnic criteria, such as "rubber-tree smallholders" or "estate laborers," much like the policy of the United Malays' National Organisation (the Malay partner in the Alliance) in the late 1960s.[56] In Means's view, Mahathir has squandered the time bought by the repression and failed to create a stable foundation for the transition to a more enduring multiethnic democracy.

Others argue that such a strategy would have been unworkable in a context of increased democracy. Mahathir's main opposition in the 1980s, for example, came not from the Chinese but from Islamic groups, which tried to outflank the relatively tepid ethnic politics of the UMNO. In order to deflect this threat, Mahathir offered interest-free loans from a state-backed Islamic bank and created an Islamic university. Switching to a nonethnic strategy would arguably have been political suicide under these circumstances.[57]

An alternative strategy is to hope that economic changes brought by several consecutive years in the early 1990s of annual growth rates over 7 percent will so transform Malaysian society as to make ethnic divisions irrelevant. For example, the liberalizing 1991 New Development Policy reduced the government's role in the economy and, consequently, lessened the impact of ethnically discriminatory state hiring rules. Likewise, economic change is promoting a variety of crosscutting economic, cul-

[56] Means, *Malaysian Politics: The Second Generation*, 313–14.
[57] Case, "Malaysia: Aspects and Audiences of Legitimacy," in Alagappa, *Political Legitimacy*, 75.

tural, class, and gender cleavages that may reduce the salience of the Malay-Chinese split.[58]

In conclusion, the paired cases of Sri Lanka and Malaysia show that democratization risks the exacerbation of ethnic tensions, especially when the most effective tools for mobilizing mass political support are traditional ethnic networks, such as those of the Sri Lankan village monks. In such cases, the truncation of democracy may be part of the solution, and not (as Human Rights Watch argues) the main problem. Sri Lanka and Malaysia offer lessons in what developing countries should avoid during democratization. India has important similarities to those cases, yet it offers more positive lessons about the creation of strong civic and journalistic institutions as a precondition to democratization in a multiethnic society.

## India: The Race between Civic Institutionalization and Ethnic Mobilization

India has a mixed record of intermittent ethnic violence punctuating a general pattern of interethnic peace. Ethnic violence was most intense at the moment of India's independence. Nearly a million were killed and 15 million uprooted in the Hindu-Muslim clashes that accompanied the 1947 partition of the British Raj into India and Pakistan.[59] Between 1947 and the 1980s, Hindu-Muslim rioting occurred from time to time in a few cities, but the overall pattern of relations among India's ethnic and religious groups was moderate and stable (see map on following page).[60]

A second spike in ethnic violence came in the 1980s and 1990s with the rising intensity of three ethnic separatist movements. Since 1989, over 15,000 have been killed and a quarter million displaced in fighting between the Indian government and Muslim rebels in the mountainous province of Kashmir, which is claimed by both India and Pakistan. Since fighting against Sikh insurgents began in the province of Punjab in 1981,

---

[58] Ibid., 79–80, 106.

[59] Radha Kumar, "The Troubled History of Partition," *Foreign Affairs* 76:1 (January/February 1997), 26.

[60] Ashutosh Varshney, *Ethnic Conflict and Civic Life: Hindus and Muslims in India* (New Haven: Yale University Press, forthcoming).

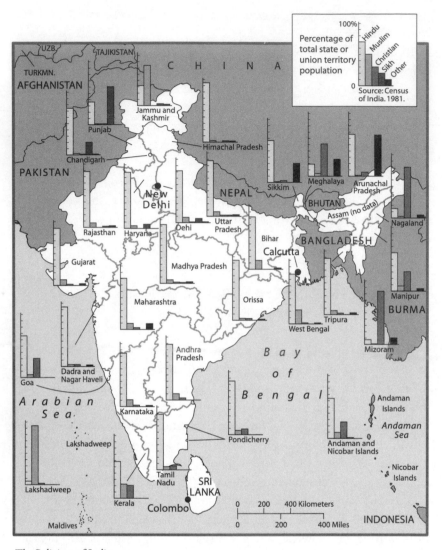

*The Religions of India*

20,000 have been killed. And in the province of Assam, 5,000 have died since 1979 in a complex struggle that has involved the Hindu Assamese, the Muslim minority, tribal peoples, and government forces.[61] At the same time, ethnic nationalism has also been on the rise among India's Hindu majority. The Bharatiya Janata Party instigated the destruction of an historic Muslim temple by a Hindu mob in 1992 and by 1998 won

---

[61] Brown, *International Dimensions of Internal Conflict*, 5.

enough votes to become the main party in India's governing coalition.

This mixed pattern of peace and violence was shaped by changes in the prevailing balance between the rising demands for political participation and the strength of civic institutions. As in Sri Lanka and Malaysia, the national elite formed during India's experience as a British colony was English-speaking, cosmopolitan, and for the most part secular. Jawaharlal Nehru, prime minister from 1947 (India's independence) until his death in 1964, struggled to establish a mass democracy based on inclusive, civic principles, in an impoverished country divided into several religious communities, that spoke hundreds of distinct languages. In light of these difficulties, India deserves to be counted as a qualified success in managing ethnic relations in a newly democratic state. Nonetheless, in recent decades a weakening in Nehru's integrative Congress Party has created an opening for ethnic politicians who seek to exploit the increased political awareness and aspirations of grassroots constituencies. Thus, the increase in ethnic nationalism and violence during the 1980s and 1990s resulted from a gap between the rising demands for participation and the declining ability of civic institutions to integrate formerly passive groups into the political life of the country.

### Ancient cultures and insecurity in their political context

Although cultural differences between Hindus and Muslims are ancient in India, it would be mistaken to attribute contemporary nationalist conflicts mainly to endemic popular animosities. India's ethnic communities have experienced periods of both peace and conflict over the centuries. Within Hinduism, an inclusive tradition of integrating the gods and cultural practices of other sects is arguably more ancient than any tradition of cultural rivalry. The reinvention of the Hindu tradition as exclusionary is a relatively recent project of Hindu nationalist politicians and writers. In the period since democratization, the level of conflict has varied so much over time and across locations that an alleged general propensity to ethnic hatred cannot explain much.[62] More revealing is how the political

---

[62] Susanne Hoeber Rudolph and Lloyd I. Rudolph, "Modern Hate," *The New Republic* 208:12 (March 22, 1993): Varshney, *Ethnic Conflict and Civic Life*; Paul Brass, *Language, Religion and Politics in North India* (Cambridge: Cambridge University Press, 1974).

context has varied in ways that sometimes fan the flames of ethnic rivalries and other times dampen them.

Likewise, it would be a mistake to explain ethnic violence in terms of security fears of India's distinct cultural groups without emphasizing that these fears are a symptom of varying political circumstances. It is true, for example, that most of the killing in 1947 occurred because of the abrupt decision to partition the Raj into Muslim Pakistan and Hindu-dominated India. Millions of Muslims living on the "wrong" side of the ethnically defined frontier suddenly felt vulnerable to exploitation by Hindu groups that competed with them for land and economic position. Because massive population movements were taking place with virtually no police or administrative oversight, violence was extensive. The deeper question, however, is how did the nature of the political system create this situation and yet still provide the capacity to dampen ethnic fears and rivalry.

The changing pattern of ethnic relations in India has been shaped by a race between the institutionalization of civic politics and an ethnic countertrend in the face of rising demands for mass political participation. Ethnic peace prevailed when India's secular elite was able to use the Congress Party and a professionalized press to accommodate moderate mass demands for inclusion in a civic form of politics. In contrast, when these secular institutions weakened and when demands for political participation increased, Hindu, Muslim, or other sectarian counterelites exploited alternative channels for political mobilization grounded in cultural differences, and as a result, ethnic conflict intensified.

### *Institutionalizing civic and ethnic political identities*

The British legacy contained elements that favored the politicization of both civic and ethnic identities. On the one hand, during more than a century of rule in India, Britain laid down an infrastructure of representative institutions, state administrative capacity, an educated elite with English as a common language, and a professionalized legal system and press, all of which provided the raw materials for a working civic polity. As a result of a 1919 reform of local governing boards, the Congress Party worked at grassroots electoral agitation, laying the groundwork to become a mass-based political party.[63]

---

[63] Manor, "Failure of Political Integration," 23. Such British policies did not pro-

On the other hand, as part of a strategy of divide-and-rule, British practices also politicized ethnic differences. Seeking to accommodate demands for popular political participation after World War I, the British established a system of separate electorates and guaranteed numbers of seats in provincial parliaments for Muslims and Hindus.[64] Traditional Muslim elites favored this arrangement, in part because they felt confident of their ability to control the choice of Muslim candidates. Since these Muslim elites were the allies of the British rulers in resisting Hindu demands for independence, the British had a stake in creating an electoral system that would strengthen Muslim autonomy vis-à-vis the Hindu majority. A unified, ethnic-blind electoral system, in contrast, would have facilitated the secular Congress Party's attempts to attract the Muslim rank-and-file.

As the political system began to democratize, this system of ethnic representation helped to channel mass loyalties along ethnic lines.[65] In 1937, the British allowed free elections for provincial parliaments, which would have substantial powers. Muslim electorates voted mainly for local Muslim parties or for the Congress Party; only 3 percent selected the Muslim League, which campaigned on a national basis for Muslim political autonomy under continued British sovereignty. This weak showing led the Congress Party to ignore League politicians in the filling of cabinet posts and to reject demands for Muslim autonomy.[66] As a result, the Muslim League began to advocate a separate, sovereign Muslim state. To gain mass support for this outcome, the League mounted a very successful campaign of grassroots organization, which soon overtook the local parties that had dominated Muslim loyalties in 1937.[67]

British policy promoted the politicization of Muslim identity still further during World War II. When Britain committed India to the war effort against Germany, without consultation, Congress Party members in the Indian government resigned en masse. Congress leaders were jailed, and the Party was unable to operate during the war. The Muslim League, however,

---

duce these same results in all of its colonies. In colonial Ceylon (Sri Lanka), for example, the English-speaking native politicians stayed aloof from local politics.

[64] Anita Inder Singh, *The Origins of the Partition of India, 1936–1947* (Delhi: Oxford University Press, 1987), 237; Peter Hardy, *The Muslims of British India* (Cambridge: Cambridge University Press, 1972), Chapter 8.

[65] H. V. Hodson, *The Great Divide* (London: Hutchison, 1969), 14–15, 48.

[66] Anup Chand Kapur, *The Punjab Crisis* (New Delhi: S. Chand, 1985), 56.

[67] Kapur, *Punjab*, 59.

continued to see Britain as its protector against the Hindu majority, and so supported the British war effort. Enjoying a clear field for political organizing without any opposition from the Congress, the League emerged from the war with a strengthened hold over the Muslim electorate.

In the post-war 1946 elections, the League gained 76 percent of the Muslim vote through its irresistible call for the creation of the state of Pakistan.[68] When in 1947 the League called for "direct action" in the streets to press the Congress for concessions on Muslim autonomy, the new electorate, its loyalties channeled by the system of representation separated by ethnicity, responded by rioting in Calcutta and in other major cities. Looking to extricate themselves through a policy of "divide-and-quit," the British abandoned India to a chaotic bloody partition of the extensively intermingled religious communities.

Despite this rocky start, at the height of the authority of Nehru and the Congress Party, India's ability to manage ethnic tension was impressive. By the time of the first postindependence elections in 1952, the Congress organization had become well established in villages and neighborhoods.[69] Traditional local leaders were recruited, by patronage, into Congress structures, which were rapidly becoming the only game in town. Congress adapted to the demands of these local elites but kept a short leash on the expression of ethnic prejudices. After 1956, for example, India deftly carried off a redrawing of many of the boundaries of India's federal units, in response to demands for linguistically more homogeneous provinces. Whereas ethnofederal border rectification is rightly viewed as a Pandora's Box of incompatible claims, the Indian central government had both the astuteness to devise reasonable rules governing adjustments and the authority to enforce them.[70] Similarly, at the 1962 National Integration Conference, the Congress leadership insisted that its local politicians refrain from recruiting support through divisive ethnic or caste messages.[71]

The dominance of central Congress authorities began to slip during the

[68] Singh, *Origins*, 243.

[69] Lloyd Rudolph and Susanne Rudolph, *In Pursuit of Lakshmi: The Political Economy of the Indian State* (Chicago: University of Chicago, 1987), 127.

[70] Myron Weiner, *Party Building in a New Nation: The Indian National Congress* (Chicago: University of Chicago Press, 1967), 50.

[71] Myron Weiner, "India: Two Political Cultures," in Lucian Pye and Sidney Verba, eds., *Political Culture and Political Development* (Princeton: Princeton University Press, 1965), 231.

1960s, bringing with it a new era of ethnic politics. In part this reflected a rivalry between traditional village notables and a new generation of upwardly mobile peasants in local Congress organizations. The older Congress bosses, who had generally attempted to bridge castes and ethnic groups, were increasingly seen as unresponsive and self-serving. Protest movements against this establishment sometimes mobilized around class appeals, but existing social networks made it easier to mobilize along ethnic lines.[72] At the top of the Congress hierarchy, Nehru's daughter, Indira Gandhi, was locked in combat with the old-boy network of the party, which was dubbed "the Syndicate." In the late 1960s and 1970s, she sought to free herself from Congress's grassroots organizational structure through direct appeals not only to religious groups but also to increasingly politicized lower-caste and lower-class segments of Indian society.[73]

These tactics encouraged the expression of political demands in ethnic terms. After Indira Gandhi agreed to change the borders of Punjab, which the dominant Sikh ethnic group there had demanded, the Sikhs increased their demands on a host of other issues. They insisted on greater financial autonomy for Punjab, a more favorable division of water rights, further border changes, and special rights for Sikhs elsewhere in India.[74]

At the same time, Indira Gandhi's tactics undercut the ability of India's centralized, secular institutions to contain these rising ethnic demands.[75] Partly in response to the Sikh crisis, she began twenty months of emergency rule in June 1975 with the jailing of scores of journalists and the dissolution of the Press Council, India's watchdog of free and fair speech. Accurate reporting on the Sikh separatist conflict was made impossible by the arrest of journalists under the Punjab Special Powers Act.[76] Once emergency rule

[72] Stanley Kochanek, *The Congress Party of India* (Princeton: Princeton University Press, 1968), 351; Francine Frankel, *India's Political Economy, 1947–1977* (Princeton: Princeton University Press, 1978), 341; Weiner, "India: Two Political Cultures," in Pye and Verba, *Political Culture and Political Development*, 210–11; Anthony Smith, *The Ethnic Origins of Nations* (Oxford: Blackwell, 1986), 146.

[73] Rudolph and Rudolph, *Lakshmi*, 128, 134–35; Frankel, *India's Political Economy*, 344–45, 386–90.

[74] Kanti Bajpai, "Diversity, Democracy, and Devolution in India," in Brown and Ganguly, *Government Policies and Ethnic Relations in Asia and the Pacific*, 71.

[75] Human Rights Watch, *Playing the "Communal Card,"* 21.

[76] Kevin Boyle, *Article 19 World Report 1988* (New York: Times Books, 1988), 135–37.

ceased, Congress leaders in Delhi found that their local networks had atrophied. Access to local information and the ability to recognize and select
good candidates and provincial ministers had been degraded.[77]

After Indira Gandhi's assassination, her son and successor Rajiv
Gandhi found himself compelled to resort to a strategy similar to his
mother's. Circumventing core Congress structures, he instead relied on
peripheral organizations like the Youth Congress, which provided what
Atul Kohli called "belligerent mass mobilization" for short-term advantages against political opponents.[78] Equally corrosive was a plan to reserve
half of the positions in the governmental bureaucracy to minorities and
formerly disadvantaged castes.[79]

As a result of this decline in India's central civic institutions, ethnic conflict has been on the rise ever since. As Susanne and Lloyd Rudolph
explain, "India's institutional assets began to dissipate as Indira Gandhi
sought to maintain power in the face of an increasingly mobilized and
demanding electorate."[80] In the race between institutions and participation, civic institutions were losing. Increasingly, local politicians, especially
in Kashmir and Punjab, resorted to the strategy of ethnic mobilization,
which helped them move into the resulting institutional vacuum. Outbreaks of violence increasingly coincided with the electoral cycle, as the
democratic process politicized dormant cultural and status cleavages.[81] In
this new environment, the Congress Party no longer attracted enough
votes to remain the governing party. Instead, recent electoral politics has
been dominated by the Hindu nationalist Bharatiya Janata Party, the winner of the 1998 and 1999 parliamentary elections, and by a conglomeration of moderate regional parties, which prevailed in the 1996 election.

### Professional versus ethnic journalism

Journalism provides another prism through which to tell the same story.
Indian professional journalism has a long tradition of high-quality report-

---

[77] Rudolph and Rudolph, *Lakshmi*, 137–38.

[78] Atul Kohli, *Democracy and Discontent: India's Growing Crisis of Governability*
(Cambridge: Cambridge University Press, 1990), 340.

[79] Rudolph and Rudolph, "Modern Hate."

[80] Rudolph and Rudolph, *Lakshmi*, 132.

[81] Austin, *Democracy and Violence*, 3, 6.

ing, which has served to keep ethnic tensions in check. However, the high-quality English-language press is running a race against inflammatory vernacular local media, which thrive on the exacerbation of ethnic tension.

By the start of the twentieth century, the English-language Indian press was already able to use the pressure of open public debate to constrain the nonelected British regime's policies.[82] By the time of independence, a number of highly professional, major urban newspapers had developed a voluntary press code for reporting on ethnic riots. Following this code, the press abjured provocative headlines, refrained from specifying casualty figures during the heat of the moment, scrupulously cited sources, and dug for accurate information on the causes of riots. These informal codes were institutionalized in the Press Council, modeled on its British forebear. The Council was given the same statutory powers as a civil court to investigate violations of the press code.[83]

The smaller, partisan newspapers, however, have often inflamed ethnic tensions. In provincial towns, publishers and journalists are highly dependent on the support of local business elites, and expedience often gets in the way of truth in reporting on interethnic relations. The vernacular language press commonly circulates false reports, inflated death figures, and unevaluated statements by ethnic leaders. This gap between the restrained, professional, statewide press and the inflammatory vernacular press has been growing over the past two decades as a result of economic change and the growth of literacy in provincial areas.[84] Social change, sharply rising newspaper readership, and the emergence of a local intelligentsia have played a central role in re-igniting ethnic conflict in Kashmir, for example.[85]

---

[82] S. N. Paul, *Public Opinion and British Rule* (New Delhi: Metropolitan, 1979).

[83] R. C. S. Sarkar, *The Press in India* (New Delhi: S. Chand, 1984), 190–93, 295–96; Moti Lal Bhargava, *Role of Press in the Freedom Movement* (New Delhi: Reliance, 1987), 336, 341–42; Allyn and Wilkinson, *Guidelines for Journalists*, Appendix.

[84] S. B. Kolpe, "Caste and Communal Violence and the Role of the Press," 342, 349, and Asghar Ali Engineer, "The Causes of Communal Riots," 36–38, both in Asghar Ali Engineer, ed., *Communal Riots in Post-Independence India* (Hyderabad: Sangam, 1984); Hamish McDonald, "Paper Tigers," *Far Eastern Economic Review* (October 5, 1995), 28–30; Zenab Banu, *Politics of Communalism* (Bombay: Popular Prakashan, 1989), p. 21.

[85] Sumit Ganguly, *The Crisis in Kashmir: Portents of War, Hopes of Peace*

In short, the case of India imparts a two-edged lesson. On the one hand, it shows that the establishment of civic institutions prior to the rise of mass politics can provide an infrastructure for a democratic ethnic peace, even in an impoverished multiethnic state with low levels of literacy. On the other hand, India's travails also demonstrate that civic institutions are fragile in such a setting, especially when schemes for minority representation in parliament or the bureaucracy create incentives for political organizing along ethnic lines. Counterelites are always ready to use ethnic appeals to fill any gap that emerges between rising demands for participation and a weakening of civic institutions.

## Rwanda and Burundi:
### The Perils of Pluralism and Powersharing

The bloodiest ethnic violence of the 1990s occurred in the central African country of Rwanda. Over a half million members of the minority Tutsi ethnic group were hunted down and slaughtered in April 1994 by squads trained by an extremist faction of the majority Hutu government and by other Hutu who joined in the genocide. In the neighboring country of Burundi, some 50,000 Hutu and Tutsi died in 1993 and 1994 in a largely separate ethnic conflict.

These two cases illustrate the danger of international efforts to promote democratization and ethnic powersharing in countries that lack an adequate institutional foundation for pluralistic politics. The violence in Burundi followed the victory of the Hutu majority candidate in a free and fair presidential election, which turned the Tutsi minority military regime out of power. Similarly, the Rwanda genocide followed the signing of an internationally sponsored agreement, which provided for increased political pluralism and governmental powersharing between Hutu and Tutsi. Both countries experienced a flourishing of independent newspapers on the eve of the violence. International organizations and the great powers had exerted strong pressure for liberalization and powersharing on the dictatorships in both countries.[86]

---

(Cambridge: Cambridge University Press, 1997), and Ganguly, "Explaining the Kashmir Insurgency: Political Mobilization and Institutional Decay," *International Security* 21:2 (Fall 1996), 76–107.

[86] For a critique of international policy toward Burundi, see Michael S. Lund,

These political changes scared powerful elements of the ruling elite of both regimes, who feared not only the loss of their accustomed privileges but also worried that new governments would prosecute them for past human rights abuses. These elements exploited the increase in freedom of the press to mount vitriolic campaigns of ethnic hatred. In Rwanda, extremists in the Hutu government saw genocide as a means to forestall the implementation of the international agreement. In Burundi, the Tutsi-dominated military resorted to massive violence only when the newly elected Hutu president tried, in the name of powersharing, to introduce more Hutu into the army.

Many observers in the international community, such as the nongovernmental activist organization Human Rights Watch, have seen Rwanda and Burundi as examples of the dangers of authoritarian elites who "play the ethnic card" in order to save their position of domination over society. Such groups argue that these cases demonstrate the need to promote democratization, free speech, civil society, and powersharing and to bring authoritarian human rights abusers to justice in order to prevent ethnic violence.[87] In fact, these cases show exactly the opposite. They demonstrate how such reforms can intensify conflict in poor, ethnically divided countries where elites are threatened by democratization, civic institutions are absent, and populations lack the education and civic skills to make democracy work.

In developing this argument, I first discuss the historical background to the Hutu-Tutsi conflict in both countries; I then show how international pressure for democratization fostered ethnic violence in Burundi in 1993–94; and finally, I show how international support for pluralism and powersharing triggered the 1994 genocide in Rwanda (see map).

### Historical rivalries

The Hutu, an agricultural people, have constituted roughly 85 percent of the population of both Rwanda and Burundi. The Tutsi, traditionally a pastoral people, have lived among the Hutu for centuries. The two groups speak the same language and have very similar cultural practices. Typically, Tutsi tend to be tall and thin, whereas Hutu tend to be short and stocky.

---

Barnett R. Rubin, and Fabienne Hara, "Learning from Burundi's Failed Democratic Transition, 1993–1996: Do International Initiatives Match the Problem?" in Barnett R. Rubin, ed., *Cases and Strategies for Preventive Action* (New York: Century Foundation Press, 1998), Chapter 3.

[87] Human Rights Watch, *Slaughter among Neighbors*, 13–32.

*Rwanda and Burundi*

However, in some areas, especially southern Rwanda, Hutu and Tutsi have intermarried extensively, and as a result, are racially indistinguishable except by their identity cards. During the 1994 genocide, patrols at road-blocks would consult identity cards in deciding whom to kill.

The Belgian colonial regime, practicing the strategy of divide-and-rule, treated the minority Tutsi as a ruling class. As a consequence, Tutsi were better educated and wealthier. On the eve of independence in 1959, the Hutu of Rwanda rebelled against their Tutsi overlords, installing a Hutu majority regime that systematically discriminated against Tutsi in education and government employment. The next three decades witnessed cycles of raids, repression, and retaliation between the government and elements of the Tutsi minority, who eventually developed a powerful military base under the protection of the friendly regime in neighboring Uganda. By 1993, this Tutsi rebel force had gained clear military superiority over the army of the Hutu regime, which depended on French backing to stave off utter defeat.[88]

In Burundi, in contrast, the Tutsi minority never fell from power. Their military regime ruled by outright repression. The worst bloodshed came in 1972, when 100,000 Hutu were killed by the Tutsi-dominated regime. Between 1972 and 1993, however, Tutsi repression was so effective in deterring Hutu resistance that the resort to violence remained comparatively limited.[89]

Thus, the rivalry between Hutu and Tutsi is historically rooted in colonial and precolonial relationships of power and economics, sharpened by the racial distinguishability of many members of the two groups. However, these historical differences have been fanned into hatreds by elites who consciously sow myths about the other group, both in the media and by word-of-mouth in refugee camps.[90] These elites exaggerate group differences, yet they also blur these differences when it is to their advantage. For example, the leader of the 1994 genocide campaign against the Rwandan Tutsi, Robert Kajuga, came from a Tutsi family that had switched its identity to Hutu after 1959 by falsifying the family's identity cards.[91]

---

[88] Gérard Prunier, *The Rwanda Crisis: History of a Genocide* (New York: Columbia University Press, 1995), Chapters 3 and 5.

[89] Réné Lemarchand, *Burundi: Ethnocide as Discourse and Practice* (Cambridge: Cambridge University Press, 1994).

[90] Liisa Malki, *Purity and Exile: Violence, Memory and National Cosmology among Hutu Refugees in Tanzania* (Chicago: University of Chicago Press, 1995).

[91] This was Robert Kajuga, leader of the militias that implemented the genocide. See Africa Rights (Rakiya Omaar and Alex de Waal), *Rwanda: Death, Despair and Defiance* (London: Africa Rights, September 1994), 108.

Thus, colonial policies of divide-and-rule and postcolonial elite manipulation of ethnic hatreds provide the historical backdrop to the ethnic violence of the 1990s in Burundi and Rwanda. The specific triggers of the violence, however, were international efforts to promote democracy and powersharing in both countries.

### Democratization and ethnic violence in Burundi

Even Human Rights Watch acknowledges that it was the free and fair election of Burundi's first Hutu president in June 1993 that set the stage for the killing of some 50,000 Hutu and Tutsi. Pressure from international donors was one of the main reasons that the Tutsi-dominated ethnic minority government of Pierre Buyoya agreed to hold these risky elections. An October 1988 mission of World Bank officials to Burundi stressed the need for "transparency in the judicial process" and a reversal of prosecutions of open critics of the government. At the same time, the U.S. House of Representatives passed a resolution urging a comprehensive reassessment of aid policies in light of human rights abuses by the Burundian military.[92] The Buyoya government responded by developing plans for more extensive powersharing with the Hutu majority and for elections. By 1992, says Réné Lemarchand, the premier student of Burundian politics, "there was more freedom of expression and association than at any time since 1972."[93]

In early 1993, on the eve of the elections, nongovernmental organizations descended on the Burundian capital of Bujumbura to facilitate the transition to democracy. The U.S.–based National Democratic Institute arrived to train election monitors. A Swedish think tank mounted a symposium on human rights and development. The African-American Institute, at the behest of Buyoya himself, held a conference on the role of the military in a democracy.[94] Thus, the financially dependent regime gave the international community what it wanted.

Buyoya seems to have been surprised when the 85 percent Hutu electorate turned his largely Tutsi regime out of office in favor of a moderate Hutu, Melchior Ndadaye. The Tutsi military, fearing that the elected gov-

[92] Lemarchand, *Burundi*, 129.
[93] Ibid., 176.
[94] Ibid., 185.

ernment's powersharing scheme would neutralize the army as a security guarantee for the Tutsi minority, launched a coup to protect its monopoly of force, touching off a series of bloody reprisals and leaving the country on the brink of all-out civil war. This was hardly unforeseeable. Indeed, on the eve of these events, even the pro-liberalization Lemarchand had warned that "how the officer corps, an all-Tutsi preserve, may react to a large influx of Hutu recruits is anybody's guess."[95]

Despite the debacle caused by international efforts to promote pluralism and powersharing in Burundi in 1993, the international community failed to learn that these policies were dangerous. Continuing to pursue a similar strategy in Rwanda, they catalyzed an even bigger human rights disaster the following year.

### Powersharing and pluralism as precursors to the Rwanda genocide

In Rwanda, as in Burundi, pressures to democratize from international donors that contributed 60 percent of the Rwandan government's revenue played a central role in triggering ethnic slaughter. The authoritarian Hutu regime of Rwandan president Juvénal Habyarimana was hard pressed on every front in the late 1980s and early 1990s. Rwanda's economy was suffering from falling coffee prices. Attacks by Tutsi rebels from bases in neighboring Uganda caused further economic disruptions. Even among Hutu, domestic opponents of the regime were calling for an increase in political pluralism. International aid donors exerted their influence on behalf of these demands.

Yielding to these pressures, Habyarimana abandoned the government's press monopoly in July 1990, which lead to "an explosion in the number of newspapers and journals" published by antigovernment groups.[96] "A vibrant press had been born almost overnight," says scholar Gérard Prunier. However, the newly free press included not only voices of moderation but also many Hutu extremist organs mounting a vituperative campaign against the Tutsi minority.[97] Moreover, Hutu extremists attached to

[95] Ibid., 187.

[96] Africa Rights, *Rwanda*, 150.

[97] Prunier, *The Rwanda Crisis*, Chapter 4, "Slouching towards Democracy," esp. 131–33, 157, on the low quality and extremism of these new entrants into public discourse.

the regime continued to monopolize the radio, a key asset among a population that was 60 percent illiterate.

Despite these limited concessions to political pluralism, pressure on the Habyarimana regime increased in the early 1990s. The Tutsi military threat intensified. Hutu opposition political parties called for democratic elections. International backers urged Habyarimana to accept a power-sharing accord with his Hutu opponents and with the armed Tutsi rebels. After a Tutsi rebel attack on the capital in 1993 was parried only with the help of French troops, Habyarimana had no alternative but to accept the internationally sponsored Arusha Accords, which provided for Tutsi participation in government and a Tutsi military unit to provide security for Tutsi politicians in the capital city of Kigali. If implemented, these accords would have excluded from the new joint Hutu-Tutsi government those Hutu extremist members of the Habyarimana regime who were mounting the hate campaign against the Tutsi.

As pressure for the implementation of the Arusha Accords increased in early 1994, the Hutu extremist faction seemed cornered. As part of the settlement, an international commission named names of highly placed Hutu extremists who had been complicit in small-scale killings of Tutsi. "Individuals named were promised an amnesty," says Africa Rights's Alex de Waal, "but knew that their actions were under scrutiny," and so distrusted these guarantees. Human rights groups were active in this period of internationally sponsored powersharing and pluralization. "Rwanda had one of the most vigorous human-rights movements in Africa," says de Waal. "Six independent human-rights organizations cooperated in exposing abuses by government and rebel forces."[98] Meanwhile, moderate Hutu from southern Rwanda, where "Hutu" and "Tutsi" were racially almost indistinguishable, began to mobilize politically against Hutu extremists in the government clique and in their northern Rwanda social base.[99]

In this setting, the extremist clique around Habyarimana had every

---

[98] Alex de Waal, "The Genocidal State," *Times Literary Supplement*, July 1, 1994, 3–4; see also Africa Rights, *Rwanda*, 30–32.

[99] Africa Rights, *Rwanda*, 30–34, 44; Bruce D. Jones, "The Arusha Process," in Howard Adelman and Astri Suhrke, eds., *Early Warning and Conflict Management in Rwanda* (forthcoming); Alan J. Kuperman, "The Other Lesson of Rwanda: Mediators Sometimes Do More Damage Than Good," *SAIS Review* 16:1 (Winter-Spring 1996), 221–40.

reason to fear democratization and calls for justice from the international community. However, the extremists still had powerful cards to play to avert the implementation of the Arusha Accords. To forestall a fall from power and subsequent judicial accountability, these officials developed a plan for mass genocide. "The extremists' aim," says Africa Rights, "was for the entire Hutu populace to participate in the killing. That way, the blood of genocide would stain everybody. There could be no going back for the Hutu population."[100] To prepare the ideological terrain for the genocide, the extremists intensified their inflammatory media campaign, playing on Hutu fears of the former Tutsi elite.

But there was a flaw in this plan. Habyarimana, heavily dependent on foreign aid to prop up his system of official patronage, balked at implementing a bloodbath that he knew would cut him off from foreign funds. The president's extremist allies in the military and security services had no such qualms. From January to March 1994, their unofficial journal *Kangura*, an example of the flowering of Rwandan media in the period of pluralism and incipient powersharing, warned Habyarimana not to flinch from the destruction of the Tutsi and predicted with astonishing accuracy the details of the president's subsequent assassination.[101] Habyarimana was killed in April 1994, apparently by his own presidential guard, upon returning from a meeting at Dar Es Salaam, where he had made renewed concessions to international donors, the UN, and the Organization of African Unity. As Alex de Waal aptly states, "Habyarimana was a victim of the international peace industry."[102]

With Habyarimana out of the way, the Hutu extremist clique unleashed militias trained in the techniques of genocide. Independent journalists were a special target in the first wave of the killings. At the same time, Radio-Télévision Libre des Mille Collines, a pseudoprivate station established earlier by Habyarimana's wife, spread the word that Tutsi rebels were about to rise up and kill Hutu, and consequently that all Hutu should join the militias in a campaign of preventive killing. The militias threatened to kill Hutu who did not participate in the genocide,

---

[100] Africa Rights, *Rwanda*, v; also 568–96; Prunier, *The Rwanda Crisis*, 170; Jones, "Arusha."

[101] Africa Rights, *Rwanda*, 66–68.

[102] de Waal, "The Genocidal State," 4; also Jones, "Arusha." On Habyarimana's death, see Prunier, *The Rwanda Crisis*, 213–29.

so it is difficult to judge how much of the killing was triggered by the radio propaganda per se. [103] Nonetheless, some observers argue that the hate broadcasts played a significant role in the second phase of the killing, after the initial militia sweeps. Holly Burkhalter, the Washington director of Human Rights Watch, argued that jamming the hate radio was "the one action that, in retrospect, might have done the most to save Rwandan lives." Instead, the transmitters were withdrawn from the path of the advancing Tutsi army into the safe haven of the French army zone, where they continued to broadcast. [104]

### Post-conflict lessons

After the genocide, non-governmental organizations (NGOs) such as Human Rights Watch and Africa Rights, as well as many independent scholars, drew the lesson that the international community still needs to encourage Rwanda and Burundi to democratize, to foster an independent press, and to bring the perpetrators of genocide to justice "to deter further slaughter." [105] However, upon closer examination, it is clear that these organizations' own analyses of the causes of the Rwandan genocide contradict their prescriptions. After the genocide, NGOs continue to advocate precisely those measures that their analyses show to have triggered the killings: an increase in political pluralism, the prospect of trials of the guilty, and the promotion of antigovernment media. [106]

The real lesson of these cases is that the ideals of democratic rights, civil society, uncompromising justice, and free speech must make pragmatic accommodations to recalcitrant reality. The examples of Rwanda

---

[103] Africa Rights, *Rwanda*, vi, 35, 37–38, 63–64, 69–72, 150; Human Rights Watch, *Slaughter among Neighbors*, 21, 23–24.

[104] Holly Burkhalter, "The Question of Genocide," *World Policy Journal* 11:4 (Winter 1994–95), 44–54, esp. 51, 53.

[105] Human Rights Watch, *Slaughter among Neighbors*, 28, 31; Africa Rights, *Rwanda*, 720; Reporters sans Frontières, *Rwanda: L'impasse? La liberté de las presse après le génocide, 4 juillet 1994–28 août 1995* (Paris: Reporters sans Frontières, 1995), 48–50; Alison Des Forges, "The Rwandan Crisis," paper prepared for a conference on Sources of Conflict in Rwanda (Washington, DC: U.S. Department of State, October 17, 1994).

[106] Compare Africa Rights, *Rwanda*, 32–34 and 720, to Des Forges, "Rwandan Crisis," 1 and 9.

and Burundi bear out the theory presented in this book: democratization is likely to spark nationalist conflict in countries that have an underdeveloped economy; a population with both poor civic skills and underdeveloped representative and journalistic institutions; and elites who are threatened by democratic change. These handicaps, especially when combined with a legacy of colonial divide-and-rule and ethnic mythmaking, made "democratizing" Burundi and Rwanda prime candidates for ethnic violence of the worst kind.

Despite this, international programs in many central African countries still attempt to foster the development of a democratic "civil society" of urban professionals. Yet this segment of society often finds that its interests lie in competing for control of a predatory state rather than in promoting the rights of the bulk of the rural population.[107] When this civil society speaks out, it is often on the wrong side of the issue.

Some NGOs do recognize this harsh reality. For example, the French journalism NGO, Reporters sans Frontières, warns that "the error committed in Rwanda, which consisted of applying the rule of 'laissez faire' in the name of the principle of liberty of the press, must not be repeated." While working to reconstitute the private news media in both Rwanda and Burundi and to bring journalists implicated in the genocide campaign to justice, the French NGO acknowledges that the thirteen newspapers it is helping in Rwanda consist primarily of opinions, not news. Realistically skeptical about some of the journalists it supports, Reporters sans Frontières conditions aid on a pledge to forswear ethnic hate speech. In Burundi, Reporters sans Frontières notes the paradox that many journalists working under a new law on press freedom are calling for an ethnic dictatorship that would shut down nonofficial expression of views. Since the invisible hand of the marketplace of ideas is so unreliable in such circumstances, Reporters sans Frontières relied also on the visible hand of two international radio stations broadcasting into Rwanda and Burundi from Zaire.[108]

In multiethnic countries that are as bereft of the preconditions of

---

[107] Robert Fatton, Jr., "Africa in the Age of Democratization: The Civic Limitations of Civil Society," *African Studies Review* 38:2 (September 1995), 67–100.

[108] Reporters sans Frontières, *Rwanda*, 6, 41–42; 52–53; Reporters sans Frontières, *Burundi, le Venin de la Haine: Étude sur les médias extrémistes*, 2d ed., (Paris: Reporters sans Frontières, July 1995), 63, 68–69; quotation on 69.

democracy as are Rwanda and Burundi, a long period of economic development and institution-building will be needed before free speech and free elections can be part of the solution to ethnic conflict, rather than part of the problem.

## Conditions That Dampen Nationalist Conflict in the Developing World

Given the potential dangers facing developing countries with weak states, it is remarkable that more of them do not foment nationalist wars or suffer from ethnic violence. Numerous developing countries are democratizing without undergoing upsurges of nationalist conflict. Why is there not more nationalist or ethnic conflict in the developing world? As in the settings analyzed in previous chapters, such conflicts are absent where mass demands for political participation remain weak, where elites are optimistic about their prospects in a democratic regime, or where the process of democratization is moving smoothly into the stage of full consolidation.

Some weak states in the developing world sit astride societies that are not highly mobilized for mass politics. These states often lack the capacity to extract taxes reliably from their society, to provide social services, to quash corruption, and to manage the tasks of economic development or military security, let alone provide effective integrative institutions for a constructive mass voice in politics. Thus, one might expect the emergence of a popular nationalist movement to strengthen the state. However, in many of these societies, the same conditions that lead to the weakness of the state also make it difficult to sustain a mass movement, whether nationalist or otherwise.

In some of these societies, levels of literacy and organizational skills are low, means of communication are underdeveloped, and would-be mobilizers of collective action lack resources to operate on a national scale. Numerous states of Central Asia and Africa are in this category. The weakness of these states may give rise to anarchical conflict, as in Tajikistan and Somalia, yet the groups may be organized around local and clan lines, rather than mainly around ethnic communities, which are more extensive "imagined communities" requiring more sophisticated forms of social capital to organize.

The obverse of weak capacity is weak motivation. States like Saudi

Arabia, which derive a substantial portion of their revenue from oil exports, may have little need to build a strong, popular state that has sufficient legitimacy to extract resources through heavy direct taxation. The same is true of some African states whose budgets are supported mainly through foreign assistance. Political entrepreneurs in such states have little motivation for nationalist mobilization.[109]

Nationalism is also weak where traditional local elites such as landowners, religious organizations, or kinship networks of small-scale merchants retain a strong enough position to block both resource extraction by the state as well as strong mass movements. This pattern is common among the weak states of the Middle East, Africa, and other parts of the developing world.[110] Ethnic or tribal groups may organize as loose lobbies to capture benefits from this kind of "soft" state, but they lack the motive or the ability to organize a nationalist state-building movement to strengthen or replace the state. In such cases, exorbitant payoffs to ethnic groups, tribes, clans, or other patronage networks keep the state weak and prevent it from investing effectively in a rationalized economy.[111] The authoritarian state may retain enough coercive power to repress opponents, including mobilizers of ethnonational and other mass movements, but may lack sufficient infrastructure-building power to solve the tasks of development.

This, then, explains why many ineffective Third World states fail to develop strong nationalisms. But democratizing states in the developing world are not of this type. They are states where political participation is expanding. Yet a significant proportion of them, too, fail to develop belligerent nationalisms or ethnic conflicts. Indeed, Samuel Huntington's book on the most recent wave of democratization stresses the remarkably low levels of violence that accompanied democratic transitions during the 1980s and early 1990s. While acknowledging that the bloodshed in Nicaragua and South Africa was part of the transition process, Huntington

---

[109] Kiren Chaudhry, *The Price of Wealth: Economies and Institutions in the Middle East* (Ithaca: Cornell University Press, 1997).

[110] Joel Migdal, *Strong Societies and Weak States: State-Society Relations and State Capabilities in the Third World* (Princeton: Princeton University Press, 1988).

[111] Goran Hyden, "Problems and Prospects of State Coherence," in Donald Rothchild and Victor Orolunsola, eds., *State Versus Ethnic Claims: African Policy Dilemmas* (Boulder, CO: Westview, 1983), 67–85; Goran Hyden, *No Shortcuts to Progress* (London: Heinemann, 1983), 19.

denies that internal violence in Guatemala, El Salvador, the Philippines, and Peru stemmed mainly from democratization.[112] Moreover, he notes, many other cases were completely peaceful. Why?

The concepts developed in earlier chapters of this book and illustrated by the historical case studies of democratization in Europe suggest two answers. The first focuses on the interests of old elites potentially threatened by democratization, and the other on the legacy of institutions from the old regime.

One reason that the most recent wave of democratizations has been comparatively peaceful is that old elites were cushioned as they fell from power. Huntington calculates that about half of the democratizations of the 1980s were initiated by the authoritarian regime itself. Another large proportion of the cases were what he calls "negotiated transplacements," whereby the new democratic elite gave the abdicating authoritarian elite credible guarantees that they would find life tolerable in the changed circumstances. Latin American militaries, in particular, were often given high degrees of organizational autonomy and assurances that they would not be seriously punished for the crimes that they committed while in power.[113] In Chile, for example, the military remained a state within the state, obedient to the former dictator Augusto Pinochet. Only a handful of military officers were prosecuted for their murderous repression of opposition, and their punishment was incarceration in luxurious, country-club-style facilities.[114] Likewise, in newly democratic South Africa, a Truth Commission offered amnesty to government officials who agreed to testify about the political crimes they had committed under the apartheid regime.[115] In contrast, where murderous elites were not offered credible exit guarantees, as in Rwanda and Burundi, democratization did sometimes trigger ethnic violence.

Second, democratization was less likely to cause nationalist or ethnic

[112] Samuel Huntington, *The Third Wave* (Norman: University of Oklahoma Press, 1991), 192.

[113] Ibid., 116, 211–15.

[114] Carlos Acuña and Catalina Smulovitz, "Adjusting the Armed Forces to Democracy," in Elizabeth and Eric Hershberg, eds., *Constructing Democracy: Human Rights, Citizenship, and Society in Latin America* (Boulder, CO: Westview, 1996), 13–38.

[115] Tina Rosenberg, "Recovering from Apartheid," *The New Yorker* (November 18, 1996) 86–95.

violence if some of the institutional preconditions of successful civic democracy were already in place before the transition. In Latin America, in particular, countries undergoing transitions in the 1980s (including Argentina, Brazil, and Chile) had had extensive experience with democratic institutions in earlier periods. Most of them had fairly well-developed party systems and professionalized journalists waiting in the wings. In many cases, these democratic institutions were reactivated during the phase of liberalization negotiated with the exiting regime. Many of the Latin American transitions shared these characteristics with the Polish and Hungarian transitions, which moved gradually out of a gestation period of "post-totalitarian" communism into roundtable discussions to design a new, democratic system.[116] Similarly, one factor in the smooth South African transition was the well-established English-language opposition press, exemplified by the Rand *Daily Mail* and its successors, which for decades had been consistently more liberal than many of its readers.[117] When the political opening in the 1990s permitted the English-language media to report more freely, television and especially print news, already staffed with a professional cadre, moved quickly toward international norms.[118] These cases, in short, shared some of the features of the British pattern of civic nationalism, where institutions of political representation and free speech were fairly well established for elites before the era of mass democracy.

This is consistent with political scientist Alexander Kozhemiakin's finding that democratization is less likely to lead to war if it subsequently becomes successfully consolidated. Of course, war itself may disrupt democratic consolidation, so the direction of causality is somewhat in doubt. But even taking this into account, the peacefulness of successful democratic transitions in Kozhemiakin's sample—e.g., Costa Rica (1949), Venezuela (1959), Portugal (1974), and Spain (1975)—is striking in comparison to the conflict-proneness of failed democratizations—e.g., France (1848–51), Germany (1919–33), Italy (1919–22), Turkey (1950–60 and 1973–80),

---

[116] Juan Linz and Alfred Stepan, *Problems of Democratic Transition and Consolidation*, 55–65, 255–343.

[117] Elaine Potter, *The Press as Opposition: The Political Role of South African Newspapers* (Totowa, NJ: Rowman and Littlefield, 1975).

[118] On the transition, see Timothy Sisk, *Democratization in South Africa* (Princeton: Princeton University Press, 1995).

and Sudan (1986–89). This finding would surely be strengthened by including successful consolidations from the 1980s, but Kozhemiakin's criterion requires twenty years of uninterrupted democracy to establish the success of consolidation.[119] When powerful elites are reconciled to democracy, and when institutions are already well established during the initial phase of the transition, this facilitates consolidation. These are also factors that short-circuit the pathologies that give rise to belligerent nationalism and war. Thus, it is not at all surprising that successful transitions are more peaceful.

In short, democratization need not lead to belligerent nationalism or ethnic conflict if elites are buffered from the effects of rising political participation or if institutions to channel participation in a civic direction are already well established. However, these conditions are all too scarce in the developing world.

## Conclusions

The developing countries' recent experiences with nationalist conflict run parallel to those of the historical European and the contemporary post-Communist states. Democratization increases the risk of nationalist and ethnic conflict in the developing world, but the strength and outcome of this propensity varies in different circumstances.

Nationalist and ethnic conflicts are more likely during the initial stages of democratization than in transitions to full consolidation of democracy. Moreover, trouble is more likely when elites are highly threatened by democratic change (as in Burundi, the former Yugoslavia, and historical Germany) than when elites are guaranteed a satisfactory position in the new order (as in historical Britain and in much of South America and east central Europe today). Uncontrolled conflict is more likely when mass participation increases before civic institutions have been extensively developed, as the contrast between Burundi and South Africa suggests. Similarly, ethnic conflict is more likely when the civic institutions of the

---

[119] Alexander Kozhemiakin, *Expanding the Zone of Peace? Democratization and International Security* (New York: St. Martin's, 1998), Chapter 5. Linz and Stepan offer different criteria for consolidation, which depend on characteristics of political behavior and institutions, not the passage of time.

central state break down at a time of rising popular demands, as in India in the late 1980s and 1990s. Finally, ethnic conflict is more likely when the channels for mobilizing mass groups into politics are ethnically exclusive. This is true whether the channeling is prescribed by the state, as in the British system of separate ethnic voting in India, or rooted in the social networks of traditional society, as in the role of the Buddhist priests in getting out the vote in postindependence Sri Lanka.

The concluding chapter examines the prescriptive implications of these findings.

# 7

## Averting Nationalist Conflict

## in an Age of Democratization

The past decade has been a time of both promise and disappointment for those who anticipated that a trend toward global democratization would strengthen world peace. On the heels of the collapse of the Soviet empire and democratic transitions in Latin America and elsewhere, Freedom House found that out of 183 countries evaluated in 1991, there were 91 democracies and 35 countries in some form of democratic transition, up from only 44 democracies in 1972 and 56 in 1980. Yet by the end of 1993, Freedom House lamented that "freedom around the world was in retreat while violence, repression and state control were on the increase in a growing number of countries."[1] As peace and democracy were becoming successfully consolidated in much of Latin America and north eastern Europe, mass electoral politics were stimulating nationalist

---

[1] James Lee Ray, *Democracy and International Conflict* (Columbia: University of South Carolina Press, 1995), 49. See also Thomas Carothers, "Democracy without Illusions," *Foreign Affairs* 76:1 (January/February 1997), 85–99.

and ethnic conflicts in the Balkans and the Caucasus, and having varied consequences elsewhere.

Liberals who have been perplexed and dismayed by this mixed out-come must confront three puzzles. First, why have the objectives so desired by liberals often produced illiberal, violent side effects? Why have the collapse of autocratic states and empires, the democratization of their successor states, the expansion of free speech, and the marketization of command economies frequently led not to peace but to nationalist con-flicts? The history of nationalism shows that when autocracies lacking popular support collapse from the toil of military and economic competi-tion, political elites will scramble to mobilize support for new states that will carry out those tasks more successfully. Nationalism has proved to be a successful ideology for attracting popular support for state-building. Since the eighteenth century, the rise of nationalism has commonly coin-cided with an increased role of the popular masses in politics.

Second, how is it that aggressive nationalism remains an attractive doc-trine, despite the fact that it has often proved costly and counterproduc-tive for its proponents and adherents? Given nationalism's disastrous track record during the twentieth century, why is it not discredited? Why are Serbs, Hutus, and Sinhalese so attracted to it? The histories examined in this book show that nationalism remains attractive in part because elite groups seeking to harness national collective action to their own parochial purposes often find nationalism a convenient ideology for ruling in the name of the people without actually granting the people full democratic rights. These elites may include not only governmental officials and other dominant groups of the old regime but also local or ethnic minority elites. When mass political participation is increasing, yet democratic institutions remain weak, these elites have the motive and opportunity both to sow myths that exaggerate the need for nationalist mobilization against threatening opponents and to minimize its costs. Once this process builds momentum, the elites that set it in motion may be unable to control mass enthusiasms. As a result, even the promoters of national-ism may incur unanticipated costs. Such risks, even when expected, may seem worth running to those hard-pressed elites who see few acceptable alternatives.

Third, why does democratization sometimes trigger nationalist con-flict, but at other times does not? A whole host of factors affect this, rang-ing from demography to the balance of power. Democratization sometimes empowers a people who harbor grudges against other nations, but such historical rivalries are also present in many cases where nationalist conflict is avoided. More often, it is the process of democratization itself that shapes the nation's consciousness and sets the pattern of its nationalist rivalries. How that process plays out is influenced by (1) the democratizing country's level and pattern of social and economic development, (2) the strength and character of its domestic political institutions, and (3) the interests of the groups that are taking the lead in nation-building. Where powerful groups find democratization to be particularly threatening because they have little hope of prospering under the new order, their incentive for nationalist mobilization will be strong. Where institutions of democratic representation and free speech are weak, such groups will have ample opportunities to hijack public debate on behalf of a belligerent nationalism. Conversely, where a large middle class commands advanced civic skills, where elite interests are adaptable, and where the institutional groundwork for democracy is well prepared before political participation expands, there is a greater likelihood that nationalism will take the more prudent civic form rather than the more reckless ethnic, revolutionary, or counterrevolutionary forms. In short, there are three principal injunctions for a happy democratization: be rich and modernized, have adaptable elites, and establish a thick web of liberal institutions before embarking on the process.

The main purpose of this concluding chapter is to assess the prescriptions that follow from my analysis of the causes of nationalist conflict during the process of democratization. In cases where favorable conditions are absent, they need to be fostered if democratization is to go smoothly. The first section of this chapter elaborates on the importance of building a supportive institutional framework before beginning the democratic transition. The second section evaluates common prescriptions for averting nationalist and especially ethnic conflicts, and finds that some prescriptions may actually increase the likelihood of conflict. The third section argues that the international setting can exert a substantial influence, for good or ill, on the course of nationalism in democratizing states. Some of this international impact may be subject to the conscious control of powerful states in the international community. A concluding section returns to the question of whether the future holds out the prospect of a global democratic peace, or whether it holds in store a clash of warring ethnodemocracies.

## Weaving a Thick Safety Net for Democratic Transitions

Some liberals think that it takes very little to establish a stable, peaceloving democracy: just get the authoritarian state out of the way, they argue, and people will have a good chance to establish a cooperative social order.[2] Other liberals argue that a long list of preconditions must be met before free voting and free speech can serve as the basis for a stable, productive, peaceful society. They stress the importance of a certain degree of wealth, the development of a knowledgeable citizenry, the support of powerful elites, and the establishment of a whole panoply of institutions to ensure the rule of law and civic rights.[3] The present study strongly supports the latter view. To minimize the risk that a democratic transition will trigger nationalist conflicts, a thick safety net of preconditions should be firmly in place. If these conditions do not exist, it may be wise to postpone encouraging democratization until they are. But how many preconditions of which kind need to be firmly in place? And does it matter in what sequence they emerge?

In designing strategies to ward off the dangers of nationalism in democratizing states, conceptions of liberalism that stress the need for a "thick" network of social supports are a good guide.[4] "Thin" understandings of liberalism hold that a liberal, democratic, peaceloving, free-market

[2] In addition to Friedrich Hayek and liberal social contract theorists from John Locke to John Rawls, note also attempts by Andrew Schotter and others to show, through game theory and other forms of rational choice theory, how social order and liberal social institutions may be provided through the interaction of rationally bargaining individuals. Free-speech absolutists in the human rights community, including Human Rights Watch, adopt some elements of this position.

[3] Pointing to various preconditions are Adam Przeworski and Fernando Limongi, "Modernization: Theories and Facts," *World Politics* 49:2 (January 1997), 155–83; Robert Putnam, *Making Democracy Work* (Princeton: Princeton University Press, 1993), Dietrich Rueschemeyer, Evelyne Huber Stephens, and John D. Stephens, *Capitalist Development and Democracy* (Chicago: University of Chicago Press, 1992), and Juan Linz and Alfred Stepan, *Problems of Democratic Transition and Consolidation* (Baltimore: Johns Hopkins University Press, 1996).

[4] For this distinction, see Ira Katznelson, *Liberalism's Crooked Circle* (Princeton: Princeton University Press, 1996). Note that Katznelson's version of thick liberalism imports cultural content from ethnic and traditional religious sources, whereas mine focuses on civic cultural and institutional elements.

society has a good chance of emerging spontaneously from the self-interested actions of calculating individuals, as long as nefarious governments
do not get in the way. This outlook may seem like a caricature that
nobody could really believe in, and stated this starkly, it probably is. Even
proponents of economic shock therapy for democratizing states, for
example, understand that the state must guarantee property rights and a
stable currency before the miracle of laissez-faire can promote economic
efficiency. Everyone knows that public opinion is sometimes warlike in
democracies. Hardly anyone thinks that a single free and fair election is
enough to guarantee that a country will remain democratic.[5] Even proponents of absolute freedom of speech agonize over the dangers of uncontrolled hate speech.[6] Nonetheless, in many quarters of contemporary
American society, there remains a bias toward thinking that "all good
things go together" and that more political and economic freedom is
almost always advantageous.[7] This bias is found in constituencies as
diverse as neoclassical economists, activists in nongovernmental human
rights organizations, foreign policy professionals, and scholars writing on
the democratic peace.

"Thick" versions of liberalism, in contrast, contend that a thick context
of liberal institutions, values, interest-group bargains, or social ties is
needed to channel mass political participation into liberal directions. Some
thinkers and activists single out one or another type of contextual factor
more than others. Samuel Huntington, for example, stresses the need for a
strong framework of state power to channel civic participation toward flexible, rule-governed compromise.[8] In contrast, Robert Putnam, like many
contemporary nongovernmental activist groups, stresses the need for a
dense web of social relationships built up through participation in nonpo-
litical voluntary organizations to establish the kind of trust needed to
make democratic compromise work.[9] Many writers on international peace

[5] Linz and Stepan, *Problems of Democratic Transition and Consolidation*, Chapters
1 and 2.

[6] Human Rights Watch, " 'Hate Speech' and Freedom of Expression," *Free
Expression Project* 4:3 (March 1992).

[7] Robert Packenham, *Liberal America and the Third World* (Princeton: Princeton
University Press, 1973); Freedom House, *Freedom in the World*.

[8] Samuel Huntington, *Political Order in Changing Societies* (New Haven: Yale
University Press, 1968).

[9] Putnam, *Making Democracy Work*.

among democracies stress the role of strong liberal norms, not simply democratic procedure per se, as an antidote to war.[10] Students of democratization in Latin America stress the importance of well-constructed political bargains between elements of the liberalizing authoritarian state and social interest groups.[11] From this standpoint, such minimal democratic attributes as free elections and free speech are far from sufficient to insure enduringly liberal, let alone pacific, outcomes, in the absence of a thick, supportive context of norms, institutions, and interests.

The findings of this book suggest that only thickly embedded liberal polities are well insulated from the risk of developing belligerent, reckless forms of nationalism in the course of democratization. This argument has a strong precedent in Karl Polanyi's analysis of the rise of fascist nationalism and the causes of the two world wars, *The Great Transformation*.[12] Polanyi was interested in the consequences of an increase in political participation in a context of inadequate political and economic institutions, precisely the dilemma that faces a number of newly democratizing states today. Polanyi saw a contradiction between the thin liberal economic institutions of the nineteenth century, including the apolitical regulation of the international economy by the unplanned workings of the gold standard, and the expansion of the electoral franchise to include the mass of the working population of the advanced capitalist states. Mass groups that suffered from the laissez-faire approach to market adjustments demanded more thickly institutionalized protection from world economic forces. In some countries, such as Germany, nationalist politicians successfully garnered support by promising illiberal schemes that used high tariffs and imperial conquest to protect the nation from painful economic adjustment. Elsewhere, however, there developed a more thickly embedded liberalism, which deployed Keynesian countercyclical economic policies, the welfare state, and state-managed bargaining between labor and capital to mitigate the pain of market adjustments. The New Deal in the United

---

[10] Bruce Russett, *Grasping the Democratic Peace* (Princeton: Princeton University Press, 1993); John Owen, "How Liberalism Produces Democratic Peace," in Michael Brown, ed., *Debating the Democratic Peace* (Cambridge: MIT Press, 1996), 116–56.

[11] Linz and Stepan, *Problems of Democratic Transition and Consolidation*, Chapter 6; Guillermo O'Donnell and Philippe Schmitter, *Transitions from Authoritarian Rule* (Baltimore: Johns Hopkins University Press, 1986).

[12] Karl Polanyi, *The Great Transformation* (Boston: Beacon, 1957; orig. ed., 1944).

States and similar govermental strategies in Europe's "corporatist" democracies, such as Sweden, are examples from the 1930s.[13] Where liberalism learned how to develop a thick context of regulatory institutions and supportive coalitions, aggressive mass nationalism was avoided. After World War II, this more thickly embedded institutional context was extended to the international dimension through the Bretton Woods economic institutions, like the International Monetary Fund and the General Agreement on Tariffs and Trade, and through security institutions like NATO.[14]

In our own day, too, democratization in weakly institutionalized settings often plays into the hands of nationalist demagogues and swaggering populists. The period since the end of the cold war shares two features of the era that Polanyi studied. The first is rising political participation in a domestic context of weakly developed democratic institutions. Germany and Japan, the imperfectly democratizing great powers that plagued Polanyi's era, have now entered the community of pacific liberal states. Today, however, Russia and China have yet to complete that passage, and their futures remain problematic, as do many new democracies in smaller states. The second common feature is the mismatch between the unit of democratic accountability, the nation-state, and the increasing globalization of economic, social, and political forces shaping people's lives in an interdependent world. Polanyi showed how people supported nationalists who promised to protect them from painful adjustments to international markets in the early twentieth century. In the era of the gold standard and the unregulated international business cycle, people sought refuge in the only institution where they could exercise their voice, their nation's state. Nowadays, in a period of even more extensive globalization, intergovernmental organizations do more than previously to regulate international markets and to soften the impact of market adjustments. Nonetheless, the mismatch between democratic norms and the governance of international markets is no less pressing than it was in the period that Polanyi studied. People living in democracies get to elect their national governments, but international organizations such as the

---

[13] Peter Katzenstein, *Small States in World Markets* (Ithaca: Cornell University Press, 1985); Peter Gourevitch, *Politics in Hard Times* (Ithaca: Cornell University Press, 1986).

[14] John Ruggie, "International Regimes, Transactions, and Change: Embedded Liberalism in the Postwar Economic Order," *International Organization* 36 (Spring 1982), 379–415.

European Union, the IMF, and the United Nations are not subject to electoral accountability. This "democratic deficit" of supranational institutions is one reason why people still try to solve their problems at the level of the nation-state.[15]

### The importance of mutually reinforcing institutions

Institutional supports and other favorable preconditions for a peaceful democratic transition should be diverse and mutually reinforcing. No single factor provides the magic ingredient that is sufficient to ward off the dangers of nationalism during a transition to democracy. The combination of very high per capita income and a large middle class probably comes close to being a sufficient cause of a peaceful transition, but not quite. By the standards of its day, Weimar Germany was an economically advanced country. Nor is a thick network of voluntary organizations in civil society sufficient in itself to ward off illiberal belligerent nationalism: voluntary nonstate groups have often been the most vociferous nationalists, as in Wilhelmine Germany. Likewise, a strong state, even one with highly developed representative institutions, may be captured by illiberal interests, as in Weimar Germany. Conversely, in a context of institutional collapse, even politicians with highly flexible interests may turn to extreme forms of belligerent nationalism, as in the French Revolution. Finally, having the leader of the country proclaim support for a civic form of nationalism will not in itself insure a good outcome if institutional supports for it are weak. Boris Yeltsin consistently argued for civic conceptions of Russian citizenship, even while prosecuting a brutal war against Chechen ethnic separatism.

In short, a broad range of institutional, civic, coalitional, and ideological supports is needed to reliably ward off aggressively nationalist outcomes. In this mutually supportive package, the lack of any one pillar creates the risk that the other elements will not work toward liberal outcomes. Because democratizing states commonly lack one or more of these supports, they are disproportionately war-prone, and in culturally plural societies, disproportionately at risk for ethnic conflict.

[15] Michael Mann, "Nation-States in Europe and Other Continents: Diversifying, Developing, Not Dying," 130, and Stanley Hoffmann, "Thoughts on the French Nation Today," 73–75, both in *Daedalus* 122:3 (Summer 1993); J. H. H. Weiler, "The Transformation of Europe," *Yale Law Journal* 100 (June 1991), 2466–74.

### *Getting the sequence right*

It matters in what sequence these preconditions appear. Since the character of a people's nationalism is profoundly influenced by the pattern of its democratization, getting the sequence right matters not only for avoiding conflict in the short run but also for shaping enduring identities in a positive way. Many of the cases in this book show that if nationalist conflict is to be avoided, the development of civic institutions should be well underway before mass-suffrage elections are held. Likewise, it is better if a strong middle class emerges before press freedom expands and civil society groups get organized, or else these may be easily hijacked by an elite with a nationalist agenda. Indeed, the most favorable sequence would begin with the emergence of a powerful elite with adaptable interests that are not threatened by the inclusion of broader social circles in the political process. If this element is lacking, threatened elites are likely to deflect ostensibly democratic developments, such as rising press freedom and burgeoning civil society organizations, toward a nationalist direction.

These insights into the conditions that promote a peaceful transition have significant implications for several current debates about the management of ethnic rivalry and other forms of nationalist conflict. The next section evaluates several of the arguments advanced in these debates, criticizing some commonly accepted solutions and proposing alternatives. A subsequent section takes up the question of whether it is realistic to think that outside assistance can supply the missing prerequisites in order to insure a peaceful transition.

## Strategies for Averting Nationalist Conflict

Each of the four types of nationalism—ethnic, civic, counterrevolutionary, and revolutionary—presents distinctive problems and thus requires specifically tailored measures to avert nationalist conflict. However, the strategies recommended for each are but variations on a single theme, which is first to contain nationalist conflict by whatever means are expedient in the short run, including coercion, and then gradually put in place a thick network of civic institutions to defuse the motives for belligerent nationalist mobilization in the long run. This strategy involves, to the extent possible, both the delay of high levels of mass political participation until later stages and the integration of the emerging civic state in a reliably supportive network of international institutions, norms, and practices.

Though this is a liberal, civic approach to the establishment of social peace and order, these specific prescriptions run directly counter to much liberal conventional wisdom. My approach is skeptical of arrangements for powersharing between cultural groups, doubtful of federalism, selective in recommending democratization, wary of proposals to expand freedom of speech, and conditionally tolerant of the domination of civil society by a strong state. Underpinning these views is the assumption that it is only after a thickly supportive structure of institutions and norms has been firmly established that "all good things go together" in liberal political systems.

I first discuss prescriptions for managing ethnic nationalism, and then turn to the problems presented by counterrevolutionary and revolutionary forms of nationalism.

## Managing ethnic nationalism

Today's headlines are filled with the difficulties of managing ethnic conflict where cultural groups inhabiting the same state hold antithetical political goals. Although some very knowledgeable social scientists have developed sophisticated solutions for this type of problem, each of the most commonly proposed solutions has as many drawbacks as benefits. Thus, debate over their relative merits still rages not only in academic journals like the *American Political Science Review* but also in pragmatic magazines like *Foreign Affairs*, which are read by policymakers.[16] I suggest ways of sequencing and adapting strategies that run counter to the common run of recommendations for minimizing ethnic conflict in transitional states.

### Hegemonic Control by the Majority
One strategy that often gets left off the list of "solutions" to ethnic conflict because of its unpalatability to a liberal audience is hegemony. In

---

[16] Arend Lijphart, "The Puzzle of Indian Democracy: A Consociational Interpretation," *American Political Science Review* 90:2 (June 1996), 258–68; Radha Kumar, "The Troubled History of Partition," *Foreign Affairs* 76:1 (January/February 1997), 26.

many multiethnic societies, one ethnic group monopolizes the power of the state and uses it to dominate other groups. In some cases, this is accomplished by outright repression; in other cases, by stratagems that divide minorities in order to conquer them. Repression can sometimes be effective in preventing ethnic conflict, if the power of the dominant group is so overwhelming as to preclude rational resistance. This worked for decades in the Soviet empire, for example. On balance, however, statistical studies show that political repression and economic exploitation tend to be associated with a greater risk of ethnic conflict.[17] Repression per se is not reliable as a strategy of ethnic conflict management.

Domination works more reliably when it is tolerated by those who are deprived of power yet decide that being second-class citizens is better than being first-class rebels. Ethnic minorities may be co-opted if they are granted benefits smaller than those of the dominant group yet greater than their next-best alternative. For example, Russians in Estonia compare their situation to that of Russians in Russia and typically decide that the lack of Estonian citizenship is not so terrible. Israeli Arabs tolerate various forms of economic and political discrimination because of the economic opportunities that Israel affords them. Similarly, ethnic Chinese in Malaysia tolerate severe discrimination in access to higher education and government jobs because Chinese businesses are booming in the pro-capitalist environment fostered by the Malaysian state. Armenians, though holding second-class status in both the Ottoman and the Russian Empires, were often loyal subjects when their community was protected from external foes or given rights to regulate their own internal affairs.

Such hegemonies work best when tangible side benefits are reinforced by ideological justifications of ethnic subordination. Sometimes this is accomplished by the fiction that status inequalities are based on neutral legal criteria, not on ethnic ascription. For example, measures excluding most Russians from Estonian citizenship are based not on ethnicity per se, but on one's ancestors' citizenship in the interwar Estonian state (before most Russians arrived) and on knowledge of the official language of the state, which happens to be Estonian. Insofar as this seemingly civic justification for ethnic exclusion might create an opening for more inclusionary outcomes in the long run, it may be reasonable for Russian-speaking

---

[17] Ted Robert Gurr, *Minorities at Risk* (Washington, DC: US Institute of Peace, 1993), Chapters 2–5.

Estonians to accept the ideology as one they can work with.[18] In another variant, Arabs who are citizens of Israel proper (i.e., not those in occupied Gaza and the West Bank) get to vote, though they are deprived of many other social and economic benefits that are distributed by the state through Jewish nongovernmental organizations or as a result of military service. In this system, discrimination is partially constrained and masked by the need to maintain the appearance of a rational-legal equality. As a result, Arabs who profit from the system have an opportunity to work the constraints to their advantage and to justify their acquiescence to it.[19]

Though such hegemonies or "ethnic control regimes" may be quite effective in moderating ethnic conflict, they nonetheless have some major drawbacks.[20] The systematic deprivation of equal civic rights to ethnic minorities creates an ideological climate in which the democratic rights of the majority are also held to be less than absolute.[21] If the collectivity is held to count for more than the individual, this insidious principle can be, and often is, used to undermine the rights of individuals of the majority ethnic group as well. In Armenia, for example, it was a short step from the expulsion of ethnic Azeris to the abrogation of democracy and journalistic freedom for ethnic Armenians as well.[22] Ethnic hegemonies are less objectionable as temporary expedients than as permanent vehicles for civic inequality. If Estonia, for example, were gradually to infuse real content into its nominally civic principles, its long-run prognosis as a liberal democracy would be good. Unfortunately, few dominant ethnic groups are prescient enough to liquidate their own hegemonic position voluntarily through gradual civic reforms. South African whites moved in that direc-

---

[18] Toivo Raun, "Ethnic Relations and Conflict in the Baltic States," in W. Raymond Duncan and G. Paul Holman, Jr., *Ethnic Nationalism and Regional Conflict* (Boulder, CO: Westview, 1994), 155–82; David Laitin, "National Revival and Competitive Assimilation in Estonia," *Post-Soviet Affairs* 12:1 (January-March 1996), 25–39.

[19] For background, see Sammy Smooha, "Minority Status in an Ethnic Democracy: The Status of the Arab Minority in Israel," *Ethnic and Racial Studies* (July 1990).

[20] Ian Lustick, "Stability in Deeply Divided Societies: Consociationalism Versus Control," *World Politics* 31:3 (April 1979), 325–44; Kenneth McRae, "Theories of Power-Sharing and Conflict Management," in Joseph Montville, ed., *Conflict and Peacemaking in Multiethnic Societies* (New York: Lexington, 1991), 93–106.

[21] Liah Greenfeld, *Nationalism* (Cambridge: Harvard University Press, 1992).

[22] Michael Specter, "Drift to Dictatorship Clouds Armenia's Happiness," *New York Times*, January 3, 1997, 1, 12.

tion, in part due to pressure from a worldwide economic boycott. Malaysia and Israel, however, have taken as many steps backward as forward in recent decades.

To prevent such backsliding, quasi-democratic ethnic control regimes should be placed under moderate but relentless pressure from the international community to breathe life gradually into the nominally civic provisions of their constitutions. International tolerance should be shown for ethnic hegemonies if their reforms are heading in the right direction, even if slowly. At the same time, the international community should be supporting the development of the institutional infrastructure that will be needed when the disadvantaged minority is finally allowed to play a full role in the civic life of the state. This means, for example, training ethnic minority journalists to take over responsible positions in mainstream media serving an ethnically mixed audience. It does not, however, mean jump-starting the creation of ethnic opposition media to give voice to the demands of excluded minorities. That would only exacerbate the segmentation of the marketplace of ideas, making it easier for ethnonationalists to sow myths unchallenged.

### Ethnic Partition

Another unattractive but important and sometimes necessary strategy is ethnic partition. One does not have to hold primordialist theories of ancient hatreds to believe that, once popular identities are mobilized to fight along lines defined by cultural differences, it will be difficult to erase fears and hatreds rooted in the memory of those conflicts. Once intermingled cultural groups have fought, it is likely that their subsequent cohabitation in the same state will be wary, and consequently that they will fight again in the future. Any of a number of triggers—retreat of the imperial order-keepers, democratization, economic changes, shifts in the demographic balance of power—may touch it off. For that reason, a number of scholars have been making the case for ethnic partition as the best solution for certain cases of very highly mobilized nationalist enmities.[23]

---

[23] Chaim Kaufmann, "Possible and Impossible Solutions to Ethnic Civil Wars," *International Security* 20:4 (Spring 1996), 136–75; and other works cited by Daniel Byman and Stephen Van Evera, "Hypotheses on the Causes of Contemporary Deadly Conflict," *Security Studies* 7:3 (Spring 1998), 49–50.

Among the objections to this strategy, the most obvious is that the creation of ethnically homogeneous states in places like the former Yugoslavia, Rwanda, Burundi, and the Transcaucasus would require the resettlement of huge numbers of unwilling people. Yet the history of many ethnic conflicts shows that separation is likely to happen anyway, but through the vilest kind of warfare if not through internationally supervised, preventive operations in peacetime. One reason for ethnic peace in much of Eastern Europe today is that the two world wars occasioned a vast "unmixing of peoples" through what today's Serbs would term ethnic cleansing.[24] Even such civilized folk as the Czechs expelled over a million Germans at the end of the war in 1945. In the present period, expulsions have accompanied many ethnic conflicts. During the breakup of the Soviet Union, hundreds of thousands of Armenians and Azerbaijanis were hounded from each others' countries by force.[25] Fighting and intimidation in the former Yugoslavia has likewise made many areas more homogeneous and thus made partition more plausible. In light of the de facto partition of Bosnia into Serbian and Muslim-Croat parts, the international community's insistence on maintaining the Dayton Accord's de jure fiction of political integration seems almost perversely designed to prevent the acceptance of an inevitable equilibrium. In future cases of this type, the UN High Commissioner for Refugees might be wise to make a preventive offer of low-interest mortgages to fearful individuals stranded in minority enclaves who wish to purchase housing in their ethnic home republic.

Opponents of this strategy argue, however, that partition rarely resolves conflicts, in part because populations often remain somewhat intermingled, and as a result, endemic conflict persists despite partition, as in, for example, Ireland, Palestine, and Kashmir. Most important, partition—and the anticipation of partition—may itself be a cause of conflict. Many more died in ethnic violence in the aftermath of partitioning India and Pakistan as a result of the turmoil and insecurities of migration, than before it. Indeed, plans to divide the former British Raj may have acted as a self-fulfilling prophecy, creating needless fears and uncertainties

[24] Rogers Brubaker, *Nationalism Reframed* (Cambridge: Cambridge University Press, 1996), Chapter 6.
[25] Barbara Anderson and Brian Silver, "Population Redistribution and Ethnic Balance in Transcaucasia," in Ronald Suny, ed., *Transcaucasia: Nationalism and Social Change,* 2d ed. (Ann Arbor: University of Michigan Press, 1996), 490–91.

about the status of religious minorities that would find themselves on the wrong side of the partition line.[26] For these reasons, while preventive partition should not be viewed as unthinkable, nor should it be seen as a preferred strategy applicable to a wide range of cases.

### Federalism

A related strategy is federalism. Instead of partitioning ethnic communities into separate sovereign states, this strategy would divide them into partially autonomous territorial subunits within the state, whose boundaries are designed to coincide with ethnolinguistic concentrations. This method has a terrible track record, yet it remains popular with liberal problem-solvers, in part because it seems to allow national self-determination without the nasty fuss and bother of full-fledged partition. In fact, ethnofederalism is frequently a recipe for subsequent partition, often needlessly so. In the wake of communism's collapse, the only states to break up were the three ethnofederal systems—Yugoslavia, the Soviet Union, and Czechoslovakia—the first two with violent consequences. Arguably, in each of these states ethnofederalism was a strategy of rule actively chosen by its Communist founders, not a necessity forced upon them by the irresistible demands of ethnic groups. As numerous studies have demonstrated, ethnofederalism tends to heighten and politicize ethnic consciousness, creating a self-conscious intelligentsia and the organizational structures of an ethnic state-in-waiting.[27] When mass political participation expands, these ethnofederal structures channel it along an ethnic path.[28] For these reasons, ethnofederalism is at best a last resort that risks fueling rather than appeasing the politicization of ethnicity.

One of ethnofederalism's very few success cases is India, which reluctantly acceded to demands to reorganize some of its provincial boundaries after 1956 to coincide more closely with linguistic divides. Nehru and the Congress Party, at this point still at the height of their authority, were adamant secularists. Thus, the central government kept a tight rein on the process of ethnofederal reorganization. Rules guiding this process stipu-

---

[26] Radha Kumar, "The Troubled History of Partition," *Foreign Affairs* 76:1 (January/February 1997).

[27] Brubaker, *Nationalism Reframed*, Chapter 2.

[28] This process has played itself out even in Québec. See Karen Ballentine, Columbia University dissertation in progress.

lated that no concessions would be made to secessionist groups, that demands for redrawing boundaries along religious lines would be rejected out-of-hand, that large-scale popular support for the change had to be demonstrated, and that reorganization had to be requested by all the affected linguistic groups.[29] Most observers credit these controlled boundary adjustments with redressing a reasonable grievance without compromising the basic principles of the centralized, secular, ethnic-blind state. Subsequent problems leading to heightened communal mobilization in Indian politics were caused by the breakdown of the Congress system at the center, not by ethnofederalism per se.

### Assimilation

The opposite strategy is the assimilation of ethnic minorities to the cultural identity of the ethnic majority. This is possible for groups that are culturally similar, such as Russians and Ukrainians, or for minority cultures that are assimilated before they achieve a literary consciousness or political organization beyond the kinship level.[30] But for most groups that are already in sustained ethnic conflicts, the window for cultural assimilation to the foe's ethnic identity has already closed.

### Powersharing versus Cross-Ethnic Alliances

The two opposite strategies of ethnic conflict prevention that have stimulated the most academic debate are (1) *powersharing* between ethnic groups and (2) institutional engineering to foster *integrative, cross-ethnic political alliances*.[31] The powersharing approach developed by Arend Lijphart takes the politicization of ethnic groups as a given in deeply divided societies, and it offers guidelines for elite-led pacts between the groups that will allow them to live in peace and mutual security.[32] In con-

[29] Paul Brass, *The Politics of India since Independence* (Cambridge: Cambridge University Press, 1990), 169, 172–73.

[30] Karl Deutsch, *Nationalism and Social Communication* (Cambridge: MIT Press, 1966), Chapter 6; Lars-Erik Cederman, *Emergent Actors in World Politics: How States and Nations Develop and Dissolve* (Princeton: Princeton University Press, 1997), 157–61.

[31] Timothy Sisk, *Power Sharing and International Mediation in Ethnic Conflicts* (Washington, DC: US Institute of Peace, 1996), Chapter 3.

[32] Arend Lijphart, *Democracy in Plural Societies* (New Haven: Yale University Press, 1977); Lijphart, "The Power-Sharing Approach," in Montville, *Conflict and Peacemaking in Multiethnic Societies*, 491–510.

trast, the integrative approach of Donald Horowitz tries to depoliticize ethnic identity by means of institutional arrangements that create incentives to align on the basis of crosscutting cleavages.[33] My findings reinforce the many doubts that scholars have expressed about elite-managed ethnic powersharing. Integrative approaches like Horowitz's are more promising for democratizing states, though these must be embedded in a broader context of supportive institutions than the constitutional and electoral schemes that Horowitz himself emphasizes.

*Powersharing.* Lijphart lists the central characteristics of powersharing as joint control of executive power of the state, substantial autonomy of ethnic groups to regulate their own internal affairs, a minority veto on important issues, and proportionality of parliamentary representation, bureaucratic appointments, and state financial benefits.[34] Underpinning these arrangements is a system of bargaining between leaders of the participating ethnic groups, and deference to those leaders on the part of each group's ethnic rank-and-file. Lijphart lists nine factors as conducive to powersharing:

1. the absence of a single majority group,
2. no economic disparity among the groups,
3. a balance of power among the groups,
4. a small number of groups,
5. a country with a small total population,
6. the existence of an external threat common to all groups,
7. overarching loyalties that reduce the exclusiveness of ethnic attachments,
8. prior traditions of compromise, and
9. geographic concentrations of ethnic residence.

However, he adds that powersharing is always the best approach in deeply divided societies, even when those factors are absent.[35]

---

[33] Horowitz, "Making Moderation Pay," in Montville, *Conflict and Peacemaking in Multiethnic Societies*, 451–76.

[34] Lijphart, "The Power-Sharing Approach," 494–95. See also Eric Nordlinger, *Conflict Regulation in Divided Societies* (Cambridge: Center for International Affairs, Harvard Studies in International Relations, 1972), 21–33.

[35] Lijphart, "The Power-Sharing Approach," 497–98; note also the list of conditions in Joseph Rothschild, *Ethnopolitics* (New York: Columbia University Press, 1981), 162–64.

The powersharing approach is especially problematic in the context of democratizing societies. Powersharing, as Lijphart conceives it, depends on mass groups deferring to the judgments of moderate elites who represent their ethnic segments. However, deference can hardly be taken for granted in democratizing societies. Mass groups clamoring for a greater say in politics will use any available argument, especially the argument that traditional elites are selling out the nation's interests by being too accommodating toward outsiders. In this context, elites jockeying for power within the ethnic group often have an incentive to be immoderate. Institutionalized powersharing exacerbates this by defining all politics as ethnic politics. As mass groups enter the political process, anyone who wants to participate must go through ethnic channels. Mobilizing support by definition means making sectarian appeals. Cross-ethnic politicking is reserved to elites, who may be too pressured from below to be accommodating toward elites of the opposing community.

The empirical record is not very favorable to powersharing.[36] Lijphart points to Belgium and Malaysia as textbook cases of successful powersharing in ethnically divided societies. Setting aside the example of Belgium, a rich country in the heart of a peacefully democratic continent, Malaysia hardly counts in favor of Lijphart's scheme. Rather than being an example of a "consociational democracy," it is instead an example of a successful ethnic Malay hegemony (with side payments to the Chinese business elite) erected by suppressing democracy and free speech. Lijphart also counts India as an example of successful powersharing.[37] Indeed, limited legal self-regulation by Muslims and linguistic federalism are powersharing elements in the Indian political system. However, the main principle of the Congress system in its heyday was secularism, the opposite of representation along religious or communal lines. Congress's success in containing ethnic and religious conflict was precisely that it encompassed all cultural groups so that communal groups were not mobilized in competition to one another. Finally, Lijphart used to claim Lebanon as the premier example of powersharing, but since the outbreak of the bloody civil

---

[36] Paul Brass, *Ethnicity and Nationalism* (London: Sage, 1991), Chapter 9; Ian Lustick, "Lijphart, Lakatos, and Consociationalism," *World Politics* 50:1 (October 1997), 88–117.

[37] Arend Lijphart, "The Puzzle of Indian Democracy," *American Political Science Review* 90:2 (June 1996), 258–68.

war there in the 1970s, he now stresses the flaws in Lebanon's consociational arrangements.[38] In fact, Lebanon, along with Yugoslavia, underscores the dangers of this approach: it locks in an ethnic definition of politics, which leads to disaster when the prospect of rising popular participation undercuts the moderation of elites, or when demographic shifts alter the ethnic balance of power.[39]

**Cross-ethnic alliances.** Horowitz's integrative approach pursues exactly the opposite strategy: it tries to depoliticize ethnicity by creating institutions that reward cross-ethnic alignments. For the most part, he suggests encouraging this through constitutional and electoral provisions. In federal systems, for example, he suggests that boundaries should not coincide with ethnic patterns of settlement but should cut across them or break them up into smaller units. He notes that Nigeria's three-province system, which corresponded with ethnic lines, broke into bloody ethnic warfare in 1967. Afterward, the new regime imposed a twelve-province scheme that successfully politicized local identities and subcleavages within the broader ethnic categories.[40] For similar reasons, Horowitz recommends electoral rules that require winning candidates to garner at least some of their votes from a different ethnicity. This can be done by requiring supermajorities larger than any single group could provide, or by requiring successful candidates to get a number of "second-preference" votes. Such a scheme was instituted in Sri Lanka in 1978, but by then, Horowitz says, politics was so polarized that electoral rules were insufficient to induce moderation.

There is not much direct empirical evidence in support of Horowitz's claims. He is no more convincing than Lijphart in asserting Malaysia as a successful test of his theory.[41] The value of the Nigerian example is mitigated by the fact that the return of outright military dictatorship, rather than clever electoral rules, had a great deal to do with the postconflict stabilization of ethnic politics. South Africa, the subject of a detailed prescriptive book by Horowitz, adopted neither Horowitz's nor Lijphart's

[38] Lijphart, "The Power-Sharing Approach," 507–8; Lijphart, *Democracy in Plural Societies*, 147–57.

[39] Ivo Banac, *The National Question in Yugoslavia* (Ithaca: Cornell University Press, 1984), 414, notes that the conditions Lijphart specifies for successful consociational powersharing were also absent in Yugoslavia.

[40] Horowitz, "Ethnic Conflict Management for Policymakers," in Montville, *Conflict and Peacemaking in Multiethnic Societies*, 122–23.

[41] See Chapter 6 in this volume.

schemes, but the country democratized successfully and relatively peacefully anyway.[42]

Horowitz is on the right track, but his institutional schemes are too mechanistic and insufficiently embedded in a broader supportive context. Cross-ethnic institutions are needed on more dimensions than just electoral and constitutional rules. For example, segmental boundaries in the marketplace of ideas need to be erased by media institutions that will serve as a common forum for the presentation and rigorous evaluation of ideas for all communities of that state. That is, in addition to Horowitz's "vote pooling," multiethnic societies also need "idea pooling." Integrative institutions are also needed in the administrative realm. In contrast to Lijphart's call for ethnic representation in state bureaucracies, what is really needed are ethnic-blind and highly professionalized courts, police, and armed forces that will carry out state policy equally toward all individuals, regardless of ethnicity.[43]

The commitment to the creation of a dense web of such ethnic-blind institutions can serve as the basis for a civic nationalism that is based not on the coexistence of ethnic groups but on the civic rights and duties of individuals. Unlike the strategy of ethnic assimilation, the promotion of civic nationalism does not require citizens to alter that aspect of their identity that is rooted in traditional culture, but simply to depoliticize it.

As a practical matter, a civic national identity can emerge in a number of ways. In the case of Switzerland, a long history of cross-cultural cooperation against outside threats created strong civic myths to underpin collective action. In a society of immigrants from many cultures, such as in the United States, loyalty to state institutions based on equal individual rights can serve as a strong foundation for a common identity. In many states, however, civic nationalism is based on a broadened redefinition of a core ethnic identity.[44] British civic nationalism, for example, grew out of a redefinition of English patriotism that stressed the centrality of individual liberties and common struggles against foreign foes, in which Scots

---

[42] Donald Horowitz, *A Democratic South Africa? Constitutional Engineering in a Divided Society* (Berkeley: University of California Press, 1991).

[43] Horowitz's own recommendations on the ethnic composition of military forces in South Africa are complex, taking into account both professionalism and representativeness. See Horowitz, *A Democratic South Africa?*, 227–31.

[44] Anthony D. Smith, *The Ethnic Origins of Nations* (Oxford: Blackwell, 1986).

and Welsh could be full participants. French national identity, though based partly on the ethnic core of the Île de France, was broadened through the experience of the French Revolution to include civic principles of equality and the rights of man. As a result, immigrants have been able to become French by integrating themselves into French civic life much more easily than outsiders could become German, for example, whose identity conception is more ethnic and exclusionary.[45]

A number of contemporary states stand at the cusp of developing civic national identities through one or another of these pathways.[46] Most may do so by making a core ethnic identity more inclusionary, whereas some may have to forge entirely new loyalties to a multiethnic territorial state. Russia and Ukraine, for example, have formed around a central core ethnic group, but apart from establishing the core group's language as the official medium for state business, they are not attempting to impose an ethnic stamp on the political system. The rhetoric of top government officials stress inclusionary loyalty to the state rather than exclusionary loyalty to the ethnic group. Over time, it is possible that Estonia may likewise broaden the core of its ethnic self-definition to take on a more civic character. Civic identity in Kazakhstan, however, seems less likely to emerge from the gradual broadening of a core ethnic identity, since two core ethnic identities, Russian and Kazakh, are regionally concentrated, numerically equally balanced, and culturally too distinct for easy assimilation. Any successful civic identity would have to be bicultural and based on loyalty to an administratively successful state. In light of that, full democratic participation should wait until Kazakhstan's state has been able to demonstrate its effectiveness and thereby generate an enthusiastic mass following.

Despite the advantages in principle of the civic solution, some caveats are in order. In some cases, as in the regime of the Slovak nationalist former prime minister Vladimir Meciar, the argument that group rights can be best guaranteed through the protection of individual rights is a rhetorical mask for a policy of majority ethnic hegemony. While touting an individual rights approach to minority safeguards, Meciar in fact failed to deliver on either individual or group rights for Slovakia's Hungarian

[45] Rogers Brubaker, *Citizenship and Nationhood in France and Germany* (Cambridge: Harvard University Press, 1992).

[46] Ian Bremmer, ed., *Understanding Nationalism* (forthcoming).

minority. He banned Hungarian street signs, gerrymandered electoral districts to reduce political clout of the concentrated Hungarian minority in
southern Slovakia, shifted economic investment to the ethnically Slovak
north, and used the state's power to hinder opposition journalism. Even
in such cases, however, the best strategy is not to promote minority group
rights to defend against such encroachments, but to insist that the majority regime implement its avowed civic principles in an effective, even-
handed way.

However, the promotion of overarching civic identities is not a short-
term possibility in circumstances where the mobilization of ethnic cleavages is already extremely intense. Civic nationalism is a nonstarter in
Bosnia today, no matter how much the promoters of the Dayton Accord
cherish that ideal. Nonetheless, short-run choices should, wherever possible, avoid expedients that make civic outcomes more difficult in the long
run. Powersharing and ethnofederalism, by locking in ethnic identities,
are in that sense steps in the wrong direction. Moderate, balanced ethnic
control regimes that contain ethnopolitical mobilization of the majority
as well as the minorities, may be a better strategy for the long run, provided it is combined with the gradual fostering of civic institutions.

### Combating Nationalist Myths in the Marketplace of Ideas

Finally, another strategy emphasizes intellectual solutions to ethnic conflict.[47] Some argue, for example, that the root cause of ethnic conflict
comes from the false historical myths that nationalists sow about the
alleged perfidies of the ethnic foe.[48] From this standpoint, mechanical
gimmicks like powersharing or electoral alliances are unworkable until
these myths are exploded, and perhaps unnecessary once that is achieved.
In this view, textbooks, not electoral laws, should be the top priority for
reform.

The findings of this book suggest that intellectual combat against falsi-
fiable myths is indeed a key instrument for containing ethnic conflict.
However, such combat can be waged effectively only in a well-constituted
marketplace of ideas. Thin liberal solutions based on free speech and the
spontaneous emergence of truth will be trumped every time unless they

---

[47] Rothschild, *Ethnopolitics*, 80–84.
[48] Stephen Van Evera, "Hypotheses on Nationalism and War," *International
Security* 18:4 (Spring 1994), 26–33.

are placed within a thickly supportive web of norms and institutions. Thus, civic identity, scrutiny of myths, Horowitzian electoral incentives, professionalized bureaucracies, and high-quality journalism must be developed simultaneously. None works effectively in isolation from the other components, and the development of the whole package may take time.

Democratization and free speech can be made compatible with ethnic harmony and the moderation of nationalist sentiment only under favorable conditions of supply, demand, and institutional regulation of the marketplace of ideas. If these conditions do not exist, they need to be created before, or at least along with, the unfettering of speech and political participation.

On the supply side, the influence of the international community may be essential to help break up information monopolies, especially in states with very weak journalistic traditions and a weak civil society. In Cambodia, for example, the UN's relatively successful media and information program was designed, according to the UN commander, to "bypass the propaganda of the Cambodian factions" by directly disseminating information about the elections. [49] However, since the broader context of Cambodian politics remained inhospitable to civic democracy, these media efforts did not have a lasting effect.

Thus, the breakup of monopoly power over politics and discourse must coincide with measures to reduce elites' incentives for nationalist mythmaking or else to eliminate their capacity to make trouble. As the Rwanda case shows, it is reckless for the international community to threaten elites with across-the-board exposure and prosecution of past crimes, unless there exists the will and capability to render harmless the likely backlash from elites who are backed against the wall. Without this will, elites who are potentially threatened by democratization and the end of censorship should be guaranteed a soft landing in the emerging open society. Many Latin American and East European countries have done well by keeping prosecutions limited. In contrast, fine moral declarations without effective actions are the worst possible policy.

---

[49] Michael W. Doyle, *UN Peacekeeping in Cambodia: UNTAC's Civil Mandate* (Boulder, CO: Lynne Rienner, 1995), 54–55. For other cases, see Dan Lindley, "Collective Security Organizations and Internal Conflict," in Michael E. Brown, ed., *The International Dimensions of Internal Conflict* (Cambridge: MIT Press, 1996), 562–67.

On the demand side, ethnically segmented markets should be counteracted by the promotion of civic-territorial conceptions of national identity. Inclusive national identities can be fostered through an integrative press that expresses a variety of outlooks on the same pages. All too often, international aid to the opposition press in democratizing countries overlooks its low journalistic quality, on the grounds that creating a pluralism of voices is the essential objective. In Romania, for example, the U.S. Agency for International Development has subsidized antigovernment newspapers that fail to meet even the most minimal standards of accuracy in reporting.[50] Instead, aid should go to forums that present varied ideas, not a single line, in a setting that fosters effective interchange and factual accuracy. In post-1945 Germany, for example, American occupiers licensing newspapers showed a strong preference for editorial teams whose members spanned diverse political orientations.[51] The international community should encourage this kind of idea-pooling through integrative public forums in order to break down the intellectual boundaries between ethnically exclusive communities.[52]

For this reason, NGOs and other aid donors should reconsider projects to provide ethnic minorities with their "own" media.[53] Instead, support should go to media that strive to attract a politically and ethnically diverse audience, invite the expression of various viewpoints, and hold news stories to rigorous standards of objectivity. This can be done by expanding existing NGO programs like the International Press Institute in Vienna[54] to train journalists from newly democratizing countries and by providing quality news organizations with equipment, subsidized newsprint, or other logistical support. Special efforts should be made to improve the regional and local press. In case after case—Weimar, India,

---

[50] Thomas Carothers, *Assessing Democratic Assistance: The Case of Romania* (Washington, DC: Carnegie Endowment for International Peace, 1996), 80–89.

[51] Richard L. Merritt, *Democracy Imposed: U.S. Occupation Policy and the German Public, 1945–1949* (New Haven: Yale University Press, 1996), 291–315, esp. 296, emphasizes the effectiveness of this strategy.

[52] On a common media as a precondition for an integrated national consciousness, see Benedict Anderson, *Imagined Communities* (London: Verso, 1983).

[53] Stephen Harold Riggins, *Ethnic Minority Media* (Newbury Park, CA: Sage, 1992).

[54] Larry Diamond, *Promoting Democracy in the 1990s* (New York: Carnegie Corporation, Report to the Carnegie Commission on Preventing Deadly Conflict, December 1995), 24–25.

Sri Lanka, and contemporary Russia—key vehicles of nationalist myth-making have been face-to-face networks and narrowly targeted, unprofessional periodicals. To provide an effective alternative to these, media projects should focus on the inclusion of local journalists in the activities of statewide media associations, mid-career training sabbaticals for grass-roots journalists, and financial subsidies to make a high-quality local press independent and affordable.

Idea pooling can also occur outside of formal journalistic institutions through face-to-face interactions of citizens. A study comparing Indian cities with low and high rates of interethnic rioting shows the crucial role played by interethnic voluntary organizations (such as Rotary Clubs, film societies, and trade unions) and other informal channels for communication in refuting myths that cause conflict spirals. When such channels existed, rumors about an interethnic rape or the desecration of a temple were nipped in the bud; otherwise, a cycle of retaliation was likely.[55] Thus, instead of partitioning society into segmented groups that communicate only with themselves, an integrated forum for discourse and information-sharing, whether through media or voluntary organizations, should be promoted.

Major efforts should also be made to promote the institutionalization of effective norms of elite discourse, journalistic professionalism, and independent evaluative bodies *before* the full opening of mass political participation. Whenever possible, market imperfections should be counteracted by decentralized institutions, not by centralized regulatory directives, and by promoting norms of fair debate, not by restricting the content of speech. In some cases, however, certain kinds of constraints on speech may be necessary in multiethnic societies while these institutions are being built, even though this idea may be ethically uncomfortable for Western liberals. Moreover, it is politically difficult to design constraints on democracy and free speech that do not play into the hands of elites who want to squelch freedom entirely. When electoral polarization touched off commu-

---

[55] Ashutosh Varshney, "Postmodernism and Ethnic Conflict: A Passage to India," *Comparative Politics* (October 1997). For similar findings, see Sherrill Stroschein, "The Components of Coexistence: Hungarian Minorities and Interethnic Relations in Romania, Slovakia, and Ukraine," in John Micgiel, ed., *State and Nation Building in East Central Europe* (New York: Columbia University, Institute on East Central Europe, 1996), 153–76.

nal riots in Malaysia in 1969, for example, the government banned public discussion of ethnic issues and imposed a regime of ethnic coexistence that insured Malay political domination and economic prosperity for the Chinese business community. After a quarter century of tight press controls, the uneasy communal peace still holds, but this interlude that might have been used to prepare an institutional infrastructure for a more durable, democratic solution has been squandered.[56]

Neither the ethnic strife unleashed by unchecked democratization in cases like Sri Lanka nor the temporary, repressive communal cease-fire in cases like Malaysia is desirable. One element of a better solution is for international donors to offer incentives to elites to develop institutions of free debate, even while tolerating the retention of some temporary limits on free expression, including limits on ethnic hate speech. Another element is to offer direct aid for professionalizing those elements of the media that are attempting to create an integrated forum for responsible, accurate debate. But when these remedies are unavailing, those who value both unfettered speech and peace must assess the trade-off between them, without illusions.

### Managing counterrevolutionary and revolutionary nationalism

Though solutions to ethnic conflict have a high priority on today's policy agenda, other varieties of nationalism may present even more important policy challenges in the future. In contemplating a future threat from Chinese nationalism, for example, it is not tensions between Han Chinese and Tibetans that are the main worry for the international community, but rather a surly, Wilhelmine-style nationalist China.[57] This is

[56] Gordon P. Means, *Malaysian Politics: The Second Generation*, (Singapore: Oxford University Press, 1991), esp. 137–38, 313–14, 418–22, 439; Karl von Vorys, *Democracy without Consensus: Communalism and Political Stability in Malaysia* (Princeton: Princeton University Press, 1975), 394–412.

[57] John Garver, *Will China Be Another Germany?* (Carlisle Barracks, PA: U.S. Army War College National Strategy Institute, 1996); David Shambaugh, "Containment or Engagement of China? Calculating Beijing's Responses," *International Security* 21:2 (Fall 1996), 185–86; Erica Strecker Downs and Phillip Saunders, "Legitimacy and the Limits of Nationalism," *International Security* 23:3 (Winter 1998–99), 114–146; Patrick E. Tyler, "Rebels' New Cause: A Book for Yankee Bashing," *New York Times*, September 4, 1996, A4; Patrick E. Tyler, "Shifting Gears, Beijing Reins in Anti-Japanese Campaign," *New York Times*, September 19, 1996, A7; Allan Whiting,

most likely to develop either through the counterrevolutionary dynamic, in which threatened military or party elites play the nationalist card to rally support in the face of roiling social change, or through a revolutionary dynamic, in which intense nationalism becomes the vehicle for reestablishing the political order in the wake of dramatic change.

To dampen counterrevolutionary nationalism, the findings of this study suggest three recommendations. The first is to provide a golden parachute for still powerful elites who are potentially threatened by democratic change. Elites facing the prospect of downward mobility, especially ones that control tanks or mass media, need to be reassured that they will find a lucrative though less commanding niche in the new order. They should be made weak but happy in the course of democratization. Insofar as the preoccupation of the Chinese People's Liberation Army with the manufacturing of pirated rock-and-roll CDs serves that end, perhaps the United States should be less exercised about such trespasses against intellectual property rights.

Second, insofar as increased trade and investment helps to create commercial wealth and build a strong middle class, it may in the long run create some of the preconditions for civic democracy. In the short run, however, increasing exposure to trade and international financial flows may favor either liberal democratic political movements or populist protectionism, depending on the precise configuration of interests at stake. Once a liberal, free-trading, democratizing coalition is in place, the example of Weimar Germany suggests that this tie needs to be well institutionalized and buffered from the vagaries of market fluctuations or political squabbles. Otherwise, swing constituencies may abandon the democratic coalition, and a nationalistic backlash may set in. What counts most in the integration of democratizing states into the world economy may be the stability and predictability of the tie. This point is further examined in the section below on the impact of trade.

Third, it is unreasonable to expect a country like Communist China to democratize successfully in a sudden big bang. Few of the components of a thickly institutionalized liberalism could be put in place quickly in China. An energetic but still comparatively small commercial class that is

---

"Chinese Nationalism and Foreign Policy after Deng," *China Quarterly* (Summer 1995); Fareed Zakaria, "Speak Softly, Carry a Veiled Threat," *New York Times Magazine* (February 18, 1996), section 6, pp. 36–37.

engaged in international trade cannot be decisive on its own, and it will, in any case, act in a liberal fashion only in an institutional setting that is conducive to its success. Otherwise, populist nationalism may be its more likely strategy for weathering the storms of social change in a largely peasant, authoritarian country with a decentralized, nationalistic military. As in Wilhelmine Germany, intellectuals and middle classes hoping to play a greater role in political life may find that authoritarian elites are more willing to tolerate expressions of nationalist outrage than calls for liberal democracy. For example, popular protests in Beijing of the inadvertent 1999 U.S. bombing of the Chinese embassy in Belgrade were not just allowed but were actively encouraged by official media, whereas the 1989 pro-democracy demonstrations, led by a similar core of student protesters, were effectively squelched.[58] With old Communist elites still able to set the terms of popular participation of politics, a sudden transition to mass politics could lead in dangerous and unpredictable directions. Consequently, China should be encouraged not to democratize abruptly, but to prepare a much more limited liberal opening, gradually installing the rule of law and more objective discussion in a professionalized press before devolving power to representative institutions.

Revolutionary nationalisms require a different approach. Once mass enthusiasm is mobilized around a nationalistic theme, fine-tuning coalition incentives through instruments such as trade is unlikely to have much impact. Rather, as Stephen Walt concludes in his wide-ranging study of revolutions and war, what is required is a patient strategy of containment.[59] Military and economic measures to constrain the expansionism of the revolutionary regime should be crafted to avoid the appearance of an offensive threat, which would only deepen the paranoia of the revolutionary mindset. Russian qualms about NATO expansion, intensified by NATO's bombing of Serbia, show how difficult it is to make defensive security preparations distinguishable from preparations for aggression, even in the eyes of a relatively moderate potential opponent. As a rule, containment should not start at the doorstep of the revolutionary nationalist state. This is also true in a case like Russia's, where ethnic nationalism

[58] Erik Eckholm, "China's Liberals Look for Silver Lining," *New York Times*, May 17, 1999, A11.

[59] Stephen Walt, *Revolution and War* (Ithaca: Cornell University Press, 1996), 342–44.

may also come into play through the urge to protect or incorporate ethnic compatriots in Russia's "near abroad."

This discussion assumes, of course, that conscious choices made by politicians can affect the likelihood of nationalist conflict, and that the international community can influence the incentives that politicians and publics face. But is this true? Even if the international community devises astute strategies grounded in an improved understanding of the factors that promote or dampen nationalist conflict during democratic transitions, can it substantially affect the outcome? How much do international incentives shape the trajectory of nationalist politics?

## International Impact on Democratization and Nationalist Mobilization

Students of democratic transitions, most of them specialists in comparative domestic politics, have tended to look for the causes of democratization in the internal characteristics of states. Samuel Huntington's list of twenty-seven alleged causes of democracy and democratization, culled from academic literature, includes only four international factors, three of them involving colonization or military occupation by a democracy. In contrast, Huntington's own research lists five factors that account for the wave of democratizations since 1974, all of them international: the legitimacy problems of authoritarian regimes on a global level; global economic growth; the liberalizing of the policies of the Catholic Church; the changes in the policies of the Soviet Union and the Western powers; and emulation of the initial democratizers at the leading edge of the wave.[60]

The international setting affects not only the likelihood of democratic transitions but also the likelihood that democratization will lead to nationalism and war. For example, democratizing states tend to be more war-prone only if they live in bad neighborhoods surrounded by autocracies. Democratic transitions are more benign when the neighbors are already democratic.[61]

---

[60] Samuel Huntington, *The Third Wave* (Norman: University of Oklahoma Press, 1991), 37; Ray, *Democracy and International Conflict*, 50–51. See also Linz and Stepan, *Problems of Democratic Transition and Consolidation*, 72–76.

[61] John R. Oneal and Bruce Russett, "Exploring the Liberal Peace: Interdependence,

Standard theories in the field of international relations point to three key international factors that affect a country's chances of democratizing and also the chance that its democratization will trigger nationalist conflict: international trade, military competition, and the international spread of ideas. In this section, I discuss the impact of these international factors on the internal variables that have played a central role in the argument of this book: the interests of groups and coalitions, the role of institutions in channeling political competition, and the impact of ideas on the resulting political struggle. Each of the theories discussed below contains an implicit policy prescription; to get a desired result, one must somehow influence the causal variable specified by that theory. Many of these implications are subtle and two-edged, however; applying them prescriptively requires sensitivity to the particular features of individual cases.

### The impact of trade

One group of theories examines the impact of trade on domestic political coalitions. What these theories hold in common is the notion that the changing costs and benefits of international trade affect the power resources and coalition incentives of political groupings inside states. Sometimes these shifts provide incentives for nationalist mobilization; at other times they may encourage the development of civic democracy.

Mature democracies tend to be free-trading. Indeed, civic nationalist states like Britain and the United States have been the leaders of the open global trading system. It is tempting to conclude, therefore, that promoting free trade with a democratizing country will increase its chance of developing a cooperative form of civic nationalism. Increased trade might strengthen the commercial middle classes needed to consolidate democracy. Lucrative trade ties might give the liberal international community a potential source of leverage to use on behalf of improving civil rights in the country. Such arguments are indeed made for increased trade with China.

These arguments, though not entirely wrong, are far too simple. While mature democracies are free-trading, statistical evidence suggests that new

Democracy, and Conflict, 1950–85," originally presented at April 1996 International Studies Association meeting.

democracies are inclined on average to become more protectionist.[62] Though some groups gain from increased trade, other may lose from it. If the average voter suffers in the short run from increased exposure to foreign competition, a backlash against free trade may develop. Nationalist politicians may then be able to win support for a program of protectionism or even of seizing foreign markets through imperial expansionism. This may be a particular danger in new democracies, where elites can take advantage of their media monopolies or their power to set agendas to determine what information and options voters consider. Thus, since increased trade can be a two-edged sword, it is important to examine more closely the conditions in which it promotes or undercuts aggressive nationalism.

Drawing on standard neoclassical economic theories of comparative advantage, Ronald Rogowski has developed an exceptionally elegant argument about the impact of changing exposure to trade, which has significant implications for the study of aggressive nationalism.[63] Analyzing incentives for coalitions among the three factors of production (land, labor, and capital), Rogowski begins with the truism that relative scarcity determines the price of the three factors. Owners of factors that are abundant locally will gain from free trade. For example, if labor is relatively abundant in the domestic market, increased trade will cause relatively cheap food and capital investments to flow into the country. As a result, workers will eat better and will find higher paying jobs. Thus, when labor is the abundant factor, workers will be free-trading. In contrast, owners of factors that are scarce locally will benefit from protectionism. If land and capital are scarce, the owners will have an incentive to keep out cheap competition from foreign farmers and capitalists, which would drive down their profits.

This logic has implications for the formation of political coalitions in democratizing countries. For example, if both labor and capital are abundant relative to land, elites who own capital will have an incentive to align with workers in a democratizing coalition against owners of scarce land who favor protectionism. However, if labor is relatively scarce, its preferences will be protectionist, so democratization will work against free trade.

[62] Edward D. Mansfield, "Democratization and Commercial Liberalization," paper presented at the 1996 annual meeting of the American Political Science Association.

[63] Ronald Rogowski, *Commerce and Coalitions* (Princeton: Princeton University Press, 1989).

Sometimes labor may be abundant and free-trading, but both land and capital may be scarce, therefore protectionist and antidemocratic, as in the German "marriage of iron and rye."[64] As I showed in the chapter on Germany, elite coalitions of this kind may use nationalist ideology to promote protectionism and to deflect demands for democratic participation.

Changes in the international environment may affect the direction and the strength of these incentives. Prussian rye-growing aristocrats were free-trading in the 1860s, for example, until North American grain flooded the European market in the decade following the American Civil War. As a result, the Prussian rye-growers switched their coalition partners and became strongly motivated to solve through politics the problems they could not solve through the free market.[65]

Rogowski acknowledges, however, that his theory predicts alignments, not outcomes. That, he says, depends on a variety of other factors, including the effects of previous institutions. For example, the fact that members of the Prussian landowning class served as high officials of the German state gave this class decisive advantages in forging a coalition that advanced its interests.[66] Outcomes may also depend on which ideas are persuasive in the coalition-making process. German industrialists, landowners, and the government officials who headed their alliance all prevailed over liberal, democratic free-traders, in part because they were able to harness protectionist and imperialist economic interests to a potent nationalist ideology. The success of this ideology depended in turn on the institutional structure of the marketplace of ideas in the German Reich and in the Weimar Republic.[67] Thus, the policy implications of a change in the incentives for trade depend not only on the logic of group interest, but also on the context of institutions and ideas that shapes and aggregates those interests.[68]

A collapse of international trade is especially likely to fuel a nationalist backlash. Peter Gourevitch's *Politics in Hard Times* shows how the so-called Great Depressions of the 1870s and the 1930s harmed relatively liberal, democratizing coalitions of export sectors and urban workers in

---

[64] Ibid., 33.

[65] Ibid., 39–40.

[66] Peter Gourevitch, *Politics in Hard Times*.

[67] See Chapter 3 in this volume.

[68] Kathryn Sikkink, *Ideas and Institutions: Developmentalism in Brazil and Argentina* (Ithaca: Cornell University Press, 1991).

countries like Germany and Japan.[69] Faced not only with collapsing markets for exports but also the drying up of foreign financing for social welfare programs or heightened foreign competition in their own domestic markets, powerful social groups—whether industrial cartels or landed gentry—switched from the promotion of free trade and the expansion of democratic suffrage to a policy of increased protective tariffs within a militarily dominated imperial market.

However, hard times caused by shifts in international markets do not always produce aggressive nationalism. Gourevitch notes that these depressions produced varying effects from country to country, depending in part on the prior structure of institutions and interests. In Britain, for example, the free-trading alliance between City of London financiers and the workers who wanted to preserve the "cheap loaf," decisively rejected Joseph Chamberlain's proposals for tariff protection and imperial expansion in the 1905 election. What shaped this outcome was not only group interests but also the comparatively advanced democratic institutions that gave the working class a decisive voice in ratifying the policy response.

Even more surprising is Jeffry Frieden's finding that economic hard times actually promoted democratization in some Latin American states in the 1980s.[70] When dramatically rising interest rates caused a ballooning debt crisis, authoritarian regimes that had lived high on cheap funds were suddenly discredited. The financial community in those countries, as well as other holders of mobile assets, had supported the dictatorship in better times; now they chafed under the costs of huge subsidies to owners of immobile assets in state-supported heavy industry. In some of these countries, mobile capital sought a democratizing alliance with the people as a way of throwing the millstone dictatorship out of power. Thus, all good things do not necessarily go together: even economic crisis can promote democracy if it undercuts an antidemocratic coalition.[71]

---

[69] Gourevitch, *Politics in Hard Times,* Chapters 3 and 4.

[70] Jeffry Frieden, *Debt, Development, and Democracy* (Princeton: Princeton University Press, 1991).

[71] For statistical findings about the relationship of economic performance and democratization, see Adam Przeworski and Fernando Limongi, "Modernization: Theories and Facts," *World Politics* 49:2 (January 1997), 155–83, and Stephan Haggard and Robert Kaufman, *The Political Economy of Democratic Transitions* (Princeton: Princeton University Press, 1995).

These theories are directly relevant to a number of policy choices on the contemporary agenda. Would reducing the European Union's high trade barriers against the agricultural products of Eastern Europe serve to solidify democratization there, or would it strengthen antidemocratic coalitions? Will dramatically increased international trade with China strengthen democrats or their adversaries? Historical precedent suggests that the effects of international trade on such outcomes can be dramatic, but they can cut both ways. Predicting political consequences requires a nuanced understanding of the interplay of groups' economic incentives, of coalition dynamics shaped by institutional pathways, and of the galvanizing effect of ideology.

### *The impact of military competition*

Military security is no less important than trade in creating the international context of democratization. Statistical studies show that involvement in warfare typically has the short-run effect of restricting democratic rights.[72] In the longer run, however, mobilization for war may promote democratization, especially if prevailing methods of military organization require a loyal, self-motivated mass army.[73] When democratization develops in a warlike formative setting, as in the French Revolution or in Serbia in the period before World War I, the popular political culture may be stamped for some time with a belligerently nationalist ethos. Similarly, NATO's bombing of Serbia during the Kosovo conflict of spring 1999 served to intensify nationalist feelings even among the democratic opposition to Milosevic's regime. Likewise, when military recruitment is one of the main vehicles for bringing the popular masses into the broader life of the nation, democratic nationalism may take on a militarized cast.[74]

---

[72] Ted Robert Gurr, "War, Revolution, and the Growth of the Coercive State," *Comparative Political Studies* 21:1 (April 1988), 45–65; Arthur Stein and Bruce Russett, "The Consequences of International Conflicts," in Ted Robert Gurr, ed., *Handbook of International Conflict* (New York: Free Press, 1980), 399–422.

[73] Stanislav Andreski, *Military Organization and Society* (Berkeley: University of California Press, 1991); Charles Tilly, *Coercion, Capital, and European States, AD 990–1990* (Cambridge: Basil Blackwell, 1990), Chapter 4; Olive Anderson, *A Liberal State at War* (New York: St. Martin's, 1967).

[74] Barry Posen, "Nationalism, the Mass Army and Military Power," *International Security* 18:2 (Fall 1993), 80–124; Eugen Weber, *Peasants into Frenchmen* (Stanford:

Conversely, a conducive international setting may institutionalize an especially pacific character in a newly democratic state. For example, the U.S. occupation was very effective in inculcating pacifist institutions, laws, and strategic culture in newly democratic Germany and Japan after World War II. Indeed, some Americans complain that Germany and Japan did not pull their weight in cold war military expenditures and had the luxury of free-riding on U.S. defense guarantees.[75]

Similar efforts after World War I had been much less effective. A favorable international security environment, including the Washington naval arms control treaty and the Locarno scheme guaranteeing French and German borders, was designed to promote liberal, democratic, free-trading coalitions in Germany and Japan in the 1920s.[76] These arrangements were not well institutionalized on either the domestic or the international plane, however, and they did not endure.

In contrast, the Bretton Woods and NATO system pioneered in the late 1940s did have a strong institutional base. Though the amount of money provided under the Marshall Plan after 1948 was probably smaller than the amount loaned to Germany under the Dawes and Young Plans in the 1920s, the different institutional context made the Marshall money more effective. Whereas Dawes and Young loans were frittered away on city services to appease labor, the Marshall Plan required the West European states to cooperate in order to break down trade barriers and establish an efficient industrial policy.[77] Likewise, the Western military alliance was better institutionalized after World War II and therefore served more effectively as a bulwark against the revival of nationalism in the separate West European states.

---

Stanford University Press, 1976); Mark Von Hagen, *Soldiers in the Proletarian Dictatorship* (Ithaca: Cornell University Press, 1990).

[75] Thomas U. Berger, "Norms, Identity, and National Security in Germany and Japan," in Peter Katzenstein, ed., *The Culture of National Security* (New York: Columbia University Press, 1996), 317–56.

[76] Jack Snyder, *Myths of Empire* (Ithaca: Cornell University Press, 1991), Chapters 3 and 4.

[77] J. Bradford De Long and Barry Eichengreen, "The Marshall Plan: History's Most Successful Structural Adjustment Program," University of California at Berkeley, Department of Economics Working Paper No. 91–184, November 1991. More generally, see Robert Keohane and Lisa Martin, "The Promise of Institutionalist Theory," *International Security* 20:1 (Summer 1995), 46–50.

Thus, democratizing countries may be less conflict-prone if their risky transition is molded to fit into a benign international framework. Those who favor the expansion of NATO and the EU to include the newly democratizing countries of eastern and central Europe rest their argument in part on this case.[78] They argue that making membership conditional upon democracy and respect for human rights will create incentives for behavior that directly reduces the risk of conflict.[79] They also argue that membership in Western organizations will lock in these practices by fostering domestic institutions that insure both civilian control over the military and legal checks on ethnic discrimination. Theoretically, this makes sense in light of the argument presented in this book.[80] In practice, however, these incentives may be too weak to override contrary pressures in immature democracies. NATO membership has not made Turkey's democracy stable, for example, nor averted repression of its Kurdish minority. Moreover, NATO and EU membership may be extended only to the easy cases—Poland, the Czech Republic, and Hungary—where pacific democracy is already well established and hardly needs to be shored up. Finally, opponents of NATO expansion feared that it would fuel a populist nationalist backlash in Russia, though this fear has turned out to be somewhat exaggerated.

Short of directly integrating newly democratizing states into Western institutions, a more oblique strategy rests on influencing coalition politics in the newly democratizing state.[81] In some situations, an aggressive nationalist coalition and a more moderate alternative may both be plausible outcomes in a democratizing state. Both potential coalitions may have plausible sources of political support. Which of the two coalitions succeeds may depend on the choices made by constituencies that could

---

[78] Richard Kugler, *Enlarging NATO* (Santa Monica: Rand, 1996).

[79] For a broader argument based on this reasoning, see Ted Hopf, "Managing Soviet Disintegration: A Demand for Behavioral Regimes," *International Security* 17:1 (Summer 1992), 44–75.

[80] For elaboration, see Jack Snyder, "Averting Anarchy in the New Europe," *International Security* 14:4 (Spring 1990), 5–41; Snyder, "International Leverage," *World Politics* 42:1 (October 1989), 1–30.

[81] Robert Putnam, "Diplomacy and Domestic Politics: The Logic of Two-Level Games," *International Organization* 42 (Summer 1988), 427–60; Etel Solingen, *Emerging Regional Orders: Politics, Economics and Security at Century's End* (Princeton: Princeton University Press, 1998).

swing in either direction. Such swing groups may be influenced by the prospect of benefits from cooperation with other states. If the leadership of the democratizing state cooperates with foreign states in ways that pay off for swing constituencies, it may be possible to lock in a moderate coalition that creates the conditions for its own perpetuation.

For example, many observers were quite fearful of a spiraling conflict between Ukrainian nationalists and Russian imperial revivalists. In the early 1990s, Ukrainian nationalists sought to use the threat of Russian encroachments on Ukrainian sovereignty to mobilize popular support for the tasks of state-building. At the same time, some Russian political figures sought to use nationalist and imperial themes to defeat democratic market reforms. For a time, it appeared that hawks in both camps might be able to create a self-fulfilling prophecy of conflict by playing upon divisive issues, such as the disposition of Soviet nuclear weapons in Ukraine, the fate of the Black Sea fleet, and the disputed status of the Crimean peninsula.[82] This has not occurred, in part because the West helped to sponsor a cooperative coalition to counter this negative spiral. Russian president Boris Yeltsin and Ukrainian president Leonid Kuchma implicitly exchanged Russian moderation on the Crimea for the Ukrainian agreement to give up nuclear weapons. Conditional Western economic aid to Ukraine helped to promote this nuclear deal, which defused the hawks' appeals. As a result, the swing electoral constituency of moderate Ukrainian nationalists in central Ukraine voted disproportionately with Russian-speakers in eastern Ukraine for Kuchma's policy of cooperation with Russia, rather than with more extreme Ukrainian ethnonationalists in western Ukraine.[83] Since newly democratizing states can evolve in either nationalist or liberal internationalist directions, it makes sense to

[82] Putnam would call this kind of self-amplifying political dynamic a "negative reverberation." On the breakup of Yugoslavia as a two-level game with negative reverberation, see Stuart Kaufman, "The Irresistible Force and the Imperceptible Object: The Yugoslav Breakup and Western Policy," *Security Studies* 4:2 (Winter 1994–95), 281–329.

[83] Putnam would call this a "synergistic issue linkage." In a similar example, Islamic fundamentalists suffered dramatically declining support in Jordan's November 1993 parliamentary elections after the conclusion of the Israeli-Palestinian peace agreement, brokered by the United States and others in the international community. Youssef M. Ibrahim, "Jordanian Vote Endorses Peace Effort," *New York Times*, November 10, 1993, A8.

try to influence the direction of that trend by targeting incentives on those swing constituencies who might prove decisive by leaning in one direction or the other.

### *The transnational impact of ideas*

The international setting may influence the development of nationalist ideas not only indirectly, by shaping institutions and coalition incentives, but also directly, by shaping the international climate of ideas. Recently, political scientists have studied how transnational currents of ideas can shape thinking, especially in newly democratizing states where ideologies are in flux. Such states tend to follow successful examples, which is one reason, says Huntington, why democratization occurs in copycat waves.[84] Also, experts from role-model states may be brought in, as they were, for example, to design radical economic reform policies in Chile or Russia, and to devise a devilishly complex scheme of proportional representation in Hungary. However, even when intentions are good, the results from directly copying what works in advanced democracies may be counter-productive. Experts in advanced democratic states who take for granted the well-developed institutions of their market economy and their "marketplace of ideas," may err by prescribing laissez-faire solutions—such as "more free speech is always better"—which work poorly in an underinstitutionalized setting.

In the security field, the ideas that are disseminated through transnational expert channels sometimes may be beneficial, such as the West European concepts for defensive military strategies that Gorbachev's new thinkers picked up from their contacts with nongovernmental arms control experts. But bad ideas can also spread. Before World War I, for example, a transnational "cult of the offensive" spread a Europe-wide professional military consensus that attacking was easier than defending, that the bonus for striking first would be large, and consequently that

---

[84] Huntington, *Third Wave*; also Timur Kuran, "Now Out of Never," *World Politics* 44:1 (October 1991), 7–48, and Renée DeNevers, book on East European transitions (Cambridge: MIT Press, forthcoming), on the dynamic of emulation in Eastern Europe. On copycat behavior in Eastern Europe in 1919 and the 1930s, see Joseph Rothschild, *East Central Europe between the Two World Wars* (Seattle: University of Washington Press, 1974), 21.

security was scarce. This notion helped to spur popular nationalist movements, which were animated in part by the notion that their governments were not doing enough to protect the nation from the urgent offensive threats posed by neighboring powers.[85] Nowadays, there seems little to fear from a transnational cult of militarism or ethnonationalism. The conditions that made Europe ripe for a continent-wide militarist cult of the offensive in 1914 are now obsolete.[86] And there is no evidence that ethnonationalism in Rwanda has anything whatsoever to do with copying from counterparts in Serbia or in Nagorno-Karabakh.

Still, other kinds of transnational ideological movements may yet affect the course of ethnonationalism. Pauline Baker notes that the international human rights movement is often at odds with the community of international conflict resolution experts.[87] The former, says Baker, are often human rights absolutists who want to punish human rights abusers and undermine authoritarian regimes, whereas the conflict resolution community is willing to deal with anyone, even a Slobodan Milosevic, who can deliver an agreement for a workable peace. Dubious tactics by both the international human rights and conflict resolution communities played exacerbating roles in the recent ethnic bloodshed in Rwanda and Burundi. Thus, the international intellectual climate may have potent and sometimes unintended effects on the conflict-propensity of democratizing states.

In sum, it would be a mistake to think that the United States or the broader community of mature democracies has the wisdom, willingness, or wallet needed to micromanage the democratization process in scores of countries around the globe. Nonetheless, it would be an equal mistake to believe that the economic, military, and ideological stances of the great powers do not exert a substantial effect, for good or ill, on the shape of nationalisms that are emerging in these states. The advanced democracies need first to understand the sometimes complex effects of their policies on political coalitions, taking into account the local context of elite inter-

---

[85] Stephen Van Evera, "The Cult of the Offensive and the Origins of the First World War," *International Security* 9:1 (Summer 1984), 58–107.

[86] Stephen Van Evera, "Primed for Peace," *International Security* 15:3 (Winter 1990/91), 7–57.

[87] Pauline Baker, "Conflict Resolution versus Democratic Governance: Divergent Paths to Peace?" in Chester A. Crocker and Fen Hampson with Pamela Aall, *Managing Global Chaos* (Washington, DC: US Institute of Peace, 1996), 563–72.

ests and political institutions. With this knowledge in hand, it may be possible to adjust policy at the margins in ways that dampen incentives for nationalist conflict.


## Ethnodemocracy: A Threat to the Democratic Peace

I have argued that a country's first steps toward democracy spur the development of nationalism and heighten the risk of international war and internal ethnic conflict. In principle, this argument need not call into question the proposition that mature democracies will never fight wars against each other. Nationalist conflict has so far been a disease of the transition, and it may remain so. But what if some of today's ethnically exclusionary democratizing regimes successfully institutionalize majority rule, yet systematically deny basic civil rights to significant minorities? If these excluded groups obtain military support from democratically elected ethnic brethren abroad, war between two institutionally mature democracies would seem likely.

One support underpinning the democratic peace is the common civic identity shared by all liberal states. If two nations' democratic identities are based instead on mutually inimical ethnic principles, a key link between democracy and peace is cut. Such ethnic identities might arise during the transition process and then get locked in as the new ethnodemocracy institutionalizes its electoral processes, political parties, and rule of law for the majority. If so, this danger places an even greater premium on averting the institutionalization of ethnicity during the early stages of democratization.

The possibility that a democratic people might coalesce around a distinctive cultural or ethnic core is hardly a new one. Implicitly, if not explicitly, Wilsonian doctrine assumed that language and ethnicity were natural criteria for defining which groups would get to exercise the right of self-determination. Democracy in Germany and Israel, not to mention the southern United States and many other states, has coexisted uneasily with ethnic favoritism. But nowadays proponents of ethnodemocracy seem more overt and assertive. More and more self-styled democratic movements—whether the Karabakh Committee in Armenia, the Popular Front in Azerbaijan, Vuk Draskovic and other democratic oppositionists in Serbia, or even the milder ethnodemocrats of Estonia—call for full civic rights for the ethnic majority only. Minorities under these ethno-democratic majorities suffer the loss of a political voice in the best cases, and the loss of life and home in the worst. Serbia's democratic opposition expressed no remorse over the expulsion of Albanians from Kosovo in spring 1999. In response to the fear of majority tyranny, more and more minorities seek self-defense through the guaranteeing of group rights; fewer are satisfied with the pursuit of individual protections. In making this choice, they are implicitly opting for a balancing of group power, a short step away from the self-help solutions appropriate to a setting of anarchical competition, rather than reliance on the rule of law.

Any movement away from civic democracy and toward ethnic democracy would undermine the democratic peace because it would de-activate the mechanisms that keep relations between democracies peaceful. Advanced civic democracies never fight wars against one another for two related reasons. First, democratic procedure, when it is well-institutionalized, confers power on the average voter who ultimately pays the price for an unnecessary, ill-considered war. Second, civic democracies, sharing inclusive ideals of civic rights for all members of society, perceive each other as having common principles that make war between them illegitimate and nearly unthinkable. The first condition may work unreliably in ethnodemocracies, since the disenfranchisement of minority voters may be merely the first step down the slippery slope of other circumventions of the democratic process. The second condition surely will not operate between two ethnodemocracies whose rival cultures preclude any pretense of a common identity. More ethnodemocracy will not make Armenia and Azerbaijan more peaceful toward each other.

In the early stages of democratization in multiethnic societies, ethnic mass mobilization is an alluring substitute for true democracy. When thick institutional ties are unavailable to underpin the democratic process, thick cultural ties may seem like the next best thing for elites who seek popular support. But in this case, second best is not good enough, if one of the goals of democratization is the promotion of peace. To achieve this goal, there is usually no substitute for the painstaking fostering of civic institutions and traditions. In many societies, the construction of these traditions will take time. Faith in either of two shortcuts—ethnic democracy or instant mechanical democracy—is misplaced. Democracy is not instant. If it came in a bottle, everyone would have it. But for the patient and persistent, the wait will be worthwhile.

# Appendix

**Selected Ethnic Wars, 1945–1999[1]**

| Country | Years | Warring Groups | No. of Deaths | No. of Displaced Persons | Status in Late 1999 |
|---|---|---|---|---|---|
| Afghanistan | 1978–99 | Various class, ethnic (Pushtun, Tajik, Uzbek), religious forces, USSR | 1,200,000 | 5,200,000 | Victory by Taliban Islamic forces contested by regional opponents |
| Angola | 1975– | Government (Mbundu), *vs.* UNITA (Ovimbundu) | 300,000 | 2,000,000 | Ongoing |
| Azerbaijan | 1988–97 | Government vs. Karabakh Armenians | 55,000 | 1,700,000 | Cease–fire holding |
| Bangladesh | 1975–89 | Government vs. Chittagong Hill peoples | 24,000 | 50,000 | Limited autonomy |
| Bosnia | 1992–95 | Serbs, Croats, Muslims | 140,000 to 240,000 | 2,500,000 | Autonomy in confederal state |
| Burma/ Myanmar | 1948– | Government vs. Karens (and other tribal groups) | 130,000 | 1,333,000 | Imminent government victory over Karens |
| Burundi | 1972 | Tutsi government vs. Hutu | 100,000 | | Hutu repressed |
| Burundi | 1993–94 | Tutsi army vs. backers of Hutu president | 50,000 to 100,000 | 700,000 | Tutsi regain supremacy |
| Chad | 1980–87 | Government vs. northern Muslim tribes | 7,000 | | Rebels defeated |

**Selected Ethnic Wars, 1945–1999[1]**

| Country | Years | Warring Groups | No. of Deaths | No. of Displaced Persons | Status in Late 1999 |
|---------|-------|----------------|---------------|--------------------------|---------------------|
| China | 1950–51, 1959–80 | Communist government vs. Tibetans | 100,000 | 128,000 | Tibetans suppressed |
| China | 1980 | Communist government vs. Uighurs, others | 2,000 | | Uighurs suppressed |
| Croatia | 1991, 1995 | Government of Croatia vs. government of Serbia, Serb secessionists | 10,000 to 25,000 | 320,000 | Croatian government victory, many Serbs flee |
| Cyprus | 1963–64 | Greek Cypriots vs. Turkish Cypriots | | | Greek–dominated regime |
| Cyprus | 1974 | Greek Cypriots vs. Turkish Cypriots, Turkey | 300,000 | | Turkey intervenes to partition island |
| Ethiopia | 1967–91 | Government vs. Eritrean, Somali, Oromo, Afar secessionists, Tigrean rebels | 700,000 | over 800,000 | Somali, Afar, and Oromo federal autonomy; Eritrea independent; Tigrean rebels victorious |
| Georgia | 1991–93, 1998 | Government vs. Abhaz, Ossets | 17,500 | 475,000 | Regional autonomy |
| Guatemala | 1965– | Government vs. Mayans, left-wingers | 150,000 | 200,000 | Conflict subsided |

| | Dates | Combatants | Casualties | | Outcome |
|---|---|---|---|---|---|
| India | 1946–48 | Hindus vs. Muslims | 800,000 or more | 15,000,000 | Partition; Pakistan created |
| India | 1952– | Government vs. Nagas, Tripuras, other Assamese tribes | 10,000 to 16,000 | 50,000 | Autonomy for some groups, 1972; Ongoing |
| India | 1965 | Government vs. Kashmiris, Pakistan | 20,000 | | Negotiated settlement of war |
| India | 1989– | Government vs. Kashmiris, Pakistan | 15,000 | 250,000 | Ongoing |
| India | 1978–93 | Government vs. Sikhs | 20,000 | 30,000 | Militants suppressed; Sikh moderates in power in Punjab |
| Indonesia | 1963–96 | Government vs. Irian Jaya (Papuans) | 10,000 to 30,000 | | Repressed; episodic resistance |
| Indonesia | 1975–99 | Government vs. Timorese | 200,000 before 1999, plus additional casualties in 1999 | | International peacekeeping force deployed |
| Indonesia | 1977–99 | Government vs. Acehenese | 15,000 | 6,000 | Repressed in 1997; conflict resumed |
| Iran | 1979–94 | Government vs. Kurds | 40,000 | 200,000 | Repressed |
| Iraq | 1980–92 | Government vs. Kurds, NATO | 215,000 | 526,000 | Internationally supported autonomy |

*Appendix*

## Selected Ethnic Wars, 1945–1999[1]

| Country | Years | Warring Groups | No. of Deaths | No. of Displaced Persons | Status in Late 1999 |
|---|---|---|---|---|---|
| Iraq | 1991 | Government vs. Shiites | 35,000 | | Repressed |
| Israel | 1948–93 | Government vs. Palestinians | 1,700 since 1968 | 3,000,000 (965,000 since 1968) | Partial autonomy |
| Kenya | 1992 | Government, Kalenjin tribe vs. Luo, Kikuyu, and other tribes | 1,500 | 45,000 to 300,000 | Subsided |
| Lebanon | 1975–90 | Christians, Muslims, Palestinians | 120,000 | | Powersharing; de facto partition |
| Moldova | 1992 | Government vs. Russian army, Dniestr separatists[2] | 1,000 | 105,000 | Regional autonomy, 1997 |
| Morocco | 1973–95 | Government vs. Saharawis | 2,000 | | Suppressed; referendum postponed |
| Nigeria | 1967–70 | Government vs. Ibos | 2,000,000 | | Defeated |
| Nigeria | 1980–84 | Government, Christians vs. Muslims | 11,000 | | Suppressed |
| Pakistan | 1971 | Government vs. Bengalis, India | 1,000 | | Bangladesh independent |
| Pakistan | 1973–77 | Government vs. Baluchis | 9,000 | | Defeated; partial autonomy, 1980 |

| Philippines | 1972–87 | Government vs. Moros | 50,000 | 900,000 | Limited autonomy, 1990 |
|---|---|---|---|---|---|
| Russia | 1994–96 | Government vs. Chechens | 35,000 | 400,000 | Autonomy; conflict resumed, October 1999 |
| Rwanda | 1963–64 | Hutu government vs. Tutsi | 10,000 | | Tutsi repressed |
| Rwanda | 1990–94 | Hutu government vs. Tutsi | 500,000 to 800,000 | 2,000,000 | Government overthrown |
| Serbia | 1998–99 | Government vs. Kosovar Albanians, NATO | 10,000 | 800,000 | Autonomy, 1999 |
| Spain | 1959–80 | Government vs. Basques | 1,000 | | Autonomy, 1980 |
| Sri Lanka | 1983– | Government vs. Tamils | 36,000 | 1,200,000 | Ongoing |
| Sudan | 1963–71 | Government vs. northern Muslims, southern animist peoples | 50,000 | | Autonomy; powersharing |
| Sudan | 1983– | Government vs. northern Muslims, southern animist peoples | 1,200,000 | 4,500,000 | Ongoing |
| Turkey | 1984– | Government vs. Kurds | 13,000 to 50,000 | estimates vary widely | Ongoing |
| United Kingdom | 1969–94 | UK government, Northern Ireland Protestants, and Catholics | 3,000 | | Peace agreement; powersharing |
| USSR | 1945–52 | Government vs. Lithuanians | 40,000 | | Suppressed; independent, 1991 |

## Selected Ethnic Wars, 1945–1999[1]

| Country | Years | Warring Groups | No. of Deaths | No. of Displaced Persons | Status in Late 1999 |
|---|---|---|---|---|---|
| USSR | 1944–50s | Government vs. Ukrainians | 150,000 | | Suppressed; independent, 1991 |

[1] Conflicts that claimed over 1,000 deaths, in which a principal basis of enmity was group identity or culture (including religion) and in which political objectives were articulated in ethnic terms. Conflicts sometimes listed as ethnic wars—but omitted here—include Liberia (warlords, not ethnic nationalists), Peru (indigenous Sendero Luminoso have class-based, not ethnic, ideology), Somalia (mainly clans of the same ethnicity), South Africa in the 1980s (deadly repression, but not warfare), and Tajikistan (see Chapter 6). Other possibly relevant cases are Algeria, 1962–63 (largely Berbers vs. Arabs); Congo, 1960–65 (ethnic element to Katanga secession); several regional and religious rebellions in Indonesia in the 1950s; Uganda, 1966 and 1980 (government vs. Baganda and other tribes). The main sources for this table are Roy Licklider, "The Consequences of Negotiated Settlements in Civil Wars, 1945–1993," *American Political Science Review* 89:3 (September 1995), 681–90, revised at http://www.rci.rutgers.edu/~lick-lidel/; Michael E. Brown, ed., *The International Dimensions of Internal Conflict* (Cambridge: MIT, 1996), 4–7; Chaim Kaufmann, "Possible and Impossible Solutions to Ethnic Civil Wars," *International Security* 20:4 (Spring 1996), 160; Ted Robert Gurr and Barbara Harff, *Ethnic Conflict in World Politics* (Boulder, CO: Westview, 1994), 160–66; Gurr, "Peoples against States: Ethnopolitical Conflict and the Changing World System," *International Studies Quarterly* 38:3 (September 1994) 369–75; Gurr, *Peoples versus States* (forthcoming), Table 23; see also Gurr's Minorities at Risk database at http://www.bsos.umd.edu/cidcm/mar. Because the classification rules used by these sources are quite varied, there is little overlap among the conflicts they list. Licklider's list includes a few "identity" wars that I omitted because they didn't meet my criteria. In most cases, figures on deaths and displaced persons are approximate and in some cases differ widely. Where no figures are given for deaths or displaced persons, reliable estimates were not available in the sources cited.

[2] See Chapter 6 for discussion of ethnic and nonethnic aspects of the conflict.

# Credits

# Index

Page numbers in *italics* refer to tables.